Social Wor... Children and ...ies

D1352468

Social Work

with
Children &
Families

Edited by
Martin Davies

palgrave
macmillan

Policy

Law

Theory

Research

Practice

First published 2012 by
PALGRAVE MACMILLAN

Palgrave Macmillan in the UK is an imprint of Macmillan Publishers Limited, registered in England, company number 785998, of Houndmills, Basingstoke, Hampshire RG21 6XS.

Palgrave Macmillan in the US is a division of St Martin's Press LLC, 175 Fifth Avenue, New York, NY 10010.

Palgrave Macmillan is the global academic imprint of the above companies and has companies and representatives throughout the world.

Palgrave® and Macmillan® are registered trademarks in the United States, the United Kingdom, Europe and other countries.

ISBN-13: 978–0–230–29385–4

This book is printed on paper suitable for recycling and made from fully managed and sustained forest sources. Logging, pulping and manufacturing processes are expected to conform to the environmental regulations of the country of origin.

A catalogue record for this book is available from the British Library.

A catalog record for this book is available from the Library of Congress.

10 9 8 7 6 5 4 3 2 1
21 20 19 18 17 16 15 14 13 12

Printed and bound in the UK by Charlesworth Press, Wakefield, West Yorkshire

For Gareth Miller
Emeritus Professor of Law at UEA, Norwich
friend of a lifetime

Brief contents

Full contents

List of figures, tables and boxes

The authors

Caroline Ball, Formerly Dean of the Norwich Law School, University of East Anglia

Janine Bolger, Senior Lecturer in Social Work, Robert Gordon's University, Aberdeen

Gary Clapton, Senior Lecturer in Social Work, Edinburgh University

Pat Dolan, UNESCO Professor and Director of the Child and Family Research Centre, National University of Ireland, Galway

Nick Frost, Professor of Social Work, Leeds Metropolitan University

Simon Hackett, Professor of Social Work, Durham University

Sally Holland, Reader in the School of Social Sciences, Cardiff University

David Jodrell, Researcher, Dartington Social Research Unit, Totnes, Devon

Christine Jones, Lecturer in Social Work, Durham University

Leonie Jordan, Lawyer, London

Seden Karakurt, Student Intern, Dartington Social Research Unit, Totnes, Devon

Andrew Kendrick, Professor of Residential Child Care, Strathclyde University

Michael Little, Director, Dartington Social Research Unit, Totnes, Devon

Cecilia Love, Doctoral Student, School of Social Sciences, Cardiff University

Jess McCormack, Social Worker, Glasgow

Alison McLeod, Honorary Research Fellow, University of Cumbria

Jeremy Millar, Lecturer in Social Work, Robert Gordon's University, Aberdeen

Kate Morris, Associate Professor of Social Work, Nottingham University

Robin Sen, Lecturer in Child and Family Social Work, Sheffield University

John Simmonds, Director of Policy, Research and Development, British Association for Adoption and Fostering, London

Joe Smeeton, Lecturer in Social Work, University of East Anglia, Norwich

Mark Smith, Senior Lecturer in Social Work, Edinburgh University

Helga Sneddon, Senior Fellow, Centre for Effective Services, Belfast

Jonathan Stanley, NCERCC, London

Preface

The world of social work is not a static system but one that is always evolving. This book is designed to explore the elements that have influenced and continue to influence that evolutionary process: policy, law, theory and research all contribute to the end product – what the frontline social worker does in practice.

One of the best pieces of advice I was given when I was an undergraduate at Liverpool University was:

> Always remember when you are reading an academic textbook, it is not like a detective story. You are not meant to read it steadily through from page 1 to page 267. Rather, you should 'manage' it in such a way that it serves your own personal interests.

This advice is especially appropriate for this book. It has a strong internal structure that enables it to be used in different ways depending on what each reader wants.

	Part I Family support	Part II Child protection	Part III Adoption and fostering	Part IV Residential child care
Policy	Chapter 1	Chapter 6	Chapter 11	Chapter 16
Law	Chapter 2	Chapter 7	Chapter 12	Chapter 17
Theory	Chapter 3	Chapter 8	Chapter 13	Chapter 18
Research	Chapter 4	Chapter 9	Chapter 14	Chapter 19
Practice	Chapter 5	Chapter 10	Chapter 15	Chapter 20

How to use this book

First, this book can be used in order to explore any or all of the four topics that are introduced – family support, child protection, adoption and fostering, and residential child care. The four parts provide comprehensive coverage of each subject. The reader who approaches it in this way will quickly experience the differences in background and style between the authors who write on the five academic spheres. Policy, law, theory and research each have their own intellectual heritage, and these are well reflected in the various contributions to this book. The practice chapters, by contrast, are down to earth and tell a number of real-life stories. By following the advice of my erstwhile teacher in Liverpool, the reader could usefully read each practice chapter first before turning to the weightier material that, in book order, precedes it. Ask yourself, then, how does the policy, law, theory or research material relate to the real world of practice that my authors have recorded for you?

A second approach that I myself tackled with fascination is to read in sequence all four chapters on each of the five relevant spheres – policy, law, theory, research, practice. For example, you can ask yourself: What are the similarities and differences between the theoretical perspectives that are outlined in respect of the four fields of social work – family support, child protection, adoption and fostering, and residential child care? You will find some similarities and some clear differences in each of the spheres. For example, the contrasts of emphasis between some aspects of residential child care and much that is written in respect of community-based social work come through strongly.

Alternatively, a concentrated reading of all four practice chapters will give the reader an illuminating glimpse of the challenges that confront the social worker every day – and of how they are being tackled.

A third approach to the book, as with all academic works of reference, is simply to go to one or more chapters in order to receive an up-to-date state-of-the-art précis of where our subject is at in the second decade of the twenty-first century. For example, with an essay to write on risk management in child care, the continuing importance of family support in social work, developments in adoption policy over 50 years, or the role of residential care today, you would be home and dry. Well, almost! Each author has provided a note about three books or papers suggested as being suitable 'for further reading'; if you tackle those with an inquiring mind, you really will be able to call yourself an up-to-date expert in that field.

You should bear in mind that this book has a companion volume, *Social Work with Adults*, and that it has an identical internal structure. It covers mental health, old age, drug and alcohol misuse, and the personalization agenda. By using the two books together, you will get a synoptic view of eight different areas of social work practice. There may be a growing distance between the various specialist fields in social work, but the work that is done shares many common features, and the two books together accurately reflect the extent to which poverty remains a powerful common factor in the majority of cases.

The authors of this book and its companion volume are based in all parts of the UK and in the Republic of Ireland. This wholly desirable fact has, however, presented the editor with a problem – especially in respect of the policy and law chapters. There are some clear and many slight differences in legislation and policy to be found in the five countries, and if this had been designed as a comprehensive textbook, they would have had to be punctiliously identified. But, as I explain in the Introduction, the book is not intended to cover every aspect of social work. My interest and, I hope, that of the book's readers is concentrated on the conceptual differences between policy, law, theory, research and practice – and these are capable of intelligent inter-pretation, whatever the national context to which they apply.

Martin Davies

Acknowledgements

From the moment of its conception, almost exactly two years before publication, this book has benefited from the intellectual imagination of a great many people. Although the component parts of the book represent familiar territory, the idea of presenting them synoptically and, to a certain extent, deconstructing them involved a degree of risk, and I am immensely grateful to my many colleagues for responding to the idea so enthusiastically.

I owe a particular debt to two people who encouraged me to move forward with the original idea. Catherine Gray of Palgrave Macmillan is one of a rare breed of publishers' editors who responds to her authors' embryonic creations with a powerful mixture of critique and inventiveness; I like to think that she brings the best out in me. Viv Cree in Edinburgh is like me in that she inhabits that dangerous and difficult territory of being a social scientist within the essentially ideological field of social work; I greatly admire her writing, and she was generous in her response to my original outline; more than that, she played a major part in the process of lining up a cast of potential authors.

Several other people helped me with the book's early development, possibly more than they realized at the time,: among them, David Howe, Cathy Humphreys, Nigel Parton, Gill Schofield and June Thoburn all enabled me to clarify my ideas.

But, of course, a book like this owes everything to its authors, and I have been blessed with an amazingly positive and committed team of colleagues. I have shared their good humoured online company for the past two years, and they have tolerated my persistence with a level of forbearance that time and again took me by surprise. Together, we have shared the highs and lows of ordinary life – theirs and mine. I thank them.

Martin Davies

Every effort has been made to contact all the copyright holders, but if any have been inadvertently omitted the publishers will be pleased to make the necessary arrangements at the first opportunity.

Introduction

Social workers have, for more than a century, been a significant and increasingly substantial occupational group in the UK and other parts of the world. From their beginnings within the framework of voluntary societies, they have moved steadily, as public employees, towards the hard centre of our democratic welfare economy. They have grown accustomed to the fact that members of society who have no need of their services may view them and their profession with some ambivalence. Thirty years ago, in *The Essential Social Worker*, I argued that they play a crucial part in the maintenance of our complex community in a state of approximate equilibrium. That remains true.

The scale and the cost of social work have risen in line with our growing population; practitioners face ever more complex problems as family structures fracture, people live longer, substance misuse disturbs the surface of people's lives, and the state commits itself to reliance on community-based, rather than institutional-based, support systems.

Against this background, and reflecting the way in which, from time to time, policy wheels turn full circle, there has been a gradual shift away from the idea of 'generic' social work – the conventional wisdom in the second half of the twentieth century. Social workers still do their basic training together, but the scale of public and political concern about the primacy of child welfare has led to a clear policy division now between 'social work with children and families' and 'social work with adults'. This book, together with its companion volume, reflects that development.

Of course, because families and indeed communities as a whole are made up of children and adults, young and old, who freely interact with and depend on each other, the division between the two books is not clear-cut. In this volume, for example, there is frequent mention in the practice chapters of the fact that mental health issues and difficulties associated with substance misuse are commonly to be found affecting families where there is concern about child welfare.

Authors were invited to tackle the question: 'How does policy/law/theory/ research affect social work practice in each of the four chosen fields – family support, child protection, adoption and fostering, and residential child care? And, in parallel to that, different authors were asked to provide material outlining the reality of practice in those same fields.

It should be said at the outset that the two volumes together are not designed to be encyclopedic or comprehensive guides to the whole field of social work practice; there are a number of other books that fulfil that aim. The intention, rather, is to see what happens when you 'deconstruct' the five elements. What are the differences of emphasis between them? How do the four 'academic' spheres feed in to the practice chapters? Through a series of questions – one in each chapter – readers are invited to join in the task of 'Making connexions'. There are very few certainties in social work; but a thoughtful and reactive reading of this text will enable the reader to form a judgement on what weight should be placed on a whole range of probabilities.

In this Introduction, I will briefly touch on some of the thoughts and ideas that have been prompted in me as a result of working with the 20 chapters. I will do so by briefly reflecting in turn on each of the five 'key elements'.

Policy

Over the years, the historical development of child care policy has been driven by forces that represent different moral, intellectual and political perspectives. In Chapters 6 and 11 respectively, Little and Simmonds identify some of them:

- feminist thinking
- medical developments
- the need felt by politicians to respond to media-driven scandals
- financial constraints.

In the light of these sometimes conflicting elements, it has proved to be extremely difficult to achieve clarity of objectives in child care practice.

In addition, in Chapter 1, Morris suggests that we have little knowledge 'about the lived experience of families who are the subject of policy concern'. In other words, we tend to be ignorant of how different families work – a shortcoming that can only become more acute in the context of increasing cultural diversity. Given that the primary focus of policy in children and families social work has been and remains to keep families together, Morris's assertion identifies a serious intellectual vacuum that cannot help but make it difficult to translate the social and political will into practice.

In Chapter 6, Little interprets the situation by saying that child care policy has traditionally been ruled by the heart, rather than the head, and he calls for a paradigm shift based largely on the development of greatly expanded research programmes using empirical methods that will allow policy-makers to judge the effectiveness or ineffectiveness of specific practice methods, although that will require some significant improvement in the process of clarifying objectives.

In the last half-century, adoption and residential child care have both experienced paradigm shifts of significant proportions, although only partly as a result of research evidence. Adoption, in particular, has changed so much that what is now called 'adoption' is, for the most part, an entirely different phenomenon from that which existed 50 years ago. It offers us an example par excellence of a policy development brought about almost entirely by external factors: developments in law and medicine (legal abortion and effective methods of contraception) and in social morality (the widespread acceptance of the right of children born 'out of wedlock' to be brought up by their birth parent(s)).

In residential child care, it is hard to escape the conclusion that what remains of it is an important but largely residual provision – the last line of defence when all family- or community-based options have been exhausted. And what does one make of the fact that the commercial sector now dominates residential care provision? This is a policy shift that has led to the public sector being largely reduced to a commissioning or regulatory role.

Law

Generally, in the field of social work, legislation flows from the public or political identification of aspects of human behaviour or circumstance that require management or intervention: the growing awareness of the existence of child abuse is one example; the perceived vulnerability of the children of asylum seekers is another. The recognition that such situations prompt, at government level, a response that is then enshrined in law gives the clearest signal possible that society accepts corporate and budgetary responsibility for creating a framework that allows its concerns to be acted on in practice. And the people who are called on to act on it are social workers, their managers and their assistants.

A crucial example is to be found in respect of 'the child in need'. But it is an example that illustrates the limitations of the law. Not only is the concept of 'need' difficult to define – it is, in fact, a rather fluid or relative concept – but the resources available to social workers, charged with assessing needs and responding appropriately, are finite, with the result that, in practice, although it may vary from place to place, the *interpretation* of what 'need' means will be made at practitioner or management level, or both, and will be at least partly driven by the social worker's awareness of the level of resources available to meet that need. Thus, in reality, as Jordan argues in Chapter 2, the legal term 'in need' becomes reinterpreted as meaning 'with higher levels of need' or even 'in need of protection'.

The field of child protection, perhaps more than any other, reflects the way in which politicians and lawyers have had to respond to high levels of public demand for legislation in order to reduce the incidence of child abuse. But, because of the sensitivity of any policy that appears to intrude upon the privacy of family life, the legislative process is by no means straightforward. Through political debate, principles are established and then legislation is passed. Sometimes it is successful: as Ball suggests in Chapter 7, many were doubtful whether the concept of 'significant harm' would prove to be viable in practice; but, she argues, it has worked well. On the other hand, although report after report, following high-profile abuse cases, have asserted the need for improved interdepartmental collaboration, the plain fact is that this is easier to ask for than to secure – as any sociologist of organizations will attest.

Law is not always the driving force in social work practice: although legislation in respect of adoption has been regularly revised, the main changes in practice have been driven by demographics, developments in medicine, changing moral values, and the dynamics of professional policy within social work itself. Similarly, the decline in the use of residential child care has not occurred because of any legislative reform; as Sen notes in Chapter 17, this illustrates the fact that 'policy and practice decisions can shape the character of social work within its given legal context'. Law provides a framework. But the social worker on the ground – for good or ill – is the frontline arbiter of how legal principles are converted into practice.

Theory

'The guiding principle of my work is the welfare of the child', says Hackett's senior social worker in Chapter 8. This idea may seem to be a self-evident and universal aspiration, but, at the very least, it is specific to a particular point in historical time. In the fifteenth century, for example, daughters of the aristocracy were betrothed (promised) to a known boy or man before their tenth birthday and were married by 13 or 14. The guiding principle was to optimize the likelihood of them bearing a male child who could maintain the line of succession. Physical abuse and sexual abuse were routine. Even in the twenty-first century, intercultural difficulties impact on the social worker's role because family values and expectations are culturally specific and may sometimes be seen to be challenging common assumptions about 'the welfare of the child'.

There is clearly a tension in contemporary social work about the nature and shape of families today. In Chapter 13, Jones quotes with approval Silva and Smart's remark (1999, p. 11) that 'families "are" what families "do"'. This socially constructed reality – no less today than in the fifteenth century – creates the private world in which adults live and into which children are born and raised, and provides the framework within which social workers pursue their policy-driven objectives.

Sociological theory provides explanatory and exploratory insights that enable the social worker to understand the context of people's lives. But when sociological thinking is applied to the world of the practitioner itself, it becomes clear that the social work role and task are central to a particular model of Western democracy, with its unambiguous commitment to the idea that everything should be done by the state to avoid or to counteract societally induced suffering. And through policy change and legislation, that role evolves in the face of changing social circumstances.

But as Hackett points out in Chapter 8, theory can exist at many different levels of specificity – what he calls meta-, meso- or micro-theory. And it is at the micro-level that attempts have been made to enable social workers to operate in the same scientific way that has delivered high-quality results in many other fields of practice in the modern world, for example engineering, dentistry, agriculture and pharmacy. It is not an impossible aspiration in some areas of practice, although the lack of clarity in the specific objectives of social work and the often long-term nature of it present understandable problems. Although examples of empirical support for particular methods, such as motivational interviewing, are to hand, Sen reminds us that some of the worst examples of abuse *within* the care setting have been associated with the use of rigidly applied quasi-scientific therapeutic methods (Chapter 17).

Theory – which can sometimes be seen as a moral or ideological dynamic – provides social workers with insights into the lives of the people they are employed to focus on; it helps them to understand their social context, and, echoing Hackett again, it can provide the social worker with a reference point from which to appraise the complex factors involved in a case and to make practice decisions.

Research

As far as child care policy and practice are concerned, the primary contribution of research over the years has not been evaluative: in the UK, randomized controlled trials (RCTs), which would lead to firm conclusions about the effectiveness or ineffectiveness of different types of social work intervention, have been thin on the ground. But, despite that, a great many research studies, using theoretical perspectives from either psychology or sociology, have been carried out in the field of social work with children and families. For the most part, they can be broadly described as exploratory, reflective, explanatory or descriptive.

It would be quite wrong to conclude that the near absence of RCT projects has meant that research has been lacking in influence as far as policy or practice are concerned. On the contrary, it is easy to pick out a number of areas where research has played a major part in the development of practice. For example:

- There was a time when the voice of the child would, in many cases, go unheard and unheeded. Research in child protection and adoption has been hugely influential in putting the child centre stage and, in some respects, leading to changes in the related legislation in order to impose a requirement on social workers to take the views of the child fully into account.
- The views and expressed feelings of parents have been highlighted as warranting full attention in social work practice. Research in respect of children with disabilities has concluded, as McLeod reports in Chapter 4, that 'social workers should listen to parents and take their views seriously'.
- Research has been instrumental in the field of adoption, says Clapton (Chapter 14), in ensuring that birth mothers are brought in from the fringes of social work practice in order to take 'their place at the table'. As a result, 'the term "the adoption triangle" (adopted people, adoptive parents and birth mothers) came into popular usage'.
- Research that highlighted the problems experienced by children leaving care has led directly to changes in legislation, policy and practice.

As far as evaluative research is concerned, there remain major difficulties. As McLeod comments in Chapter 4, 'social work does not have outcomes you can easily count'. To talk of 'doing research into child abuse' is roughly equivalent to the idea of 'doing research into adult ill health'. There is clearly a need to achieve much greater specificity of focus, specificity of method and specificity of intended outcome if the concept of 'social work intervention' is ever to achieve intellectual respectability as a result of demonstrable research conclusions.

How do you judge what counts as 'successful' in social work? In Chapter 19, Kendrick reflects on the problem in respect of residential child care: 'We need ... to avoid broad generalizations in favour of a more nuanced approach about what works for whom in what circumstances'. It may well be, as Sneddon suggests in Chapter 9, that social work places less reliance on research evidence than other professions, but that should not be taken as a damning criticism of social workers, nor is it necessarily a fault of the researchers. The shortcoming (if it is one) has to be laid at the door of those who put in place the policies that lead to publicly funded activity in areas of profound social and psychological complexity, often on the grounds of nothing more sophisticated than: 'Something should be done about it'.

At the very least, research has thrown a great deal of light in areas where previously there was darkness; it has produced knowledge where there was ignorance; and it has gone some way towards requiring policy-makers and practitioners to have more clear-cut objectives.

Practice

There is one massive difference between the world of social work practice and the academic fields referred to above: whereas policy, law, theory and research deal in generalities, practice focuses always on one child or one family in a particular social context. Practice is concerned with the specifics of a unique situation; it is a situation that will develop in unpredictable ways, a situation that will be influenced, not just by the social worker, but by all the people caught up in it, and, almost always, it will be an evolving situation that may defy any attempt on the social worker's part to identify specific objectives – however much researchers would like that to be done. No wonder Smeeton draws to our attention the idea of dealing with the messy complexities of practice through maintaining a position of 'respectful uncertainty' (Chapter 10).

This is especially so when the social worker engages in the crucial task of assessment. There are two reasons why social work assessment in the field of child care is difficult: first, the practitioner is simultaneously aiming to draw conclusions both about the needs of the child (which may point in one direction) and about the risks presented by people or situations close to the child (which may suggest a diametrically opposite conclusion); and any action taken on the basis of the assessment will almost certainly have consequences that will affect the child, for better or worse, for the rest of their lifetime. Although the court plays the legally decisive role when it comes to the crunch, the reality is that the court's decision is heavily dependent on conclusions drawn by the social worker.

After assessment, what then? The nature of social work intervention has moved a long way from the days when, in some spheres, it was thought of as being a form of one-to-one counselling. The fields of fostering and adoption, family support and, even more so, that of residential child care involve complex interactive relationships that encroach on the everyday world of children and their families. Life story work, proactive liaison with doctors and teachers, vigorously securing improved benefits: they are all part and parcel of ground-level social work, and they all demand a high level of skill in empathizing with children and adults alike.

Developments in social work practice are sometimes prompted by research – as with the solution-focused approach – but, more often, they are influenced by the way in which our society itself is changing. The often transient nature of family structures, the widespread use of drugs, the increasingly varied ethnic mix, the presence of large numbers of asylum seekers – all have had an impact on the ways in which social workers respond to new situations.

It is possible, but wrong, to take the simplistic view that social work practice is or should be 'policy put into operation'. Of course, on one level, that is true. But the nature of the social work role and of the complex situations facing it means that, although policy, law, theory and research have an influential part to play, the creative and empathetic skill of the practitioner is the essential catalyst that makes the difference between success and failure – and that difference can have life-enhancing consequences for some of the most vulnerable people in our society.

Part I
Social Work and the Provision of Family Support

There is a sense in which the idea of family support underpins all aspects of social work with children and families. Family support is often regarded as a desirable form of partnership-based practice designed to avoid unnecessary receptions into state care and/or child protection-led interventions. As Alison McLeod says in Chapter 4, 'there seems … to be flawed thinking in the idea that supporting families and protecting children can be separate, unconnected activities'. But conceptually, there is clearly a linguistic difference between the act of 'supporting' and that of 'protection', even if the two are closely intertwined.

As Kate Morris demonstrates in Chapter 1, the reality of 'family support' is complex. Not only is the meaning of 'family' far from straightforward, but the policy context is subject to frequent political review. Practitioners face difficult challenges because the main focus of their work tends to be on families who are either socially excluded or are seen to be antisocial. Such families may require assertive or even coercive 'support', with significant implications for the nature of practice.

In Chapter 2, Leonie Jordan explores the legal framework surrounding family support practice – essentially contained in the Children Act 1989 and the associated regulations and guidance. The Act gives discretion to local authorities, within reason, 'to set the threshold for access to … support services'. As a result, professional social workers and their managers are inevitably 'gatekeepers' for the provision of services, which are finite, often time limited and not necessarily ideally suited to the needs of the families concerned. Jordan argues that the 1989 Act 'provides a sound legal foundation for family support services', but that the reality of resource constraints means that there is often a gap between what families 'need' and what can be provided.

In exploring the theoretical foundations of family support work in Chapter 3, Nick Frost and Pat Dolan outline a matrix of interventions, differentiating between support initiatives that are statewide, community based or family focused. Social work practice tends to be concentrated in the last of these, and the authors emphasize the crucial importance of reflective practice as a key component in the provision of family support at this level.

Alison McLeod's research chapter (Chapter 4) reports a wide range of empirical material, but she acknowledges that 'evaluating the evidence on the effectiveness of family support can be challenging, as it is difficult to make a clear link between intervention, costs and outcomes'. Consequently, 'the evidence on the effectiveness of family support is less clear than that on how it should be delivered'. This should not, however, blind us to the valuable feedback on social work practice that research studies have provided as a result of focusing on the opinions of families and children themselves.

In the practice chapter (Chapter 5), Jess McCormack paints a vivid and wide-ranging picture of what social workers actually do when they provide family support. She describes four family settings, with circumstances ranging from the plight of a pregnant East European migrant to an 11-year-old schoolboy accused of disruptive behaviour in class but unable to communicate effectively with his deaf parents. In all four case scenarios, McCormack describes the nature of the social work interventions that were designed to provide support.

Nick Frost

1

Family support: policies for practice

K**ATE** M**ORRIS**

The policy context for the development of family support services has changed significantly during recent years. Family support now sits within a very different context; indeed, questions can be asked about the usefulness of the term in contemporary family-minded policy and practice. In this chapter, the changes are described and their implications for services and practices considered. Central to this discussion is the diverse meanings given to the idea of 'family' by policy-makers and practitioners. There are multiple understandings in policy and practice of 'family', and these generate challenges and tensions for those concerned with family support and family-minded practice.

The complexity of the policy context for family support presents questions for the maintenance of informal responsive interventions and the services that can support change within families and promote good long-term outcomes for children.

Understanding the meaning of 'family'

Generically, the focus of family-minded policies and practices is less than clear. It is, therefore, useful to try to establish some clarity in what is experienced by practitioners and service users as 'family' in family support policy and practice. A review of the recent literature concerned with approaches to vulnerable families identified that the majority of services labelled as 'family services' are, at the point of delivery, concerned with the immediate carers of a child. Indeed, there is an argument that, in service provision, the primary focus of concern and intervention is the mother (Gillies, 2005). There is evidence of an interchangeable use of the terms 'parents' and 'family' in family services, such as family centres, and in many models in practice engaged with parents and parenting. The child's extended network is rarely visible in the service provision (Morris et al., 2008).

Policy

Therefore, in contemporary family support policies and practices, the use of the word 'family' is worth careful scrutiny. There is limited evidence of services seeking to engage with the extended network of a child, of which parents are often only one part. Policy-makers rarely articulate a working definition of family and, as a result, assumptions are made about the appropriate recipients of family services. The focus of concern in family support needs teasing out, and this has important implications for the effectiveness of the services.

Conceptual understandings of family are contested. As Williams (2004) suggests, family-focused research has moved beyond a traditional concern with who constitutes the family to exploring family practices. The 'how' as well as the 'who' is now also the subject of theoretical and empirical study. The evidence from those services and practices that are actively concerned with children's networks suggests that, for children and families, understanding of family is a fluid and broad notion. Family networks are not restricted by geographical location, blood ties or proximity. The children's 'family', revealed by models of family engagement (such as family group conferences), includes a diverse range of related and unrelated members and reflects the child's history, traditions and experiences. Thus, the focus in service delivery and social work practice on a limited number of network members (usually mothers and/or parents) may not reflect the lived experiences of family life for children.

The introduction into the UK of the Family Nurse Partnership programme (DH, 2011) provides a useful example of the confusion between the labelling of policy streams and initiatives as 'family minded' and the reality in the practice of family at the point of service delivery. The initiative's name implies that the family of a child will be the focus of intervention. Studies here and elsewhere – the initiative has its origins in the USA – reveal a practice focus on mothers, with a limited amount of paternal engagement (Olds, 2006). The inclusion of grandparents, adult siblings and significant others is not set out in the programme design, nor in its translation into practice. As a result, the opportunities to promote skills and care within the extended network may well be overlooked, as will the types and forms of wider family practices that require intervention and change.

The theoretical and empirical work that explores the value of harnessing the child's network in promoting care and protection is well documented (see, for example, Folgheraiter, 2004). But policy and practice developments in family support have not yet fully engaged with this body of knowledge, nor have they explored wider involvement with the child's networks. Research suggests that, in policy and practice, the use of 'family' may be experienced as a narrow focus of intervention, involving only limited engagement with family members.

While the policy context has been the subject of considerable attention and change, at the point of service delivery, 'family' is translated into practices that work with parents and primarily mothers. Fathers have, historically, been either overlooked or more actively excluded from family support services (Featherstone, 2009). In part, this is attributed to the role fathers have played in family problems, but it is also rooted in traditional views of the responsibilities and functions of fathers and mothers in child rearing. Recent developments have sought to promote the involvement of men in family support provision. But this is as yet an underdeveloped area of policy and practice.

What is apparent is that, in any analysis of family support policies, the reality of provision at the point of service user engagement will need to be considered.

The changing policy context for family support

The implementation of the Children Act 1989 (CA 1989) alongside the commissioning and publication of a body of research during the early 1990s fuelled a debate about the focus of child welfare provision (DH, 1995). The research raised concerns about the professional preoccupation with child protection at the expense of support services to children in need. This research evidence revealed the extent to which children and their families accessed services through a series of assessments concerned with risk. Those demonstrating insufficient risk were often left to one side without alternative or helpful services (Gibbons et al., 1995), the risk being that families then re-entered the child welfare systems at a later stage with increasingly acute needs. Families also reported the absence of helpful early services and described the requirement for a crisis to develop before local authority services could be accessed (Lindley, 1994). The economic and human consequences of this emphasis on high-risk situations led to what is often referred to as the 'refocusing debate': the challenge of supporting a shift towards prevention while delivering services that met existing child protection responsibilities. The focus for prevention was on family support delivered within the framework of Part III of the CA 1989, with an anticipated development of services for 'children in need' (Morris et al., 2009).

The election of the Labour government in the UK in 1997 brought with it a new policy focus on prevention within the context of social exclusion (Barnes and Morris, 2009). This, in turn, had significant implications for the arrangements for family support, and the manner in which services were developed. The previous arrangements for family support had been framed by the CA 1989, which sought to promote the maintenance of children within their families and the provision of services to support children where there were additional needs (Ryan, 1989). The tenor of the legislation was reflective of a policy concern with negotiated provision, professional/family partnerships and the development of approaches that located rights and responsibilities within children's families. It is worth noting that, in the light of the discussion at the start of this chapter, this was, in reality, a focus on parental rights and responsibilities.

Early into their first term, the UK Labour government initiated a series of cross-cutting reviews led by policy action teams (PAT), one of which focused on children 'at risk' (SEU, 2000). The review raised concerns about the extent to which the CA 1989 had been able to promote early support and helpful informal services. The policy analysis was that the Act had failed to deliver the support needed by families to ensure long-term good outcomes for children. Instead, services had been focused on children with high-level needs and there had been a failure to develop holistic preventive family support services (SEU, 2000, p. 76):

> PAT believes the philosophy which lay behind the Children Act 1989 has never been put into practice for a combination of reasons:
>
> - the fact that the costs of crisis intervention fall on different budgets from those that might fund earlier preventative activity – and services that might fund earlier preventative activity would not receive any payback from it;
> - the way the priorities for services for young people are set out in legislation and policy guidance, and the consequences this has for their deployment of resources; and professional cultures.

The policy direction for family support changed in the wake of the various central government reviews. The focus became children's pathways into and out of social exclusion. The drivers for family-minded support services were embedded in an understanding of social exclusion as the key threat to children's long-term wellbeing. A discourse of risk and protective factors became a central theme (France and Utting, 2005). While the evidence base for accurately predicting outcomes for children was embryonic, there was a growing emphasis on understanding the exclusionary and inclusionary processes that led to poor outcomes for children:

> Proponents of the paradigm acknowledge that there is much still to be learned about the influence of individual risk factors, including their salience at different stages in children's lives, and the ways that they interact and contribute to poor outcomes. (France and Utting, 2005, p. 79)

The changing policy context relocated families as partners in developing socially and economically viable future citizens and in addressing the risks of the outcomes of social exclusion. Family involvement and support were assessed to be central to the development of protective factors. Fawcett et al. (2004) suggest that we saw the emergence of the 'social investment state', where families were responded to within a context of their role as supporters of future pathways out of the long-term effects of social exclusion. Specifically, families were positioned as partners in the production of socially and economically viable citizens. From this preoccupation with the consequences of social exclusion and the long-term outcomes for children came a broad policy drive towards an integrated approach to meeting the needs of children and their families. The CA 1989 was primarily concerned with individual assessments of need and individual responses to these needs, although provisions were made for the multi-agency involvement of local authority services. This approach to 'in need' services was largely replaced by the *Every Child Matters* change agenda. The *Every Child Matters* policy stream required support and welfare services to develop holistic responses to need for all children:

> The vision we have is a shared one. Every child having an opportunity to fulfil their potential. And no child slipping through the net. (DfES, 2004, p. 5)

Interagency working become a central theme in the policy framework, and legal and policy guidance enforced the bringing together of services around the child (the Children Act 2004). Thus the policy framework for family support moved from individual understandings of support and risk to one of broader concerns focused on generic indicators of outcomes for children. Within this context, traditional approaches to family support became subsumed within wider developments for prevention and risk management.

As a result, the policy and practice focus moved away from family support delivered in the context of children in need towards a national, centrally led set of preventive initiatives aimed at responding to the perceived risks of social exclusion. The government funded a raft of preventive programmes that targeted, primarily by geography, those children and families at the greatest risk of social exclusion. Prevention programmes, such as Sure Start, the Children's Fund and Connexions, were all funded centrally and rolled out nationally. But evaluations attached to these initiatives revealed that those families with high levels of need and more complex and enduring difficulties struggled to take up the preventive services provided. These were the families that social work has historically been concerned with, families with ongoing multiple needs who require a range of social work and social care responses. Family services had, in policy terms, again failed to reach those who most needed them and, as a result, new policy discourses emerged. The failure of the CA 1989 to produce early responses to children in need was compounded by a failure of the prevention programmes to engage those most in need. Family support had experienced a changing policy context, but still struggled to be an effective response for complex and multifarious reasons.

The families with chronic levels of need who were not evident in the take-up of preventive services were the new focus of policy concern. They were explicitly targeted as families with needs that presented high costs to society (SEU Task Force, 2008). They were presented as unwilling or unable to fulfil their role in the partnerships needed to address social exclusion. Highly targeted policies were developed that were argued to be necessary to respond to the 4% of families who presented multiple, complex needs and who were not responsive to existing preventive programmes. The Respect agenda and the Think Family policy stream became new contexts for family support and family-minded services.

For social work, there were issues of uncoordinated but overlapping policy and practice domains. As Spratt (2009) points out, families with multiple and enduring needs are frequently known to social work services, and thus they form a part of the caseload of social work practitioners. But the preventive programmes developed failed to engage with social work practitioners and services, as well as failing to engage with their clients. Social work was not evident in the practitioner groups involved in the prevention programmes (Frost and Parton, 2009) and social work knowledge and skills in engaging the most marginalized families were not utilized.

Think Family was the primary policy response to this apparent failure in family support responses to reach the most marginalized and excluded of families. This policy

Policy

stream sought to bring together previously segregated service arrangements (adult services and children's services) and develop a holistic approach to families with complex and enduring needs (SEU Task Force, 2008). Within this policy stream were specific initiatives aimed at supporting families who were deemed to be at high risk of poor outcomes. Examples included the extension of the Family Intervention Projects and the introduction of Family Nurse Partnerships and Family Pathfinders. The new targeted initiatives overlapped with traditional family support spheres of practice. The families who were the subject of the new family-minded interventions were families whose children were at risk of entering the care and protection systems, who experienced drug and alcohol problems, who lived with violence and poverty, and whose children had been the 'children in need'. The relationship between these new policies and services and existing family support services was unclear. For some localities, these additional support services were used to enhance provision, for others it led to a reduction in the more traditional services as funding moved to the new arrangements.

The confusing and at times contradictory set of policy drivers for some aspects of family support have emerged alongside changes in the arrangements for other, mainstream family support services. Support services such as Sure Start and children's centres have a chequered policy history, with changes to their remits and funding. The original intentions for these family services were concerned with easily accessible, preventive provision that sought to help families develop their skills in developing pathways out of poverty and social exclusion. Although drawing on a genre of US evidence-based prevention programmes, the UK Sure Start model can also be argued to be within a tradition of helpful, negotiated support services. As with Part III of the CA 1989, the tone and tenor of the Sure Start policy and programme was that families, with help and support, were best placed to help children achieve their potential. The model sought to assist families in rearing children to become social and economically viable citizens. While there is little evidence of strong connections between the family support services within social work and the Sure Start practitioners in the early planning of the initiative, there is evidence of Sure Start diverting children from more intensive social work intervention and of practitioners responding positively to the support provided by Sure Start centres to children and families (Tunstill et al., 2005).

In summary, the policy context surrounding families and family support has experienced significant changes since 1997. There has been a flurry of policy and service developments aimed at 'at risk' families. The resulting myriad of policies, services and interventions presents families with complex choices (Morris and Featherstone, 2010) and leaves practitioners with difficult challenges in bringing together multiple interventions stemming from different central and local policy streams.

The policy discourses: how families are understood

The apparent failure of Sure Start (and other allied preventive programmes) to reach all needy families generated policy concerns about the most marginalized and vulnerable families. There was a careful but clear delineation between mainstream families who wanted to 'do right' by their children and those families that were failing in their child-rearing responsibilities. The construction of 'good' and 'bad' parents was refined and enhanced by the growing body of legislation focused on antisocial behaviour and troublesome children (Cleland and Tisdall, 2006).

In the analysis of the plethora of family-minded policies surrounding family support, it is possible to identify discourses that suggest particular categories for conceptualizing families. These identities are then reflected in the type and tone of services provided and in the responses of practitioners. Murray and Barnes (2010) suggest that family-minded policy developments can be grouped around four 'identities' for families:

1 *The resourceful family:* families that can be expected to meet children's needs and can appropriately manage risks and care needs.
2 *The responsible family:* hard working, able to play their role as active citizens and meet a set of expectations about child rearing and parenting.
3 *The socially excluded family:* vulnerable, multiple need families that require intensive support and may reflect generations of disadvantage.
4 *The antisocial family:* families who are experiencing exclusion and presenting risky, difficult behaviours.

These categories are not mutually exclusive, and can represent some confusing realities for families. For example, families may simultaneously be expected to offer kinship care placements for children in need (resourceful), and yet be members of a family deemed to be antisocial or excluded by virtue of some family members being unable to care safely for children. The value of this analysis lies in its representation of the new discourses that surround family support. The point of engagement for families needing support – this may be antisocial behaviour or requirements to offer kinship care – will determine the subsequent practice and services responses.

Family support as a conceptual framework in child and family policy-making has therefore changed. It is no longer a localized process to assess children and provide their families with services based on thresholds of need. Instead, families are a site for intervention and for partnership, whether cooperatively or coercively. Families are seen as central to the future production of responsible and productive citizens, and family support is now set within a very different agenda. Understandings of family have also shifted. The policy developments now more clearly promote specific responses to families according to judgements about need and capacity. For family support, it can be argued that the identification in family-minded policies of a category of family that requires assertive, at times coercive 'support' services is of greatest significance and has substantial implications for future family support practice.

Models and approaches

As the body of literature concerned with family support suggests (Aldgate and Tunstill, 1995; Tunstill, 1997), the manner in which services have been provided has rested on a negotiated voluntary approach. While in reality the CA 1989 may have been primarily concerned with assessing needs for high thresholds, its intentions were to promote helpful responses that prevented further difficulties. In this context of responsive, informal family support provision, third sector involvement has had an important role. Large and small charitable organizations have traditionally sought to provide services that were concerned with alleviating family problems and preventing the escalation of need.

The policy focus on the development of large-scale preventive programmes resulted in an increased emphasis on the role of the third sector. Initiatives such as the Children's Fund (which covered England and Wales) placed an expectation on local areas to include voluntary sector organizations in the partnerships established to plan and deliver services to children at risk of social exclusion (Edwards et al., 2006). The connections with third sector provision at a local level gave a voice and an increased profile to community-based support services that were led by traditionally marginalized groups (Beirens et al., 2006). Black and minority ethic organizations were able to access funding to develop services, such as supplementary schools, family centres, school home partnerships and out of school schemes (Morris et al., 2006). These services reflected the needs of the communities that stimulated their development, but faced real problems in maintaining long-term provision, given the short-term funding streams attached to many of the initiatives. The 'policy churn' (Warren et al., 2006) meant that while the voluntary sector did achieve a higher profile in delivering support services during the Labour government's focus on prevention programmes, this was not sustainable as funding switched to other policy developments.

But models of provision of family support, irrespective of the policy context, have struggled to be experienced as 'family minded' at the point of service delivery (Morris et al., 2008). The earlier discussions identified the limited understandings of family utilized by policy-makers and practitioners. This is reflected in the models and approaches adopted in the configuration of family support services and the arrangements for family engagement. Whole family approaches, that is, those services that seek to work with the family rather than the individual(s) within the family, are relatively rare. Hughes (2010) proposes that existing family-minded provision can be best understood by adopting a series of categories. Reviews of the literature reveal that there are four approaches to responding to families in need. The first category sees no involvement of the extended family network. The services are only concerned with the presenting individual. Hughes (2010, p. 545) suggests three other categories:

1   approaches seek to strengthen the ability of family members to offer support to a primary service user within that family
2   family members are recognized as having their own specific and independent needs arising out of their relationship with the primary service user
3   includes 'whole family approaches' focused on shared needs and strengths that could not be dealt with through a focus on family members as individuals.

These categories helpfully reveal the limits in existing approaches and practices with families. In family support terms, the categories capture the different models of practice. While not mutually exclusive, those services focused on the child and working with adults insofar as they care for the child fall within the first category (parenting classes, home school learning partnerships, out of school schemes). The services that work with individuals with needs arising from their roles within the family reflect the second category (support work with mothers of young offenders, partners of drug and alcohol addicts, young carers). The family-based provision that seeks to engage the family as a whole sits within the final category (family group conference services, family therapy). The paucity of services within the final category is as a result of a long history of family support services being focused on individuals, particularly mothers.

In part, the limits to the models rest on the absence of a robust knowledge about the lived experiences of families who are the subject of policy concerns. The translation of family policy into parent or mother provision has meant that any empirical data about service use or user needs has focused on these groups within a child's network. While there is a growing evidence base about the characteristics and prevalence of families with multiple needs, this is not accompanied by a better understanding of the lived experiences of families with complex needs. Without this knowledge, family support services and the policies that surround them will, by necessity, have to make assumptions about family life and family practices. And these assumptions focus on parents – and particularly on mothers, with the absence of fathers in family support provision acknowledged but not as yet fully addressed (Featherstone, 2009).

The evidence from those adopting a whole family approach indicates that families are willing and able to engage positively with the opportunities such approaches present (Morris and Connolly, 2010). This is not to negate the needs within families for some individuals to be the focus of specific interventions. It also presents challenges for practitioners in developing skills in working with the multiple and sometimes conflictual identities and needs within a family. But new models and approaches to family engagement indicate that family support has new directions to travel, and innovative developments are possible.

New challenges and opportunities

The current legal framework for family support sets out expectations and requirements for the support families should receive and the rights and responsibilities professionals and families should assume. The preceding analysis of the policy context for family support has suggested that there is a tradition of responsive negotiated provision set within a permissive legal framework. Family support has historically been characterized by informal services that sought to support families to care for children. While the wellbeing of children was the focus of the services, the activity was primarily concerned with helping families care better rather than undertaking early intervention to prevent the longer term outcomes of social exclusion.

More recently, this tradition was accompanied by an assertive policy approach to identify and target those families that presented what was judged to be high risks and costs. This focus on specific groups of families facilitated the introduction of evidence-based prevention programmes. Policy attention turned towards understanding the effect and outcomes of defined programmes that fixed on early intervention to achieve long-term change for children. These programmes have a set of common characteristics; primarily those of being evidence-based, tested and targeted interventions with a predetermined model that requires fidelity in implementation:

> Evidence-based programmes are interventions that have a proven impact on children's health and development. All have been tested in experimental conditions to see if the desired effect is achieved. Most share several common features. They are targeted at a clearly defined problem and population and are underpinned by an articulated causal process, comprising a statement of logic about what is to be achieved, how and why. Some seek to prevent impairment before it occurs; others intervene early in its gestation, while others treat entrenched problems or prevent them from getting worse. (Axford and Little, 2010, p. 2)

Proponents argued for the feasibility of adopting tried-and-tested prevention programmes that could result in specified outcomes for children. These programmes and this policy stream are not the focus of this discussion. However, the growing prevalence of evidence-based early intervention in debates about family-minded responses will mean that existing family support services and practitioners will have to engage with this development and reflect on its relationship to established family support approaches.

> **Making connexions**
>
> To what extent and in what circumstances should social workers provide support to families where there is no identified child protection issue?

There is also a further, complicating policy discourse that has emerged. The purpose of family support – historically the maintenance of children within their network through family assistance – has been questioned and interrogated in the light of a series of tragic child deaths. The death of Peter Connelly, as a result of violence and neglect perpetrated by his immediate carers, caused widespread public outcry. The revisiting by Lord Laming of the provisions in England and Wales for safeguarding children led to a series of recommendations about procedures and practices (Laming, 2009). Alongside this focus on professional processes and arrangements, a discourse emerged concerned with the feasibility and appropriateness of social workers seeking to maintain children within their families:

> Repairing families cannot be the primary, if rarely expressed criterion for success. But when the wake of Baby P has subsided we shall return to the status quo in which social workers who intervene to remove children from parents face vilification. The emphasis is – too much in my view – on fixing families. (Neary, 2009, p. 180)

This discourse has significant implications for family support. In reality, families have struggled to be able to access or be offered comprehensive well-funded support services. In 2005, the Family Policy Alliance (2005, p. 2) described the ongoing difficulties families faced in accessing support services, and argued strongly for legislative change to ensure that assessments and services for children need were not curtailed:

> the reality is that many children, and families in need do not receive even minimal support and many have difficulties in accessing such services that are available.

In this analysis, family support policy and practice faces double jeopardy. Social workers are criticized for providing support for too long when earlier decisive action should be taken. Yet simultaneously, support services are criticized as inadequate and sparse. There may well be a reality within this paradox for families of 'too little for too long'.

In response to this challenge of inadequate and inappropriate support, there is a growing body of work concerned with better understanding of families experiencing ongoing and multiple difficulties. The study of the prevalence and experiences of families facing adversity presents methodological challenges (Devaney, 2008; Clarke and Hughes, 2010). However, without a greater body of knowledge, the capacity of family support services to provide effective responses to families in need will be curtailed. While prevention programmes have been the subject of quasi-scientific interrogation and evaluation, support services remain relatively underexplored. The rapidly changing policy context has inhibited the opportunities to carefully capture the impact and experiences of sustained support. Indeed, debates about the appropriateness and feasibility of enduring family support services continue, as Neary's quote above illustrates. Family responses to services reveal the value and importance of flexible, responsive services that can provide ongoing assistance and support. There is a political debate to be had about the willingness to provide such services, set within the policy context of a preference for evidence-based structured interventions.

Conclusions

This analysis of family support policies has described rapid change, with limited sustained activity. It is, without doubt, a confusing picture. The short-term funding of family-minded initiatives, coupled with the susceptibility of this area of policy to political change, has resulted in a complex history. There is now a lack of clarity about the role of family support in the current landscape. Early intervention prevention programmes are different in tone and content from the traditional support services but are a dominant theme in current policy discussions (Allen, 2011). The inadequate implementation of Part III of the CA 1989, followed by the political preference for rapid policy developments in prevention and social exclusion, has left family support struggling for an identity and at times a political and policy legitimacy. There is a renewed focus on families, but what the result of this will be for family support is, as yet, unclear.

Further reading

■ Frost, N. and Parton, N. (2009) *Understanding Children's Social Care.* London: Sage.

Provides a comprehensive overview and critical analysis of children's social care in England following the introduction of *Every Child Matters* in 2003 and the 2007 *Children's Plan*. Examines the key issues surrounding child care policy, politics and legislation, and their implications for practice.

■ Katz, I. and Pinkerton, J. (2010) *Evaluating Family Support: Thinking Internationally, Thinking Critically.* Chichester: Wiley.

The delivery of effective family support is a key global child welfare issue, yet there is little consensus on what constitutes family support or what the best ways are to evaluate it. Offers a review of the conceptual and operational problems involved in this complex and topical field.

■ Morris, K., Mason, P. and Barnes, M. (2009) *Children, Families and Social Exclusion: Developing New Understandings for Prevention.* Bristol: Policy Press.

Illustrates and explores the experiences of children and families who are most marginalized, using evidence from the National Evaluation of the Children's Fund. Considers the historical context of approaches to child welfare, and presents a new framework for understanding and developing preventive polices and practice within the context of social exclusion.

References

Aldgate, J. and Tunstill, J. (1995) *Section 17: The First 18 Months.* London: HMSO.

Allen, G. (2011) *Early Intervention: The Next Steps. An Independent Report to Her Majesty's Government.* London: HMSO.

Axford, N. and Little, M. (2010) 'Let's walk before we run', *Journal of Children's Services*, **5**(4): 2–3.

Barnes, M. and Morris, K. (2008) 'Strategies for the prevention of social exclusion: an analysis of the Children's Fund', *Journal of Social Policy*, **35**(2): 251–70.

Beirens, H., Hughes, N., Mason, P. and Spicer, N. (2006) *The Children's Fund and Refugees and Asylum-seekers.* Birmingham: NECF.

Clarke, H. and Hughes, N. (2010) 'Family minded policy and whole family practice: developing a critical research framework', *Journal of Social Policy and Society*, **9**(4): 527–31.

Cleland, A. and Tisdall, K. (2005) 'The challenge of antisocial behaviour: new relationships between the state, children and parents', *International Journal of Law, Policy, and the Family*, 19, 395–420.

Devaney, J. (2008) 'Inter-professional working in child protection with families with long-term and complex needs', *Child Abuse Review*, **17**(4): 242–61.

DfES (Department for Education and Skills) (2004) *Every Child Matters: The Next Steps.* London: DfES.

DH (Department of Health) (1995) *Child Protection: Messages from Research.* London: HMSO.

DH (2001) *Children Act Now: Messages from Research.* London: HMSO.

DH (2011) *The Family Nurse Partnership Programme,* http://www.dh.gov.uk/en/Publicationsandstatistics/Publications/PublicationsPolicyAndGuidance/DH_118530.

Edwards, A., Barnes, M., Plewis, I. and Morris, K. (2006) *Working to Prevent the Social Exclusion of Children and Young People: Final Lessons from the National Evaluation of the Children's Fund,* Research Report 734. London: DfES.

Family Policy Alliance (2005) *Supporting Children and Families,* briefing paper. London: FPA.

Fawcett, B., Featherstone, F. and Goddard, J. (2004) *Contemporary Child Care Policy and Practice.* Basingstoke: Palgrave Macmillan.

Featherstone, B. (2009) *Contemporary Fathering: Theory, Policy and Practice.* Bristol: Policy Press.

Folgheraiter, F. (2004) *Relational Social Work: Toward Networking and Societal Practices.* London: Jessica Kingsley.

France, A. and Utting, D. (2005) 'The paradigm of "risk and protection-focused prevention" and its impact on services for children and families', *Children and Society,* **19**(2): 77–90.

Frost, N. and Parton, N. (2009) *Understanding Children's Social Care.* London: Sage.

Gibbons, J., Conroy, S. and Bell, C. (1995) *Operating the Child Protection System.* London: HMSO.

Gillies, V. (2005) 'Meeting parents' needs? Discourses of "support" and "inclusion" in family policy', *Critical Social Policy,* **25**(1): 70–90.

Hughes, N. (2010) 'Models and approaches in family-focused policy and practice', *Social Policy and Society,* **9**(4): 545–55.

Laming, Lord (2009) *The Protection of Children in England: A Progress Report.* London: TSO.

Lindley, B. (1994) *On the Receiving End.* London: Family Rights Group.

Morris, K. and Featherstone, B. (2010) 'Investing in children, regulating parents, thinking family: a decade of tensions and contradictions', *Social Policy and Society,* 9, 557–66.

Morris, K., Mason, P. and Barnes, M. (2009) *Children, Families and Social Exclusion: Developing New Understandings for Prevention.* Bristol: Policy Press.

Morris, K., Warren, S., Plumridge, G. and Hek, R. (2006) *Preventative Services for Black and Minority Ethnic Children: A Final Report of the National Evaluation of the Children's Fund.* London: DfES.

Morris, K., Hughes, N., Clarke, H. et al. (2008) *Think Family: A Literature Review of Whole Family Approaches.* London: Cabinet Office.

Murray, L. and Barnes, M. (2010) 'Have families been rethought? Ethic of care, family and "whole" family approaches', *Social Policy and Society,* **9**(4): 533–44.

Neary, M. (2009) 'The case for care', *Public Policy Research,* **15**(4): 180–1.

Olds, D. (2006) 'The nurse-family partnership: an evidence-based preventive intervention', *Infant Mental Health Journal,* **27**(1): 5–26.

Ryan, M. (1989) *The Children Act 1989: Putting it into Practice* (2nd edn). London: Ashgate.

SEU (Social Exclusion Unit) (2000) *Young People at Risk: Policy Action Team Report 12.* London: SEU.

SEU Task Force (2008) *Reaching Out: Think Family.* London: Cabinet Office.

Spratt, T. (2009) 'Identifying families with multiple problems: possible responses from child and family social work to current policy developments', *British Journal of Social Work*, **39**(3): 435–50.

Tunstill, J. (1997) 'Family support clauses of the 1989 Children Act', in N. Parton (ed.) *Child Protection and Family Support: Tensions, Contradictions and Possibilities.* London: Routledge.

Tunstill, J., Allnock, D., Akhurst, S. et al. (2005) 'Sure Start local programmes: implications of case study data from the National Evaluation of Sure Start', *Children & Society*, 19, 158–71.

Warren, S., Apostolov, A., Broughton, K. et al. (2006) 'Emergent family support practices in a context of policy churn: an example from the Children's Fund', *Child Care in Practice*, **12**(4): 331–46.

Williams, F. (2004) *Rethinking Families.* London: Calouste Gulbenkian Foundation.

Policy

2

The legal foundations of family support work

LEONIE JORDAN

Part III of the Children Act 1989 (CA 1989), when implemented in 1991, created the foundation for the responsibility of the state to provide support services to children who were considered to be 'in need'. This was achieved by establishing a carefully considered set of duties and powers given to local authorities. These duties supplemented the duties the state nationally retained for what we usually refer to as 'welfare benefits' – broadly direct and indirect financial supports for adults who are not in employment or who need assistance with the cost of housing. The premise of Part III of the CA 1989 is that children do best if they grow up in their family, preferably cared for by parents or by family members. This premise is consistent with social and family policy, which recognizes that early intervention to support families and children who may be experiencing challenges and difficulties is more likely to prevent or reduce longer term impairment to a child's development. It is also likely to reduce the need for the child to be removed from their parents' care.

The CA 1989 gave to local authorities a general duty to children in their locality to provide a range of family support services to assist families whose children had needs beyond universal needs and where there were particular concerns about their health and development. However, the duty is a general or overall duty and is not an individual duty owed to each individual child in the local authority's area, so an individual child cannot directly claim a right to services from the local authority. Thus, how many children are defined as being 'in need' and therefore entitled to access support services is, in reality, 'rationed' or 'targeted'. This chapter will examine the present legal framework for the support services provided by local authorities. It will identify how these provisions have been interpreted by the courts and how they have been carried out in practice by professionals acting on behalf of the local authority. The challenge for professionals and for families caring for children is how best to 'target' the finite resources of the local authority and how to manage the tensions between partner agencies when deciding who has the responsibility for providing a service or any service at all.

The expectation was and remains that local authorities will systematically identify broadly the number of children in their locality whose health and development are being compromised by their individual or family circumstances and the types of need these children have, so that a wide range of services is developed or commissioned from partner agencies, including the voluntary or private sectors. The core principle remains that 'need' will be identified through a process of assessment by the social worker, in partnership with the parents or carers of the child, together with the child or young person. The assessment should be completed by the social worker, consistent with statutory guidance (DH, 2000), to clarify what the child's health and development needs are, so that services may then be identified to address those needs. Best practice assumes that services funded through the children's service funding stream of the local authority will be provided, where appropriate, in conjunction with services funded through adult care services, when the parent or carer has needs in their own right, and also in partnership with other agencies, such as health, education and housing. The Children Act 2004 (CA 2004), which must be read in conjunction with the duties in the CA 1989, aimed to strengthen the responsibility of the director of children's services to ensure more effective corporate sharing within the local authority of the duty owed to children 'in need', as well as strengthening cooperation with other agencies for 'improving the wellbeing of children', not just to safeguard and promote the welfare of children, in other words, to extend clearly the responsibility beyond a child protection remit (CA 2004, ss. 10(1), 14(1)).

For the purpose of clarity and simplicity in this text, the term 'parent and carer of a child or young person' includes any person who is bringing up a child, not just a person with 'parental responsibility' (CA 1989, s. 3 defines parental responsibility). Thus, the term includes a step-parent, co-parent, a family member or friend taking on the day-to-day parenting role, whether under a court order or informally. The term 'family' embraces many arrangements within which children grow up and is defined widely in the CA 1989 to include 'any person who has parental responsibility for the child and any other person with whom he has been living' (CA 1989, s. 17(10)). I will use the term 'child' to include all minors unless I am specifically talking about young people in a particular context.

What are the local authority duties for family support services?

Part III of the CA 1989, which needs to be read with Schedule 2 and 3 of the Act, sets out a framework for community-based family support services – such as family centres and after-school provision – as well as the support service of accommodation, whereby, in agreement with a parent with parental responsibility, the local authority provides a place for the child to live and be cared for as well as maintenance for the child's care. The CA 1989 also sets out, together with the Children (Leaving Care)

Act 2000 and the Children and Young Persons Act 2008, responsibilities on the local authority for young people who have been 'looked after' by the local authority (sometimes referred to as being 'in the care of the local authority'), provided certain criteria are met.

Inherent in the CA 1989, which built on earlier legislation requiring local authorities to provide family support services, is the issue about which children are owed this support duty and what is the extent of the duty owed. Professionals and their managers talk in terms of thresholds for access to services and inevitably are 'gatekeepers' for finite, often time-limited and not necessarily ideal services from the family and community's viewpoint. The legislation contains a concept of targeted services, with discretion to the local authority, within reason, to set the threshold for access to and the terms and duration of the services. This is an inevitable source of tension between the child's family and the professionals involved and their managers about whether a child is first identified as being a child 'in need' and provided with services at all. If the child is identified by the local authority as being 'in need', there is sometimes disagreement about what kinds of services will be provided and which are likely to be useful.

Section 17(1), Children Act 1989 states:

It shall be the general duty of every local authority (in addition to the other duties imposed on them by this Part) –

(a) to safeguard and promote the welfare of children within their area who are in need; and
(b) so far as is consistent with that duty, to promote the upbringing of such children by their families, by providing a range and level of services appropriate to those children's needs.

An important decision interpreting the provisions in section 17(1) was made by the House of Lords when it considered three appeals made on behalf of children about whether, when the local authority had identified a particular need as part of an assessment of a child, it was under a duty to provide to the individual child the service or resource to meet that need (*R (on the application of G)* v *Barnet London Borough Council*; *R (on the application of W)* v *Lambeth London Borough Council*; *R (on the application of A)* v *Lambeth Borough Council* [2003]).

A majority of the House of Lords decided that the duty under section 17 was a 'general' duty owed to all children who were 'in need' in the area of the local authority. The duty was described as:

an overriding duty, a statement of general principle. It provides the broad aims which the local authority is to bear in mind when it is performing the 'other duties' set out in Part III. (CA 1989, para. 85)

This general duty is targeted to children in the area who have broadly higher level needs (described usually as children 'in need'), as defined in sections 17(10) and 17(11) of the Act. These needs are beyond those which can be provided for by universal education and health services. The House of Lords said that the duty owed to an individual child or family was limited, which means that neither the child nor the family can require the local authority to provide one of their services or 'buy in' an appropriate service: 'the child in need does not have an absolute right to the provision of any of these services', meaning the services under Part III of the Act. Thus even if the child and their family are assessed and meet the 'in need' criteria, they may not get the type of social care support services they consider would assist their child.

The court took the view that Parliament had intended that the local authority had a degree of discretion, in view of its finite resources, to make judgements about what kinds of support services it would provide overall either directly itself or commission from other providers, and the kind and level of service it would provide to any child assessed as being 'in need'.

The definition of 'need' and 'in need' in sections 17(10) and 17(11) is also drawn widely.

Sections 17(10) and 17(11), Children Act 1989 state:

(10) … a child shall be taken to be in need if –

(a) he is unlikely to achieve or maintain, or to have the opportunity of achieving or maintaining, a reasonable standard of health or development without the provision for him of services by a local authority under this Part;

(b) his health or development is likely to be significantly impaired, or further impaired, without the provision for him of such services; or

(c) he is disabled

…

(11) … a child is disabled if he is blind, deaf or dumb or suffers from mental disorder of any kind or is substantially and permanently handicapped by illness, injury or congenital deformity or such other disability as may be prescribed; and in this Part –

'development' means physical, intellectual, emotional, social or behavioural development; and
'health' means physical or mental health.

The definition of 'disabled' comes from the National Assistance Act 1948. Families generally understand the concept of 'in need', with its focus on health and development, to mean that without extra support services, their child's wellbeing will deteriorate or not improve or that their child will be denied the opportunity to have

Making connexions

In what ways do social workers have discretion in determining the presence of 'need' in a child's situation? How likely is it that there will be variations in different workers' interpretation of 'need'?

the advantage of the extra support from the local authority or some other service provider. The words that give the local authority some degree of discretion about how or whether to exercise this targeted duty are 'reasonable standard' (CA 1989, s. 17(10)(a)) and 'significantly' (s. 17(10)(b)). These words enable professionals to make judgements about where to set the threshold or entry point for access to support services under Part III.

Definitions of 'development' and 'health' are the same as the definitions for the terms found in section 31 of the CA 1989, which sets out the grounds for care proceedings – a judicial application by the local authority to remove a child from their family without the parents' agreement. The link between being a child 'in need' and a child needing protection is thus established in the legislation, consistent with the concept of a child's development and health needs being along a continuum. This is reflected in professional judgements made after the child's needs are identified and the capacity of the child's carer to meet these needs taken into account. The question, then, for professionals is whether the child needs support through a 'child in need' plan, or protection and support services within a 'child protection plan' and the child protection regulatory framework. The 'in need' of social work support services threshold tends to be set by local authorities at a relatively high bar. Families may find that they are directed to other agencies to have the child's 'additional needs' – needs over and above universal health and education needs – supported, and may not be able to access the expertise of professional social work support. In reality, the threshold in some authorities may be so high that in practice only the children who are at risk of being a child protection concern are offered family support services.

When a parent or person with parental responsibility is aggrieved about what they see as a failure or refusal to provide any or a suitable family support service, they are entitled, along with the child, to make representations and complaints to the local authority (CA 1989, s. 26(3)). However, this is limited to children already identified as being 'in need' or who are already 'looked after' by the local authority. Families in dispute about getting to first base for services, where the dispute is about whether or not their child is within the definition of 'in need', are obliged to resort to the general social care complaints procedure.

Respect for private and family life and nondiscriminatory service provision

The family support provisions in the CA 1989 are consistent with the duty on the local authority as a 'public authority' to comply with the Human Rights Act 1998 (HRA 1998) and particularly the provisions of Article 8 – respect for private and family life. This Act also applies to child health and education providers as well as the police service; HRA 1998 section 6 applies the Act to 'public authorities'.

The HRA 1998 overarches the provisions of the CA 1989 and subsequent amending legislation, which means that child welfare legislation must be interpreted consistent with European convention rights enshrined in the HRA 1998.

Article 8 does not give an absolute guarantee to family life and therefore to services from these agencies to support a family in all situations to bring up their children. It is a 'qualified' right and the state and its agencies have to balance the child's entitlement to grow up cared for by their own family, who may at times need support services to do so, against the duty to protect and, if necessary, remove the child from their family. In such a situation, the local authority must follow a fair and transparent process, including an application to court if the parents do not agree with the local authority's proposals for the care of their child.

The duty on the director of children's services to plan jointly with partner agencies, to commission and provide support services to promote children's wellbeing must comply with both international obligations and domestic law on ensuring that services are nondiscriminatory. The HRA 1998 and its enshrined conventions, as well as the Equality Act 2010, create the framework for delivering these responsibilities: at the front line, it is the professionals working with children and their families who are the interpreters and decision-makers as to how services to enhance the wellbeing of children are delivered, as well as acting as the gatekeepers to resources.

Law

Human Rights Act 1998

This Act applies the rights contained in the European Convention on Human Rights 1950 to legislation passed by the UK Parliament and includes duties on the state to:

- secure the right to life – Article 2
- protect citizens from inhuman or degrading treatment and torture – Article 3
- ensure security and liberty – Article 5
- provide the right to a fair hearing if civil or criminal charges are made by the state – Article 6
- respect family life and private life – Article 8
- protection from forms of discrimination – Article 14

International treaties creating obligations on the state include:

- European Convention on Human Rights 1950 – see www.coe.int
- United Nations Convention on the Rights of the Child 1989 – see www.unicef.org

To ensure that the views and wishes of children and young people are given proper weight by the local authority when a decision is being made about whether to provide support services, the local authority is required to find out their views 'as far as reasonably practicable and consistent with the child's welfare' and give 'due consideration' to these views 'having regard to the [the child's] age and understanding' (CA 1989, s. 17(4A), amended by the Adoption and Children Act 2002, ss. 116(1), 148(1)). At the very minimum, the local authority must be able to demonstrate that it has found out what the child actually thinks about the services. Because a child or young person may have, for example, a communication barrier – through disability or where the child's and family's language may not be English – this is not an adequate reason not to find out their wishes and views. Particularly for young people, providing services that are not seen as helpful to either them or their family leads to potentially serious consequences for them.

The range of family support services: duties and powers

Considerable discretion remains with the local authority, subject to statutory guidance – that is, guidance issued under the Social Services Act 1970 with which local authorities must comply – about how to plan for and develop local family support services. A number of the duties are qualified. For example, the duty in section 18 of the Act to provide daycare for preschool children who are 'in need' – already giving scope to assess need and potentially restrict access – is further qualified by the phrase 'as is appropriate', giving the local authority, within reason and in compliance with its nondiscrimination obligations, the power to make the decision about what are suitable daycare services, who will provide these and the frequency and duration of these services for an individual child.

Part I of Schedule 2 of the CA 1989 sets out in greater detail the duties in relation to the range of family support services. It includes duties, often qualified, and powers or discretion to provide services. For example, the local authority is required to have a register of all children with disabilities – as defined in section 17(11) of the CA 1989 – in their area: this is aimed at ensuring present and future planning and commissioning of services for this group of children 'in need'. This duty is not qualified (CA 1989, Schedule 2, Part I, para. 2). The local authority is required to 'take reasonable steps' to provide services to prevent neglect and abuse, giving the local authority some autonomy about the kinds of services it develops and whether the services are provided in partnership with other agencies or delegated to other agencies to deliver (CA 1989, Schedule 2, Part I, para. 4). The local authority has a power, not a duty, to provide alternative accommodation, including cash assistance, where a person is posing or likely to pose a risk of significant harm to a child and agrees to live in accommodation other than the child's home (CA 1989, Schedule 2, Part I, para. 5). This structure of duties, often qualified by phrases like 'as they consider appropriate' or 'as far as is reasonably practicable', and powers or discretion to provide additional services, if it is consistent with their primary duty to protect children, set down the foundation for family support services.

Research studies into the barriers to providing and sustaining family support services have identified this ambit of discretion as central to the experience of children and their carers. For example, Aldgate and Statham's (2001) overview of the government-funded studies examining the implementation of the CA 1989 concluded that preventive services as envisaged in Part III of the Act are provided in 'a climate of intense competition for resources for public welfare services', with the inevitable outcome that services targeted to children 'in need' tended to be directed towards the most needy children and, even more so, to children 'at risk of significant harm'.

The service of accommodation for children and young people

Section 20 of the CA 1989 gives both a duty and a power to the local authority to provide for parents and carers a support service whereby, with the agreement of the parent, a child who is 'in need' can be 'looked after' by the local authority to assist, for example, a parent who needs a period in hospital because of their own ill health. Section 20 is sometimes misunderstood in terms of its purpose and its implications.

When the CA 1989 was being considered in Parliament, section 20 was the subject of considerable debate. Those supporting the provisions as drafted were clear that the intention was to give the parent an entitlement, subject to certain criteria, to ask for and receive the service of accommodation for their child – in other words, the local authority taking on, with their agreement, the day-to-day task of caring for their child. Unlike in earlier legislation, the parent who made the arrangement is not restricted in ending this service arrangement. The parent with parental responsibility or any other person holding parental responsibility under a court order, regardless of the duration of time the child has been looked after, usually by a foster carer, can request their child to be returned immediately to their care. If the local authority considers this is not in the child's interests, the local authority is required to make a court application for permission to refuse the parent's request by seeking an interim care order, or if there is immediate risk of significant harm to the child, an emergency protection order, provided the court is persuaded that the grounds for making such an order are met.

To access the service of accommodation, the child must be assessed by the local authority as being 'in need' and requiring accommodation for one of the reasons in section 20(1).

Section 20(1), Children Act 1989 states:

Every local authority shall provide accommodation for any child in need within their area who appears to them to require accommodation as a result of –

(a) there being no person who has parental responsibility for him;

(b) his being lost or having been abandoned; or

(c) the person who has been caring for him being prevented (whether or not permanently, and for whatever reason) from providing him with suitable accommodation or care.

Law

If the child gets through the gate of being identified as 'in need', the grounds for accommodating the child thereafter are broad. Local authorities become responsible for providing services to children and young people who have no identified carer – this may include asylum-seeking or refugee children – as well as those whose parent is not able to care for them at the time of the request, whether in the short or longer term.

However, as the arrangement is based on consensus or agreement between the parent and the local authority, the parent must have the capacity to make such an agreement and understand its implications. A parent who has, for example, a serious mental health issue that is preventing them from caring for their child may not have, at the time of making the request, the capacity to give an informed agreement to the proposed care arrangements. When accommodation under section 20 is provided, the parent keeps their parental responsibility but may delegate it, or such as is agreed, to the local authority, who will arrange for the child's day-to-day care. The local authority cannot withhold from the parent information about where the child is living (CA 1989, Schedule 2, Part I, para. 15), must comply with any contact orders that may already be in place, and cannot make major decisions about the child's care without the parents' agreement. The local authority is not permitted to provide the service of section 20 accommodation if the parent or any other person with parental responsibility for the child is 'willing and able' to either provide accommodation for the child or arrange for another person to do so. The local authority, similar to the situation when agreeing section 17 family support services, is required explicitly to ascertain the child's 'wishes and feelings' about the proposal to accommodate them under section 20 (CA 1989, ss. 20(6), 22(5)).

Section 20(3) imposes a duty on the local authority to provide accommodation under section 20 for 16- and 17-year-old young people if the criteria of being 'in need' and the consequence of having nowhere to live is likely to 'seriously' prejudice their welfare, in the opinion of the local authority.

Section 20(3), Children Act 1989 states:

Every local authority shall provide accommodation for any child in need within their area who has reached the age of sixteen and whose welfare the authority consider is likely to be seriously prejudiced if they do not provide him with accommodation.

This duty has significant ramifications for young people and local authorities and is the source of considerable tension about the way the local authority exercises its decision-making as to, first, whether the young person is 'in need' and, second, whether their welfare is likely to be seriously prejudiced by their present circumstances of having nowhere to live. The Act provides that young people aged 16 and 17 can agree the service of section 20 accommodation directly with the local authority, which does not need to have the agreement of the young person's parent. The parent has no right to discharge the young person from this section 20 accommodation arrangement.

Local authorities have been challenged about the way they exercise their discretion in relation to their duties and powers under section 20. The courts have taken a robust and at times pragmatic view of what 'in need' and 'prejudice to welfare' mean from the standpoint of young people. The court has observed that if a young person is 'sofa surfing', sleeping in cars and thus unable to eat well, take part in education or employment and is at risk, then they are likely to be both 'in need' and because of their lack of somewhere to live, their welfare is likely to be compromised significantly if the local authority does not provide suitable arrangements for them under section 20. Authorities have been reminded that it is unlikely to be reasonable corporate behaviour towards young people to 'bounce' them between housing services and children's services (see, for example, *R (on the application of G)* v *London Borough of Southwark* [2009]; *R (A)* v *Croydon London Borough Council* [2008]). The resource implications for local authorities are considerable and a continuing source of professional tension.

In some circumstances, to avoid the inevitable outcome of a child being separated from their parent or carer by being provided with accommodation under section 20, the local authority may choose to support the family by using its powers under section 17(6).

Section 17(6), Children Act 1989 states:

The services provided by a local authority in the exercise of functions conferred on them by this section may include providing accommodation and giving assistance in kind or, in exceptional circumstances, in cash.

This section was amended by the Adoption and Children Act 2002 (ss. 116(1), 148(1)) to include the power to provide accommodation – in other words, housing – to the child and parent or carer so that the family could remain together. Local authorities may be reluctant to take on such a commitment under section 17(6), especially where it may turn out to be a longer term commitment and when social housing resources are frequently limited or not available. Changes in benefits entitlements are also likely to make local authorities disinclined to use this power. However, a local authority could provide for a deposit to enable a family to rent in the private sector or could support rent payments for a period. Social workers may find it difficult to get managers to sanction either direct financial support – which may have conditions as to repayment – or to fund long-term housing arrangements or to actually access housing provision for a child and their family.

Services for disabled children and their family

Children with disabilities who are assessed as coming within the definition of 'disabled' in section 17(11) of the Children Act 1989 (see above) are children 'in need' and are entitled to support from the local authority's children's services. Some parents and professionals may consider that including these children within the group of targeted, 'in need' children has potentially constrained the expansion of support services for disabled children and their families in the struggle within the local authority for the allocation of funds between support and protection services. The CA 1989 has been amended (by the Health and Social Care Act 2001, s. 58) to enable parents of disabled children to request that the local authority make 'direct payments' to them, so that instead of receiving services from the local authority, the parent can purchase the kinds of services that the local authority is under a duty to provide (CA 1989, ss. 17A, 17B). However, the funding stream to provide for these arrangements is not secure and may change at any time. There is a view that this provision may have led to a degree of inequality in services for such children, as some families are more effective at purchasing services, mainly from the voluntary sector, than other families for whom dealing with service providers' application and review systems is challenging.

Supports for a family member taking responsibility for children under private law court orders

What is referred to as 'kinship' or 'family and friends' care has expanded since the implementation of the special guardianship order in 2005 (CA 1989, ss. 14A–14G, inserted by the Adoption and Children Act 2002; see also Jordan and Lindley, 2006). This order is more usually made to enable a family member to acquire parental responsibility for a child. It gives parental responsibility to the child's special guardian, which can be exercised to the exclusion of all other persons holding parental responsibility. In some cases, it may be granted to a person who was previously the foster carer of the child. The reality is that many of the children subject to this order are likely to be children with a significant level of needs, because of the history of care they received, either before the order was made or when they initially became 'looked after' by the local authority.

From its inception, the CA 1989 gave a power, not a duty, to the local authority to pay what is referred to as a 'residence order allowance' (Schedule 1, para. 15) to a person who is not a parent of the child but is caring for the child under a residence order, a private law order made under section 8 of the Act. Thus, local authorities have the discretion to support family members who take on day-to-day responsibility for a child. The power is discretionary: there is wide variation between local authorities as to the circumstances in which an allowance is paid and the amount paid. Many authorities had no clear policies and this has been criticized by the courts both for lack of transparency and potentially unfair decision-making. Most local authorities now have schemes that provide for both means testing and an annual review of the allowance paid, which creates a degree of uncertainty for these carers. Some of the children, who will have a considerable and enduring level of need, may well come within the definition of 'in need' in sections 17(10) and 17(11), although authorities are often reluctant to accept this. This arrangement raises the question of the role of the state to support a child who cannot live with one or both of their parents and the role of the family who take on the care of children within their family network. Some of these carers, based on their personal experience, would argue that not only does the state have a responsibility to assist these children and their carers, but that it would be a better and fairer system if it was provided for at national level, rather than devolved to local authorities, thus avoiding the potentially divisive struggle with other children 'in need' for finite resources.

The debate has become more pressing in recent years as local authorities seek to find long-term and secure family care arrangements for children, where either their parents agree they cannot bring them up or a court has decided that the child cannot grow up in the care of their parents. There are broadly two groups of children who are likely to become the subject of a special guardianship order:

1 those where a family member or a person connected to the child have come forward to offer to care for the child with the agreement of the parents, thus avoiding the need for the local authority to obtain a care order
2 those children who the local authority is already looking after – either in section 20 accommodation or as a result of a care order made in care proceedings – and who exit from local authority care status by being placed in the care of a family member or friend, who is usually supported to apply for a special guardianship order.

The provisions in the CA 1989 and the Special Guardianship Regulations 2005 create an additional set of duties on the local authority to provide a range of support services to the child, to the special guardian and to the child's parents, including, although subject to means testing, financial support. These support services include support with promoting contact arrangements and therapeutic supports. While there is a duty on the local authority in the case of a child who has been looked after and who is now going to live with a family member to assess the child's, carers' and parents' needs, there is no duty to provide for all the needs identified, subject to the local authority making a 'rational' decision.

A similar range of duties apply when a child is adopted either by a person within that child's family network or outside the family.

Family support services: what next?

The CA 1989 provides a sound legal foundation for family support services. The delivery of the services – by whom and what kinds of services – is inevitably subject to government policy about how the state prioritizes the health and development needs of children and young people, and the importance of supporting families, all of whom may, for many differing reasons, face challenges in bringing up their children. The debate about whether the state's responsibility should be devolved to a local authority is likely to continue. Some policy thinkers consider that to reduce the competition for resources between family support provision and child protection responsibilities, it is time to split the functions and remove family support provision from local authorities' remit. This viewpoint may not sufficiently acknowledge the reality of the continuum of health and development needs that children have and the fluid thresholds between needs above universal needs, high level of needs and needs arising from child protection risks and responses by the local authority.

Discussion about whether the family should be able to self-assess to identify need under sections 17(10) and 17(11) is an important part of the debate to review again whether there are restrictive barriers and invisible thresholds to services. Part III of the CA 1989 is imbued with the principle of partnership between the service provider and the child, the young person and their carer when family support services are put in place. The duties and powers give to professionals working with children and their families the levers with which to advocate and negotiate support services: the central issue remains – are there a sufficient range of useful support services available to the child and family at the time when they request and need these?

Appendix 2.1 Table of cases

R (A) v Croydon London Borough Council [2008] EWCA Civ 1445
R (on the application of G) v Barnet London Borough Council
R (on the application of W) v Lambeth London Borough Council
R (on the application of A) v Lambeth London Borough Council [2003] UKHL 57, 1 All ER 97
R (on the application of G) v London Borough of Southwark [2009] UKHL 26

Further reading

■ Brayne, H. and Carr, H. (2010) *Law for Social Workers* (11th edn). Oxford: OUP.

Substantial text giving social workers a detailed account of the legal framework for social work practice for children and adults; includes case studies, discussion points and exercises, which embed legal concepts into day-to-day professional decision-making.

■ Moran, P., Ghate, D. and van der Merwe, A. (2004) *What Works in Parenting Support? A Review of the International Evidence*. London: DfES.

Provides helpful context in understanding some of the practice dilemmas for practitioners when working with children and families to provide support services, and offers an understanding of what parents and carers find helpful and barriers to accessing services.

■ Morris, K. (ed.) (2008) *Social Work and Multi-agency Working: Making a Difference*. Bristol: Policy Press.

Considers, from a perspective of partnership practice, the challenges for current social work practice in working in multi-agency settings where agencies have differing legal responsibilities and professional approaches.

References

Aldgate, J. and Statham, J. (2001) *The Children Act Now: Messages from Research*. London: DH.

DH (Department of Health) (2000) *Framework for the Assessment of Children in Need and their Families*. London: DH.

Jordan, L. and Lindley, B. (eds) (2006) *Special Guardianship: What Does it Offer Children Who Cannot Live with their Parents?* London: Family Rights Group.

Law

3
The theoretical foundations of family support work

NICK FROST AND PAT DOLAN

The seemingly straightforward concept of 'family support' contains within it many challenges, complexities and practice dilemmas. 'Family support' also comprises a number of diverse practices and thus it is difficult to define it or theorize about it. As a consequence of this complexity, it is sometimes referred to as a 'slippery concept' (Frost et al., 2003, p. 7) and because it encompasses so many meanings, 'it is difficult to disentangle them' (Penn and Gough, 2002, p. 17).

Despite this complexity and ambiguity, family support has a central and crucial role within child welfare and, in most social democratic societies, is embodied in legislation – such as in section 17 of the Children Act 1989 in England and Wales, reflecting the 'right to family life' enshrined in the United Nations Convention on the Rights of the Child.

As a diverse and difficult-to-define concept covering a range of practices, it is unsurprising that family support is underpinned by a number of theoretical approaches. In order to understand family support, it is important to examine theories about the 'family' as a social construction and theories around the idea of 'support'.

Ideas around family support and the related concept of 'early intervention' raise profound theoretical challenges about the relationship between childhood, families and the state. All of us will have strong opinions on these relationships: some of us will be more interventionist, others less so. Within this context, the aim of this chapter is to share theoretical perspectives on family support in order to enhance and develop practice, and to reflect on the value base that underpins family support.

Theories of the family

Family support is concerned with our understanding of the family and how we understand family forms and family change. Issues about the family are frequently highlighted in media and political debates: the publication of official statistics or new research is often greeted by headlines about the 'decline of the family', 'poor parenting skills', the 'increase in divorce' or the 'number of children born out of wedlock' and so on. When the original research or statistics are consulted, it is often the case that these headlines are exaggerations and that media responses can be understood as 'moral panics'. A moral panic was defined definitively by the sociologist Stan Cohen (1973, p. 9) as a situation where 'a condition, episode, person or group of persons emerges to become defined as a threat to societal values and interests'.

Moral panics are frequently focused on the family, particularly around single parenting and family breakdown – concerns that lie at the heart of family support practice. Carol Smart (2007, p. 10) reflects on these debates around the family:

> Perhaps the most significant of these debates around family life have been those between (1) ideas of the demise of the extended family and the rise of the 'modern' nuclear family; (2) the decline of marriage as an economic contract and the rise of companionate relationships between spouses; (3) the changing status of childhood and the growth of child-centredness; (4) and latterly the decline of the nuclear family and the rise of fluid family practices.

The approach taken by Smart and others is influenced by feminism and the 'family practices' school. The family practices perspective emphasizes that there are many ways of being connected with others and thus that 'family' is defined by what we do:

> The concept of 'family practices' … focuses on the everyday interactions with close and loved ones and moves away from the fixed boundaries of co-residence, marriage, ethnicity and obligation that once defined the … nuclear family. It registers the ways in which our networks of affection are not simply given by virtue of blood and marriage but are negotiated and shaped by us, over time and place. (Williams, 2004, p. 17)

This perspective is contested by those who we may identify as 'traditionalist' in their approach to the family, including writers such as Patricia Morgan (1998, p. 66), who complains that:

> Where the definition of family is stretched to cover any household, where any living situation and all transitional states are equally 'families', there is nothing to decline or dissolve, only movement between ever-transmuting 'family forms'.

Morgan (1998, p. 74) argues that the traditional dual parent family unit promotes the best interests of children, as it is a:

> *fact* that family structures may differ in the opportunities they offer to growing children … the number of children with psychosocial disorders has grown over the same time as families have increasingly fractured and fragmented … lone parenthood is the strongest socio-demographic predictor of childhood injury … children are more likely to go into care following a crisis when the family is 'reconstituting' itself.

Theory

In terms of a theory to underpin family support, it is argued here that perhaps the most useful theoretical framework is the 'family practices' approach, because the concept of 'family practices' captures the complexity of modern family life that confronts family support professionals every day in their practice.

Another useful way of thinking about the family comes from sociologist Anthony Giddens. Giddens and related theorists, who reflect on modernity, risk and change, argue that family change can be unsettling and brings with it many problems. Giddens is keen to establish that, while family change brings challenges, this does not mean that such change should be regretted, as family change has brought with it more freedom and equality for both women and children. Giddens (1999, p. 63) utilizes the idea of the 'democratic family', where there is:

> a democracy of the emotions in everyday life ... this applies as much in parent-child relationships as in other areas ... they should assume an in principle equality ... in a democracy of the emotions, children can and should be able to answer back.

Giddens is often identified as a 'communitarian', a theory that can be clearly related to family support practice. This idea influenced Tony Blair, British prime minister from 1997 until 2007, and can be seen in many aspects of family policy adopted by the New Labour government. Communitarians place an emphasis on both 'rights' and 'responsibilities' in the links between the community and the family.

Etzioni (1993, p. 54), American communitarian theorist, represents a trend within communitarianism that places a strong emphasis on responsibilities, and thus argues that: 'making a child is a moral act. Obviously it obligates the parents to the child. But it also obligates the parents to the community.' Etzioni (1993) emphasizes that the needs of children should be prioritized: parents have a moral responsibility to the community to invest themselves in the proper upbringing of their children.

Communitarianism provides a potential framework for reflecting on how the state and the family relate to each other, and the crucial role that family support practice has at the interface between the two.

Family support: the research base

The starting point for many family support debates is often the US project, the High-Scope Perry Preschool Program. It is worth rehearsing the history of the HighScope programme at some length, as, in many ways, it provides a theoretical template for other family support programmes, certainly in research terms.

The programme ran in Perry Elementary School in Ypsilanti, Michigan in the 1960s. It consisted of an intervention with 123 low-income African American three- to five-years-olds. This was made up of 2.5 hours of high-quality daycare for the children during the week, drawing on an active learning/child-centred model. The daycare took place alongside a home-visiting programme.

Perhaps the most remarkable element of the programme was an extensive research process, which followed up the children at 15, 19, 27 and, most recently, at 40 years of age. The findings are extensively reported and the data analysis is both complex and sophisticated.

Children were allocated to an intervention group and a control group. There were 58 children in the intervention group and 65 in the control; the attrition rate is remarkably low, with the researchers being in contact with about 90% of the group at the 40-year follow-up.

Here we can only provide a summary of the evaluation findings and will focus on crime and financial impacts. Heckman et al. (2009, p. 11) undertook a secondary analysis of the statistics and they are critical of some of the original research methods, but nevertheless conclude that: 'crime reduction is a major benefit of this program'. An example of the statistics that back up this assertion include:

> The program group had fewer arrests overall than the control group (averages of 1.3 versus 2.3 arrests per person), fewer felony arrests (averages of 0.7 versus 2.0 arrests per person), and fewer juvenile court petitions filed (averages of 0.2 versus 0.4 petitions per person). (Parks, 2000, p. 2)

Bellfield et al. (2006) undertook an overall cost–benefit analysis and estimate that $12.90 is saved from public costs for every dollar invested and argue that these gains come mainly from reduced crime by males. Cunha and Heckman (2006, p. 1), drawing on the HighScope Perry programme data and other programme data, argue that 'the most effective supplements supply family resources to young children from disadvantaged environments'. Most commentators, including Cunha and Heckman (2006, p. 60), argue the social gains are related to educational change, so that, in American terms: 'completing high school is a major crime prevention strategy'.

The research evidence here seems to be persuasive, but, as we have seen, the family is often a site of debate and controversy: debates about the family tend to be controversial and ideological. This point is demonstrated by some of the controversies flowing from the HighScope programme evidence. Reflecting on some of the same data reported above, one commentator argues that, as a result of the HighScope programme, 'the children from this program have in reality become welfare moms and hardened criminals' (Peters, n.d.). This position draws on the same data discussed by Bellfield, Heckman and others – so we can trace the strong impact of ideology and differing value positions here.

While the US research base is strong, it contrasts with the situation in other parts of the world. In the UK, for example, the Social Care Institute for Excellence stated that 'primary research in the areas of early intervention and of integrated working are in their infancy, and there is, therefore, limited direct evidence' (Wolstenholme et al., 2008, p. 3). Along similar lines, a senior manager in Birmingham, England, recently stated: 'Because we couldn't find any evidence on cost effectiveness of early interventions in this country, we went overseas (Cooper, 2010, p. 18). We clearly have an evidence deficit on this side of the Atlantic. The

Theory

evidence challenges in relation to family support were illustrated by the experience of evaluating Sure Start, which was powerfully critiqued by Michael Rutter (2007). The evaluation evidence was mixed, with even some negative impacts being identified following Sure Start intervention.

Family support: the theory base

Having explored an example drawn from the research base, we now go on to explore some of the theoretical underpinnings of family support. Within the HighScope programme, we can begin to detect the basics of a theory of family support:

- it is based on early intervention, which may refer to early in the life of the child and/or early in the emergence of the identified social problem

> **Making connexions**
>
> This chapter suggests that, in the wake of the HighScope Perry programme, 'we can begin to detect the basics of a theory of family support'.
>
> Think about the six elements identified. How many of them involve the social worker? What other services play a part?

- is an active process that engages with the parent and/or child
- attempts to prevent the emergence of problems and to promote better outcomes for children
- works in some form of partnership and agreement with the family
- draws on a theory of change – that the intervention leads to some change in the family
- generates social benefits, such as future savings in public expenditure, or decreases in social problems such as crime.

Theories of family support

Family support programmes can exist on many levels so far as their location is concerned:

- *Statewide initiatives:* such as anti-poverty programmes or political programmes that have fundamentally attempted to change childhood. We tend not to think in such terms but countries such as the post-revolutionary Soviet Union (Bronfenbrenner, 1974) or China (Xhou and Hou, 1999) were effectively attempting profound and overarching 'family support' programmes that were political and ideological in nature.
- *Community-based or neighbourhood initiatives:* such as Sure Start in the UK. These initiatives have universal intentions in that they are intended to reach every family in their identified geographical areas. They have ambitious aims in terms of bringing about area-based change that would improve the way of life for families in that locality. The nature of this ambition is reflected in a comment made by the London Metropolitan Police commissioner: 'We need the long-term activ-

ities using the facilities that are already in place, making sure that things such as Sure Start are there … they are equally as important as my officers on the street' (*Daily Telegraph*, 18 August 2010).

- *Family-focused initiatives:* such as parenting programmes or those designed to tackle key challenges such as domestic violence or substance abuse. These initiatives tend to be focused on families with identified issues.

Family support can thus be understood using a typology in terms of the location of the intervention: statewide, community based or family focused. But family support can also be understood in terms of the intentions or level of the intervention. Traditionally, intervention programmes tend to be identified using three levels:

1   *Primary prevention:* usually universal programmes, often area based, working on a voluntary basis with a wide range of families. The aim is to prevent the emergence of family problems.
2   *Secondary prevention:* generally aimed at families with challenges, who usually recognize these issues themselves and wish to work with agencies towards the achievement of change through a support and partnership model.
3   *Tertiary prevention:* is at the 'heavier' end of family support. It may focus on issues such as drug and alcohol misuse or domestic violence. It may involve working with children in state care or towards such children returning home.

This interplay between the location of the intervention and the level of intervention is represented in Table 3.1.

Table 3.1 A matrix of family support interventions

	Primary	Secondary	Tertiary
Statewide initiatives	Parenting helplines	Mediation schemes	
Community-based initiatives	Play schemes	Targeted work in children's centres	Domestic violence programmes
Family-focused initiatives	Advice 'drop-ins'	Home Start and related home-visiting schemes	Family Intervention Projects

Theorizing the matrix

Levels of intervention for family support

Levels of intervention to support children and families are generally viewed as forming 'dosages'; they range from small amounts of intervention to many people (universal provision) to large amounts of intervention to few people (targeted provision). This links levels of need to incremental service provision and the associated costs.

Theory

The primary/secondary/tertiary model typology is the oft-cited Hardiker model (Hardiker et al., 1991):

1 *Primary family support* includes universal interventions such as a visit from a public health visitor to all parents through a postnatal programme, or school inoculations and other universal health services. These operate on the principle that by preventing or intervening early (both in terms of early years and early in the development of a problem), the later onset of greater problems can be averted, thus leading to financial savings for health services as well as – equally if not more important – social gain for families and society more widely.

2 *Secondary family support* seeks to identify and intervene at an early stage in the onset of problems in the lives of children, families and communities. Usually through domiciliary or community-based services, professionals seek to provide time-limited help to enable families to cope, become resilient and better linked with primary support. Home Start, the international voluntary organization that provides a service based around home visiting, is a useful example of this level of family support. The assumption that underpins secondary interventions is that if problems or issues are addressed through strengths building in children, parents and families, the need for more intensive interventions, including out-of-home placement of children, can be averted.

3 *Tertiary family support* is often perceived as remedial, in that it typically includes intensive actions by professionals addressing severe social or personal problems. Such interventions may, for example, include domestic violence and substance abuse programmes; or they can involve children being placed away from their home and parents through kin-based, foster or residential care, as well as more intensive monitoring by professionals. The creative care of children in respite, foster or residential care can be an important element of family support practice at this level. Stein and Rees (2002) highlight the fact that better outcomes post-placement are achieved where children in the care system receive support from their families.

Similarly, even in the context of serious child protection issues, support from responsive and safe family members is crucial for children who have been abused (Buckley, 2003; Thompson, 2009).

Sites of intervention for family support

Statewide initiatives

Statewide initiatives aim to provide some support to all families on the basis not just of common good but on the underlying assumption that a low dosage of support to all families will lessen the need for more expensive interventions later. Such initiatives vary from country to country but usually combine a mixture of regular support to children by means of payment to the parent(s) of some form of children's allowance, or through tax credits. Alternatively, some initiatives may focus on the early years of childhood through the provision of free or low-cost child care provision. It is noteworthy that, whereas there is generally a focus on the universal provision of support to families with young children, the support from the state tends to wane as children get older and move into the teenage years – a time which can be far more costly to parents.

Community-based initiatives

Community development and capacity building is well established, and in many ways represents a form of collective support for families (Chaskin and Baker, 2004). In recent years, some initiatives have focused on targeting support to specific families in need in local communities and ensuring that wider local social capital improves, for example the Communities that Care programme, introduced to Britain from the USA (Hawkins and Catalona, 2002). This is sometimes referred to as 'progressive universalism' (Frost and Parton, 2009).

There is, however, a tension within this approach. Families can be seen as being best supported in communities by building on the community's own strengths, through, for example, better housing and employment opportunities. Conversely, some approaches to community-based initiatives target disadvantaged localities and work with the identified set of families known by professionals to be in most need of support, for example the Springboard Family Support programme in the Republic of Ireland (see McKeown et al., 2000).

Whereas these two approaches to community-based family support may seem as being somewhat in opposition or 'polar' in terms of policy, it can be argued that both approaches are required. Universal community development projects that step back and help all can complement more immediate specific supports to targeted children and families in need. This connection needs to be in partnership with stakeholder participation, respectful and discrete, thus enabling a tide that can 'lift all boats' in terms of giving real meaning to community regeneration when it is required.

Family-based initiatives

Family support initiatives tend to focus on parents as key agents in enabling resilience and overall coping capacity. For example, well-established international family-based programmes, including Family Nurse Partnerships (Olds et al., 1997) and Incredible Years (Webster-Stratton, 1992), both well known and fully evaluated, operate on the principle of a strong partnership with parents. However, the same level of attention to connectivity with parents tends to be less evident in programmes for teenagers, which, it can be argued, sometimes can exclude familial carers. The need to identify parents as key supporters to teenagers and as active family support agents has been highlighted by James Whittaker (2009), particularly when helping 'high-risk' youth. Even in terms of enabling civic engagement in youth as a method to ensure their better wellbeing, youth civic action programmes need to include parents and family as a central aspect of the process (Dolan, 2010).

Theory

Youth mentoring programmes such as Big Brothers Big Sisters, which has been in existence for over 100 years, are well proven as an effective adult friendship model for youth in need (Tierney et al., 1995). In recent times, implementation of Big Brothers Big Sisters has been advocated as needing wider models of progression, so that young people can move on to other forms of support (Rhodes and Lowe, 2008). This has been manifested in Ireland where the programme has involved strong connections to parents and communities by providing it as an 'add on' to youth work rather than a stand-alone programme (Brady and Dolan, 2007). Just as community-based initiatives may best achieve community capacity building by including an element of specific family support infusion, so family-based initiatives may need to combine working with parents and older children on similar models to work with early years children.

Underpinning family support with reflective practice

Positive close personal relationships underpin the presence and prevalence of family support (Cutrona, 2000); and it is well established that better mental health is associated with perceived support from the family (Pinkerton and Dolan, 2007). Improved wellbeing (Dolan, 2010) and stronger resilience (Ungar, 2008) have been identified as other key benefits of positive familial and friendship relationships. In this context, supportive interventions from professionals and services that are strengths based (Saleeby, 1996) achieve positive outcomes for children and families through family programmes; this has been strongly emphasized in UK research (Belsky, 1997) and internationally (Barnes, 2003).

Increased emphasis is being placed on evidence-based services, which contribute to proven outcomes in relation to family support (Daro and Donnelly, 2002). However, although the need for evidence and proven programmes to support families is desirable, in themselves 'programmes do not make the worker'. The core issue of responsive relationships between professionals and the children and families they work with and for is crucial in building an effective partnership.

Reflective practice connects how service users receive an intervention from a range of professionals to the type and level of support on offer (Dolan et al., 2006). Thus the professional utilization of Kolb's model of thinking in action in a reflective and questioning mode is strongly encouraged (Kolb, 1984). Rather than seeing reflective practice as depending on a purely subjective judgement by frontline workers, perhaps counterbalancing fidelity to tightly scheduled and manualized, almost 'robotic' programmes, a balance or mixture is required. This includes the capacity of workers to support families by a process of distilling benefits from programmes but with an awareness of their effect on those they work with (Canavan et al., 2009).

A simple framework for building family support from interventions (what is intended) to outputs (what is done) to outcomes (what is effective) is outlined in Table 3.2. This attests to an emerging theoretical idea that connects the provision of family support to bonding social capital (or 'getting by') and bridging social capital (or 'getting ahead') (Putnam, 2000). In terms of interventions, this allows a comparison between the work of professionals who see their role as limited to ensuring they connect with service users in the first instance (bonding social capital) or aim for more radical change and improvement in terms of bridging social capital.

Thompson (2009) has argued that responsive and reflexive professionals are those who aim for higher targets for those they work with. This being the case, the importance of hidden practical help is known to be more effective than explicit advice from professionals (Bolger and Amarel, 2007). However, using the 'getting ahead' target in family support interventions, and through the use of a reflective practice approach, more outputs can be achieved by simply matching support needs to the support provided, including the provision of emotional advice linked with practical help.

In terms of outcomes, the approach of professionals in the provision of family support can involve ensuring that service users are able to cope – a goal which in itself should not be undervalued. However, through the use of a cocktail of the best elements of proven programmes with an ongoing reflective practice vision, which includes the aim of achieving substantial improvement, high-quality practice can be envisioned. These relationships are presented in Table 3.2.

Table 3.2 Conceptualizing family support

Family support orientation	Getting by – bonding capital	Getting ahead – bridging capital
Interventions	Connecting	Changing
Outputs	Practical support (hidden)	Multiple forms of help
Outcomes	Coping	Improvement

Conclusion

We have seen in this chapter that the concept of 'family support' is complex and difficult to define. We have argued that family support can be underpinned by two forms of theory – theories about the family and theories about how support actually works. We have also seen that family support exists at the complex interface between the state and the family. As a result of this interface, family support practice can be both political and controversial. As family support is multilevel and multifaceted, it is the case that no one theory or one theoretical framework is adequate to understand or conceptualize it. A comprehensive approach to family support needs to draw on wider social theories (around equality and social change), mid-range social theories around communities and social resilience, and micro-theories concerned with bringing about change in individual families through one-to-one or therapeutic approaches.

This theoretical pragmatism – not unusual in social work – is helpful, as family support has to address a number of social challenges in many different contexts. If such an approach is underpinned by research evidence and reflective practice, this can help professionals to utilize theory and research in the best interests of families.

Further reading

■ Allen, G. (2011) *Early Intervention: The Next Steps. An Independent Report to Her Majesty's Government.* London: TSO.

Influential government-commissioned study of early intervention, suggesting innovative methods underpinned by a rigorous evidence base.

■ Dolan, P., Canavan, J. and Pinkerton, J. (eds) (2006) *Family Support as Reflective Practice.* London: Jessica Kingsley.

Interesting and engaging collection of papers, with an international flavour, in which the editors propose a 'reflective practice' approach delivering family support.

■ Williams, F. (2004) *Rethinking Families.* London: Calouste Gulbenkian Foundation.

Short, readable book that provides new ways of thinking about families and family change, drawing on innovative social research and theory.

References

Barnes, J. (2003) 'Interventions addressing infant mental health problems', *Children & Society*, 17, 386–95.

Bellfield, C.R., Noves, M. and Barrett, W.S. (2006) *High/Scope Perry Pre-School Program: Cost Benefit Analysis Using Data from the Age 40 Year Follow Up*. New Brunswick, NJ: NIEER.

Belsky, J. (1997) 'Determinants and consequences of parenting: illustrative findings and basic principles', in W. Hellinckx, M. Colton and M. Williams (eds) *International Perspectives on Family Support*. Aldershot: Ashgate.

Bolger, N. and Amarel, D. (2007) 'Effects of social support visibility on adjustment to stress: experimental evidence', *Journal of Personality and Social Psychology*, **92**(3): 458–75.

Brady, B. and Dolan, P. (2007) 'Exploring good practice in Irish child and family services: reflections and considerations', *Practice*, **19**(1): 5–18.

Bronfenbrenner, U. (1974) *Two Worlds of Childhood*. Harmondsworth: Penguin.

Buckley, H. (2003) *Child Protection Work*. London: Jessica Kingsley.

Canavan, J., Coen, L., Dolan, P. and Whyte, L (2009) 'Privileging practice: facing the challenge of integrated working for outcomes for children', *Children & Society*, 23, 377–88.

Chaskin, R.J. and Baker, S. (2006) *Negotiating Among Opportunity and Constraint: The Participation of Young People in Out of School Time Activities.* Chicago, IL: Chapin Hall Center for Children at the University of Chicago.

Cohen, S. (1973) *Folk Devils and Moral Panics*. London: Paladin.

Cooper, J. (2010) 'Can preventive services survive?', *Community Care*, 3 June, pp. 3–5.

Cunha, F. and Heckman, J. (2006) *Investing in our Young People*. Chicago: University of Chicago.

Cutrona, C.E. (2000) 'Social support principles for strengthening families: messages from America', in J. Canavan, P. Dolan and J. Pinkerton (eds) *Family Support: Direction from Diversity*. London: Jessica Kingsley.

Daro, D. and Donnelly, A.C. (2002) 'Charting the waves of prevention: two steps forward, one step back', *Child Abuse and Neglect*, 26, 731–42.

Dolan, P. (2006) 'Assessment, intervention and self-appraisal tools for family support', in P. Dolan, J. Canavan, and J. Pinkerton (eds) *Family Support as Reflective Practice*. London: Jessica Kingsley.

Dolan, P. (2010) 'Youth civic engagement and support: promoting wellbeing with the assistance of a UNESCO agenda', in C. McAuley and W. Rose (eds) *Child Well-being: Towards a Better Understanding of Children's Lives*. London: Jessica Kingsley.

Dolan, P., Canavan, J. and Pinkerton, J. (eds) (2006) *Family Support as Reflective Practice*. London: Jessica Kingsley.

Etzioni, A. (1993) *The Spirit of Community: Rights, Responsibilities and the Communitarian Agenda*. New York: Simon & Schuster.

Frost, N. and Parton, N. (2009) *Understanding Children's Social Care*. London: Sage.

Giddens, A. (1999) *Runaway World*. London: Profile Books.

Frost, N., Jeffery, L. and Lloyd, A. (2003) *The RHP Companion to Family Support*. Lyme Regis: RHP.

Hardiker, P., Exton, K. and Barker, M. (1991) *Policies and Practice in Preventive Child Care*. Aldershot: Avebury.

Hawkins, D. and Catalano, R. (2002) *Communities that Care: Action for Drug Abuse Prevention*. London: Wiley.

Heckman, J., Moon, S.H., Pinto, R. and Savelyev, P. (2009) *The Rate of Return of the High/Scope Perry Pre-School Program*, Discussion Paper 4533. Bonn: IZA.

Kolb, D. (1984) *Experiential Learning as the Science of Learning and Development*. Englewood Cliffs, NJ: Prentice Hall.

McKeown, K. (2000) *Supporting Families: A Guide to What Works in Family Support Services for Vulnerable Families*. Dublin: TSO.

Morgan, P. (1998) 'An endangered species?', in M. David (ed.) *The Fragmented Family: Does It Matter?* London: Institute for Economic Affairs.

Olds, D., Eckenrode, J. and Henderson, C. (1997) 'Long term effects of home visitation on maternal life course and child abuse and neglect: fifteen-year follow-up of a randomized trial', *Journal of the American Medical Association*, 278, 637–43.

Parks, G. (2000) *The HighScope Perry Preschool Project*. Ypsilanti, MI: Juvenile Justice Bulletin.

Penn, H. and Gough, D. (2002) 'The price of a loaf of bread: some conceptions of family support', *Children & Society*, **16**(1): 17–32.

Peters, B. (n.d.) *Preschool's Magic Black Box: Critique of High/Scope Perry Preschool Claims*, www.iche-idaho.org/issues/34/.

Theory

Pinkerton, J. and Dolan, P. (2007) 'Family support, social capital, resilience and adolescent coping', *Child & Family Social Work*, 12, 219–28.

Putnam, R. (2000) *Bowling Alone: The Collapse and Revival of American Community*. New York: Simon & Schuster.

Rhodes, J. and Lowe, S.R. (2008) 'Youth mentoring and resilience: implications for practice', *Child Care in Practice*, **14**(1): 9–17.

Rutter, M. (2007) 'Sure Start local programmes: an outsiders perspective', in J. Belsky, J. Barnes and E. Melhuish (eds) *The National Evaluation of Sure Start: Does Area-based Early Intervention Work?* Bristol: Policy Press.

Saleeby, D. (1996) 'The strengths perspective in social work practice: extensions and cautions', *Social Work*, **41**(3): 296–305.

Smart, C. (2007) *Personal Life*. Cambridge: Polity Press.

Stein, M. and Rees, G. (2002) 'Young people leaving care and young people who go missing', in J. Bradshaw (ed.) *The Wellbeing of Children in the UK*. London: Save the Children.

Thompson, N. (2009) *Practising Social Work: Meeting the Professional Challenge*. Basingstoke: Palgrave Macmillan.

Tierney, J., Grossman, J. and Resch, N. (1995) *Making a Difference: An Impact Study of Big Brothers Big Sisters of America*. Philadelphia: Public Private Ventures.

Ungar, M. (2008) 'Resilience across cultures', *British Journal of Social Work*, **38**(2): 218–35.

Webster-Stratton, C. (1992) *The Incredible Years: A Trouble Shooting Guide for Parents of Children Age 3–8*. Toronto: Umbrella Press.

Whittaker, J.K. (2009) 'Evidence-based intervention and services for high-risk youth: a North American perspective on the challenges of integration for policy, practice and research', *Child & Family Social Work*, **14**(2): 166–77.

Williams, F. (2004) *Rethinking Families*. London: Calouste Gulbenkian Foundation.

Wolstenholme, D., Boylan, J. and Roberts, D. (2008) *Factors that Assist Early Identification of Children in Need in Integrated or Inter-agency Settings*, Research Briefing 27. London: SCIE.

Xhou, X. and Hou, L. (1999) 'Children of the cultural revolution: the state and the life course in the People's Republic of China', *American Sociological Review*, **64**(1): 12–36.

4
What research findings tell social workers about family support

ALISON MCLEOD

Family support in its different guises has a long history in our society. In Jane Austen's novel *Emma*, first published in 1816, there is a delightfully observed scene where the heroine engages in what might be termed 'family support'. The squire's daughter in a country village, Emma, who has reasons of her own for walking across the village and appearing charitable, sallies forth laden with provisions to visit a family in need. The family's problems are identified as sickness and poverty, ignorance and 'temptations', and Emma's solution is to offer them a combination of handouts plus advice: 'the distresses of the poor were as sure of relief from her personal attentions and kindness, her counsel and her patience as from her purse' (Austen, 1933, p. 86). What difference, if any, her ministrations make and what the family think of them is not recorded: these are not Emma's concerns.

By the middle of the twentieth century, our understanding of how to support families in difficulties had become less top down: an account of wartime Pacifist Service Units' work with 'problem families' states: 'Family case-work is more than the distribution of relief or advice. It is a matter of helping one's neighbours out of difficulties, enabling them to live fuller and more satisfying lives' (Stephens, 1947, p. 45). Stephens (1947, p. 46) stresses that, while the worker can encourage and assist families, 'he cannot inflict his remedies on them nor coerce them'. The 'rehabilitation' of families in difficulty, he argues, can be achieved in an environment of interagency cooperation through practical and material assistance combined with social and domestic education, provided all services are delivered in a genuinely respectful manner, which helps people whose self-confidence is at a low ebb to seek their own solutions to their problems. The elements of what might still be seen now as good practice in supporting families can already be seen here. However, what

Stephens lacks is the modern emphasis on demonstrating effectiveness: there is no attempt in his book to provide evidence that his approach works, or works better than any other.

In our more utilitarian age, particularly in the face of a shrinking public sector dominated by cuts in government spending, it has become essential for social care agencies to justify all expenditure. To this end, practitioners need to know what research can tell them about which interventions are likely to have the most positive long-term outcomes for service users. Managers and others responsible for budgets will also be asking which approaches are most cost-effective. This chapter tries to draw together and summarize the current state of knowledge on what works when supporting families so that practitioners and managers know where to find the evidence that will back up their choice of interventions.

One of the first obstacles one faces when researching family support is that there is no consensus on what the term covers. To quote Penn and Gough (2002, p. 17): 'Family support is one of those phrases that is used so often it has almost lost its meaning, or rather it encompasses so many meanings that it is difficult to disentangle them.' For a start, the meaning of the phrase differs according to who you ask. Penn and Gough demonstrate clearly that families in need may have quite a different conception of the sort of support they need from staff in the agencies that are there to support them.

Family support can be either informal – provided by friends, relatives and neighbours – or formal – provided by public, private or voluntary organizations. The coalition government elected in 2010 is keen to maximize the use of informal support to reduce costs, but Ghate and Hazel (cited in Quinton, 2004) have found that most families using formal services are already accessing high levels of informal support as well; it is, therefore, hard to see where such savings will be made. Nevertheless, we can learn from the way informal services operate. Quinton (2004, p. 78) argues that formal services should aspire to some of the qualities that families appreciate in informal ones: individual, relationship-based, flexible, respectful and empowering: 'The need to feel competent and in control is just as important in people's relationship with formal as it is with informal sources of support.'

In many agencies within children's social care, family support is taken to mean interventions with families where there is a relatively low level of need – levels 1 and 2 of Hardiker's model (Hardiker et al., 1991), that is, universal services or services for children and families needing extra support. Such work is often allocated to unqualified staff and would by definition exclude children in public care or those with child protection plans. 'Family support' can also be used synonymously with early intervention or 'preventive' work: 'better a fence at the top of the cliff than an ambulance at the bottom' (Sinclair et al., 1997, p. 8). Earlier intervention, it is claimed, can save money as well as lives (Laming, 2009, p. 23). However, this begs the question: prevention of what? Work with children with child protection plans can prevent admission into the care system; work with families of looked after children can prevent the children staying in care long term; and in both cases this would be work at Hardiker's levels 3 and 4: services for children and families needing intensive assistance or urgent intervention. In Quinton's (2004) summary of research in the field, *Supporting Parents*, research on supporting foster carers and pregnant teenagers in care is included: neither of these groups would fall into the category of early intervention.

There seems to me to be flawed thinking in the idea that supporting families and protecting children can be separate, unconnected activities. As *Messages from Research* (DH, 1995a) demonstrated, a narrow focus on an alleged incident of ill-treatment, ignoring the wider needs of the family, can be traumatic and unhelpful for both child and parents. On the other hand, as serious case reviews have proved over the decades, from Maria Colwell and Jasmine Beckford to Peter Connelly (DHSS, 1974; London Borough of Brent, 1985; Haringey LSCB, 2009), ignoring the child's perspective and focusing on the needs of the parents can have catastrophic outcomes. I would argue that family support and child protection must be two sides of the same coin. The child's welfare should be paramount, even for staff working primarily with the parents; equally, promoting best outcomes for children at risk of significant harm requires the worker to pay attention to the needs of parents, supporting them and working in partnership with them, as far as is compatible with the child's welfare (Thoburn et al., 1995; DCSF, 2009; Kendall et al., 2010).

In this chapter, I consider the evidence on the effectiveness of formal services aimed at supporting children who are living with their families in the community, whatever their perceived difficulties and whether or not they are perceived to be at risk of significant harm. I examine different approaches to delivering support to families and then look at what research says about support needed by parents and children with different problems. A number of cross-cutting themes will emerge, including the need for a holistic approach, the importance of partnership and the value of timely intervention. These will be drawn together at the end.

Evaluating the evidence

As in all social work research, evaluating the evidence on the effectiveness of family support can be challenging, as it is difficult to make a clear link between intervention, costs and outcomes. Social work does not have outcomes you can easily count and proving cause and effect can be tricky since humans are complex and are influenced by many factors (McLaughlin, 2007). Even deciding whether or not an intervention has achieved its objectives may be hard, since participants' views about both objectives and outcome may differ (Triseliotis et al., 1995; Aldgate and Bradley, 2001). There can be ethical as well as practical issues in denying intervention to a control group, so large-scale randomized controlled trials are relatively rare in UK social work research generally, although interest in them is growing (Axford and Little, 2008). Some would argue that all quantitative research in social care is flawed (Thorpe, 1994), and it is the case that much of the research base on family support has a qualitative methodology.

As a result of the predominance of research using 'soft' qualitative data, we have a much clearer understanding of how service users would like us to intervene than we have of which interventions lead to the best outcomes. Such 'soft' data should not be rejected. According with service users' wishes involves listening to them and taking their views seriously, sharing information, treating each service user as an individual and working in partnership: this chimes clearly with social work's value base (GSCC, 2002), and it may also make service users more willing to engage with practitioners and so enhance the chance of interventions being successful. Nevertheless, there are limits to how much notice must be taken of service users' views. As Everitt et al. (1992) make clear, consumer opinion has its limitations: there is not one service user voice but many; the interests of different service users may conflict, for example what is best for the child may not accord with the parents' wishes; and consumer opinion tends to be conservative. Quinton (2004, p. 193) observes that some service users' expectations of services were unreasonable, leading him to conclude that 'users' views *on their own* may not always be a reliable guide to improving services'.

The evidence on the effectiveness of family support is less clear than that on how it should be delivered. Although there are a large number of studies indicating that carefully thought-out interventions can assist troubled families, the data are complex and conclusions qualified. In Quinton's view (2004, p. 203), the research shows that 'parents can be helped directly with their parenting, but also that the ecology of parenting and the direction of influences within it are very complex'. Kendall et al. (2010) illustrate this graphically: in their study of multi-problem families, although nearly half of the families benefited from support services, issues in about one in five of the families actually became *worse*, not better, following the intervention. The authors attribute this finding to the fact that hitherto unknown difficulties came to light once agencies engaged with the families. The timing of the intervention appears to be critical. Moran et al. (2004), in their review of international evidence on parenting support, found that while early intervention produced the best results, late intervention was better than none at all. They also found that longer interventions with follow-up were required for more entrenched situations where families had multiple problems.

Although early intervention is hailed as a money saver for taxpayers – 'the poppy in the battlefield of expenditure cuts', according to MP Graham Allen (Joswiak, 2010) – evidence on whether family support interventions are cost-effective is limited. Stevens et al. (2010) reviewed a range of approaches including home visiting for new parents, parenting programmes for parents of young children, cognitive behavioural therapy (CBT) and mentoring schemes for adolescents with problem behaviour. They concluded that there was evidence that all could be effective, but evidence on cost-effectiveness was thin on the ground. The main problem here was the difficulty of predicting potential future costs in a social care context. Views differ on this issue. Kendall et al. (2010, p. 22) report 'preliminary and illustrative findings' that for every million pounds spent on supporting families with multiple problems, there is the potential to save £2.5 million.

It is often argued that 'it is no longer acceptable for services to be commissioned that do not either use evidence-based programmes or evaluate alternatives in rigorous trials' (Hutchings et al., 2008, p. 24). Indeed, to use untested methods is to risk wasting one's time and perhaps doing more harm than good. Best social work practice requires the practitioner to keep up to date with the latest research and rigorously evaluate their own practice (Everitt et al., 1992). Nevertheless, a cynic might point out that the most rigorous evaluations are often carried out in situations where someone stands to gain financially from demonstrating that an intervention is effective: parenting programmes are international money-spinners, so it may be no coincidence they are the interventions that have been most rigorously tested and hence have the strongest evidence base (Stevens et al., 2010). Many aspects of family support work merit further research (Statham and Smith, 2010); nevertheless, the families we work with need help now and social workers cannot wait until research has answered all the questions. Meanwhile, we must do our best, armed with what research has discovered so far.

Approaches to family support

The concept of family support encompasses a wide range of interventions, and research on each technique has come up with different indicators for best practice. Some of the most used approaches are discussed below.

Parenting programmes

Parenting programmes have been a growth area in the past two decades. They vary but are generally delivered to groups of parents, using group discussion, role-playing and videos to teach 'positive parenting'. This involves spending 'quality time' with the child, giving encouragement and rewards for desired behaviour, avoiding physical punishment or aggression in response to misbehaviour, and promoting responsibility and age-appropriate independence. Some of these programmes have been more rigorously researched than others. Such programmes require facilitators to be specially trained and to stick closely to a prescribed programme. Whether the less rigorously evaluated programmes are actually any less effective is debatable.

There is a wealth of evidence indicating that parenting programmes can reduce parental stress and improve children's behaviour and emotional wellbeing (Hutchings et al., 2008), but they do not benefit all families equally. Parents with the most entrenched problems are least likely to attend, and, if they do, least likely to stay the course (Moran et al., 2004). Such parents need a more holistic approach to their problems, what Fox and Holtz (2009) have termed 'wrap-around family support'. This might include, for example, a programme of constructive activities, problem-solving training and literacy support for the children (Scott and Sylva, cited in Quinton, 2004). For some parents, including those with learning difficulties and those with complex problems, individual work at home covering the same material as the group parenting programmes may be more effective (Fox and Holtz, 2009).

Research

Home visiting

Home visiting, whether by qualified or unqualified staff or volunteers, is another common component of family support programmes. This has the benefit of giving the parent individual time and attention: 'What parents and children in need of support often appreciate most is someone who has time to sit down, listen, treat them with respect and help them to find solutions to their own problems' (Statham and Biehal, 2004). The home visitor may also offer practical support with parenting tasks, which is appreciated by many harassed parents (Ghate and Hazel, cited in Quinton, 2004). Statham and Smith (2010) identify that health visitors, providing as they do a universal, non-stigmatizing home-visiting service for all families with young children, are well placed to support families where there are difficulties, but they argue that in areas of high deprivation, the normal service may need to be increased if it is to have any impact. Targeting vulnerable groups, for example teenage parents, can also yield promising results. The use of volunteers in home-visiting schemes is appealing because it is seen to be cost-effective. Volunteers can listen, advise and befriend without stigma, particularly when they come from the local community and have faced similar difficulties themselves (C4EO, 2010), but they need to be trained, supported and used with caution. Statham and Smith highlight conflicting research into the efficacy of home visiting by volunteers, and Moran et al. (2004, p. 4) conclude: 'Supporting families without compromising their autonomy is a demanding and delicate job and highly skilled and appropriately trained staff will get better results.'

Home visiting is, of course, the bedrock of a traditional family casework approach to social work, but it can involve an element of challenge as well as support. Searing (2003, p. 314) argues that 'the aim is to get beyond normal politeness and to be able to raise sensitive subjects, ask probing questions and explore things more deeply'. If family support is all carried out by people without professional qualifications, this element of possibly uncomfortable but necessary intrusiveness may be lost. However, if child protection work is seen as a separate activity from family support, there is a risk of losing the central psychosocial relationship between social worker and client: 'Basic skills such as sharing information and listening continue to be key in achieving change – such skills are rooted in respect and empathy' (Morris and Shepherd, 2000, p. 173). Forrester et al. (2008), however, researching communication between social workers and parents in child protection scenarios, found that the social workers were better at clarifying their concerns than communicating empathy for the parents' situation. They argue persuasively that this can be counterproductive.

Direct interventions with children

While parenting programmes and home-visiting schemes target the parents, some approaches to supporting families are addressed more specifically at their children. The promotion of language development in toddlers and early years child care provision can both aid children's all-round development. Families facing the highest levels of deprivation are, however, least likely to access these services (C4EO, 2009; Speight et al., 2010). Statham and Smith (2010) refer to evidence indicating that groupwork can assist the social and emotional development of children identified as shy or withdrawn, and that CBT can be effective in building children's emotional resilience. Buchanan and Ritchie (2004) survey the literature on the effectiveness of therapies and behavioural interventions with children, and conclude that CBT is the best evidenced type of therapy, but that many approaches to direct work with children have little, if any, support from research. This may, of course, reflect the absence of relevant research and the difficulty of evidencing change in emotional wellbeing rather than actual ineffectiveness.

For children with more complex difficulties, multifaceted interventions are most likely to be effective. Fox and Holtz (2009) describe an effective approach to work with toddlers who were living in poverty and exhibiting behaviour problems. This combined individual work with both parents and children and incorporated nondirective play and parenting training carried out at home. Incentives in the form of food coupons were offered to parents for completing the programme. Similarly, Rose et al. (2009) report 'modest but promising' results for a project intervening with children under 12 with challenging behaviour, where group and individual work was carried out with both parents and children. Biehal (2005) studied specialist support teams offering short-term intensive interventions with families with teenagers at risk of coming into care. These teams focused both on changing the adolescent's behaviour and on modifying parenting style. The most successful interventions were long rather than short term, offered multiple approaches and were linked to good relationships between the worker, the young person and the parents and to changes in the environment, for example a change of school. Situations where interventions were least likely to be successful were characterized by longstanding, entrenched difficulties, marital conflict or parental mental health problems and/or the young person identifying with an antisocial peer group. The key variables were found to be the parents' and child's motivation to change and the worker's skills.

Promoting access to finance and services

Income support may not be the responsibility of many agencies offering family support, but ignoring the impact of poverty on parenting does parents a disservice. Penn and Gough (2002, p. 30) argue that:

> Poverty is overwhelming for those who experience it, yet most family support measures do not address it. Poverty has repercussions for health and for the take-up of preventive health measures as well as for participation in wider leisure activities.

Research

They conclude that services will be ineffective unless they address the full range of resources that families need. Quinton (2004, p. 83) agrees: 'Tackling poverty and lack of resources is a key part of tackling parenting problems.' Having good knowledge of the benefit system and of local resources is clearly going to be important for practitioners supporting families. Good information about services, accessibility, assisting with transport and providing incentives for accessing services each has a part to play. It can also be argued that family support agencies should look more widely at a family's needs and help them, for example, to take up literacy and numeracy classes (C4EO, 2009) or healthcare (Penn and Gough, 2002).

Accessibility of services is a recurrent issue in the research. One problem, not just for parenting classes and home-visiting schemes but common to all services aimed at supporting families, is that men are much less likely to engage with them than women. Penn and Gough (2002, p. 19) comment that although agencies talked about working with 'parents', in fact, they aimed their services at mothers, and engaged fathers were 'treated as a prize catch'. Statham and Biehal (2004) suggest that agencies should develop a strategy for engaging fathers, provide tailored services and activities for them, and give a specific staff member the role of encouraging the engagement of fathers. Providing ethnically sensitive services is another challenge for agencies: satisfaction with services among some minority groups, especially where there are language differences, is low. This mirrors the many access barriers preventing people with any sort of disability from receiving the services they need. Quinton (2004) highlights poor interpreting services, indifferent communication, serious issues with access, fragmented services, buck-passing, lack of resources, and high thresholds for involvement. There is clearly much more that agencies could do to make family support available to all.

Nevertheless, Quinton (2004, p. 170), summarizing research on four other groups who may be 'hard to reach' – pregnant teenagers in care, young fathers in prison, rejecting parents and 'multi-problem' families – concludes that while 'support for them is indeed in short supply … this is not entirely the fault of the services', since they frequently rejected help that was offered, refused to acknowledge concerns, saw the child and not themselves as the problem, were 'overdependent' or wanted services only on their own terms. 'In short, these were often difficult families to 'support' and work with.'

Children's centres, with their philosophy of providing a range of non-stigmatizing community-based resources for families often delivered by unqualified staff and volunteers, are frequently held up as a better way of delivering support than high-tariff, high-cost, statutory social work teams. However, Quinton (2004, p. 170) found that families already receiving services from the centres 'were strikingly unwilling to see services extended to other groups of needy parents'. This suggests again that the notion of providing services through volunteers and community groups may not work well for families with more complex difficulties.

Reorganizing services

Following the publication of *Messages from Research* (DH, 1995a), local authorities were urged to 'refocus' their services towards family support. Dartington Social Research Unit (DSRU, 2004) summarizes findings on how to reorganize services to redress the balance from 'heavy end' interventions towards preventive services. It advises a thorough structural reorganization using good evidence about local patterns of need, with involvement from all relevant agencies. This should be planned carefully following consultation with both service users and staff, giving attention to political support, funding and ongoing training needs. Following reorganization, changes must be monitored and evaluated. The authors signal a note of caution, however: 'There is little evidence of any impact of organization per se on child outcomes … it is only ever part of the solution' (DSRU, 2004, p. 2). This reflects findings by Kendall et al. (2010) and Biehal (2005) that all models of service provision had weaknesses as well as strengths and no one organizational structure could be linked to greater effectiveness. Reorganizing services is no substitute for good professional judgement, supported by insightful and challenging supervision.

> **Making connexions**
>
> What does research tell us about what makes for good social work practice in the provision of family support?

Supporting families facing particular issues

Much of the research into supporting families is not about preventive work in general, but about the specific types of support needed by families facing particular challenges. The following sections summarize the evidence on what works best in different circumstances.

Children with disabilities

Children with disabilities are defined within the Children Act 1989 as automatically coming under the category of 'children in need' and so are entitled under the same Act to support services from local authorities to help them achieve their potential while continuing to live with their families. Such support can be valuable: 'It can take just one professional who is committed to working with a family on their terms to make a great, positive and lasting benefit to them' (Clavering, 2007, p. 41). Research into current service provision can make depressing reading, however. Quinton (2004) identifies problems with planning and coordination, poor information, a lack of partnership with parents, and culturally insensitive services dominated by a medical model.

Nevertheless, there has been a substantial amount of research indicating what makes for good practice: Abbot et al. (2005) found that the best approach involved joined-up multi-agency services with a specific key worker to coordinate service delivery to the family and a holistic attitude: not just emotional support but practical and financial help too, together with promotion of the child's healthcare needs and education. Clavering (2007) reports on the views of parents of disabled children and concludes that social workers should listen to parents and take their views seriously, spend time getting to know the child and be knowledgeable about disability. At the same time, they should see the whole child, not just the impairment, and see the whole family, not just the disabled child. Parents, she found, want social workers to provide practical and emotional help and to fight their corner. Mitchell and Sloper (2001) found that disabled children want to feel welcome and included, to see their friends, to get out, meet people and join in leisure activities, and Franklin and Sloper (2006) add that they wish to be involved in decisions and to be given choices. Naylor and Prescott (2004) researched the views of siblings of children with disabilities and found that they were looking for people who understand, opportunities to express their feelings, more time to themselves away from their disabled sibling, and more individual attention from adults.

Families with a disabled parent

Quinton (2004, p. 129) reports poor practice in families with a disabled parent too: 'Services often concentrated on parents' disability and ignored their needs as parents'; the deficits in their parenting were highlighted and their needs for support in parenting tasks not acknowledged. Access, stigma and poor information created unnecessary barriers. Services, he found, worked better where there was a key worker system, and staff needed to be emotionally supportive as well as technically skilled. Morris and Wates (2006) look at the needs of parents with physical disabilities and sensory impairments. Practical aids, adaptations and assistance with everyday parenting tasks such as taking the child to school were high on their list of wants, together with information, workers who were well informed about their particular needs, advocacy and effective access to services. For example, deaf parents benefited from a specially tailored parenting programme, rather than just an interpreter, if they were to get most benefit from the course. It was important that staff considered the adults' needs for parenting support, not just for healthcare and social support relating to their disability.

Parents with learning disabilities

The Social Care Institute for Excellence (SCIE, 2005a) summarizes research findings on parents with learning disabilities, demonstrating that they face negative attitudes from agencies, fragmented services, and are often passed backwards and forwards between adult and children's services. Individual home-based programmes have been found to work better for this group of parents than centre-based/group parenting courses. Social support networks are particularly important for their psychological wellbeing, although it is not clear that this makes them better parents. As in so many other situations, a holistic approach is indicated, bearing in mind that poverty, unemployment and single parenthood can increase parenting stress; the authors warn against assuming that all the parents' difficulties stem from their learning difficulties.

Parents with mental health problems

Similar findings emerge from Diggins' (2009) review of research on working with parents with mental health problems. She urges professionals from all agencies to consider the needs of the whole family, not just concentrate on, for example, the health of the parents or the safety of the children. Services should work together. The children want information, want to be heard and want opportunities to make friends, while their parents want quality practice to address their health needs but are reluctant to engage with children's services for fear that their children will be removed. Agencies need to tackle stigma, she concludes.

Parental substance misuse

Parental substance misuse has been a topic arousing increasing concern nationally in recent years, but services have been slow to respond. Forrester and Harwin (2004) identified low levels of knowledge about drug and alcohol misuse among staff working with children and families. Social workers, they found, often underestimated the dangers of alcohol and were slow to remove children from substance-misusing parents and overhasty to return them from care. Barlow (2004), researching services in Scotland, found poor coordination between child care and substance abuse agencies and patchy, inconsistent family support services that did not reflect local needs.

While services may still have some way to go, there is at least a growing literature on best practice. Tunnard (2002) points out that parental problem drinking can be a hidden or taboo issue, which has to be brought out into the open if it is to be addressed. She recommends separate services for women and interpretation and mother tongue services for linguistic minorities. Young people need information and a listening ear: Tunnard recommends the use of support groups for children of problem drinkers. She also highlights the value of local voluntary services including faith-based ones in supporting people affected by substance abuse. Like many other writers, Tunnard stresses the need for coordinated multi-agency services to meet the needs of all family members.

Copello et al. (2005) focus on how working with family members can help reduce the level of substance misuse as well. They quote 'robust' evidence that giving family members space to talk leads to a reduction in family stress, which, in turn, leads to reduced substance misuse and a greater likelihood of treatment entry and maintenance. Positive outcomes have been reported for children whose parents use substances if they are involved in groupwork, given social support, skills training, and help with emotional problems.

Research

Velleman and Templeton (2007, p. 79) look in more depth at what sort of work can directly benefit the children in families where there is parental substance misuse, regardless of whether or not the parents are engaging with treatment services. They conclude that 'there are clear ways that practitioners can intervene to reduce risk, and to increase resilience'. Resilience is identified as the capacity of an individual to survive adversity. A growing research base demonstrates that resilience can be enhanced through promoting security and stability, self-esteem, self-efficacy, and problem-solving skills. Educational achievement, having hobbies and skills, and being supported by an adult mentor who believes in the child and will fight their corner are all associated with resilience (Gilligan, 2009). Velleman and Templeton (2007) marshal evidence of the efficacy of a range of practical approaches to supporting such children. As well as working on family relationships, issues of separation and loss, and poor parenting, the worker can:

- promote relationships with an adult (parent, relative or other mentor) who does not misuse substances
- build links with wider family members and community networks
- encourage school attendance and achievement
- help the child to pursue hobbies and interests
- be responsive to the child as an individual and build on their strengths.

The promotion of resilience should take place alongside a careful assessment of risks and a programme of work aimed at reducing them. The greatest risks, Velleman and Templeton (2007) argue, arise not directly from the substance misuse but indirectly, through family disharmony, violence and conflict, separations or inconsistent parenting, so that an important part of the work involves addressing these issues.

Young carers

There are some issues that are common to families where parents are disabled or mentally ill and to those who misuse alcohol or drugs. One of these is that children in these families may assume the role of young carers. Such children frequently take on responsibilities beyond their years, whether for the health needs of their parents, the care of siblings or the maintenance of the household (Diggins, 2009). Their needs can be overlooked:

> The nature of caring is often such that young carers can disappear from the 'normal' social radar to the extent that they become a 'seldom heard' group within the overall population. If they continue to fulfil the caring role and do not demand interventions in their own right, there is often little likelihood that they will come to the attention of anyone outside their immediate domestic circle. (Roberts et al., 2008 p. 4)

This is particularly the case for young people from ethnic minorities where the stigma of illness may be higher and knowledge of services lower. Young carers' school attainment and leisure activities can suffer because of the pressures of caring; this can mean they have reduced long-term life opportunities. Naylor and Prescott (2004) highlight the benefit for young carers of supportive groupwork with others in similar circumstances. Increasing research on the needs of young carers since the mid-1990s (Dearden and Becker, 2000; SCIE, 2005b; Roberts et al., 2008) has highlighted other effective approaches: information, involvement in planning, a flexible attitude from schools, befriending schemes, support to pursue out-of-home interests, and advocacy and advice services.

Child neglect

A second issue that can be common to children whose parents have a range of difficulties is that they can be at risk of neglect – either physical or emotional. This may not be deliberate on the part of the parent and it may arise in a number of different ways. In most cases, what is needed is for the worker to identify the aspects of parenting that are more difficult for this parent to carry out effectively and then make arrangements for the affected aspects of the child's needs to be met in some other way, for example via aids and adaptations or through the attentions of the other parent, a relative or a service such as a playgroup or parenting course. Neglect, however, can be an insidious form of ill-treatment, hard to spot because it may be low key and slow growing, yet devastating in its long-term effects (Brandon et al., 2008). It is important that staff working in family support are aware of its manifestations and are prepared to respond to it as seriously as they would to more obvious forms of maltreatment. Brandon et al. (2008) highlight the particular risks of what they call 'start again syndrome', where workers may ignore a long history of neglect and attempt to start with 'a clean slate'. There is a dearth of useful research into what does work with neglectful families, but there are some useful findings:

- This is a long-term problem. Short-term interventions have little impact on entrenched problems: early and sustained interventions are needed and these need to be based on a thorough assessment, taking account of the whole family history.
- Parents need help with their own problems: finance and housing issues must be addressed and building up families' support networks can be helpful.
- Children can benefit from direct work to build their resilience.
- These are not easy families to work with and practitioners can mirror the chaos and confusion of the families: good supervision is the key to good practice (Howe, 2005; Taylor and Daniel, 2005).

Domestic violence

Exposure to domestic violence is now recognized as having a harmful effect on children (Calder, 2004), which extends beyond vulnerable early childhood into

Research

adolescence and beyond (Biehal, 2005). Domestic violence might seem to be different in nature from the other issues discussed so far, yet there can be parallels in its influence on children's development. In Cleaver et al.'s study of the impact of parents' issues on children, they describe the impact on children of parental mental illness, problem alcohol and drug use and domestic violence together, arguing that 'a review of the evidence ... suggests that the effects on children's development may have many features in common, irrespective of the cause of the problem' (Cleaver et al., 1999, p. 52). These effects can include prenatal damage, attachment difficulties, high stress levels, emotional and behavioural problems, stigma, social exclusion, poverty, poor school attainment and long-term poor life chances. Many of the interventions workers can offer, for example assessing and managing risk or promoting resilience, mirror those already described.

However, domestic abuse does differ in certain crucial aspects. First, there is a strong link between parental violence against a partner and physical and emotional abuse of their children (Rose and Barnes, 2008), plus a weaker link with sexual abuse (Humphreys and Mullender, 2000). Brandon et al. (2008), in their review of cases where children had been killed or seriously injured through abuse and neglect, found that a history of parental violence was present in over 70% of cases.

Second, domestic abuse is a strongly gendered issue: much evidence indicates that it is disproportionately inflicted on women by men (Cleaver et al., 1999). Most family support services, however, as we have seen, are aimed at women. Women, while victims in the situation and often unable to protect themselves (Humphreys and Mullender, 2000), tend to be seen as the primary carers responsible for children's safety, and may be blamed for failing to protect. This leads Worrall et al. (2008, p. 4) to characterize the situation as one of 'culpable women, invisible men'. It is perhaps not surprising that women living through domestic violence fear statutory child care services and may be reluctant to seek help from them. The dilemma for social workers can be acute, however, as, while they may wish to treat all family members humanely, the child's welfare has to be their paramount concern. Worrall et al. (2008, p. 5) conclude that all interventions should aim to promote three ends simultaneously: the protection of the children, the empowerment of the victims of the violence, and the accountability of the perpetrators. They recognize, however, that there are tensions between these three aims, which can argue against each other.

Responses to domestic violence must be multi-agency, since housing, health and education issues are important as well as child protection and criminal justice. Support for victims might include building up links with relatives or community networks as well as the provision of safe housing, alarms and special protection in court. Training is needed for all staff, and ethnically sensitive services are needed in response to the particular issues for women from minority groups.

Services for perpetrators of domestic abuse usually take the form of groupwork using a CBT approach combined with awareness-raising on attitudes related to gender. Evidence on their effectiveness in changing men's attitudes is mixed, however (Worrall et al., 2008). One aim of work with perpetrators is to prevent the transmission to the next generation of an attitude that violence is an expression of masculinity; boys, in particular, can benefit from seeing their fathers accept responsibility for their violence and change their behaviour (Worrall et al., 2008). Children exposed to domestic violence have an overwhelming need to talk about their experiences (Humphreys and Mullender, 2000; Calder, 2004); 'in order to do this, however, they need to feel safe, be respected, listened to and helped to understand what is happening in their families' (Worrall et al., 2008, p. 7). Group or individual work can assist them; the focus should be on expression of feelings, building self-esteem, reassuring them they are not to blame for the violence, and helping them develop plans that will keep them safe in future.

Cross-cutting themes

Key issues emerge from the literature on family support, not so much about what to do, but about how to do it. Just as the impact on children can be similar, whatever the cause of their problems, so good practice in family support tends to look rather the same, whatever the setting. These themes are:

- *Comprehensive assessment:* Families requiring support services are typically complex. All family members may have particular individual needs and sometimes their needs conflict (Forrester and Harwin, 2004; Worrall et al., 2008). The solutions to their difficulties are not straightforward, otherwise they would probably have found solutions themselves and not needed to access formal support services (Quinton, 2004). Planning interventions cannot be done effectively unless there is a thorough assessment first, taking into account the developmental needs of each child, the capacity of each parent to meet those needs, and the support available from wider family and community (DH, 2000).
- *Holistic approach:* It is not just the assessment that must consider the needs of each family member and the whole family within its social context. Interventions too need to be holistic if they are to be effective (Penn and Gough, 2002; SCIE, 2005a; Diggins, 2009). This involves addressing issues relating to poverty (Penn and Gough, 2002; Quinton, 2004) and stigma (Worrall et al., 2008; Diggins, 2009), and providing practical as well as emotional support (Selwyn et al., 2006; Velleman and Templeton, 2007).
- *Skilled, well-supported staff:* The skills required for working with these needy families are considerable; it cannot all be delegated to unqualified staff and volunteers (Moran et al., 2004; Biehal, 2005). Social workers need to be well trained and understand the specific issues for the families they are supporting (Barlow, 2004; Morris and Wates, 2006; Clavering, 2007). The work is stressful and can involve the delicate balancing of needs and rights. Good supervision is a vital element in best practice (Wonnacott, 2003).

Research

■ *Interprofessional working:* The difficulties of these families extend across all areas of their lives and typically require services from a range of agencies (Barlow, 2004; Abbot et al., 2005; Rose et al., 2009). It is a nonsense, therefore, for agencies to operate in isolation from each other. Despite the proliferation of guidance on multi-agency communication and collaboration (HM Government, 2010), practice across the sector still appears to be poor. One of the reasons for this may be the number of agencies that can be involved with one family and the fact that some staff see their clients as being primarily the adults while others focus on the needs of the children. Promising approaches involve building links between adults' and children's services (Kendall et al., 2010) and the use of a key worker system (Quinton, 2004; Abbot et al., 2005).

■ *Partnership with parents:* As well as respectful collaboration with other professionals, it is essential that practitioners work in partnership with parents (Thoburn et al., 1995; DCSF, 2009; Kendall et al., 2010). This involves listening to their views, taking their concerns seriously and having empathy for their perspective even when challenging them on aspects of their parenting (Forrester et al., 2008). Social workers should recognize parents' expertise as the people who know their children best (Quinton, 2004; Clavering, 2007) and build on their strengths. Parents will need good information about services and options if they are to make informed choices: planning should be done *with* them rather than *for* them. Staff may need to advocate for them and should keep them informed on progress and outcomes (DH, 1995b).

■ *Engagement with children:* Vital as partnership with parents is, there is a possibility that if a worker focuses too strongly on the parents, the child's perspective may be missed. This could potentially be dangerous. Rose and Barnes (2008) argue that this is a particular risk in cases of chronic neglect, and as we have seen, neglect can be a feature in many families where support agencies are involved. In any case, children deserve to be listened to and respected in their own right, irrespective of the needs of their parents (McLeod, 2008). There is overwhelming evidence that children in need want their own voices to be heard, and do not want workers to engage only with their parents (Tunnard, 2002; Copello et al., 2005; Franklin and Sloper, 2006; Diggins, 2009). It is also clear that direct work with children, whether as individuals or in groups, can be a key aspect in alleviating families' overall difficulties (Mitchell and Sloper, 2001; Velleman and Templeton, 2007; Worrall et al., 2008), as well as in promoting the children's own wellbeing (DCSF, 2009).

■ *Early intervention:* Intervening early can prevent an escalation of problems, reducing stress and distress:

> The most striking message is that early intervention clearly works – when it is an appropriate intervention, applied well, following timely identification of a problem; and the earlier the better to secure maximum impact and greatest long term sustainability. (C4EO, 2010, p. 4)

It would appear common sense that this would also save money in the long term, since it should do away with the need for more intensive services at a later date. There is some evidence of this (Kendall et al., 2010; Stevens et al., 2010), although it is hard to quantify the cost of something that did not happen. What is clear from a number of studies, however, is that where problems are complex or longstanding or where parents have learning difficulties, brief interventions will not make much impact. Such families will require support services over lengthy periods if they are to function effectively (Moran et al., 2004; SCIE, 2005a).

And finally

Reading the research on family support can at times seem discouraging, given that it so often highlights poor practice. It is also easy to become despondent in an era of cuts to services. However, we should not underestimate the value of an effective service, and such services do exist. Selwyn et al. (2006, p. 260) studied support services for families who had adopted older children and found that:

> adopters singled out some social workers for particular praise. These were workers who were seen to be champions for the child and who listened respectfully to the carers' views. They also understood the reality of how difficult parenting could be and offered concrete advice and support.

I conclude with the views of some parents who have accessed support services at children's centres in one area in northern England (Aitken, 2011):

> The Children's Centre helped me when I was on my own with my first child. They helped me become a good parent and also to believe in myself to become more successful as a person. I now own my own successful business.

> I can see a big difference in [child]'s development and playing with other children since she started using the service.

> It has helped me with a whole range of issues related to my parenting and the children's development … they have a lot to offer parents of children with difficulties.

> Calming, professional, helpful, friendly, essential, brilliant, perfect. Godsend!

Further reading

■ Allen, G. (2011) *Early Intervention: The Next Steps: An Independent Report to Her Majesty's Government.* London: TSO.

A politician argues passionately and persuasively the case for earlier intervention so as to enable all children to reach their potential.

Research

■ Munford, R. and Sanders, J. (1999) *Supporting Families.* Palmerston North: Dunmore Press.

Useful account of how research findings on family support can be integrated into a strengths-based, reflective approach to practice; although hailing from New Zealand, is equally applicable in a UK context.

■ Quinton, D. (2004) *Supporting Parents: Messages from Research.* London: Jessica Kingsley.

Discusses in greater depth a range of research findings on the effectiveness of different approaches to family support

References

Abbot, D., Watson, D. and Townsley, R. (2005) 'The proof of the pudding: what difference does multi-agency working make to families with disabled children with complex health-care needs?', *Child and Family Social Work*, **10**(3): 229–38.

Aitken, R. (2011) Barnardo's Sure Start in Cumbria: A Survey of Service-users' Views, unpublished report. Barnardo's.

Aldgate, J. and Bradley, M. (2001) 'Supporting families through short-term fostering', in J. Aldgate and J. Statham (eds) *The Children Act Now: Messages from Research.* London: TSO.

Austen, J. (1933) *Emma.* Oxford: Oxford University Press.

Axford, N. and Little, M. (2008) 'Less heat, more light', *Journal of Children's Services*, **3**(2): 3.

Barlow, J. (2004) 'The interface between substance misuse and child-care social work services: can workers co-operate?', in R. Phillips (ed.) *Children Exposed to Parental Substance Misuse: Implications for Family Placement.* London: BAAF.

Biehal, N. (2005) *Working with Adolescents: Supporting Families, Preventing Breakdown.* London: BAAF.

Brandon, M., Belderson, P., Warren, C. et al. (2008) *Analysing Child Deaths and Serious Injury through Abuse and Neglect: What Can We Learn?* Nottingham: DCSF.

Buchanan, A. and Ritchie, C. (2004) *What Works for Troubled Children?* London: Barnardo's.

C4EO (2010) *Grasping the Nettle: Early Intervention for Children, Families and Communities.* London: C4EO.

Calder, M. (2004) *Children Living with Domestic Violence: Towards a Framework for Assessment and Intervention.* Lyme Regis: Russell House.

Clavering, E. (2007) 'Enabling carers to care: processes of exclusion and support for young disabled children', *Benefits*, **15**(1): 33–44.

Cleaver, H., Unell, I. and Aldgate, J. (1999) *Children's Needs – Parenting Capacity: The Impact of Parental Mental Illness, Problem Alcohol and Drug Use and Domestic Violence on Children's Development.* London: TSO.

Copello, A., Velleman, R. and Templeton, L. (2005) 'Family interventions in the treatment of alcohol and drug problems', *Drug & Alcohol Review*, 24, 369–85.

DCSF (Department for Children, Schools and Families) (2009) *Promoting the Emotional Health of Children and Young People.* Nottingham: DCSF.

Dearden, C. and Becker, S. (2000) 'Listening to children: meeting the needs of young carers', in H. Kemshall and R. Littlechild (eds) *User-involvement and Participation in Social Care: Research Informing Practice.* London: Jessica Kingsley.

DH (Department of Health) (1995a) *Child Protection: Messages from Research.* London: TSO.

DH (1995b) *The Challenge of Partnership in Child Protection.* London: TSO.

DH (2000) *A Framework for the Assessment of Children in Need and their Families.* London: TSO.

DHSS (Department of Health and Social Security) (1974) *The Report of the Committee of Inquiry into the Care and Supervision Provided in Relation to Maria Colwell.* London: HMSO.

Diggins, M. (2009) *Think Child, Think Parent, Think Family: A Guide to Parental Mental Health and Child Welfare.* London: SCIE.

DSRU (Dartington Social Research Unit) (2004) *Refocusing Children's Services towards Prevention: Lessons from the Literature.* Dartington: DSRU.

Everitt, A., Hardiker, P., Littlewood, J. and Mullender, A. (1992) *Applied Research for Better Practice.* Basingstoke: Macmillan – now Palgrave Macmillan.

Forrester, D. and Harwin, J. (2004) 'Social work and parental substance misuse', in R. Phillips (ed.) *Children Exposed to Parental Substance Misuse: Implications for Family Placement.* London: BAAF.

Forrester, D., Kershaw, S., Moss, H. and Hughes, L. (2008) 'Communication skills in child protection: how do social workers talk to parents?', *Child and Family Social Work,* **13**(1): 41–51.

Fox, R. and Holtz, C. (2009) 'Treatment outcomes for toddlers with behaviour problems from families in poverty', *Child and Adolescent Mental Health,* **14**(4): 183–9.

Franklin, A. and Sloper, P. (2006) *Participation of Children and Young People in Decision-making Relating to Social Care.* York: University of York Social Policy Research Unit.

Gilligan, R. (2009) *Promoting Resilience: Supporting Young People who are in Care, Adopted or in Need.* London: BAAF.

GSCC (General Social Care Council) (2002) *Codes of Practice for Social Care Workers and Employers.* London: GSCC.

Hardiker, P., Exton, K. and Barker, M. (1991) *Policies and Practices in Preventive Child Care.* Aldershot: Avebury.

Haringey LCSB (Local Children Safeguarding Board) (2009) *Serious Case Review: Baby Peter.* Haringey: LCSB.

HM Government (2010) *Working Together to Safeguard Children: A Guide to Inter-agency Working to Safeguard and Promote the Welfare of Children.* Nottingham: DCSF.

Howe, D. (2005) *Child Abuse and Neglect: Attachment, Development and Intervention.* Basingstoke: Palgrave Macmillan.

Humphreys, C. and Mullender, A. (2000) *Children and Domestic Violence.* Dartington: Research in Practice.

Hutchings, J., Bywater, T., Eames, C. and Martin, P. (2008) 'Implementing child mental health interventions in service settings: lessons from three pragmatic randomized controlled trials in Wales', *Journal of Children's Services,* **3**(2): 17–27.

Research

Joswiak, G. (2010) 'Interview with Graham Allen, chair, independent commission on early intervention', *Children and Young People Now*, 28 September.

Kendall, S., Rodger, J. and Palmer, H. (2010) *Redesigning Provision for Families with Multiple Problems: An Assessment of the Early Impact of Different Local Approaches.* London: DFE.

Laming, Lord (2009) *The Protection of Children in England: A Progress Report.* London: TSO.

London Borough of Brent (1985) *A Child in Trust.* London: Borough of Brent.

McLaughlin, H. (2007) *Understanding Social Work Research.* London: Sage.

McLeod, A. (2008) *Listening to Children: A Practitioner's Guide.* London: Jessica Kingsley.

Mitchell, M. and Sloper, P. (2001) 'Quality in services for disabled children and their families: what can theory, policy and research on children's and parents' views tell us?', *Children and Society*, **15**(4): 237–52.

Moran, P., Ghate, D. and van der Merwe, A. (2004) *What Works in Parenting Support: A Review of the International Evidence.* London: DfES.

Morris, J. and Wates, M. (2006) *Supporting Disabled Parents and Parents with Additional Support Needs.* London: SCIE.

Morris, K. and Shepherd, C. (2000) 'Quality social work with children and families', *Child and Family Social Work*, **5**(1): 169–76.

Naylor, A. and Prescott, P. (2004) 'Invisible children? The need for support groups for siblings of disabled children', *British Journal of Special Education*, **31**(4): 199–206.

Penn, H. and Gough, D. (2002) 'The price of a loaf of bread: some conceptions of family support', *Children and Society*, **16**(1): 17–32.

Quinton, D. (2004) *Supporting Parents: Messages from Research.* London: Jessica Kingsley.

Roberts, D., Bernard, M., Misca, G. and Head, E. (2008) *Experiences of Children and Young People Caring for a Parent with a Mental Health Problem.* London: SCIE.

Rose, W. and Barnes, J. (2008) *Improving Safeguarding Practice: Study of Serious Case Reviews 2001–2003.* Nottingham: DCSF.

Rose, W., Aldgate, J. MacIntosh, M. and Hunter, H. (2009) 'High-risk children with challenging behaviour: changing directions for them and their families', *Child and Family Social Work*, **14**(2): 178–88.

SCIE (Social Care Institute for Excellence) (2005a) *Helping Parents with Learning Disabilities in their Role as Parents.* London: SCIE.

SCIE (2005b) *The Health and Well-Being of Young Carers.* London: SCIE.

Searing, H. (2003) 'The continuing relevance of case-work ideas to long-term child protection work', *Child and Family Social Work*, **8**(4): 311–20.

Selwyn, J. Sturgess, W., Quinton, D. and Baxter, C. (2006) *Costs and Outcomes of Non-infant Adoptions.* London: BAAF.

Sinclair, R., Hearn, B. and Pugh, G. (1997) *Preventive Work with Families.* London: National Children's Bureau.

Speight, S., Smith, R., Lloyd, E. and Coshall, C. (2010) *Families Experiencing Multiple Deprivation: Their Use of and Views on Child-care Provision.* London: DFE.

Statham, J. and Biehal, N. (2004) *Research and Practice Briefing: Supporting Families.* Nottingham: Research in Practice.

Statham, J. and Smith, M. (2010) *Issues in Earlier Intervention: Identifying and Supporting Children with Additional Needs.* London: DCSF.

Stephens, T. (ed.) (1947) *Problem Families: An Experiment in Social Rehabilitation.* Liverpool and Manchester: Pacifist Service Units.

Stevens, M., Roberts, H. and Shiell, A. (2010) 'Research review: economic evidence for interventions in children's social care: revisiting the *What works for children?* project', *Child & Family Social Work,* **15**(2): 145–54.

Taylor, J. and Daniel, B. (2005) *Child Neglect: Practice Issues for Health and Social Care.* London: Jessica Kingsley.

Thoburn, J., Lewis, A. and Shemmings, D. (1995) *Paternalism or Partnership? Family Involvement in the Child Protection Process.* London: HMSO.

Thorpe, D. (1994) *Evaluating Child Protection.* Buckingham: Oxford University Press.

Triseliotis, J., Borland, M., Hill, M. and Lambert, L. (1995) *Teenagers and Social Work Services.* London: TSO.

Tunnard, J. (2002) *Parental Problem Drinking and its Impact on Children.* Dartington: Research In Practice.

Velleman, R. and Templeton, L. (2007) 'Understanding and modifying the impact of parental substance misuse on children', *Advances in Psychiatric Treatment,* 13, 79–89.

Wonnacott, J. (2003) *The Impact of Supervision on Child Protection Practice: A Study of Process and Outcome.* Brighton: University of Sussex.

Worrall, A., Boylan, B. and Roberts, D. (2008) *Children and Young People's Experiences of Domestic Violence Involving Adults in a Parenting Role.* London: SCIE.

Research

5
Family support work in practice

JESS MCCORMACK

'What is it that social workers actually do?' I have been asked this question many times and I still struggle to provide a simple accurate explanation. The social worker's role has so many dimensions but at its heart is always *support* – support for people of all ages and backgrounds, people with situations and vulnerabilities unique to each individual. Family support social work teams work to protect the vulnerable while simultaneously enhancing family relationships and empowering people to effect the change required for a safe and healthy existence. Family support social work does not function in isolation, but complements the work achieved under child protection and vulnerable adult procedures.

The case studies outlined in this chapter tell the stories of four different families. Each case study describes how they came to be known to social work, describes the information that had to be gathered during initial assessment and gives an account of the intervention provided to assist them and to promote the changes felt to be needed in their lives.

Practice example 1   Natalia

Assessment

The assessment of Natalia's safety and wellbeing began before she was born. Her mother Monika was an EU migrant, who had entered the UK from Slovakia at age 18, while pregnant with Natalia. Shortly after arriving in the UK, Monika attended A&E at her local hospital and reported feeling unwell. Hospital staff noted the absence of sufficient prenatal care and informed social work of Monika's vulnerable status as a young expectant mother.

A multi-agency pre-birth assessment was undertaken. The social worker was the lead worker in the assessment and met Monika on a number of occasions during the later stages of her pregnancy. It emerged that Monika did not have any other family members in the UK. She was unwilling to discuss the father of her unborn child, saying that he remained in Slovakia. At the start of the assessment, Monika was living with 'friends'. She was reluctant for the social worker to see her accommodation. Monika accepted help in approaching a homeless accommodation provider and was allocated a temporary one-bedroom tenancy.

As the assessment progressed, the absence of a support network for Monika and her baby remained a significant cause for concern. Although she appeared to be managing financially, Monika was not working nor claiming state benefits. She explained to the social worker that she had brought money with her from Slovakia. The source of her income remained unclear and there were suspicions about the role of older Slovakian males, seen on occasion by workers in Monika's tenancy. Workers were concerned that Monika may have been involved in or was at risk of involvement in prostitution.

Throughout the pre-birth assessment, there was a lack of clarity about Monika's circumstances. This was caused, in part, by the language barrier and cultural differences. Monika identified herself as part of the Slovakian Romany community and said that the discrimination she experienced in her own country as a result of her ethnicity led her to relocate to the UK. Workers had an awareness of potential differences in Monika's values and ideas about child care as a result of her background, but they were clear that she must meet the standards of child care and protection outlined by legislation and policy in the UK.

Towards the end of her pregnancy, despite advice and support from different professionals, Monika failed to make sufficient practical arrangements for the arrival of her baby, including acquiring basic equipment and clothing for the baby. There was evidence that she was not consistently occupying her homeless tenancy and she continued to be unreliable at attending appointments with health and social work professionals. At a pre-birth case discussion, it was decided that the baby would be placed with foster carers upon discharge from hospital and an intensive package of support would be put in place with a plan to rehabilitate the baby to Monika's care.

Intervention

Natalia was born without any complications and Monika consented to her being placed temporarily in foster care. Intensive contact between mother and child was facilitated in the family home and was fully supervised by social workers. Workers provided Monika with support and advice on how to meet Natalia's needs, including modelling behaviours such as feeding, changing and interacting with Natalia. Monika's commitment to contact was positive and she was available for all planned sessions. However, workers noted that although able to manage practical tasks such as feeding and changing Natalia, Monika often required prompting to meet other basic needs. She was either unable or unwilling to interact with Natalia through eye contact and basic vocalizations. Monika eventually confided in workers that talking

Practice

to Natalia made her feel 'stupid' and that she didn't see why it was important. Workers attempted to educate Monika on the developmental benefits of such behaviour, but she remained resistant to change.

When Natalia was approximately one month old, workers raised concerns about an older Slovakian male, who appeared to be residing in Monika's tenancy, although he always left the property when they arrived with Natalia. Monika was vague about the man's role in her life and described him as a 'friend'. Given that the care plan was still to return Natalia home, a background check was undertaken, and this revealed that Monika's 'friend' Igor had been charged with offences against children (physical assault of a 15-year-old) and was therefore considered a significant risk to both Monika and Natalia. Monika was asked to ensure that Igor moved out of her tenancy because of this risk. It was also pointed out that his presence in the tenancy was contrary to the homeless accommodation policy.

Monika's commitment to contact with the social worker remained positive, but there was no improvement in her interactions with Natalia and there was evidence that Igor remained in her tenancy. Monika acknowledged that she had to make a choice between having Igor or Natalia in her life. She was offered support from a local voluntary organization with the aim of undertaking educative safety work about the risk to children from violent males. Monika attended all appointments but was reported to engage only superficially in the work.

When Natalia was three months old, a holistic assessment of her circumstances was presented at a multi-agency review meeting. It was noted that Natalia was a healthy child who was meeting her developmental milestones. There was evidence that she had formed a secure attachment to her foster carer and was benefiting from a stable routine. However, Monika had failed to demonstrate effective parenting skills during contact and remained resistant to taking on board advice. She was also unable or unwilling to remove risk factors (namely Igor) to allow Natalia to return home. When considering environmental factors, it was noted that Monika was isolated in her homeless accommodation, which was located in an area with high rates of crime and violence. Monika resisted attempts to integrate her into the local community; for example, she was unwilling to attend a local parent and child group with Natalia as she didn't want other parents to know her child was in foster care. Natalia's routine was being disrupted by contact, and although it was enabling her to maintain a link with her birth mother, she was not otherwise receiving any benefit due to Monika's inhibited interactions. Consequently, there was a lack of evidence to support Monika's ability to care for and protect Natalia. So the decision was made to pursue permanent care arrangements through the court and to seek an adoptive placement for Natalia.

Monika did not oppose the plans for Natalia's adoption. This was seen as further evidence of the absence of an attachment between mother and child, but Monika said that no one had given her the chance to bond with her child. She appeared unable to engage in the creation of a memory box for Natalia and indicated that, from conception, her life story was too painful to tell.

Practice example 2   Laura, Joe and Luke

Assessment

Laura (aged 5), Joe (aged 3) and Luke (18 months) were referred to children and families social work by addiction services who were working with their mother Alison and her partner Derek (father to Luke). Alison's addiction worker raised concerns about her increasing use of illicit diazepam, although it was noted that she had been stable on a methadone prescription since she became pregnant with Luke. Alison was engaging positively with her addiction worker and reliably attended all appointments. She often brought Luke with her to her appointments and her worker had noted a recent decline in his physical presentation.

Information from Derek's addiction worker suggested a similar pattern of substance misuse. His worker advised that Derek had a history of violence and aggressive behaviour towards professionals and was particularly resistant to social work support with regard to the children.

A social work records check revealed that support had been provided for just over a year following Joe's premature birth. Concerns at the time surrounded Alison's drug misuse and Joe's father's violent behaviour. From birth, Joe had had a number of health and development concerns, including needing to be tube fed. Joe had been diagnosed with global developmental delay, a visual impairment and mobility difficulties. Social work records indicated that Alison's relationship with Joe's father had ended shortly after his birth and she subsequently made significant positive progress in terms of minimizing her drug use. She also demonstrated her ability to meet Joe's complex needs, along with caring for Laura. Alison engaged positively with all relevant professionals and the children's case was closed to social work when Joe was one year old. He continued to receive a high level of support from a team of health professionals.

At the point of re-referral, Joe's GP reported an increase in missed health appointments and said that concern had been expressed about Derek's presentation and behaviour at a recent hospital appointment. Hospital staff reported that he appeared to be under the influence of drugs or alcohol and, when challenged, became verbally aggressive and was asked to leave.

Initial inquiries revealed that Laura was attending the local primary school and making slow but steady progress. School staff reported that her attendance was acceptable, with occasional absences and late arrivals. Her physical presentation was described as poor and she had been noted to arrive without a coat on cold winter mornings.

Joe was attending the nursery attached to the school and the staff were extremely pleased with his progress. Much of the intervention from health professionals was taking place in the nursery. Luke's name was on the waiting list for the nursery. Staff reported that Alison had been attending all relevant meetings but noted that Derek was generally uncommunicative when collecting the children.

Practice

Intervention

To intervene successfully in this case, it was crucial to build a trusting relationship with Alison and, particularly, Derek. An honest, open approach, with clear role clarification, helped them to feel more in control and less threatened by social work involvement. Some time was spent exploring their fears and their past experiences with social work, as well as co-defining some goals and areas for change.

Although initially defensive, Derek responded well to a solution-focused approach and communicated his view that their difficulties stemmed from inadequate housing, which required Laura and Joe to share a room. Part of Joe's disability meant that he rarely slept for more than two hours at a time and was consequently disruptive to Laura, as well as Alison and Derek. They said that their illicit diazepam use was to help them cope with ongoing sleep deprivation and explained that one of them would use the drug to assist sleep while the other stayed awake to meet the children's needs. They felt that if Joe could have his own room, his needs would be easier to manage. A letter of support was completed by the social worker, with contributions from health professionals, and the family's needs were reassessed by the housing association, resulting in them being placed higher up the list for a bigger property.

It was clear from the initial assessment that the family had a limited income. Neither parent worked because of their child care commitments and because of Derek's own health issues, which appeared to stem from years of substance misuse. The family was referred to an independent financial advisory service, which assisted their claim for maximum benefits, including a higher rate of disability living allowance for Joe. Further financial support was sought from local charities, which led to the funding of the purchase of new bedroom furniture for Joe and Laura.

The social work department began providing transport for Joe's hospital appointments and his attendance consequently improved. It was, however, important not to create an unnecessary dependence on support services, so Alison was asked to contact the social worker prior to each appointment in order to make travel arrangements.

A multi-agency case discussion was convened by Joe's nursery in order to ensure that all relevant supports were in place. Both Alison and Derek were invited to the meeting and they asked that the social worker should also attend to offer support; this reflected significant progress in respect of their willingness to work with social work and also effectively illustrated to the family that all agencies communicate with each other and have the same goals for the support and protection of their children.

Additional intervention was provided for Laura, who appeared to have low self-esteem and a tendency to get 'lost' in the family dynamic. Laura herself identified gymnastics as an activity she would like to try and the family was supported to ensure that she attended a local class. She particularly enjoyed the one-to-one time this afforded her with the parent who escorted her to and from the class.

During the initial assessment, it was noted that Luke was delayed in meeting some developmental milestones including walking and talking. This delay appeared to result from a lack of stimulation in the home, as Alison and Derek's focus was frequently on meeting Joe's needs. With some encouragement, Alison agreed to attend a local parent/toddler group while Joe was at nursery, which ensured that she spent some time each week focusing solely on Luke. Derek remained resistant to joining the group, but appeared to acknowledge the need for him to spend more time with Luke in order to encourage his learning and development.

Both parents continued to test positively for diazepam use at their weekly addiction appointments. However, their parenting of the children continued to improve. Laura, Joe and Luke's needs were assessed as being adequately met by Alison and Derek and social work began to withdraw.

Practice example 3   David

Assessment

A referral was received from a local primary school for 11-year-old David, who was in his final year at the school. The head teacher described David as 'out of control' and provided examples of his disruptive behaviour in class. She believed that the staff had 'tried everything' to improve David's behaviour in school but said that he was not sufficiently 'high tariff' to warrant the involvement of educational psychology, as there was no evidence of a learning difficulty. The referral to social work followed an incident in which David pulled down his trousers and underwear and exposed himself to his female teacher in front of the class.

The head teacher had made several unsuccessful attempts to meet David's parents, who had never attended a parents' evening or other school function. The emergency contact for David was his paternal grandmother, who lived nearby.

A records check revealed previous social work input for David's parents from a community care team. This information showed that both David's mother Claire and his father James had hearing impairments and communicated using sign language.

A home visit was arranged to meet David's parents while he was at school. A sign language interpreter was requested and a letter sent to Claire and James advising them of the visit.

Information gathered during the visit indicated both strengths and vulnerability factors for David and his family as a whole. The family home was well maintained and furnished and was in a quiet but well-resourced area. Neither Claire nor James worked but they appeared to manage their finances well. They were part of an active deaf community and said that they felt happy and settled in the local area. They did not feel able to attend school meetings or functions without an interpreter and said that the head teacher had advised them that the school did not have sufficient finances to provide one.

Claire spoke openly about her increasing difficulties with managing David's behaviour at home. She described how he often left the house without her knowledge and did not adhere to the boundaries she attempted to set. He refused to help out around the house and spent all his time at home in his bedroom, usually watch-

Practice

ing TV or playing on one of his three games consoles. Claire explained that David had never learned sign language, but she and James were able to lip-read when David spoke, although only if he was looking directly at them. Claire and James agreed to the social worker meeting David in school.

David presented as an intelligent and articulate child. He expressed remorse for his inappropriate behaviour in school and told the worker that his classmates 'dared' him to expose himself to the teacher. He appeared to understand why school staff were concerned by his actions. He described school as 'boring' and said he was looking forward to moving on to high school and appeared to see this as a fresh start.

David seemed to feel that his difficult behaviour in school was necessary to make and maintain friendships within his class. He spoke about being bullied in school and in the local community because of his parents' disabilities. David felt he couldn't take friends home because his parents were 'embarrassing'. He indicated that he was frustrated by attempts to communicate with his parents and appeared to be angry with them for the impact their needs had on his life.

David spoke enthusiastically about his talents and interests and his desire to join a local football club. However, he also believed this would never happen because one of his parents needed to take him along.

Initial information thus indicated that David's behaviour at school was problematic and included an apparently isolated incident of sexualized behaviour. However, as the assessment progressed, other needs emerged. David's lack of knowledge of sign language impacted on his ability to communicate with his parents. His consequent frustrations were manifested in difficult behaviour at home; this included leaving the house late at night, which was seen as placing him at significant risk in the local community. James and Claire felt their strengths as parents had been in ensuring David had everything he wanted, including numerous expensive toys and games. However, these furthered the gap between parents and child, enabling David to isolate himself within his room and communicate even less with his parents.

David was also socially isolated and felt unable to participate in community activities as a result of his parents' disabilities. He was bullied in school and in the local community and expressed a desire to belong. David's behaviour in school could have been seen as an expression of his need to fit in. He was also at risk of being caught up in local gang activity.

The family was supported by James's mother, who was usually the person they turned to in times of crisis – including seeking her support when David's behaviour became unmanageable.

Intervention

Intervention from social work in this case was planned collaboratively with David and his parents. It was important to acknowledge James and Claire's needs, but the worker's focus had to remain on the impact that their disabilities had on David's life. Communication between parents and child was a significant issue. David agreed to attend a children's sign language course run by a local charity and it was hoped this would also be an opportunity for him to meet other children in similar situations.

A referral to a local family centre was accepted and David was offered a place in a social skills group, offering him opportunities to make new friends and learn new skills. The centre also offered James and Claire places in a parenting group and arranged for an interpreter to be present.

Claire and James gained confidence in their parenting ability: they began to use the withdrawal of privileges as a consequence for David's failure to adhere to rules and boundaries within the home. This included removing his TV and games consoles from his bedroom, which encouraged him to spend time with his parents in the shared spaces within the home.

David was still keen to join the football club and was ultimately able to go along and register with the support of a befriender from a young carers' organization. His dad went along too and the football club eventually became a positive shared activity between father and son.

David's grandmother agreed to provide more consistent support instead of just being called upon in a crisis. It was decided that David would stay with his grandmother every Friday night, and this provided both him and his parents with important respite. David enjoyed the additional anonymity that high school provided and found a new peer group through the use of his football skills.

Practice example 4   Tony

Assessment

Tony has been known to social work since before he was born, as there were concerns for the welfare of his older brother due to his parents' substance misuse and mental health difficulties. Tony was allocated a new social worker at age nine. At the point of transfer, he was 'looked after' and accommodated in a residential school in a rural area approximately 30 miles from the city in which he was born and raised. Tony had been living at the school for nine months following the breakdown of his foster placement. He was described as a bright, confident child with a great deal of potential, but staff in the school believed that his progress, both academically and socially, was hampered by his tendency to have aggressive outbursts on an almost daily basis; these frequently involved violent behaviour towards both staff and peers. Tony's behaviour was significantly limiting the potential for new foster carers to be identified and consequently his long-term care plan was not progressing.

Tony presented as an articulate child and engaged positively with his new social worker. He spoke openly about life in the residential school, including his frustrations with the rules. It became apparent that Tony had a clear sense of right and wrong and found perceived injustice overwhelming. He identified this as a frequent trigger for his outbursts – a feeling that something 'wasn't fair'. Staff noted that Tony often unnecessarily involved himself in conflicts between other boys and seemed to feel compelled to make sure things were fair. In spite of this, his peer relationships were superficial. Tony said that he did not feel that he had anything in common with the other boys in his unit and did not view them as his friends. He also had a sense of the school as a temporary home and seemed reluctant to settle. Tony verbalized his need to move on and to be part of a family again.

A psychologist's assessment suggested that Tony's behaviour resulted from his complex emotions about his past experiences. His behaviour had led to the breakdown of his previous foster placement and Tony appeared to feel he himself was responsible for being in the residential school. It was noted that he needed help to make sense of his circumstances and to recognize his role in and responsibility for decisions that had been made about his life. From initial conversations with his new social worker, it was clear that Tony lacked knowledge about his background, as his previous foster carer had struggled to provide him with such sensitive information.

Intervention

Following a period of relationship building, the social worker's focus moved to creating a life storybook for Tony, with his agreement. The practical completion of the book was secondary to the process of gathering information, both independently and collaboratively with Tony, and the collective sharing and exploring of this information.

The social worker was able to gather a large amount of background information from social work records and this was used to compose a 'timeline' with Tony. He chose to start his story from the day he was born and work forwards to the present day. Tony was surprised to find out that he was born 10 weeks prematurely. He was able to integrate this positively into his sense of self by using words like 'fighter' and 'survivor'.

Tony had always been aware that his surname differed from that of his siblings and he had asked his previous foster carer to change his name to match that of his siblings. He had not been aware that his name differed because his parents were separated when he was born. This helped him to understand that his different name was simply circumstantial and did not mean he was less a part of the family. Tony actually went back to using his original surname after finding out about his numerous cousins on his mother's side of the family, all of whom shared his name. He proudly displayed a family tree on his bedroom wall and was keen to know all about his cousins.

Tony found it difficult when he heard that his parents hadn't visited him in hospital when he was a baby and that he had needed medication because of the drugs his mother had taken during pregnancy. He also struggled to accept that his father had been in prison, although he was able to express his anger towards his father productively by writing him a letter, which was incorporated into his life storybook.

When Tony had been born, his older brother Dylan (then aged 4) was in foster care due to child protection concerns. After his mother failed to visit him in hospital, Tony was placed with different foster carers, Colleen and Jim. Tony remained in

Colleen and Jim's care until he was 18 months old. During the life story work, Tony said that he didn't know he had been in foster care as a baby and had no memory of Colleen and Jim. He was keen to find out more and the social worker was able to take Tony to visit his first foster carers. This was an incredibly emotional and powerful reunion for all involved. Colleen and Jim told Tony that he was the first baby they had cared for and proudly pointed out a photograph of him still displayed on their wall. Colleen wrote Tony a long letter about his time in their care, and, with this, he was able to fill in a lot of the gaps about his early months, including his first word, his first holiday, the food he liked to eat and the age at which he took his first steps. Colleen gave Tony an album of photographs to supplement the letter.

Tony and his social worker spent time discussing the information that Colleen had provided, together with his thoughts and feelings about the visit. Along with a trip to see and photograph the site of the hospital where he was born (since demolished) and the exterior of his parents' home at the time of his birth, Tony was able to begin to build a picture of his early childhood.

Social work records showed that, when Tony was 18 months old, a decision was taken to return him and Dylan home because their parents had been successfully parenting their younger sister Katie for six months. Tony met both Dylan and Katie for the first time when he returned to his parents' care, aged 18 months.

A large part of Tony's life story was focused on his perceptions of and feelings about his siblings and their relationships. He only lived with Dylan for two years before all three children were again removed from their parents' care. Tony struggled to understand the reasons why they were removed a second time; this was, in part, due to a lack of information recorded by workers at the time. Tony and Katie were placed together with a foster carer named Susan where they remained until Tony moved to the residential school. Katie stayed with Susan.

Tony had contact with Dylan following their separation, but it was stopped two years later as it was felt to be too disruptive to the children. Both Tony and Dylan were keen for renewed contact and this was consequently carefully planned and arranged between their respective carers and social workers. The contact was positive for both boys and Dylan was able to tell Tony stories about their time in their parents' care as, being four years older, he was able to remember more about it. Tony spoke about his life feeling like a jigsaw puzzle that was being gradually pieced together.

Exploring his sibling relationships meant that Tony was forced to confront his feelings about Katie remaining with Susan and the sense he had of being rejected by Susan and her wider family. Tony spoke candidly about feeling that Katie was always treated differently by Susan and that, as the 'baby of the family', she always 'got away with things' and that this 'wasn't fair'. Tony himself identified this as the source of much of the anger and frustration that led to the behaviours that ended the placement. Through the life story work, Tony was able to begin to grieve for his losses, including the loss of Susan and Katie, although direct contact continued. Through their continued contact, Susan was supported to give Tony permission to move on to a new family, as well as crucially taking back some of the responsibility for the

Practice

failure of his placement with her family. Tony began to understand that his placement ended partly due to Susan's inability to manage his behaviour and to make him feel safe and loved.

Tony's deepened understanding of his life and his exploration of his losses afforded him greater genealogical completeness and a clearer sense of self and identity. He was able to form a new perception of himself as a 'survivor' and embraced the uniqueness of his story. This enabled him to explore with his social worker the kind of foster family that would best suit him and be able to meet his needs. This helped Tony to feel he had some control over his life and plans for his future.

New carers were identified for Tony and he made a successful transition to their home and to a mainstream primary school. He thrived in his new home environment and benefited considerably from being the only child in placement. The true life story work that Tony completed was achieved through the relationship he built with his social worker. Although the information provided was significant, it was through the trusting relationship with his social worker that Tony was able to explore his thoughts and feelings about his story and integrate these into his sense of self.

Tony worked with his new carers to develop strategies to cope with his difficult feelings and no outbursts were noted once he moved to their care. He had a rougher start in his new school but eventually settled and began to make exceptional progress towards his long-held ambition to become a police officer.

> **Making connexions**
>
> How many examples can you find in these four cases of workers using their knowledge of developmental psychology?

Discussion

The four families whose stories have been recounted in this chapter were diverse in many ways, including their composition, background and vulnerabilities. The intervention provided by the family support social workers may seem equally diverse on a practical level but the support provided in each case shared a number of common themes.

Building relationships

Essential to successful and supportive intervention was the worker's ability to build trusting relationships with the parents and, where possible, with the children. The positive working relationship with the social worker enabled the parents of Laura, Joe and Luke to accept social work intervention; it assisted David and his parents to access support from a variety of agencies; and it facilitated Tony's learning and understanding of his life story. In Natalia's case, the initial care plan of rehabilitation may not have been fulfilled, but through Monika's relationship with the social worker, she was able to accept her limitations and consent to the adoption of Natalia; their professional relationship also had the potential to be a valuable source of support for Monika in coping with the loss of her child. The value of a positive working relationship in family support cannot be overestimated, but, in the real world, the high turnover of social workers, foster carers and other professionals impacts on the consistency of such relationships. Such disruption may be an inevitable and integral part of the provision of support in the public sector, but even if the working relationship lacks longevity, professionals can still make a significant difference to family life. In the case of Laura, Joe and Luke, their parents' positive experience of social work involvement is likely to make them less anxious and less resistant to intervention in the future.

Subjectivity

Considering one of the greatest tools in social work to be the worker themselves, the role of assessing and intervening in family life is inevitably a subjective one. The case studies illustrate the practice dilemma of applying thresholds to unique circumstances. For example, what constitutes 'good enough parenting'? Can you be an adequate parent and continue to use illicit drugs? The legal threshold for child care and protection measures is 'at risk of significant harm', but what constitutes 'significant harm'? The social worker's own values are a factor in assessing each individual situation, and while it is good practice to be aware of these and to use them to inform assessments, it is important not to impose personal values on others. In Natalia's case, the worker needed an understanding of the differences between her own values and thresholds and Monika's, as these may have been affected by the traditionally transient nature of the Romany culture.

Thresholds and boundaries

Thresholds in social work are also relevant when considering when to involve external agencies or when to invoke certain internal procedures. For example, when would the sexualized behaviour in David's case be considered a child protection issue and consequently fall under a different set of internal procedures? In some of the case studies, there is a clear overlap with other services from the start: in Natalia's case, with fostering and adoption and pre/postnatal healthcare; in respect of Laura and her siblings, with addiction, education and health services; and in David's situation, with community care support for his parents. This highlights the importance of working on a multi-agency basis to provide the best possible package of support for a family.

Collaboration

Better outcomes are achieved when the design of a package of support is done collaboratively with a family: this enables family members to feel they have some control over the professionals who are entering their lives. It is interesting to reflect on the number of referrals made to different agencies in David's case, and to consider how many referrals would be too many to the extent that it could overwhelm a family.

Practice

Avoiding dependency

It is crucial to achieve a balance between providing sufficient support while not creating a dependence on services. The social worker's aim with Laura and her siblings was to empower the parents to achieve the required change independently.

Clarifying objectives

What, then, were the workers' aims in the provision of family support in each of these four cases? The overall aim in Natalia's case was to ensure that she was safe, well cared for and able to achieve her developmental potential. In Laura, Joe and Luke's case, the worker was tasked with assessing and promoting their parents' ability to care adequately for and to protect them. David's behaviour in school indicated that he needed some help in order to achieve his potential and the social worker sought to provide this by supporting his parents to improve the way in which they cared for and protected him. In Tony's case, the social worker's aim was to support him to make the required changes in his behaviour so that he could return to a safe and nurturing family environment.

The overall aim in all four cases was to support and promote the family unit and to help people, wherever possible, to stay together as a family. Throughout all the assessments and the interventions, it was crucial to continue to consider the impact of each factor on the child: the impact of Monika's choices on Natalia's safety and wellbeing; the impact of parental drug use on Laura, Joe and Luke; the impact that David's parents' disabilities had on his wellbeing; and the impact of Tony's circumstances on his ability to fulfil his potential in life.

Further reading

■ Daniel, B. and Wassell, S. (2002) *Assessing and Promoting Resilience in Vulnerable Children*, vols I, II and III. London: Jessica Kingsley.

Series of three practical workbooks packed with tools for measuring and promoting resilience in children and young people, along with easily accessible theory into attachment, resilience and child development.

■ Goodhart, G. (2003) *You Choose*. London: Random House Children's Books.

A children's book, one of the most useful tools I have had for engaging with children and young people of all ages. The brightly coloured illustrations and composition of the book provide a fabulous opportunity to explore children's perspectives, dreams and goals.

■ Hughes, D.A. (2006) *Building the Bonds of Attachment: Awakening Love in Deeply Troubled Children*. Lanham, MD: Rowman & Littlefield.

Fantastic case study-based text detailing an intensive method of supporting a child affected by significant trauma and neglect. Combines theory into attachment and child development with a practical guide to developing a model of intervention.

Part II
Social Work and Child Protection

Child protection is the area of social work most often subject to the public gaze; its mention invariably evokes an emotional response. *The Munro Review of Child Protection* (Munro, 2011) calls for a reorientation away from technical-rational managerial drivers and a return to relationship-based social work practice, and Part II of this book enables readers to locate themselves within that debate.

In Chapter 6, Michael Little and his co-authors place child protection in a policy context often driven by people's emotional reaction to the idea of harm occurring to any child or by their reaction to the state's intrusion into the private world of the family. They provide a commentary on how the UK child protection system has developed into its current form and how policy responses have impacted on practices that seek to address policy-makers' concerns.

Caroline Ball shows in Chapter 7 how the tension between the need to protect children and the reality of unwanted intrusion in 'private and family life' is reflected within the legislative framework that empowers the social worker to act on behalf of the state. The reader is engaged in an examination of the extent to which the law has succeeded in managing this tension and striking a balance between the conflicting elements.

Chapter 8 deals with the question of how practitioners rely on theoretical perspectives in their practice and how they use them in order to understand family life and their own role in the process of protecting children. Simon Hackett draws on his experience of teaching post-qualifying courses to child protection social workers in order to outline some practice examples of theory being effectively used in direct interventions. The reader is introduced to ideas of eclectic and specialist use of theory to inform practice that allows practitioners to develop a relationship-based approach to interventions with families.

The challenge of research use in child protection is explored by Helga Sneddon in Chapter 9. She provides a broad introduction to the research evidence that can inform policy and practice development and underpins the knowledge base of practitioners. This is balanced with a recognition of the difficulties faced by practitioners in keeping up to date with research and the fact that research itself doesn't always take on board practice realities or the needs of practitioners.

Chapter 10 uses four case scenarios to indicate some of the practice realities faced by social workers as they try to understand and engage effectively with families in which children are at risk of harm. They serve as examples of the messy complexities that face practitioners every day. Joe Smeeton invites readers to reflect again on the tensions identified in the previous chapters – especially in respect of the conflict between the task of advising and supporting families and that of engaging in unwanted statutory intervention with the aim of protecting children from harm.

The Munro Report succeeded in emphasizing to policy-makers that there is no single process or procedure that will keep all children safe from harm: even in the most robust of child protection systems, employing the most expert practitioners, some children will still die at the hands of the adults who should be caring for them. The challenge for social workers lies in breaking away from a reliance on feeling satisfied that they have 'done things right' and moving towards a point where they can say that they have 'done the right thing'. This shift can only be achieved by reflexive practitioners constantly testing and revising their assumptions and awareness of the impact their practice is having on the children and families with whom they work.

Joe Smeeton

Reference

Munro, E. (2011) *The Munro Review of Child Protection: Final Report – A Child-centred System*, Cm 8062. London: DfE.

6

Social policy and child protection: using the heart and the head

MICHAEL LITTLE WITH DAVID JODRELL AND SEDEN KARAKURT

Child protection is now at the core of public policy for children. It has bothered policy-makers for more than a century, evidenced by the national societies, for example the National Society for the Prevention of Cruelty to Children, calling for a better response to child maltreatment from the 1880s onwards. But it has become a focal point, at times a lightning rod of public policy, since about the 1960s when recognition of physical and sexual maltreatment increased and governments were impelled to develop child protection systems.

Public policy is the product of many forces. There is the need to accommodate the ethical and moral concerns of a society, and clearly the public has become more concerned about child maltreatment in the past half-century. There is no evidence that the problem has increased, just that we are more knowledgeable about and less tolerant of the abuses visited on children. There are pragmatic judgements that policy-makers have to make about how to manage scarce resources, protect narrow interests, and defend the boundaries around government departments. These politics deal with the role of local government and the social sector, as we are now learning to call the voluntary or 'third' sector.

One might argue that the ethical, moral and pragmatic dimensions of public policy-making are bound up in human relations, manifest in power politics and, as such, form the less rational components of the task. This is the part of public policy formation driven by the heart. Then there is the head. There is evidence about the causes of the problem, its epidemiology, and the most beneficial and cost-effective strategies for finding a solution. Increasingly, public policy-makers are also learning to listen to the consumers of services, in this case children who have been maltreated as well as their family members who, in most cases, will be fundamental to finding a positive resolution.

In this chapter, I argue that child protection policy is ruled by the heart more than the head, that is, it reflects the less rational aspects of policy-making. I show that child protection reflects five decades of reactions by central and local government administrators, with some involvement of politicians, that partly mollify the moral concerns of nations and are pragmatic in the sense that services reach many children with relatively few resources and minimize the damage to elected politicians, although less so for bureaucrats who are periodically asked to fall on their swords as a palliative for the sins of others.

I show that policy-making has turned a blind eye to advances in science and other high-quality evidence, for example about 'what works'. As importantly, because child protection has become a series of responses crudely bound up in systems for poor children, those from economically disadvantaged backgrounds, the voice of the consumer is more or less ignored.

While the historical development of child protection is understandable in social policy terms, it is fundamentally flawed. I argue for a paradigm shift that puts the needs of children and families first, driven by a hard-headed determination to understand better and effectively respond to the maltreatment of children.

Historical development of child protection policy

In a necessarily brief overview of child protection, I draw out what I consider to be the major drivers behind child protection policy over the past half-century.

Feminism has been one. Chronicles vary, but most historians of the subject agree that women meeting to discuss matters of importance to women in the 1960s became an important watershed of collective understanding, which produced a realization that domestic violence and sexual maltreatment were much more widespread than had been thought. Importantly, and ironically, given the eventual direction of public policy, this new understanding included a realization that sexual abuse was not just a matter of incest in odd, mostly deprived families but extended into ordinary families across the classes.

Emerging along with other civil rights movements, feminists drew a broad range of women into public discussion groups. Their focus was partly on the poor response to crimes against women such as rape and other sexual assaults. These led to the establishment of rape crisis centres and, later, to domestic violence shelters. These conversations began to cover the likely incidence of sexual abuse within families, and generating advocacy, training and technical assistance on the issue.

Another fault line in the shifting plates of child protection policy was the acceptance by medical doctors that a proportion of the broken bones, burns and internal bleeding they treated in A&E was not the result of accidents but of violence in the home. The paper 'The battered child syndrome' by paediatrician Henry Kempe et al. (1962) changed the way in which child maltreatment is identified and recognized around the world. It brought the high incidence of physical abuse to the attention of, first, the medical profession and later the media. Kempe subsequently worked tirelessly to introduce child abuse reporting laws, which were eventually adopted in all 50 US states.

Feminists and doctors shook the moral structures on which Western societies, particularly the USA, are based. In time, left alone, these structures might have settled on something akin to their original foundations. But another public policy driver began to exert pressure.

Over the past five decades, children's services have been driven by successive scandals that have captured the news headlines. Sometimes the outrage concerned an *omission* by children's services professionals, a failure to notice that something was awry, the absence of sharing information that would have brought a problem to attention or the simple lack of action when something was known to be wrong. The general public have been offended by the death of children, victims of gross abuse, who were known to children's services. At times, public ire has fallen more strongly on public agency heads and practitioners than on the people who killed the child.

Less frequently, the scandal concerns *commission*, for example unnecessarily removing children from their parents, and is bound up in the preparedness of public agencies and the people they employ to get involved in the private lives of families. In 1987, two paediatricians working at a Cleveland hospital in northeast England diagnosed 121 cases of suspected child sexual abuse (Campbell, 1988). They partly based their conclusions on a diagnostic technique known as 'reflex anal dilatation'. After much court activity, nearly 80 of the proceedings were dismissed. A media outcry resulted in a judicial inquiry led by Elizabeth Butler-Sloss (1988), which neither vindicated nor vilified the behaviour of the paediatricians. The case was significant in a number of respects. It reflected a concern that professionals were doing too much, not too little. The case brought into view the power of a single profession to dictate the response of other professions and the courts. Cleveland also tested the limits of society's ability to acknowledge the prevalence of sexual abuse.

A common denominator in these scandals has been a focus on children from poor, often extremely poor, economic backgrounds. It is the suffering of children who have had a precarious start in life that has been brought to attention, no doubt adding to the offence taken by the public.

Public policy-makers have been required to respond to these scandals. Generally speaking, they have been on the back foot, reacting as problems occur. In the UK, for example, major reviews have taken place in each of the decades from the 1960s onwards, and while each inquiry has added some new perspectives, there is a significant amount of repetition. Every review, for example, tends to conclude with the need for professionals to collaborate and share information more readily.

In the UK, there have been major pieces of legislation changing the relationship between state and family, for example the Children Act 1989 in England. These Acts have been influenced in part by the growing recognition of child maltreatment.

But for the most part, inquiries result not in legislation but in guidance. It is civil servants, including those qualified to practise, social workers for example, who have taken the lead in responding to the findings of successive inquiries. The product has been increased guidance to the professions. When Eileen Munro undertook her review into child protection in 2010, she found that the checklists and guidance had mushroomed from 7 to 390 pages in just a few decades (Munro, 2010). She might also have said that the language in the guidance has changed also. It is almost as if the state, powerless to tell the public how to bring up its children, has put all its energies into telling social workers, health visitors and teachers what to do.

An unintended consequence has been a mushrooming of process and a relative lack of attention given to how professionals should intervene. For example, in England, social workers are required to gather and record huge amounts of information on children. Some see their job as processors of information. Most cases viewed as risky are referred to a child protection conference at which representatives from several agencies will gather to decide what has happened, what might happen in the future and, on the basis of this analysis, what to do. As Farmer (Farmer and Owen, 1995) found in the mid-1990s, about 50 minutes of every hour of a child protection conference will be devoted to working out whether or not a child has been maltreated, leaving 10 minutes to decide what action to take. With or without a case conference, there will be a lot of sharing of information across agencies, a process that is complicated by negotiation over who will pay for any intervention and who will hold responsibility for the case.

From time to time, there will be a broader reflection on child protection policy. In the mid-1990s, for example, I was involved in a three-year review that used the evidence of 16 studies commissioned by the Department of Health. Researchers and policy-makers met at Dartington, twice a year, and an overview study, *Child Protection: Messages from Research* (DH, 1995), brought the findings together. There was a tension between those advocating greater intervention in family life and those calling for greater support of families. That tension was relieved in part by showing how family support was effective in responding to potential maltreatment. The report was well received but evaluation of its dissemination found that it tended to confirm not challenge existing behaviours (Weyts et al., 2000). In short, the Blue Book, as it became known, was all things to all people.

Summing up this brief history, it is probable that rates of child maltreatment have changed little over the past century, but awareness of the problem has peaked in the past 50 years. Social policy reaction means that many more children are identified as being at least 'at risk' of abuse than would have been the case 50 or more years ago. The management of this risk is shared across children's services agencies, with social work doing most of the heavy lifting. The behaviour of agencies and professions is dictated by increasing amounts of guidance prepared by central government, operating within a broader legislative framework that establishes the relationship between state and family.

One can see how the moral indignation of society and the pragmatic responses of policy-makers have helped to forge this history. The role of evidence is more sketchy. The perspectives of people caught up in the process are more or less absent, despite the efforts of telephone helplines for children.

The status quo

And the product of this history? Undoubtedly, it has led to much effective work. Many children who would have died have not. Many have been saved from sexual maltreatment. And given what has been shown by follow-up studies, it seems highly probable that many thousands have been protected from emotional abuse and subsequent mental health problems.

On the other side of the coin is a system that is designed for children from economically poor families, and one that better off families view with deep distrust and see as largely irrelevant to their own lives. On this side of the coin is a set of arrangements that is strong on sharing information across agencies and devotes a lot of time to trying to discover, often unsuccessfully, whether or not maltreatment can be established, which provides little in the way of support for the majority of families, but engages in highly intrusive interventions for a minority of families, such as separation of the child into foster or residential care.

Eileen Munro's review found that from 2009 to 2010, over six hundred thousand children were being drawn into the social care process in England. Roughly speaking, that is 1 child in every 20. My own, much less reliable estimate suggests that 1 in 3 children is referred to health, education, social care, police and youth justice services each year for a social need, or for some threat to their health and development. The state therefore 'knows' something about these children, and so potentially holds some responsibility for their safety.

A decision to engage with so many children and families demands a lot of precision in working out whether or not there is a risk of maltreatment. Ironically, although there has been a huge increase in the amount of information collected on families, only a small proportion of this relates to the question of abuse, or the risk of impairment to a child's health and development. I think of these lines in the sand as 'pure thresholds', and in England they relate to the legal requirement that, over and above universal services, the state should intervene when there is impairment to a child's health and development, or there is risk of impairment.

Instead of pure thresholds, we have what I call 'process thresholds', which are geared to helping agencies and practitioners know whether or not they should intervene. There is a commonly held belief that 'pure' and 'process' thresholds are aligned. They are not. The great majority of children who have been maltreated are not supported by children's services. A significant proportion of children thought by children's services to have been maltreated have not, unless one draws the threshold so broad as to include every minor misdemeanour against children.

From the perspective of children's services, this is not a healthy state of affairs. They 'know' a lot of children who may have been abused. In this context, it is surprising that there have not been more scandals. The data certainly help to explain why there has been no change over the past five decades in the mortality rate among children known to children's services. The figure runs at about 80–90 per year in England. Nor should there be any surprise at the failure to reduce the number of children who die at the hands of their abusers. These tally to about 45 per year in England (Laming, 2009).

If one looks at it from the perspective of the families involved, most get drawn reluctantly into the child protection process. Most will have something to be guilty about, since that is the nature of family life. Because they are poor, most will be wanting some kind of extra support, primarily economic but also to address mental health problems or the child's schooling. The majority will find themselves answering necessary but nonetheless highly intrusive questions. Most will wait many weeks and sometimes months for the system to respond. The great majority will find that the system cannot come to a conclusion. Few will get any help.

If families knew the systems they were encountering, they would know why they were so unlikely to get any support:

1   There are too many cases chasing the limited pot of money available. The pot is not small but it will never satisfy the needs of the half a million or so families in the child protection system alone.
2   The objectives of agencies that operate and practitioners that work within the child protection system are no longer clear:
    – Is it to prevent child maltreatment?
    – Is it to respond to maltreatment once it has occurred, with the goal of preventing impairments to health and development?
    – Is it to respond to the impairments consequent on child maltreatment so that they do not impede the child in later life?

Probably agencies and practitioners would claim all three, but finding a correspondence between claim, policy and practice is difficult.

Missing links

Looked at cold, these arrangements are found wanting. There is no evidence that they get to the right children, or that they are having any effect on the incidence of maltreatment. The process is a harbinger of scandal. It leaves a lot of families deeply dissatisfied, and, it should be said, also causes a lot of misery for policy-makers and practitioners.

It is relatively straightforward to point out the irrationality of large systems. It is harder to say what one would do about it. There is much that could be done. But pursuing the theme of the chapter, I examine how an extra dose of evidence would potentially reform some of these arrangements. I do not have space to go into the perspectives of children and families caught up in the process. It is plain that the application of evidence is only going to be effective if allied to the voice of children and families.

The place of evidence

The term 'evidence based' has become commonplace, as if there were a place for policy or practice that is not supported by knowledge. Few people bother to say what they mean by evidence. For the purposes of this chapter, I am going to apply a high bar. I am going to focus on the best epidemiology on the causes of child maltreatment, and the most robust tests of whether or not an intervention works. Some will read these lines and presume that attention to the best evidence implies no place for other kinds of knowledge. That would be a mistake.

The causes of maltreatment

There has been surprisingly little investigation into the incidence and likely causes of child maltreatment. Severe physical abuse, for example, is thought to affect between 4 and 16% of children in economically developed countries, with elevated rates in transition countries, such as Ukraine, and higher again in the global South, Ghana for example (Gilbert et al., 2009; Akmatov, 2011). There is much discussion about the validity of the assessment of these rates, and their links to potential causes such as socioeconomic status, parents' education and mental health, and their use of drugs and alcohol.

Other researchers have taken another tack by looking at ordinary household behaviours and their links to impairments to children's health and development. Straus (1979), for example, has analysed the way in which conflict is resolved within families, between adult partners and between the adults and their children. He starts from the premise that conflict is ubiquitous. Disagreements occur when people are in relationships. Those disagreements have to be resolved. Some families resolve these conflicts solely through negotiation. This turns out to be rare, occurring in less than 10% of families (Berry, 2008). More common is psychological aggression and minor physical violence affecting approximately 60% of children (Cawson, 2002; Creighton et al., 2003). Then there is the use of severe violence. This too is unusual but still affects about 7–9% of children (Cawson, 2002; Creighton et al., 2003).

Ordinary family behaviour can be correlated with measures of child wellbeing. This reveals that rates of conduct disorder, to take one indicator, are elevated 10 times for children who experience severe violence in their families. Rates for those experiencing psychological aggression or minor physical violence are elevated 3.5 times over families who negotiate conflicts consensually (Berry, 2008). There is also an association between ordinary family relationship practices and ordinary functioning of children, that is, the more conflict resolution techniques resort to different forms of aggression and violence, the worse behaved and the less happy the children will be. Figure 6.1 summarizes this relationship.

These correlations are moderated by socioeconomic risks such as poverty: poor children do worse when exposed to violence (Katz et al., 2007). Violence is not uncommon in rich families (Cawson, 2002) and is related to the same poor behaviour. So what? If these data are reliable, and they have been replicated now in many countries, they indicate a new avenue for child protection policy. As well as responding to severe cases of maltreatment, there may be benefit in a public health-style approach that encourages all families to use more consensual conflict resolution techniques, and to resort less to the psychological aggression and minor physical violence that has become normative in many economically developed countries – and possibly globally.

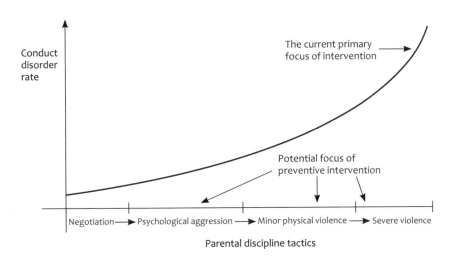

Figure 6.1 The relationship between parental discipline tactics and conduct disorder

The result of dragging the distribution in Figure 6.1 to the left would probably be better behaved, happier, more social children, which in turn would produce better school performance. It would also lead to lower levels of mental ill health. There is no proof that such a public health strategy of bringing child protection to all children would work. But it is a testable proposition.

What works?

At about the same time that child protection was demanding the attention of public policy-makers, another movement was getting underway. From the 1970s onwards, a small group of scientists began to translate what they had learned from their studies into the development of programmes that they then rigorously evaluated to find out if they had any impact on child outcomes. The adverb 'rigorously' generally implied a randomized controlled trial or at least a study with a reliable control group comprising children who did not get the intervention. These interventions, which eventually reached all aspects of children's health and development, took on the epithet 'evidence-based programmes'. In recent years, several groups, Dartington Social Research Unit included, have prepared standards that establish which programmes are evidence based and which are not (DSRU, 2010; Allen, 2011).

There are several programmes that both meet these high thresholds and impact on outcomes of interest to child protection policy-makers and practitioners:

1 There are efforts to change what happens across a community by taking a public health approach not unlike that advocated above. Typical in this category would be the application of all versions of the Triple P parenting programme in the US state of South Carolina, which produces the equivalent of 700 less child maltreatment cases and 240 fewer separations into out-of-home care for every community of 100,000 people (Prinz et al., 2009).

2 There are health visiting programmes such as the Nurse Family Partnership in the USA (known as Family Nurse Partnership in England). This early intervention approach is targeted at teenage mothers and, among a range of benefits to parent and child, results in reductions of 48% in reported rates of child abuse and neglect by the time the child is 15 years of age (Olds et al., 2007).

3 There is support in the early years, such as Sure Start children's centres. A long-term follow-up of children attending Chicago child parent centres, for example, compared to a control group getting services as usual demonstrated a reduction in the incidence of child abuse, which was linked to better parental involvement in the child's development and eventually better school and youth justice outcomes (Reynolds et al., 2004).

4 There are parenting programmes. Parent–child interaction therapy, which is applied to families caught up in the child protection system, produces reductions in re-referrals for maltreatment of two-fifths compared to families receiving standard interventions (Chaffin et al., 2004).

5 There are therapeutic models such as infant–parent psychotherapy (Cicchetti et al., 2006) and trauma-focused cognitive behaviour therapy (Cohen et al., 2005), both of which have been used with some effect with children who have been badly maltreated.

The same standards of evidence used to discover what works can be applied to the task of figuring out what does not work, that is, what interventions leave children worse off than if they had been left alone. There have been less than promising results from programmes that have tried to keep families intact where there is a high risk of severe maltreatment. The majority of intensive family preservation services, for example, do not adhere closely to the homebuilders model and have, in turn, been shown to have limited or negative impacts on family preservation (Nelson et al., 2009). There are some indications of iatrogenic effects from processes like family group conferences that try to get families to sort out the source of their problems and engineer appropriate solutions (Sundell and Vinnerljung, 2004; Berzin, 2006).

The challenge of evidence

Evidence-based programmes like those described above are not a panacea for child protection. The advantage of proven impact has to be balanced against their disadvantages. None of the approaches will be 100% successful. Most of the models are designed in the USA, meaning some preparation and translation may be required to allow UK practitioners and families to 'own' the approach. The standard of proof represents a threat to the majority of child protection services that have not been rigorously evaluated but, theoretically at least, may be as beneficial. Very few of the programmes described above have been successfully delivered on a large scale. Furthermore, in order to replicate gains achieved under trial conditions, it is necessary to maintain high levels of fidelity to the model, which has proved elusive in the context of UK children's services (Little, 2010).

Nonetheless, it is remarkable that so few of the products of the evidence-based movement are delivered to protect children from abuse. The very things known to work are the least likely to gain the support of policy-makers.

A paradigm shift

The failure to fully incorporate quality evidence and consumer perspectives into the making of child protection policy will cause it to become unsustainable. Bringing more children into the child protection system, providing few with any service, never mind a service that might prevent or ameliorate the effects of abuse, increases the risk of system failure manifested in scandals. Current arrangements are bad for the adults working in the system and for society as a whole. Not using technologies such as the evidence-based programmes described above means there is little likelihood of child abuse and neglect being prevented, which is, of course, bad for children and families.

It is easy to criticize the status quo but it is more difficult to say what should be put in its place. From my perspective, a paradigm shift is required. A starting point should involve building a common purpose, and securing some agreement from policy-makers, practitioners, scientists, consumers and the public about what the child protection system in trying to achieve. At the moment, the objectives are not clear.

One might assume that most people with an interest in child protection would put child outcomes near the top of the list of objectives. I would argue for two goals to have primacy:

1   Child protection should reduce the maltreatment of children, whether that be severe violence, sexual or emotional abuse, or neglect. Activity should prevent maltreatment and lower the rate of reoccurrence when it is identified.
2   Child protection should minimize the consequences of maltreatment once it occurs. This means breaking the links between abuse and mental health problems, or school failure or, in adulthood, that fewer victims become perpetrators.

There should be a presumption in the new paradigm that child protection would address children's rights, as well as their needs. Naturally, it should also address family rights. Readers will have noted that although the experience of severe violence in the home greatly increases the likelihood of a child developing a mental health disorder, most of those exposed to the risk do not develop the negative outcome. By this definition, there are no needs to be met. But children have a right not to experience severe violence.

Making connexions

This chapter suggests that child protection would benefit from the implementation of a public health-style policy; for example, just as sewage systems are instrumental in reducing the incidence of disease.

Do you agree? And, if so, what would such a policy look like?

The paradigm should shift so that child protection extends to all children, not just poor children. Of course, there is no legal distinction between poor and better off families. But in practice, the allocation of child protection to social work as the lead agency means that few middle-class children are inconvenienced by the system, and most that do quickly escape its grasp.

The arguments for a child protection system for all children are not just a matter of equality or protecting the economically advantaged from abuse. Some aspects of maltreatment, psychological aggression or minor physical violence, for example, are commonplace in families and therefore have the potential to respond to public health interventions. These change the distribution of ordinary behaviours so that, over time, actions at the extreme of the distribution, such as severe violence to resolve family conflict, are reduced.

A paradigm shift would need to find a more effective balance between the process of finding out who has been abused and action to prevent or address that abuse. As has been seen, at present there is lots of sifting and not much interceding. Currently, agencies wait for someone, usually a practitioner, to knock on the door to report a concern about possible abuse. If society could agree on the objectives of child protection, would it not be possible also to decide who we can help and how, and then go and knock on the doors of those eligible for this help?

No parent wants the intrusion of a practitioner telling them about their mistakes in bringing up their children. But most parents will respond to the offer of effective help with common errors, such as the use of psychological aggression or minor physical violence in the context of conflict resolution, or a range of other ineffective parenting techniques that border on or eventually lead to maltreatment.

There should be more space for policies, programmes and practices that are proved to work and take on the adjective 'evidence based'. The Family Nurse Partnership will not eradicate child abuse. But, properly implemented, it has the potential to prevent about half of the maltreatment that would be visited on children born each year, to roughly 60,000 teenage mothers. At present, only about 7% of eligible mothers receive the programme. The same problem of reach can be said of the other evidence-based programmes described above. Reach is not an issue for routine child protection practices, most of which are unproved, some of which are potentially harmful.

A paradigm shift should include a scientific approach to learning from mistakes. Every year, children die or are seriously injured as the result of maltreatment in England. About 130 of these children will be known to children's services. In England, such tragedies result in what is known as a 'serious case review'. This involves a close scrutiny of all that has gone wrong with the intention of learning from what happened to prevent it happening again. From time to time, policy-makers and practitioners are vilified in the media, and lose their jobs as a consequence for their actual or perceived mistakes.

The serious case review helps society to find the people who will be blamed for serious child maltreatment. The reviews, and the four overviews of them that have taken place over the past decade (Sinclair and Bullock, 2002; Rose and Barnes, 2008; Brandon et al., 2008, 2009), have been valuable but have not produced any change in the rate of children dying or being seriously injured as a result of catastrophic error by the system.

What would a more scientific approach designed to gradually reduce the incidence of the problem look like? The response to fatal air accidents is analogous. Here, there is a comprehensive, well-funded, routinized analysis of the causes of the accident. There is a separation of analysis and blame – nearly half of plane crashes are due to pilot error but there are no media witch-hunts of the professionals involved. The approach involves preventive as well as reactive elements. Accident investigators regularly fly in the cockpit to observe and report on mistakes. Their anonymized reports are used by pilots to reduce future error.

The results of these and other techniques have reduced fatal airline accidents from 9.5 per million miles travelled to 0.2 over the past half-century. Pilot error now accounts for 46% of accidents, a fall of 8%.

Conclusion

Systems to protect children in most economically developed nations have a vintage of about 50 years. They were initiated by the promptings of feminists and medical doctors. They reflect a necessity to act, to do something to address the maltreatment of children that had been brought into public view by advocates in the 1960s. These systems are sustained by the moral indignation of the public, and a desire, vaguely expressed but real nonetheless, that children deserve to be protected from the worst abuse. This indignation and desire generally relates to other people's children, not one's own. The response of the state has been pragmatic. The arrangements put in place reach a lot of children with a limited amount of resources. The state has become much more ready to intervene in family life, or at least in the lives of economically poor families.

Current child protection is a reflection of the heart of a nation. This chapter has called for the head to have a greater say in the future alignment of child protection. By the head, I refer to the place of evidence and the perspective of the consumer, including those children and other family members caught up in child protection inquiries and proceedings. I have argued that this rebalancing amounts to a paradigm shift in the way societies think about and deliver protection from abuse for children.

It would be wrong, however, to characterize any change in terms of an all-or-nothing development. Unhealthy systems can endure for centuries. The ability to systematize is both a virtue and a fatal flaw of systems. Once created, they are not easily swept away.

At the very least, there should be some openness to reform to produce three results:

1 It seems reasonable to expect a child protection system to demonstrate increasing numbers of ordinary children being safeguarded from maltreatment, including psychological aggression and minor physical violence.
2 Although more difficult to achieve, a decline in the numbers of children known to child protection systems who die or are severely injured as a result of maltreatment should be possible.
3 A healthy system would not only achieve these first two ends but would also demonstrate some indication of consumer satisfaction among the general public and those caught up in an investigation. Whether such changes occur depends much on the extent to which child protection is seen as meeting the needs of children over and above the needs of adults.

Further reading

■ Allen, G. (2011) *Early Intervention: The Next Steps*. London: Cabinet Office.

Influential government-commissioned study of early intervention, suggesting innovative methods underpinned by a rigorous evidence base.

■ Little, M. (2010) *Proof Positive*. London: Demos.

Monograph exploring two questions. First, how do we get proven practices embedded into services for children? Second, what is the scope for reforming children's services systems in other ways to improve child outcomes?

■ Munro, E. (2010) *The Munro Review of Child Protection. Part One: A Systems Analysis*. London: TSO.

Government-commissioned report assessing the health of child protection systems in England.

References

Akmatov, M. (2011) 'Child abuse in 28 developing and transitional countries: results from the Multiple Indicator Cluster Surveys', *International Journal of Epidemiology*, **40**(1): 219–27.

Allen, G. (2011) *Early Intervention: The Next Steps*. London: Cabinet Office.

Berry, V. (2008) The Relative Contribution of Family Conflict to Children's Health and Development, unpublished PhD thesis, University of Bath.

Berzin, S. (2006) 'Using sibling data to understand the impact of family group decision-making on child welfare outcomes', *Children and Youth Services Review*, **28**(12): 1449–58.

Brandon, M., Bailey, S., Belderson, P. et al. (2009) *Understanding Serious Case Reviews and their Impact: A Biennial Analysis of Serious Case Reviews 2005–2007*. Nottingham: DCFS.

Brandon, M., Belderson, P., Warren, C. et al. (2008) *Analysing Child Death and Serious Injury Through Abuse and Neglect: What can we Learn? A Biennial Analysis of Serious Case Reviews 2003–2005.* Nottingham: DCFS.

Butler-Sloss, E. (1988) *Report of the Inquiry into Child Abuse in Cleveland 1987,* Cm 412. London: HMSO.

Campbell, B. (1988) *Unofficial Secrets: Child Sexual Abuse: The Cleveland Case.* London: Virago Press.

Cawson, P. (2002) *Child Maltreatment in the Family: The Experience of a National Sample of Young People.* London: NSPCC.

Chaffin, M., Silovsky, J., Funderburk, B. et al. (2004) 'Parent-child interaction therapy with physically abusive parents: efficacy for reducing future abuse reports', *Journal of Consulting and Clinical Psychology,* **72**(3): 500–10.

Cicchetti, D., Rogosch, F. and Toth, S. (2006) 'Fostering secure attachment in infants in maltreating families through prevention interventions', *Development and Psychopathology,* **18**(3): 623–49.

Cohen, J., Mannarino, A. and Knudsen, K. (2005) 'Treating sexually abused children: one year follow-up of a randomized controlled trial', *Child Abuse and Neglect,* **29**(2): 135–45.

Creighton, S., Ghate, D., Hazel, N. et al. (2003) 'Putting the conflict tactics scale in context in violence from parent to child', in R. Lee and E. Stanko (eds) *Researching Violence.* London: Routledge.

DH (Department of Health) (1995) *Child Protection: Messages from Research.* London: HMSO.

DSRU (Dartington Social Research Unit) (2010) *Standards of Evidence for the Greater London Authority: An Evaluation Standard Produced as Part of the Project Oracle Evaluation Toolkit.* Dartington: Social Research Unit.

Farmer, E. and Owen, M. (eds) (1995) *Child Protection Practice: Private Risks and Public Remedies.* London: HMSO.

Gilbert, R., Widom, C., Browne, K. et al. (2009) 'Burden and consequences of child maltreatment in high-income countries', *The Lancet,* **373**(9657): 68–81.

Katz, I., Corlyon, J., La Placa, V. and Hinter, S. (2007) *The Relationship between Parenting and Poverty.* York: Joseph Rowntree Foundation.

Kempe, C., Silverman, F., Steele, B. et al. (1962) 'The battered-child syndrome', *Journal of the American Medical Association,* **181**(1): 17–24.

Laming, Lord (2009) *The Protection of Children in England: A Progress Report.* London: TSO.

Little, M. (2010) *Proof Positive.* London: Demos.

Munro, E. (2010) *The Munro Review of Child Protection. Part One: A Systems Analysis.* London: TSO.

Nelson, K., Walters, B., Schweitzer, D. et al. (2009) *A Ten-year Review of Family Preservation Research: Building the Evidence Base.* Seattle: Casey Family Programs.

Olds, D., Sadler, L. and Kitzman, H. (2007) 'Programs for parents of infants and toddlers: recent evidence from randomized trials', *Journal of Child Psychology and Psychiatry,* **48**(3): 355–91.

Prinz, R., Sanders, M., Shapiro, C. et al. (2009) 'Population-based prevention of child maltreatment: the U.S. Triple P System Population Trial', *Prevention Science,* **10**(1): 1–12.

Reynolds, A., Ou, S. and Topitzes, J. (2004) 'Paths of effects of early childhood intervention on educational attainment and delinquency: a confirmatory analysis of the Chicago Child-Parent Centers', *Child Development*, **75**(5): 1299–328.

Rose, W. and Barnes, J. (2008) *Improving Safeguarding Practice: Study of Serious Case Reviews 2001–3*. Buckingham: Open University Press.

Sinclair, R. and Bullock, R. (2002) *Learning from Past Experience: A Review of Serious Case Reviews*. London: DH.

Straus, M. (1979) 'Measuring intrafamily conflict and violence: The Conflict Tactics (CT) Scales', *Journal of Marriage and Family*, **14**(1): 75–88.

Sundell, K. and Vinnerljung, B. (2004) 'Outcomes of family group conferencing in Sweden: a 3-year follow-up', *Child Abuse and Neglect*, **28**(3): 267–87.

Weyts, A., Morpeth, L. and Bullock, R. (2000) 'Department of Health research overviews – past, present and future: an evaluation of the dissemination of the Blue Book, *Child Protection: Messages from Research*, *Child and Family Social Work*, **5**(3): 215–23.

7
Legal perspectives on social work in child protection

CAROLINE BALL

Child protection law (the so-called 'public' child law) regulates at the profoundly difficult interface of the individual's right to 'private and family life' under Article 8 of the European Convention on Human Rights (ECHR), and the duty of the state to protect its most vulnerable citizens from abuse or neglect.

The dilemma to be resolved is how the legal framework, and the legal process, can best reconcile safeguarding children from suffering significant harm with the obligation to respect personal autonomy and family privacy (Hayes, 1997). In order that this dilemma can be resolved, the child protection powers provided to local authorities, and exercised by social workers, have to be sufficiently broadly framed to encompass the range of possible harm, but have also to be subject to stringent control. They have to be wide enough to allow immediate short-term protection in an emergency and to provide courts with the power to make care orders when children have to be removed from their families. These orders allow local authorities, until the order is revoked or the child reaches the age of 18, to exercise parental responsibility, and in extreme cases, where it is considered that the child cannot return to their birth family, to place the child for adoption.

It is hard to conceive of powers that more starkly interfere with 'private and family life' than these. Hence, increasingly, with the development of international treaty obligations recognizing human rights and the rights of children, greater controls on the exercise of discretionary powers have been apparent over the past half-century (Ball, 1998). In particular, a clear policy shift is discernible between the greater child protection powers provided to local authorities under the Children Act 1975 and the emphasis on, where possible, working in partnership with parents and avoiding court proceedings in the Children Act 1989 (CA 1989).

This chapter is underpinned by awareness of the difficulty of achieving a legislative and practice balance between the exercise of child protection powers and the rights of children and families. A brief look at the state of public child law prior to the reforms introduced by the CA 1989 will set the context for a more detailed consideration of the current legal framework of child protection. The chapter concludes with exploration of the extent to which the dilemma posed by Hayes (1997) is resolved in current child protection law and the legal process.

Child protection legislation and its administration prior to the Children Act 1989

Prior to implementation of the Children Act 1989 in 1991, the public and private law relating to children was contained in separate statutes and administered in different courts. The private law, not in such a parlous state as the public law but still unsatisfactory, was the subject of detailed review by the Law Commission, which published a series of working papers and by the end of the 1980s had clear proposals for the private law relating to children.

The need for reform of the public law was clearly articulated in evidence from a group of lawyers and social workers quoted in the influential report *Children in Care* from the House of Commons Social Services Committee (House of Commons, 1984, p. 118):

> The present state of children's legislation can only be described as complex, confusing and unsatisfactory … the effect and implication of this on children is diverse with far-reaching consequences for their welfare.

The dire complexity of the public law was compounded by the fact that it had its roots in separate but closely entangled strands of legislation: one strand had its origins in Poor Law relief for destitute children, the other in the quasi-criminal provisions for the protection or control of abused or unruly children, each regulated through separate, much amended statutes from the Children Act 1908 onwards. The extent to which the close entanglement of these strands contributed to the confused state of the public law was clearly identified in the report to ministers *Review of Child Care Law* (DHSS, 1985), which informed the proposals for reform of the public law in the White Paper *The Law on Child Care and Family Services* (DHSS, 1987). A few of those 'far-reaching consequences' are evidenced in the reports of child abuse inquiries.

Child death inquiries

During the 1970s and 80s, successive inquiries into the deaths of children at the hands of their parents or carers identified how particular weaknesses in the legal framework contributed to the circumstances surrounding the child's death. Some of these reports made specific recommendations relating to changes in the law. The names of the children will be familiar to many, the legal issues associated with them possibly less so.

Maria Colwell died at the hands of her stepfather and her mother in 1973. The facts of that case starkly demonstrated the extent to which proceedings under the Children and Young Persons Act 1969, which were essentially between the local authority and the parents, precluded the child's voice being heard. An application to discharge the care order under which Maria was living with relative carers, which was not opposed by the local authority, resulted in her being moved from the carers with whom she wanted to stay to her mother and stepfather's care. The appointment of an independent guardian ad litem, now a Child and Family Court Advisory and Support Service (CAFCASS) children's guardian, to safeguard the welfare of the child in care or discharge proceedings, followed a recommendation in the report into the circumstances surrounding Maria's death (Field-Fisher, 1974).

It was the apparent inadequacy of the emergency protection provisions in the Children and Young Persons Act 1969, and the extent to which they were open to diverse interpretation, that was the key issue in the case of Kimberley Carlile who died, well known to social workers but not seen by them at critical times, in 1986. The extent of Kimberley's abuse and neglect were not seen because the social worker was only allowed to see her through frosted glass and was advised that without her being seen, there was no evidence on which to ground an application for a place of safety order. Much of the detail in the current emergency protection order provisions is based on the recommendations in the report of the inquiry into Kimberley's death (Blom-Cooper, 1987).

Paradoxically, at the same time in Cleveland, a widespread diagnosis of child sexual abuse led to many children being made the subject of place of safety orders, on medical evidence alone, for the permitted maximum of 28 days with no arrangements in place for any contact between the children and their families. The report of the statutory inquiry into this episode made robust recommendations as to the need for legal controls on the abuse of emergency protection powers (Butler-Sloss, 1988).

Other deficits in the legal framework and legal process

In addition to issues raised by the inquiries, what were the major concerns about the legal framework and legal process? The list is not exhaustive, but they centred on:

- the extent to which the law militated against local authority social workers working in partnership with families
- the inadequacy of the courts
- the limited and inflexible range of orders available in care proceedings
- the overuse by local authorities of the High Court's wardship jurisdiction
- the lack of any legal framework to support continued contact between children in care and their families.

Legal barriers to partnership working

Under the Children and Young Persons Act 1969, the way in which the provisions relating to care proceedings were framed made it difficult for local authorities to establish the grounds for a care or supervision order if the child was already accommodated by the local authority under a voluntary arrangement. This had the effect of discouraging partnership working in all cases in which there was a possibility that an order would need to be sought in the future.

The courts

Prior to 1991, only the magistrates' juvenile court had jurisdiction in care proceedings. This meant that, however complex the issues or technical the medical evidence, only laypeople with, then, minimal training could make decisions concerning the removal of children from their families into public care or supervision. In addition, the juvenile court in care proceedings was exercising a quasi-criminal rather than a civil jurisdiction, albeit using the civil standard of proof. Appeals, as in criminal proceedings, were heard in the Crown Court, hardly an appropriate forum for sensitive family matters.

Orders available in care proceedings

Under the Children and Young Persons Act 1969, care proceedings were in two parts, analogous to a criminal trial: proof of the grounds as set out in section 1 (finding of guilt), followed by a care or supervision order or the binding over of parents (sentence). There was no flexibility to make any other order or no order.

Wardship

The prerogative power of the High Court to exercise the inherent jurisdiction in wardship gives parental rights to the judge to approve all important decisions in the ward's life. The jurisdiction, in which the criteria for decision-making was that the child's welfare should be the court's first and paramount consideration, was infinitely flexible and historically used to protect the property of minor landowners or prevent the marriage of young heiresses to fortune hunters. In a somewhat bizarre development, it was creatively and increasingly used throughout the 1970s and 80s by local authorities seeking care of deeply disadvantaged, abused or neglected children. This use of wardship, while understandable in view of the shortcomings of the only other available forum, the magistrates' juvenile court, was massively disadvantageous to children and families: it was only available to local authorities, was costly, very slow, and required minimal scrutiny by the courts when the jurisdiction, which took immediate effect, was first invoked. Too often, by the first substantive hearing often as much as two years later, the child was so well settled with foster carers that, applying the welfare test, upsetting the status quo was not in the child's best interests, even if, as in some cases, there was otherwise no reason why the parents or other family members should not care for the children (Morton and Masson, 1989).

Parental contact with children in care

Prior to 1991, the management of what was then called 'access' between children in care and their families was left to the professional judgement of social workers and could not be challenged by families. Despite departmental guidance, issued in recognition of the validity of research findings regarding the extent to which the failure to maintain active links between children in care and their families was linked to lengthy care episodes with little hope of rehabilitation, little priority was given by social work managers to maintaining such links (Millham et al., 1986, 1989). It was recognized that substantial reform, putting the regulation of contact between parents and their children in care on a statutory basis, with a presumption in favour of contact, was needed.

The Children Act 1989

The chance sequence of events that led to the reform of most of the public and private law relating to children being regulated within a single Act are well documented (see, for example, Hoggett, 1989; Ball, 1990). The basic principles that underlie the Children Act 1989 are:

- local authorities working in partnership with parents and avoiding court proceedings where possible, and the courts only making orders where an order is necessary
- parental responsibility, rather than parental rights
- a single welfare principle being applied to all decisions regarding a child's upbringing, income or property
- a flexible range of orders, with almost all orders being available in all proceedings
- recognition that delays in court proceedings are likely to prejudice the welfare of the child
- the law providing a minimum threshold before courts can justify the removal of a child from home or the imposition of compulsory supervision.

The CA 1989 is in 12 Parts: Parts I and II set out the principles that underpin the Act, define parental responsibility and detail the range of private law orders, which are also available to courts in public law proceedings. Parts III to V, with accompanying schedules and regulations, lay down local authorities' duties, powers and responsibilities in regard to child care and protection. As well as the Act, which has been frequently amended since its implementation in 1991, social workers have to work within the five volumes of the revised *Children Act 1989 Guidance and Regulations* (DCSF, 2008, 2010a; DfE, 2010, 2011a, 2011b) and the detailed guidance for multi-agency child protection practice set out in *Working Together* (DCSF, 2010b, Chs 1, 2, 5, 6).

Both public and private law proceedings under the CA 1989 are administered in three tiers of courts: the magistrates' family proceedings court; the county court; and, exceptionally, the Family Division of the High Court. In public law proceedings, cases are allocated according to complexity.

The current legal framework

Services for children in need

Under the CA 1989, the presumption is that social work intervention, when needed, will wherever possible be in the form of the provision of supportive services to children and their families on a partnership basis. Part III, section 17 lays a general duty on local authorities:

(a) to safeguard and promote the welfare of children within their area who are in need; and

(b) so far as is consistent with that duty, to promote the upbringing of such children by their families, by providing a range and level of services appropriate to those children's needs.

This can be seen as the cornerstone of the CA 1989 so far as the care and protection of children is concerned.

Under section 17(10), a child is defined as being 'in need' if:

(a) he is unlikely to achieve or maintain, or have the opportunity of achieving or maintaining, a reasonable standard of health or development without the provision for him of services by a local authority … ;

(b) his health or development is likely to be significantly impaired, or further impaired, without the provision for him of such services; or

(c) he is disabled.

Disability is widely defined and '"development" means physical, intellectual, emotional, social or behavioural development; and "health" means physical or mental health' (s. 17(11)).

Of course, resources can never match the demand for the services that local authorities are empowered to provide under Part III and all authorities apply strict criteria for eligibility. However, as they will fall within the definition of 'children in need', services such as accommodation away from home can be provided for children in need of protection, provided families are willing to accept such a service. If they are unable or unwilling to do so, depending on the severity of the situation, court orders may have to be sought on the basis that the child is suffering or likely to suffer significant harm unless the order is made. These include brief duration orders under Part V available in an emergency and longer term care and supervision orders under Part IV.

The concept of 'significant harm'

Prior to 1991, compulsory intervention, whether in an emergency or care proceedings, required proof of the existence of specified grounds detailed in the legislation. Under the CA 1989, separate grounds are replaced with a single threshold test: that the child is suffering or is likely to suffer significant harm from which they cannot be protected without the granting of the order applied for. Despite considerable professional consternation regarding the apparent imprecision of the term 'significant harm' prior to implementation of the Act, in practice, recognition of harm as significant appears to have caused few problems.

Making connexions

How does the social worker set about the task of deciding whether the harm suffered by a child is 'significant' or not?

Law

The paramountcy of the child's welfare

Having established the threshold conditions, before making a care or supervision order (or orders in many other proceedings under the Act), the court has to consider the order to be made, if any, having regard to the 'checklist' of issues relating to the child before the court, set out in section 1(3) of the Act. The test to be applied is that the child's welfare is the court's paramount consideration.

The protection of children in an emergency

The protection of children from significant harm in an emergency situation stands, in policy and legal terms, at the interface of the state's duty to its vulnerable citizens and the rights of individuals to 'private and family life'. It will be readily understood that the immediate protection of children in any kind of emergency can only be achieved by the provision of widely defined powers, available without delay, either to ensure that the child is removed from a situation of danger, or can be secured in a safe place, such as a hospital, when threatened with removal.

The powers that allow such actions are necessarily draconian. Respect for human rights requires that abuse of such powers be prevented by ensuring that they are only exercisable in circumstances in which immediate protection of the child cannot be secured in any other way, last for the minimum necessary time, and are open to challenge at the earliest opportunity. Contrasting the brief and imprecise place of safety provisions in the Children and Young Persons Act 1969 with the minute detail regulating emergency protection in Part V of the CA 1989 provides a clear demonstration of the recognition of the need to curtail widely discrepant and at times abusive practice in this area.

Emergency protection orders

The powers set out in sections 44 and 45 of the CA 1989 are intended only for use in real emergencies: anyone may apply to a court or, with leave of the justices' clerk, to a single justice who is a member of the family proceedings panel for an emergency protection order (EPO), without notice to anyone who might oppose the application, on the grounds that:

there is reasonable cause to believe that the child is likely to suffer significant harm if –

(i) he is not removed to accommodation provided by or on behalf of the applicant; or

(ii) he does not remain in the place in which he is then being accommodated;

or where inquiries are being made by a local authority, anyone authorized by it, or by the NSPCC, and they are denied access to the child (s. 44).

Throughout the country, justices' clerks have arrangements in place to ensure that applications for EPOs can be made at any time.

An EPO may be made for up to eight days and may be extended once for up to seven days if the court is satisfied that there is reasonable cause to believe that the child will suffer significant harm unless an extension is granted. While it is in force, the EPO operates as a direction to any person in a position to do so to produce the child; it authorizes the removal of the child to accommodation provided by the applicant and being kept there, or prevents removal from hospital or any other place where they were immediately before the order was made. It also gives parental responsibility, limited to making day-to-day decisions regarding where the child will live, and medical and other assessments, to the local authority for the duration of the order. It is also possible to order an abuser to leave the home for the duration of the order.

There is a presumption of reasonable contact between the child and his family; however, the court may lay down requirements as to contact, including that there shall not be any. The court also has to authorize more than routine medical treatment or investigation, and a child 'of sufficient understanding to make an informed decision' has a statutory right to refuse (s. 44(7)); however, such refusal can be overridden by the High Court exercising its inherent jurisdiction (*South Glamorgan County Council* v *W and B* [1993]). Courts may also add directions concerning the provision of information regarding the child's whereabouts.

There is no right of appeal against the making or refusal of an EPO, although the child or anyone with parental responsibility has a (rarely exercised) right to apply for discharge of the EPO. The only recourse for a local authority refused an EPO is to make an emergency application for an interim care order to a higher court.

Police warrants

Where it is apparent, either at the time of the application or subsequently, that anyone attempting to exercise power under an EPO is being, or is likely to be, denied entry to premises or access to the child, a court or single justice may issue a warrant authorizing a police constable to exercise those powers using force if necessary.

Police protection

Since the nineteenth century, successive statutes have given the police extrajudicial powers to provide emergency protection for children in an emergency. The provisions in the CA 1989 provide, as with EPOs, powers that are as broad in their scope, but more restricted in their duration and application, than those they replaced. Under section 46, where a constable has reasonable cause to believe that a child would otherwise be likely to suffer significant harm, the officer may remove the child to, or ensure that he remains in, a place of safety. The section details the steps that must be taken by the constable to ensure that the parents, local authority and the designated officer responsible for inquiring into the case are informed and that the child's wishes and feelings are considered. Police protection may only last for up to 72 hours. Research findings suggest a discrepant use of police powers, with some good practice, but also considerable ignorance of the powers and an underrecording of the informal exercise of police protection (Masson et al., 2001).

Child assessment orders

The rarely used child assessment order may be of more value in terms of the persuasive power of the possibility of an application than actual use might suggest (only 82 applications in England and Wales in 1994, dropping to 44 in 2008). The order under section 43 has no parallel in previous legislation. It may be applied for only in court, on notice, by a local authority or the NSPCC on the grounds that there is reasonable cause to believe that the child is suffering or likely to suffer significant harm; that an assessment of the child's health and development are necessary, and that it is unlikely that a satisfactory assessment will be made in the absence of an order. The order, which lasts for seven days from a date specified, requires production of the child and authorizes the carrying out of the assessment.

Care proceedings

Under the CA 1989, a care order under Part IV is the only means whereby a local authority can acquire parental responsibility for a child for longer than a very short term in an emergency. Care orders can only be applied for by a local authority or the NSPCC on the basis that the threshold conditions set out in section 31(2) are satisfied, the detailed checklist of factors relating to the child's welfare set out in section 1(3) of the CA 1989 have been considered, and that the order is likely to contribute positively to the child's welfare (s.1(5)).

The threshold conditions (CA 1989, s. 31(2)) are that:

A court may only make a care order or a supervision order if it is satisfied –

(a) that the child concerned is suffering, or is likely to suffer, significant harm; and
(b) that the harm, or likelihood of harm, is attributable to –
  (i) the care given to the child, or likely to be given to him if the order were not made, not being what it would be reasonable to expect a parent to give him; or
  (ii) the child being beyond parental control.

If the court does not find the threshold conditions satisfied, it may not make a care or supervision order. However, since the proceedings are 'family proceedings', the court can, either on application or on its own initiative, make one of the private law orders available under section 8 of the Act, instead of the order applied for.

Care proceedings are commenced in the magistrates' family proceedings court and are generally heard in that court, although because of complexity, they may be transferred to the county court care centre, and, exceptionally, from there to the Family Division of the High Court. The distribution of care proceedings heard at each level of court has remained remarkably consistent since 1991. In 2010, there were 16,010 applications made, of which 84% were heard in the magistrates' court, 15% in the county court, and 1% in the High Court.

The effect of a care order

The care order, which lasts until the child is 18 unless discharged earlier, gives the local authority parental responsibility and hence the power to determine where the child will live, go to school and all other day-to-day decisions, including consent to most medical treatment. The parents retain the right to exercise any aspect of parental responsibility that is not in conflict with local authority decisions in respect to the child's upbringing, and retain their rights in regard to fundamental aspects of parental responsibility, such as change of the child's religion, the appointment of a guardian in the event of their death, and consent to the child's adoption.

There is a presumption in favour of reasonable contact between children in care and their families, and courts making care orders have to be satisfied as to the arrangements. Except for up to seven days in an emergency situation, the only way that a local authority can lawfully refuse contact is by means of a successful application to court for permission to terminate contact (s. 34).

Supervision orders

A supervision order can only be made if the threshold conditions for making a care order are satisfied. The order puts the child under the supervision of a designated local authority for up to a year and may be extended for up to three years. It may include conditions as to where the child shall live or that the child shall comply with directions from the supervisor to participate in specified activities for up to 90 days, but does not give the local authority parental responsibility. Concerns regarding the threshold conditions for making supervision orders are discussed later in this chapter.

Interim orders

Prior to the final hearing, an interim care or supervision order, or any of the private law orders, may be made on the basis that there is reasonable cause to believe that the threshold conditions exist. The first interim order may be for up to eight weeks and there may be subsequent interim orders for four weeks. Despite the statutory presumption that delay is harmful for children (s. 1(2)), many care cases do not reach a final hearing without several interim orders.

Recently, the Court of Appeal has subjected the grounds for making or refusing interim care orders to rigorous examination on the basis that an interim hearing is not a full hearing. In line with the quest for proportionality between respect for family life and the right of the child to protection from inhuman and degrading treatment, the Court of Appeal has emphasized that an interim order should only be made if, in the court's opinion, the child's safety demands immediate separation (*Re H* [2001], [2002]; *Re L* [2008]; *L-A (Children)* [2009]).

Procedure under the Public Law Outline

In 2005, the report of a judicial review of child care proceedings in England and Wales made several recommendations aimed at improving the system for children and families subject to care proceedings (HM Court Service, 2005). The review encouraged early intervention to find resolution before cases reached court, identified ways to improve local authority applications and recognized that the court process could be simplified and that case management procedures could be improved. The Practice Direction on the *Public Law Outline [PLO]: Guide to Case Management in Public Law Proceedings*, which applies to all care and supervision proceedings and as far as practicable in all public law proceedings (except EPO applications), was issued on 1 April 2008 to replace the earlier Public Law Protocol. Following a review of the way the PLO was working in practice, it was revised and simplified and a new Practice Direction issued in April 2010 (Ministry of Justice, 2008, 2010).

The PLO is a detailed case management tool designed to reduce the number of hearings and to ensure that, by the time of the hearing, only key unresolved issues are before the court. It requires local authorities to write a 'letter before proceedings' to parents setting out the concerns that have led them to decide to apply for a care or supervision order, and to undertake considerable amounts of work, including kinship and residential assessment, before making an application. The key case management emphasis is that the timetable for the proceedings should be a 'timetable for the child' based on the needs of the child subject to the proceedings. This information has to be included in the local authority's application and regularly updated.

Section 31 care plans

As has been suggested earlier, care orders represent a substantial infringement of the right to family life. This can be justified provided three conditions are satisfied: the infringement has to be in accordance with law; in pursuit of one of the legitimate aims provided for in the article; and, necessary in a democratic society. In line with earlier legislation, the CA 1989 initially allowed no judicial scrutiny of local authorities' practice in relation to a child made the subject of a care order once the order was made.

Section 31A was introduced into the Children Act 1989 by the Adoption and Children Act 2002 in response to judicial criticism in the Court of Appeal of the extent to which local authorities possibly breached Article 8(2) of the ECHR if they failed to follow a care plan that formed the basis of the court's decision to make a care order (*Re W and B (Children) (Care Plan)* [2001]). When rejecting the Court of Appeal's creative attempt to remedy this deficit as being clearly contrary to Parliament's intention as expressed in the CA 1989, the House of Lords recognized the need for the possibility of external review of local authorities' functions in respect of children in care, and urged the government to give urgent attention to the problem (*Re S (Children: Care Plan) Re W (Children: Care Plan)* [2002]).

In response, the government introduced section 31A, which requires a court to consider a care plan prepared by the local authority (a section 31A plan) before making a care order. The local authority is placed under a duty to prepare, review and where necessary modify the care plan within the timescale set by the court, and to keep the plan under review and amend it if necessary. An independent reviewing officer has to oversee the review process, and if concerned that the care plan is not being followed to the detriment of the child's welfare may, after exhausting other remedies, refer the case to CAFCASS, which may, as a last resort, refer the case back to court.

The Munro Review of Child Protection

In June 2010, early in the life of the coalition government, the secretary of state for education commissioned Professor Eileen Munro to review child protection. The Munro review is unusual among the many reviews of child protection during the past 50 years in that it is the first one since the 1960s that has not been undertaken in the frenetic political atmosphere of public demand for an effective response to the highly publicized child abuse cases referred to earlier.

Professor Munro published the first two stages of her review as they were completed, and the main report with recommendations for reform in May 2011 (Munro, 2010, 2011a, 2011b). Her wide-ranging recommendations for reform 'geared towards creating a better balance between essential rules, principles and professional expertise' were accepted by the government with very few reservations (DfE, 2011c). Implementing a few of the recommendations requires legislation; most will be dealt with through substantial incremental revision of the statutory guidance *Working Together to Safeguard Children* (DCSF, 2010b) and *The Framework for the Assessment of Children in Need and their Families* (DH, 2000), as well as changes in social work training and the support of frontline practitioners.

Conclusion

As we have seen, before 1991, there were many deficits in the legal framework identified in child death review reports and through research. What about the legal framework under the Children Act 1989?

When Victoria Climbié died in the London Borough of Haringey in 2000 at the hands of her great-aunt and her partner by whom she was privately fostered, she was well known to many agencies. While Lord Laming found the legal framework in relation to intervention in an emergency and for care proceedings largely adequate, he recommended review of the law in regard to private foster carers, which, despite amendments included in the Children Act 2004, is still not robust. He also identified the need to strengthen interagency cooperation in child protection practice. During the previous decade, the weakness of the nonstatutory area child protection committees with responsibility for coordinating child protection policies, procedure and practice among local agencies had already been recognized. Lord Laming recommended that the work of such bodies was so important that it should be put on a statutory basis, and included a recommendation to this effect among his many other recommendations for ensuring political accountability and improving child protection practice in all the agencies. The membership and responsibilities of Local Safeguarding Children Boards are prescribed in the Children Act 2004 and its accompanying regulations and guidance (DCSF, 2010b, Ch. 3).

In 2008, following the death of the toddler Peter Connolly, also in Haringey and also following high levels of contact with children's services, health and the police, Lord Laming was asked by the secretary of state for children, schools and families to prepare an urgent report on the progress being made across the country to implement effective arrangements to safeguard children. In contrast to the earlier cases, when commenting on the law, he was clear that the legislative framework for protecting children and keeping them safe from harm is comprehensive and 'further legislative change is not what is needed' (Laming, 2009), a view echoed by Munro (2011b).

Is that so? It is suggested that further legislative change may be needed to allow for children with parents unwilling to cooperate with children's services and about whom there are significant concerns, but insufficient evidence to satisfy the section 31(2) threshold. This would afford the children some protection rather than none.

The threshold conditions for making a supervision order

Currently, courts can only make a supervision order in civil proceedings if the threshold conditions in the CA 1989, section 31(2) are established. While it has not attracted attention as a key issue in any of the recent reviews, anecdotal evidence from practitioners suggests that the high threshold conditions for making a supervision order should receive further scrutiny in order to redress an imbalance between the Article 8 (ECHR) rights of parents and those of children.

The Review of Child Care Law (DHSS, 1985) rejected proposals that the grounds for making a supervision order should reflect the fact that, by not removing the power to exercise parental responsibility from parents, it was less disruptive to 'private and family life' than a care order. The reasoning was that a supervision order still represented a substantial intrusion into family life. That decision possibly represents a high point in the placing of parents' rights over those of children.

The rigorous test in relation to care orders is unarguable, but, in cases where the local authority has serious concerns that would satisfy the 'reasonable grounds for believing' test, such a high threshold leaves children without the protection that regular social work contact under a supervision order might allow (Hayes, 1997).

The legal process

The legal process encompasses the range of procedures from the institution of proceedings to the court hearing, the judicial decisions made, and the effect of any order. This discussion will focus on a key issue at the heart of the difficulty of achieving the necessary balance between the right of the child to protection and the right of the family to 'private and family life' – judicial efforts to avoid delays:

> Two months of delay in making decisions in the best interests of a child or young person equates to one per cent of childhood that cannot be restored. (Judge Nick Crichton, Wells Street Court, July 2010)

The problem for the courts is reconciling the child's need for a speedy resolution of cases with the parent's right to a hearing that may, for instance, involve several experts. Despite enshrining the principle that when determining any question with respect to the upbringing of a child, 'any delay in determining the question' is 'likely to prejudice the welfare of the child' in legislation (CA 1989, s. 1(2)), reducing delay in care proceedings has proved an intractable problem. Three separate bodies undertook reviews between 2004 and 2007 but their efforts were badly hampered by a limited evidence base and flawed approaches to accurately identifying the problems and devising solutions (Masson, 2007).

The primary aim of the 2003 *Protocol for Judicial Case Management in Public Law Children Act Cases* was to 'improve outcomes for children by reducing unnecessary delay' through requiring local authorities to set out their case in much more detail than previously, and 'active case management by a specialist judiciary'. The target was to complete care cases within 40 weeks. The timetable required the speedy appointment of a CAFCASS children's guardian, the availability of expert legal advice, and the timely completion of reports by expert witnesses. Although many family proceedings courts were able to complete cases well within the allowed period, the most complex cases in chronically understaffed care centres and the High Court frequently lasted for more than 18 months.

The working of the protocol was subsequently reviewed and it was replaced by the PLO described above. Although proceedings are now progressed on the basis of a timetable for the child, the bombardment on local authorities and the courts following the death of Peter Connolly and other factors makes it unlikely that lengthy delays will be avoided in the foreseeable future (Masson, 2008).

It is suggested that the dilemma identified by Hayes at the start of this chapter may be partially resolved, but that a perfect balance is almost certainly not attainable.

Appendix 7.1 Table of cases

Further reading

■ Katz, S.N., Eekelaar, J. and McLean, M. (2000) *Cross Currents: Family Law and Policy in the US and England.* Oxford: Oxford University Press.

The chapter on state care and child protection in this collection provides an exceptionally rich resource for readers interested in the development of child protection policy and law in England during the second half of the twentieth century.

■ Masson, J., Bailey-Harris, R. and Probert, R. (2008) *Principles of Family Law* (8th edn). London: Sweet & Maxwell.

Relevant chapters in this work (or a later edition) set the current law on child protection within the historical and policy context of its development.

■ Probert, R. (2009) *Cretney and Probert's Family Law.* London: Sweet & Maxwell.

Relevant chapters in this text provide an informed and accessible analysis of current child protection law.

References

Ball, C. (1990) 'The Children Act 1989: origins, aims and current concerns', in P. Carter and T. Jeffs (eds) *Social Work and Social Welfare Year Book, No. 2.* Milton Keynes: Open University Press.

Ball, C. (1998) 'Regulating child care: from the Children Act 1948 to the present day', *Child and Family Social Work*, **3**(3): 163–71.

Blom-Cooper, L. (1987) *A Child in Mind: The Report of the Commission of Inquiry into the Circumstances Surrounding the Death of Kimberley Carlile.* London Borough of Greenwich.

Butler-Sloss, E. (1988) *Report of the Inquiry into Child Abuse in Cleveland 1987*, Cm 412. London: HMSO.

DCSF (Department for Children, Schools and Families) (2008) *Children Act 1989 Guidance and Regulations*, vol. 1: *Court Orders.* London: DCSF.

DCSF (2010a) *Children Act 1989 Guidance and Regulations*, vol. 2: *Care Planning, Placement and Case Review.* London: DCSF.

DCSF (2010b) *Working Together to Safeguard Children: A Guide to Inter-agency Working to Safeguard and Promote the Welfare of Children.* London: TSO.

DfE (Department for Education) (2010) *Children Act 1989 Guidance and Regulations*, vol. 3: *Planning Transition to Adulthood for Care Leavers*. London: DfE.

DfE (2011a) *Children Act 1989 Guidance and Regulations*, vol. 4: *Fostering Services*. London: DfE.

DfE (2011b) *Children Act 1989 Guidance and Regulations*, vol. 5: *Children's Homes*. London: DfE.

DfE (2011c) *A Child-centred System: The Government's Response to the Munro Review of Child Protection*. London: DfE.

DH (Department of Health) (2000) *The Framework for the Assessment of Children in Need and their Families*. London: TSO.

DHSS (Department of Health and Social Security) (1985) *Review of Child Care Law: Report to Ministers of an Interdepartmental Working Party*. London: HMSO.

DHSS (1987) *The Law on Child Care and Family Services*, Cm 62. London: HMSO.

Field-Fisher, T.G. (1974) *Report of the Committee of Inquiry into the Care and Supervision of Maria Colwell*. London: HMSO.

Hayes, M. (1997) 'Reconciling protection of children with justice for parents in cases of alleged child abuse', *Legal Studies*, **17**(1): 1–20.

HM Courts Service (2005) *Thematic Review of the Protocol for Judicial Case Management in Public Law Children Act Cases*. London: HMCS.

Hoggett, B. (1989) 'Family law in the 1990s', *Family Law*, 19, 169–208.

House of Commons (1984) *Second Report from the Social Services Committee Session 1983/4: Children in Care*, HC 360. London: HMSO.

Laming, Lord (2009) *The Protection of Children in England: A Progress Report*. London: TSO.

Masson, J. (2007) 'Reforming care proceedings: time for a review', *Child and Family Law Quarterly*, **19**(4): 411.

Masson, J. (2008) 'Improving care proceedings: can the PLO resolve the problems of delay?', Part 1, *Family Law*, 38, 1019–23, Part 2, 38, 1129–32.

Masson, J., Oakley, M.W. and McGovern, D. (2001) *Working in the Dark: The Use of Police Protection*. Warwick: Warwick University School of Law.

Millham, S., Bullock, R., Hosie, K. and Haak, M. (1986) *Lost in Care: The Problems of Maintaining Links between Children in Care and their Families*. Aldershot: Gower.

Millham, S., Bullock, R., Hosie, K., and Little, M. (1989) *Access Disputes in Child Care*. Aldershot: Gower.

Ministry of Justice (2008) *Public Law Outline Practice Direction*. London: Ministry of Justice.

Ministry of Justice (2010) *Public Law Practice Direction*. London: Ministry of Justice.

Morton, S. and Masson, J. (1989) 'The use of wardship by local authorities', *Modern Law Review*, 52, 762.

Munro, E. (2010) *The Munro Review of Child Protection, Part One: A System's Analysis*. London: DfE.

Munro, E. (2011a) *The Munro Review of Child Protection, Part Two: The Child's Journey*. London: DfE.

Munro, E. (2011b) *The Munro Review of Child Protection: Final Report – A Child-centred System*, Cm 8062. London: DfE.

8

The place that theory plays in child protection work

Simon Hackett

The following quotation from a practising senior social worker demonstrates that the stakes involved in protecting children at risk of harm are high, both in terms of the children and families involved and for the workers and organizations charged with safeguarding responsibilities:

> Social work isn't easy. I am challenged daily with decisions concerning people's lives and making the wrong choice could have serious, even shocking outcomes. Consequently, the guiding principle of my work is the welfare of the child and I stress the importance of a sound theoretical base to the work that I and my team carry out.

Protecting children is perhaps the most sensitive, contested and debated area of current social work practice. The legacy of decades of inquiries into the serious injury and death of children at the hands of their carers, despite the interventions of social workers, means that public perceptions of the entire social work profession are often defined by highly publicized failings. Awareness of the nature of the harm from which social workers seek to protect children has grown significantly over the past two decades. Social workers in child protection are therefore working on constantly shifting sands, dealing with complex and multidimensional cases in an increasingly bureaucratized system that has all too often emphasized procedural compliance and process over quality of service and outcome.

    The senior social worker cited above recognizes the importance of a sound theoretical base to her work and she links the application of theory to the achievement of the welfare of the child. In this sense, theory, knowledge and research evidence provide the essential glue for effective practice. However, using theory in such an uncertain and changing practice landscape is a significant challenge. Recently I met one of my former social work students at a conference. She told me that when she had qualified, she was filled with optimism and energy about the work she would be able to undertake. Four years later, she said, she now feels demoralized and deskilled. She said she is committed to long-term positive outcomes for children rather than short-term government targets, but 'it seems that these are often the measure of success and failure'. Tellingly, she said she had been forced to put aside knowledge and theory in favour of form filling.

This chapter is concerned with the place of theory in this difficult contemporary landscape. Rather than attempt to give what would be an inadequate summary of major theories for practice, I am concerned here with understanding the *place* of theory in practice:

- What do we mean when we talk about theories in child protection and how should we understand them?
- What theories are used in practice and how?
- How do social workers make choices about what theories to use and in what circumstances?
- Should social workers be eclectic or specialist in their adoption of theoretical ideas?

In order to try to answer these questions, I offer reported experiences and examples from 48 social workers working in the safeguarding children field. The workers were part of post-qualifying programmes in child care social work across two universities. As part of my teaching on the relationship between theory and child protection practice, I asked the social workers to consider the range of theoretical ideas they draw on, to write about how they use them in their practice and to identify the challenges they face in applying them.[1] Their experiences have taught me much about the use of theory in real-life practice situations and, offering them here, I hope that others will benefit from their reflections.

What are theories and what place do they occupy in child protection work?

At their most basic, 'theories are guesses about what might be true' (Gambrill, 1997, p. 172). As such, theorizing is not restricted to social work or indeed any other area of professional practice, but is a process central to how all people assess life situations and make decisions. In social work with children and families, theories can provide the social worker with a reference point from which to appraise the complex factors involved in a case and to make practice decisions. Stepney and Ford (2000, p. viii) suggest that 'theory is a framework for understanding the clustering of ideas that attempt to explain reality in a self-conscious way'. This is a helpful definition. Theories therefore differ from research evidence as they represent a *clustering* of ideas from research that is developed into a coherent *explanatory framework*. Good theories are therefore evidence based, in other words, they draw on the best available evidence in relation to a given issue. Poor theories are speculative and based on weak evidence. In other words, poor theories are poorly informed guesses.

Using Stepney and Ford's definition, a good example of a coherent explanatory framework is that of motivational interviewing (MI), proposed initially by Miller in 1983 as a consequence of his work with problem drinkers. MI is a goal-directed, client-centred approach designed to elicit behavioural change by helping people to explore and resolve their resistance and ambivalence. In developing the theory, Miller drew on his own practice experience and also ideas from social psychology, building on the work of, among others, Bandura (1977) on self-efficacy and Rogers (1957) on empathic processes. Although not originally based on empirical data, the approach quickly drew considerable interest from practitioners working in situations where clients were resistant to change, the child protection field included. Considerable revisions to the original MI theory have since been articulated (Miller and Rollnick, 1991; Rollnick and Miller, 1995), and an extraordinarily wide range of studies have now been undertaken to validate the framework across different practice contexts (for example McMurren, 2009; Lundahl and Burke, 2009).

Howe (1987) suggests that theories help people do four important things: describe, explain, predict, and control and bring about. Thinking about these in a child protection context, the relevance of these differing functions of theory for practice becomes clear:

1 *Description:* theory can help to describe the factors commonly associated with a problem or child protection concern. This is useful as individual social workers may have experienced only a small number of situations where similar concerns were present. Theoretical frameworks developed from a larger number of similar cases can help provide a broader reference point for the social worker and can assist with assessment and the identification of need.

2 *Explanation:* theory can help to provide hypotheses about why a particular problem or concern has developed.

3 *Prediction:* theory can assist in the identification of the likely future progression of a problem or condition.

4 *Control and bringing about:* theory has the potential to identify the interventions most likely to bring about change or alter the course of the problem.

For example, a social worker recently came for advice about a case involving a 15-year-old young man who had engaged his 12-year-old niece in a range of coercive and abusive sexual behaviours. The social worker asked what theories could be recommended to help determine the response to the family concerned. Using Howe's model above, it is clear that theoretical frameworks might help the social worker in a number of ways:

1 In terms of *description*, there is often confusion about the nature of sexual behaviours in such cases. A range of theoretical models have been proposed to help distinguish between young people's normative and abusive sexual behaviours, such as Ryan's (2000) 'red flag' model or my own continuum model of sexual behaviour (Hackett, 2011). Both of these theoretical models are under-

pinned by empirical evidence from demographic studies describing the sexual behaviours of young people across contexts. Alternatively, theories such as Finkelhor's (1987) traumagenic dynamics model of child sexual abuse could help the social worker to understand the possible impact issues for the girl who has been abused.

2   Relating to *explanation*, theoretical models have been proposed to inform understandings of why adolescents sexually abuse, including, for example, Ward and Siegert's (2002) developmental pathways model.

3   Assessment models such as AIM (Print et al., 2000) or J-SOAP (Righthand et al., 2005) can assist in *predicting* the likelihood that the abusive behaviours will be repeated or will develop in frequency or nature over time.

4   Theories relating to intervention models such as multisystemic therapy (Swenson et al., 1998) can help determine the best ways of *bringing about change* to help the young person to move away from future abusive behaviour.

This one brief example highlights the varied ways in which theory can assist practitioners. For almost any practice issue across the broad child protection field, it would be possible to similarly identify a range of potentially useful theories to inform practice at the various levels of description, explanation, prediction and control. The example demonstrates the richness of theory across the field. However, this richness also brings with it a number of challenges. One is the need for practitioners to be specific about the kinds of questions they are hoping to answer through the application of theory. For instance, approaching the above practice example with the question 'what theories are there about adolescent sexual offending?' would probably generate a long list of potential theories, which are either too general to help with specific practice questions or of marginal significance in individual cases. Using Howe's model as outlined above can help practitioners to be more precise in their search for useful and informed theories. A second and related challenge is to find the best informed and most promising theories in any given situation and then to subject their use to an ongoing process of review and reflection. As Gambrill (1997, p. 173) states: 'If we do not critically evaluate our theories (assumptions), they function as prisons that limit our vision rather than as tools to discover what is false.' For example, in drawing attention to the theories above, I am confident that these models represent some of the most useful and best evidenced ideas in the field currently, but they will be developed and eclipsed as new knowledge about child sexual abuse is generated. The challenge is not to rely just on the theories that we have used in previous cases, but to use our skills in critical analysis to search for new ideas and evidence. As one social worker stated:

> I would say that I use the theories I have found families respond to positively and that have appeared to work for me historically. I cannot say if a different approach would have been any more effective in these circumstances due to my use of familiar approaches.

The application of theory to practice situations is clearly a complex process. The choice of theory for workers should be guided by the individual needs of the case, underpinned by knowledge of the best available evidence. However, as Macdonald (2001, p. 31) states:

> The choices we make are just as likely to be influenced by chance factors as by the quality of the underpinning evidence. For example our views of the causes of parental ill-treatment may be influenced by who and what we are exposed to during training, as well as our personal experience and beliefs.

Towards a model of theories in child protection

One of the significant consequences of the history of high-profile serious case reviews and inquiries into child deaths has been that child protection practice has become enormously regulated by procedure and bureaucracy. In view of the way in which child protection practice has become bureaucratized, it is ironic that the theoretical basis for much of what practitioners do remains largely unchallenged. This point is made strongly by Macdonald (2001, p. 32), who states:

> In the absence of agreed ground rules about how one *should* make choices [about theory], such a 'laissez faire' approach to knowledge leaves workers with rather more professional freedom than is probably justified by our current knowledge base. The situation is made serious by the predominant location of child protection within bureaucratic structures in which management – even when concerned with quality audit and assurance – is preoccupied with process, rather than content. *What* one chooses to do, *how* one chooses to formulate a problem, are rarely challenged.

Macdonald agrees with Sheldon (1978), who suggests that we currently have not so much a knowledge base in social work with children and families but a 'knowledge pile'. In other words, the problem is not that we lack theory in child protection – far from it – but that it is nonintegrated. As an example, Macdonald (2001, p. 31) goes on to cite the following list of theories, which appears in an (unnamed) introductory volume on child abuse and neglect:

- ethnological and sociobiological perspectives
- the psychodynamic perspective
- behaviourism and learning theory
- family dysfunction theory
- sociological theory
- the feminist perspective
- children's rights.

Macdonald outlines how all these theories appear in a chapter in the book entitled 'Alternative theory bases in child abuse', the underlying assumption being that the

Theory

theories provide equally valid alternative frameworks for understanding child abuse. This, she suggests, is hugely problematic because, while some theoretical perspectives are complementary:

> some of these theories are inherently contradictory and cannot be espoused at the same time, at least not by anyone who wishes to make even a modest claim to clear thinking. To believe one is to regard the other as invalid. (Macdonald, 2001, pp. 31–2)

Additionally, one of the problems social workers sometimes encounter in making sense of this large knowledge pile is the difficulty of comparing theories with other theories, or understanding the relationship between different theoretical ideas. I have found it helpful for practitioners to have a model that differentiates levels of theory and helps them to distinguish between:

- *meta-theories:* broad, general, high-level theoretical traditions, for example psychodynamic theory
- *meso-theories:* mid-range, derivative perspectives, for example attachment theory
- *micro-theories:* contextual, situational, practice-directed models, for example Fahlberg's arousal-relaxation cycle.

This model is depicted in Figure 8.1, which demonstrates how some micro- or meso-level theories draw on multiple higher level theories. One example would be cognitive behavioural therapy as a meso-level theory, which clearly has its roots in the higher meta-level traditions of cognitive psychology and behavioural theories.

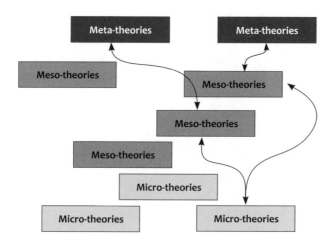

Figure 8.1 Conceptualizing levels of theory

The model can be further used to articulate the relationship between overall theoretical orientation, intervention approaches and specific techniques, as outlined in Figure 8.2.

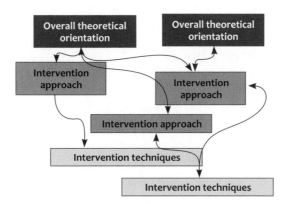

Figure 8.2 Conceptualizing intervention theories, approaches and methods

I have found that sharing this model with practitioners has been a useful way for them to be able to break down the 'knowledge pile' relevant to child protection work. For example, one social worker was able to identify that the macro-level theory she was drawing on was behavioural theory, but she was informed by 'modelling drawing on Bandura' and 'family process theories drawing on Scott' and, at a more micro-level, 'behavioural parenting training'. In reflecting on her use of theory, she said:

> I had never thought through my approach to theory before. It was really useful to be able to see the connections and contradictions between all the models I have clung to over the years.

What theories are used in child protection practice and how?

In his 1987 text on social work theory, Howe (p. 15) quotes one social worker who told him: 'If you asked me to state a theory here and now, I wouldn't have a clue.' This reminds me of my own social work training when, on the first day of one of my assessed practice placements context, my supervisor told me that he was confident that his practice experience would benefit me, but that he was going to have to read up on social work theory to supervise me. He felt I would know more than him about theory and research, as it was a while since he had completed his own training. This social worker saw theory as separate from practice, rather than an integral part of it. He told me that he preferred to work on the basis of 'practice wisdom' rather than 'theories'. Although this social worker was in many respects an excellent practitioner, it is clear that not all practice *experience* constitutes practice *wisdom*. In fact, in our subsequent supervision sessions, it was clear that my supervisor used knowledge and theory to inform his practice much of the time, but he did so largely in an implicit way. The theories had become such an automatic part of his work that it was only when asked to stand back from his practice and discuss his approach that he realized he was drawing on a wide range of theoretical frameworks.

Theory

In my work with social workers on the links between theory and practice, I have found that it is important to give workers the space to do the same. I asked the group of 48 social workers to consider

Making connexions
Considering any current or recent case of yours, what theory or theories did you actively draw on in your practice?

their *current* caseloads and to make a list of the theories they are *actively* drawing on in their work, then to write down examples. This was done individually and without consultation with the other members of the group, although we then discussed the results within the two groups from the two universities. By asking the social workers to consider their use of theory in current cases, I was interested in their real-life application in practice rather than how they might describe their overall theoretical orientation in abstract terms. Table 8.1 shows all the theories actively being used by the social workers in their current work, together with the number of people who listed the theory in question.

Table 8.1 Application of theory in practice

Theory	Number of people
Solution-focused brief therapy	28
Systems/ecological theory	13
Cognitive behavioural theory	12
Task-centred casework	9
Signs of safety	8
Strengths-based/resilience theory	7
Transtheoretical model of change	6
Psychodynamic/psychosocial theory	5
Attachment theory	5
Anti-oppressive practice	4
Behaviour modification	3
Crisis intervention	3
Child development theories	2

To be eclectic or specialist?

The results of this exercise appear to bear out that, far from being atheoretical in their work, practising social workers draw on a diversity of theories. This reinforces the view that most general social work practice is eclectic, although workers in some specialist settings and with particular remits may specialize in a particular theoretical approach (Payne, 2005). It is not surprising that most of the practitioners here, working in the broad safeguarding field with diverse cases, described themselves as eclectic in their approach, with the following quotation as indicative:

In my current role I would describe my approach as eclectic. I have found that certain theories are helpful to families in particular situations and consequently I use these theories frequently. But, it could be argued that dipping in and out of theories and approaches instead of using an intervention thoroughly and having a good understanding of it is not very helpful because it does not embrace the whole theory.

As Payne has helpfully highlighted, the debate about eclecticism or theory selection rests not so much on the benefits or otherwise of one specific approach, but on the question of *how* theory is used. Payne (2005, p. 31) warns against 'the danger of confusion in combining and adapting theories, if we pick up ideas from different places, it is important to be aware of the sources, values, methods and objectives of the basic theories we are borrowing from', and further suggests that eclecticism should be managed so that workers do not use theories in ways that are internally inconsistent or that 'debase the theory'. Reflecting on my model of theories presented above, few social workers in my survey described their practice as underpinned by an overarching macro-level theory. It was much more common for practitioners to use micro-level techniques to pragmatically inform their specific responses in individual cases. In this sense, many workers saw theory as contributing to their overall toolkit of interventions, as will become clear in the three specific practice examples I offer below. At the same time, there was frustration expressed by some workers by the limitations placed on them by their role, which, they felt, mitigated against a more rigorous approach to theory:

> I continue to find it difficult to embrace a whole theory and model due to the limitations and constraints placed on me in my workplace and its culture, which does not promote working with theories and approaches in such a way.

Being theoretically eclectic was a decision that most social workers took for themselves rather than as a consequence of direction provided by their supervisor or agency. Indeed, using a range of theories was seen as one way of challenging the poor and uncreative practice elsewhere in their agency:

> I wonder whether it is less to do with rigid adherence to a theoretical approach and more to do with my personality and my willingness to 'have a go', challenge the established order and create an environment for change?

A clustering of core theories and techniques

By far the most frequently cited theoretical framework identified by my group of 48 social workers was that of solution-focused brief therapy and its specific child protection model 'signs of safety' (Turnell and Edwards, 1997), frequently used in combination with ideas from systems theory and more general strengths-based approaches. Why was solution-focused brief therapy the most cited approach for this group of social workers? Some workers said that this framework helped them to

Theory

frame their practice approach to child protection explicitly within their underpinning social work values:

> A solution-focused approach allows clients to negotiate their own goals rather than having them imposed and solutions are co-constructed so that the solution becomes their own.

Another worker from a long-term child protection team reinforced this:

> There continues to be an overwhelming opinion that child protection work is dogmatic in its approach; however, using solution-focused models can help me focus on interpersonal skills instead of bureaucracy.

This worker went on to describe how there was significant interest developing among her colleagues in embedding the use of the signs of safety assessment model across the team's work. In one case that she felt had become 'stagnant', with professionals having lost sight of the purpose of the intervention, the use of scaling, goals and exception questions allowed her and other professionals to have a balanced perspective on the family's competences, needs and risks. In this case, the child was ultimately removed from her parents' care:

> Even though statutory intervention occurred as a result of the signs of safety assessment, the professionals involved were able to ensure a cooperative relationship with the child's parents who were able through the assessment tool to accept that their child had been placed at risk and to identify the key tasks they needed to complete prior to the child being returned to their care.

Another worker talked about her use of signs of safety in similar terms:

> The signs of safety approach provides practice principles that can enable me to build a partnership with the family. By creating a sense of hope and possibility and by respecting the family, I try to maintain a position that the family is capable of change, by building relationships with family members and without condoning any abuse and by acknowledging that all families have some signs of safety, competences and strengths.

Although my group of 48 social workers can hardly be considered representative of the whole field, it is interesting to note the degree of support within this group of social workers for the use of this theoretical framework. There appears to be a real, growing hunger for this strengths-based model as an antidote to more orthodox risk/deficit approaches to child protection work and as a means to promote meaningful collaboration with service users:

> In the majority of cases where I have employed solution-focused therapy, service users have commented on the way in which they are encouraged to work jointly with professionals at a time when they may be faced with worry and dread. Good

social work practice should mean improved client wellbeing and an equal balance of power and this is clearly facilitated through solution-focused work.

This social worker went on to describe how she had practised for a number of years with a more traditional deficit paradigm and that she had initially been cynical of an approach that attempted to shift the emphasis in favour of strengths and solutions, as opposed to current risk factors. She said that the model was not applicable in all cases and with all service users, particularly those who refuse to engage with workers, but even in these cases, she said the model resulted in her being more focused in her work.

One further surprising element about the use of solution-focused approaches was the degree to which workers stated frequently that they felt more *confident* as professionals through its use:

> Solution-focused practice gives me confidence in my work with carers because it gives me a sense of enjoyment in my work ... I personally find this to be a much more egalitarian and collaborative way of working.

Three examples of the use of theory in practice

Having discussed the place of theory in child protection practice and the range of theories that practitioners have prioritized, I offer three short examples of the use of theoretical ideas in practice. These examples give a sense of how different theories are being incorporated into the daily work of social workers, in their own words.

Carpeting the stairs

Here, a social worker from a referral and assessment team talks of her use of solution-focused theories, in particular scaling questions, in a case where a five-year-old was identified for severe neglect:

> I asked the five-year-old to tell me on a scale of 0–5 (where 5 is the happiest he could be) how happy he was at school and then at home. He rated himself a 5 at school and a 4 at home. When I asked him to consider what would need to happen in order for him to feel a 5 at home, he said, 'for Dad to paint the sitting room' and to 'have the stair carpet fitted'. The miracle question provided the same answer, with the child identifying that the stair carpet would be laid when he woke up. When a child who is faced with such harsh home conditions identifies a simple task, it is clear that what may be perceived as trivial is instead paramount. On discussion with his parents, they could identify with his request as they realized that the child had witnessed regular arguments between his mother and father in relation to the decorating and fitting the stair carpet. The parents quickly completed the task. The forthright nature of their child identifying ways in which his happiness could improve was a catalyst for these parents to bring about change.

Theory

Visiting the beach

Here, a social worker working with looked after children uses a behavioural approach with a 13-year-old, L, who had been placed in a foster placement following abuse at home:

> The [foster] family was due to go on a seaside holiday when L stated that she did not want to go. In discussion with her carers, it became clear that L was frightened of the beach. L told her carers that as a young child she remembered having gone to the local beach where she wandered away from her mother, becoming lost. When found, rather than showing relief at her return, her mother had been extremely angry and abusive. L's apparent irrational fears therefore stemmed from her terrifying experience. I suggested to the carers that they should apply the process of gradual exposure with L. Thus L was gradually reintroduced to the seaside by initially looking at pictures of beaches with her carers. I then worked with L and her carers to devise a written safety policy regarding L, including what to do if she became lost. The carers then took L to the beach but did not get out of the car. Proceeding at L's pace, the family engaged in activities at the beach, increasing her confidence and security. By using this technique, together with changing her thoughts about what would happen if she became lost, L's interaction with her environment at the beach was changed from a negative to a positive experience.

Eating the elephant

Here, a female social worker from a long-term child protection team provides an example of a cognitive behavioural intervention with a young woman in her early teens who was removed from home due to sexual abuse and neglect, but whose safety in the looked after system was under threat due to her own sexualized behaviours and drug misuse:

> I asked her if I cooked an elephant for her dinner that night, how she would plan to eat it. It would be a full-size elephant, but I really wanted to know how she would eat it. We drew a picture of an elephant together. She said that she would not be able to eat it all at once as it was too big and she would have to do it bit by bit. I then asked her to consider the elephant as her behaviours and how she could think about breaking them down into smaller pieces by thinking about what was happening when she behaved in certain ways.

The importance of worker characteristics and approach

Even the best-evidenced theoretical frameworks can be applied poorly. Understanding theory is only one part of the challenge of applying it for the benefit of children and families. As one social worker highlighted: 'Clients' lives are not led in laboratory conditions and are influenced by the dynamics of their relationship with others including the social worker.' As the brief examples above show, the successful use of theory in practice rests to a large extent not on formulaic, prescribed techniques, but on the skills and interpersonal approach of the worker using them:

> Practice in my mind must be respectful and to achieve respect I have to totally understand the model, technique and the method which I choose to apply. I am also aware that effective communication enhances intervention as this can ensure autonomy to the child and family.

It has long been recognized that therapeutic techniques and relationships cannot be mutually exclusive (Mahoney and Norcross, 1993). Indeed, certain worker characteristics have been shown to be related to effective intervention outcomes over and above theoretical modality. For example, in a study of behavioural interventions, Alexander et al. (1976) found that 60% of the variance on outcomes measures was accounted for by practitioner features. In a study of practitioners working with sex offenders, Marshall et al. (1999) investigated the effect that personal worker characteristics played in mediating the effectiveness of cognitive behavioural interventions with sex offenders. They found a range of reliably identified features that appeared to enhance the effectiveness of the interventions. These included:

- the worker's ability to empathize with the position of the client, while not colluding with their abusive behaviour
- being respectful of the person and warm in their approach
- being sincere and genuine
- encouraging the offenders to face up to their problem and rewarding them when they made positive progress
- encouraging clients' active participation in the work and being interested in them as people
- using nonconfrontational, nonaggressive methods to challenge the offenders, promoting self-challenge where possible
- being sensitive to offenders' frustrations and difficulties
- spending appropriate time on issues associated with their abusive behaviours
- being confident in their own professional skills and abilities.

Although these factors are derived from research with a particular user group, they seem to me to encapsulate the kind of interpersonal approach necessary for the effective application of theory in child protection practice. Marshall et al. (1999, p. 44) conclude:

> From the client's perspective, these features of the [worker] translate into a number of characteristics. Clients do best ... when they feel supported and are comfortable discussing personal problems without feeling attacked, and they do better when they perceive the [worker] as sympathetic, warm, understanding, empathic, and confident. In most studies, clients report that they desire advice and direction.

Theory

Conclusions on the use of theory in child protection

In this chapter, I have sought to demonstrate that theory plays an important part in child protection practice and that far from being atheoretical, social workers draw on many theoretical constructs that help them to make sense of complex practice situations and guide their interventions. Rigid, dogmatic use of theory is not supported by the majority. Most social workers feel that they require a range of approaches and frameworks that they can use as part of their practice toolkit, tailoring them to the needs of individual children and families. The three short examples cited above show this process in action.

Some social workers are able to draw on theoretical ideas as a way of staying creative and invigorating their practice. In particular, social workers using strengths- and asset-based approaches were more likely to express positive views about the quality of the service they offer, even though their cases are often complex and emotive. This is a surprising finding for me and I have not seen this written about previously. Rather than a bolt-on or a luxury, these social workers saw theory as a way of staying true to their social work values, driving positive relationships with users and giving purpose to their work. The application of theory in practice not only benefited the users, it also sustained these workers in a difficult practice context. As a result, these workers felt more effective and confident in their work.

Why was it that some workers valued theory as the 'essential glue' of practice more than others? How had they managed to locate theories and approaches that were effective in their work? Few, it seemed, had been directed to use particular theories through agency policy. In some cases, workers had been trained in particular methods as part of their social work training and continued to use these same theories in their practice. Others were exposed to new theoretical ideas in the context of short, post-qualifying training courses or through colleague recommendation within and across teams. The challenge, therefore, is to make the acquisition and application of theory less random and haphazard. This will require sustained effort not just on the part of individual social workers and their supervisors, or even social work educators, but also at an organizational and policy level. As Payne (2005, p. 66) states: 'social work theory has to have a future, because all activities are informed by theory'.

Note

1   I am particularly grateful to the three social workers who gave permission for me to include examples of their use of theory.

Further reading

■ Macdonald, G. (2000) *Effective Interventions for Child Abuse and Neglect*. Chichester: Wiley.

Sourcebook for evidence-based social work children and families.

■ Payne, M. (2005) *Modern Social Work Theory* (3rd edn). Basingstoke: Palgrave Macmillan.

Classic text on theory in social work practice, detailing a range of theoretical approaches and models.

■ Turnell, A. and Edwards, S. (1999) *Signs of Safety: A Solution and Safety Oriented Approach to Child Protection Casework*. New York: Norton.

Solution-focused model of child protection practice, much favoured by social workers in my survey.

References

Alexander, J.F., Barton, C., Schiavo, S. and Parsons, B.V. (1976) 'Systems-behavioral intervention with families of delinquents: therapist characteristics, family behaviour and outcome', *Journal of Consulting and Clinical Psychology*, 44, 656–64.

Bandura, A. (1977) 'Self-efficacy: toward a unifying theory of behaviour change', *Psychological Review*, 84, 191–215.

Corby, B. (2000) *Child Abuse: Towards a Knowledge Base*. Buckingham: Open University Press.

Finkelhor, D. (1987) 'The trauma of child sexual abuse: two models', Journal of Interpersonal Violence, **2**(4): 348–66.

Gambrill, E. (1997) *Social Work Practice: A Critical Thinker's Guide*. New York: Oxford University Press.

Hackett, S. (2011) 'Children and young people with harmful sexual behaviours', in C. Barter and D. Berridge (eds) *Children Behaving Badly: Peer Violence between Children and Young People*. Chichester: Wiley.

Howe, D. (1987) *An Introduction to Social Work Theory*. Aldershot: Wildwood House.

Lundahl, B. and Burke, B.L. (2009) 'The effectiveness and applicability of motivational interviewing: a practice-friendly review of four meta-analyses', *Journal of Clinical Psychology*, **65**(11): 1232–45.

Macdonald, G. (2000) *Effective Interventions for Child Abuse and Neglect*. Chichester: Wiley.

McMurran, M. (2009) 'Motivational interviewing with offenders: a systematic review', *Legal and Criminological Psychology*, **14**(1): 83–100.

Mahoney, M.J. and Norcross, J.C. (1993) 'Relationship styles and therapeutic choices: a commentary', *Psychotherapy*, 30, 423–6.

Marshall, W., Anderson, D. and Fernandez, Y. (1999) *Cognitive Behavioural Treatment of Sexual Offenders*. Chichester: Wiley.

Miller, W.R. (1983) 'Motivational interviewing with problem drinkers', *Behavioral Psychotherapy*, 11, 147–72.

Miller, W.R. and Rollnick, S.R. (1991) *Motivational Interviewing: Preparing People to Change Behavior*. New York: Guilford Press.

Payne, M. (2005) *Modern Social Work Theory* (3rd edn). Basingstoke: Palgrave Macmillan.

Print, B., Morrison, T. and Henniker, J. (2000) *Working with Children and Young People Who Sexually Abuse: Procedures and Assessment*. Manchester: AIM project.

Theory

Righthand, S., Prentky, R., Knight, R. et al. (2005) 'Factor structure and validation of the juvenile sex offender assessment protocol (J-SOAP)', *Sexual Abuse: A Journal of Research and Treatment*, **17**(1): 13–30.

Rogers, C.R. (1957) 'The necessary and sufficient conditions for therapeutic personality change', *Journal of Consulting Psychology*, 21, 95–103.

Rollnick, S.R. and Miller, W.R. (1995) 'What is motivational interviewing?', *Behavioral and Cognitive Psychotherapy*, 23, 325–34.

Ryan, G. (2000) 'Childhood sexuality: a decade of study. Part 1 – research and curriculum development', *Child Abuse and Neglect*, **24**(1): 33–48.

Sheldon, B. (1978) 'Theory and practice in social work: a re-examination of a tenuous relationship', *British Journal of Social Work*, **8**(1): 1–18.

Stepney, P. and Ford, D. (2000) *Social Work Models, Methods and Theories*. Lyme Regis: Russell House.

Swenson, C., Henggeler, S., Schoenwald, S. et al. (1998) 'Changing the social ecologies of adolescent sexual offenders: implications of the success of multi-systemic therapy in treating serious antisocial behaviour in adolescents', *Child Maltreatment*, **3**(4): 330–8.

Turnell, A. and Edwards, S. (1997) 'Aspiring to partnership: the signs of safety approach to child protection', *Child Abuse Review*, 6, 179–90.

Ward, T. and Siegert, R.J. (2002) 'Toward and comprehensive theory of child sexual abuse: a theory knitting perspective', *Psychology, Crime, and Law*, 9, 319–51.

9
The challenging nature of research in child protection

Helga Sneddon

There are thousands of pieces of research evidence that could potentially inform what social workers do in the realm of child protection. Child maltreatment is multifaceted and different service approaches are likely to be effective with different types of family at different stages of recognition of actual or likely maltreatment (Thoburn, 2010). The evidence base reflects this diversity: studies differ in terms of focus, methodological strengths, the populations studied or techniques used. Research has mainly focused on issues like prevalence, determinants and health and social consequences. The disciplines and methodologies used to produce the research evidence are diverse and include:

- psychobiological studies of the effect of neglect on the brain, or of how childhood maltreatment can cause physiological changes
- psychological studies of inter- and intrafamilial risk and protective factors
- psychosocial studies of the mediating and moderating factors that influence outcomes
- qualitative investigations of victims' and perpetrators' perspectives
- public health approaches to prevention programmes
- organizational studies that help us to understand when and why systems are not working together
- systems analyses designed to identify training needs for practitioners and help them learn how to listen to the experience of service users.

This chapter will review some of the types of research evidence that apply to different questions impacting on the field of child protection. The questions include how many people experience child maltreatment, what are the consequences of this, what are effective ways to prevent maltreatment, and how to intervene most effectively once maltreatment has occurred. Major challenges surround the process of producing research evidence; there are significant legal, ethical and methodological obstacles in undertaking research in this area, in addition to problems in generalizing results to different contexts (Lewig et al., 2010).

Research evidence is, of course, only one particular form of knowledge – most useful in order to shed light on particular questions or areas of practice. In understanding what research can 'tell' social workers, one must recognize that there are influences on how prepared or able practitioners may be to 'listen' to the evidence. Research sits alongside policy knowledge and practice knowledge in terms of influencing what we do, and what it tells us is sometimes at odds with these other forms of knowledge.

Other issues surround how we interpret and utilize research evidence as practitioners, researchers, parents and individuals. Significant barriers have been identified, which influence whether research has an impact on social work practice. These are discussed in this chapter because, with respect to knowledge transfer, it is not only what the evidence can tell us, but how prepared and able we are to listen and act on the evidence.

Prevalence: how many people experience child maltreatment?

Although child maltreatment is believed to be prevalent in most countries, there is often a scarcity of verifiable, national statistical data. The formulation and implementation of policies and plans, as well as the development and implementation of effective programmes and services need to be informed by scientific evidence that answers key questions:

- How many people will need to be reached by the services?
- Who are the victims of maltreatment?
- What are their characteristics and needs?

Better information on the prevalence, nature and scale of child maltreatment can inform planning for the costs incurred by individuals, families and society at large, and ultimately how to resource such systems and target interventions effectively.

Research can provide baseline data for abuse and neglect that allow the monitoring of change in the treatment of children over time (Sneddon et al., 2010; Cawson et al., 2000).

Estimating the prevalence of abuse is far from simple, however, and there are several reasons for this:

1 The source of the information used. Official statistics are likely to underestimate true prevalence rates because they are usually based on cases that have been brought to the attention of statutory authorities; these will tend to be more severe cases and will not include those that have not come to the attention of the authorities. For example, most cases of child sexual abuse, ranging from fondling

through to complete penetration, go unreported to authorities (Wyatt et al., 1999, reported in Zwi et al., 2009).

2 Statutory definitions of child abuse and neglect can sometimes be vague and will vary from one jurisdiction to another (Heller et al., 1999).

3 Child protection registers are not intended to be a list of all children in an area who have suffered or are likely to suffer significant harm, but are those for whom there is a need for a child protection plan.

The scale of the discrepancy was highlighted in the recent NSPCC (2011) maltreatment prevalence study in the UK. It indicated that almost one million secondary school children have been seriously physically or sexually abused or neglected at some point during childhood. With around 46,000 children of all ages currently on a child protection plan or register, the NSPCC cautioned that this indicates that the vast majority of maltreated children are not getting the help they need.

Akmatov (2010) undertook an analysis of child abuse in 28 developing and transitional countries using results from the Multiple Indicator Cluster Surveys. These surveys were conducted in 53 countries in 2005 and 2006 to provide nationally representative data regarding women's reproductive health and child health. The prevalence in developing and transitional countries showed that child abuse is still common practice, but there were considerable variations in prevalence of different forms across countries and regions. The most frequent form of child abuse used by parents in most countries was psychological abuse, and the least frequent form was severe physical abuse.

Kelly et al. (1991) found that 1 in 2 girls and 1 in 5 boys in the UK had an unwanted sexual experience before the age of 18 years. A decade later, May-Chahal and Cawson (2005) found that 16% of young people had been sexually abused as children – 11% of boys and 21% of girls. In a review of studies conducted outside the USA, estimated prevalence rates of 20% for females and 10% for males were considered realistic by Finkelhor (1994). Physical abuse and neglect comprise the largest categories of reported abuse in all countries where monitoring statistics are collected (Cawson et al., 2000). Studies of emotional abuse from different countries report rates varying from less than 1% to more than 25%, depending on the definition used and population studied (Cawson et al., 2000).

Although it has long been recognized that there are differences between the types of maltreatment that a person may experience, research has not focused on all the subtypes with equal interest. The majority of prevalence studies have examined sexual abuse, even though it is understood to be the least prevalent type of abuse. In contrast, neglect is the least researched, despite being much more prevalent, a phenomenon dubbed the 'neglect of neglect' (Dubowitz, 2007).

A major challenge is the issue of how to define maltreatment in precise, measurable ways, and this is commonly discussed in most investigations. Which behaviours should be included, or, in the case of neglect, which behaviours should be omitted? What is the threshold for harm? What constitutes each type of maltreatment? Studies

Research

have used a variety of measures to record prevalence rates, but it is a particularly acute problem in the study of neglect when one must measure the absence of culturally accepted parental behaviours (de Bellis, 2005). It is increasingly recognized that the traditional model of commission/omission is insufficient to capture what is now known about maltreatment. For example, while sexual abuse, emotional abuse and physical abuse are all acts of commission and directed against the child, and neglect is commonly considered an act of omission (failing to do something for the child), evidence suggests that witnessing domestic violence (where it is not directed at the child and therefore is neither an act of omission nor commission) can be equally damaging (Wilson et al., 2011).

What is the source of information about the abuse experience?

Self-report studies are valuable but they can be limited by biased samples. For example, many retrospective studies include only undergraduate students and their results are therefore not generalizable to the population as a whole. Alternatively, samples may be drawn from specific populations, for example those receiving counselling or those who may have committed offences, but their characteristics and needs may not be representative of other groups. The reality of self-selection among participants may influence the accuracy of the results if respondents decide not to participate in the research because of the subject matter; the non-respondents may be quite unrepresentative of the population as a whole. Studies may have to rely on small sample sizes and on retrospective accounts, when incidents of abuse may have been forgotten over time. There may be differences in recall rates depending on the age at which the abuse was experienced, the duration and intensity of the abuse, the nature of the abuse or the victim's relationship to the perpetrator.

Retrospective studies on adults are likely to be limited in several important ways. Few adults have detailed memories of their lives before the age of five, but it is known that more serious child maltreatment, especially physical abuse, is likely to be experienced by younger children (Cawson et al., 2000; May-Chahal and Cawson, 2005). This is likely to lead to underestimations of the true prevalence. Older adults have accumulated other major life events, in particular parenting experiences, which may affect recall of their childhood (Hobbs, 2005). There will always be some element of non-report of maltreatment by some individuals because they are not comfortable with discussing these childhood experiences with a stranger or because of feelings of loyalty to parents and family.

The NSPCC (2011) undertook a prevalence study of abuse in the UK, which attempted to address many of the methodological challenges inherent in this type of work. This involved a large random probability sample of the general population covering abuse both inside and outside the family. One in 4 young people aged 18–24 reported experiences of severe physical violence, sexual abuse or neglect during their childhood. The prevalence of abuse in this sample was compared to those of an earlier NSPCC study (May-Chahal and Cawson, 2005), and results suggested that many childhoods in the UK have changed for the better over the past 30 years. Although the 1,761 young people interviewed were relatively young, their answers about their childhood may still have been biased by recall issues, although this bias should be less than asking older people for retrospective accounts. To address this criticism, a further sample of 2,275 children aged 11–17 were interviewed to give an insight into the current prevalence of severe maltreatment in the UK. Around 1 in 5 children (18.6%) had been physically attacked by an adult, sexually abused or severely neglected at home. One in 14 of the 11- to 17-year-olds (6.9%) had been physically attacked by an adult, most commonly a parent or guardian (55% of cases). Physical attacks included those resulting in injuries such as broken bones or black eyes, being knocked unconscious and/or the use of a weapon such as a knife, gun, rock, stick or bat. The study found that 1 in 20 children (4.8%) had been severely sexually assaulted (including rape or attempted rape), or had endured forced sexual contact by an adult or child, or contact sexual abuse by a parent, guardian or sibling, or contact sexual abuse by an adult to a person under 13, or contact sexual abuse by an adult relative to a person under 16. Three per cent of children had been raped or forced into sex by another child and 2% had been sexually abused by an adult. Children were responsible for perpetrating two-thirds (65.9%) of contact sexual abuse. Sexual abuse became more common during teenage years up to age 17, and girls were the main victims. The most common form of severe maltreatment was severe neglect, experienced by 1 in 10 children (9.8%). This included severe emotional neglect and lack of physical care or supervision that would place a child at risk.

An alternative to self-report studies has been to use professional informants, for example national incidence studies in the USA. This approach has been successfully used in Europe: for example, in Holland, more than 1,100 carefully selected professionals from various occupational branches reported their suspicions of child maltreatment. The random sample of organizations, the broad representation of occupational branches, the nationally representative distribution of the sentinels, and the training in reporting child maltreatment cases are among the merits of this approach (Euser, 2009).

The effects of abuse

Different types of maltreatment are known to have different outcomes on behaviour and development. These may occur immediately and be short term, or they may manifest for several years after the abuse has occurred. Problems may include externalizing problems – conduct difficulties, risky sexual behaviour and aggression – and internalizing problems – depression, self-harm and suicidality (Sneddon, 2003; Wilson et al., 2011). The UK study (NSPCC, 2011) found that severely abused and neglected children were almost nine times more likely to try to commit suicide and almost five times more likely to self-harm compared to children who had not been severely abused or neglected. As well as behavioural and psychological outcomes, an increasing number of studies have investigated the neuropsychological effects of child maltreatment, particularly with respect to how the biochemical stress response system in the brain may change the ways in which a maltreated individual is able to respond to stressors throughout their lives – the traumatic stress response. Wilson et al. (2011) reviewed the research in this area and concluded that vulnerable brain regions (including the hypothalamic-pituitary-adrenal axis, amygdala, hippocampus and prefrontal cortex) may be linked to children's compromised ability to process both emotionally laden and neutral stimuli in the future. They note that much debate still surrounds the correlational nature of empirical studies, the potential of resiliency following childhood trauma, and the extent to which early interventions may facilitate recovery.

Certain types of abuse are thought to be more commonly associated with particular outcomes. For example, neglect is known to have negative outcomes particularly in the cognitive domain but also in behavioural and socioemotional functioning; some studies have linked the experience of neglect to more severe psychological problems than physical abuse (reviewed in Sneddon, 2003; Euser, 2009). Neglected children have been shown to have behavioural problems and conduct disorders, problems in social relationships and less competent behaviour (Kendall-Tackett and Eckenrode, 1996; Kendall-Tackett, 1997).

The experience of physical abuse may be associated more commonly with aggression towards others. Physically abused children have been found to be more highly aggressive than other children, as well as more prone to oppositional behaviour, delinquency and criminality. These children may show self-injurious and suicidal behaviour, substance abuse, emotional problems, and difficulties in relationships such as fighting with peers and being defiant towards teachers. There may also be reduced academic achievement. Many of these problems are long-lasting, extending well beyond childhood and adolescence into the adult years (Prino and Peyrot, 1994).

Children who are psychologically maltreated are likely to have low self-esteem, to be depressed, to perform poorly at school, to have greater difficulty in getting along with peers and to show other behaviour problems.

Sexual abuse may be associated with sexually deviant behaviour and emotional abuse with low adult self-esteem (Euser, 2009).

Forms of abuse are not mutually exclusive and a child may be the victim of multiple types of abuse (Higgins and McCabe, 2000), although this is not always sufficiently investigated in research studies. Manly et al. (2001) highlighted the infrequency of single subtype occurrence of maltreatment. They found that among 492 maltreated children, only 8% of physically abused children had physical abuse as a single subtype and only 5% of sexually abused children had sexual abuse as a single subtype. This suggests that focusing on a single subtype will ignore the contribution of other experiences; it also makes it difficult to know whether combinations of different kinds of abuse will affect children differently than the independent effects of a particular form of abuse (Manly, 2005). It is difficult in retrospective accounts to differentiate sufficiently well between types of maltreatment that are experienced at the same time (concurrently) and those that are experienced during childhood but at different times (consecutively). It is widely acknowledged that unpicking the shared variance between different subtypes of maltreatment is complex and challenging. Many other variables influence the impact on the child such as the frequency, intensity and duration of abuse, the type of relationship between perpetrator and victim, and how the victim perceives the abuse.

There is wide variation between research studies as to what constitutes a good outcome following maltreatment, that is, they do not show symptoms of serious psychological harm (Kendall-Tackett et al., 1993). The variation in outcomes between the victims of maltreatment may reflect many factors:

- psychological wellbeing, for example levels of depression
- whether victims reach a certain level of educational attainment
- the range of variables to measure, for example self-esteem, social skills, cognitive ability (Heller et al., 1999)
- true variations in how well victims of abuse cope with their maltreatment (Jacelon, 1997; Masten et al., 1999; Clark and Clark, 2000), and this 'coping' or resilience may vary at different times.

Resilience

The possible resilience of victims will be influenced by at least five broad classes of variables (Budd and Holdsworth, 1996):

1 *The nature of the abusive act:* for example, the use of violence or forced sex, as well as its frequency, intensity and duration. On the whole, single stressful experiences that occur in isolation are thought to be less damaging than cumulative stresses. Timing is also important: at particular stages, a child may be developmentally more protected or developmentally more vulnerable to adversities.

2 *Individual characteristics of the victim:* for example, their age or a tendency to self-blame. Individuals may have biological traits that make them more or less likely to respond positively or negatively to personal adversities. Not all victims will show the same outcomes and this can be due to resilience (Rutter, 1990, 1995). Stress-resistant children show better outcomes in environments of stress or adversity. But it must be remembered that no one has absolute resistance to stress. The following factors have been found to be associated with resilience in victims (Fonagy et al., 1994; Heller et al., 1999):

  - higher socioeconomic status
  - the absence of neurobiological problems
  - the possession of an easy temperament
  - the absence of early loss and trauma
  - secure attachment
  - positive social support
  - good educational experience

Research

- a high IQ
- a good problem-solving ability
- task-related effectiveness
- high self-esteem
- autonomy and self-control
- social understanding
- awareness and empathy
- the ability to plan
- a good sense of humour.

3   *The nature of the relationship between the victim and the perpetrator:* for example, whether the perpetrator is a sibling or a step-parent.

4   *The response of others to the abuse:* for example, the provision of social support, or the use of legal or psychological intervention. Compensatory experiences such as a good relationship with a significant other (parent, teacher, therapist) do not necessarily have to take place at the same times as the risk (Fonagy et al., 1994). Early or later experiences may compensate for the cumulative effects of the risk factors.

5   *Other factors correlated with abuse* that may exacerbate its effects or may account for some of the putative consequences of abuse: it is important to better understand how experiencing abuse interacts with other possible risk factors. For example, Rind et al. (1998) found consistent confounding between child sexual assault and family environment and concluded that family environment explained more variation in adjustment at adulthood. However, a subsequent study reported that when potential confounders such as family and social backgrounds were controlled, the association between child sexual assault and adult psychopathology was reduced but not eliminated (Zwi et al., 2009).

Risk factors for abuse

Since many acts of maltreatment occur away from the public gaze, in secrecy and in private spaces, it may be useful to understand the risk factors for abuse. This may help guide prevention programmes as well as help practitioners in the identification of families who may need additional support or investigation. Risk factors for child abuse include:

- being male (particularly for severe physical abuse)
- living with many household members
- poorer economic status, although the relationship is complex and other factors such as parental violence during childhood and cultural beliefs about the need for physical punishment may be more influential (Maker et al., 2005)
- having a disability
- having separated parents or parents with mental health, drug or alcohol problems (Akmatov, 2010; NSPCC, 2011).

Specific risk factors for sexual abuse include:

- being female
- domestic violence
- poor parental attachment
- parental alcoholism
- social isolation, which almost doubles the risk
- specific ages – pre-adolescent children aged 10–12 years are most at risk followed by children aged 6–7 years
- the perpetrator is most likely to be a family member or family acquaintance known to the child (Zwi et al., 2009).

Risk factors for experiencing multiple forms of abuse include:

- being a child with special educational needs
- a longstanding disability or illness
- having a parent with enduring physical, learning or psychiatric problems (NSPCC, 2011).

It is important to emphasize that these are risk factors – not factors that predict with absolute certainty. One factor that has raised considerable professional and public interest is whether individuals who were abused themselves are at a higher risk of later becoming abusive or offending sexually. Jespersen et al. (2009) undertook a meta-analysis of sexual abuse history among adult sex offenders and non-sex offenders. They concluded that there was support for the sexually abused abuser hypothesis, in that sex offenders were more likely to have been sexually abused than non-sex offenders; they were not, however, more likely to have been physically abused. The authors acknowledge that the intergenerational relationship is complex and that the mediating factors are not understood; it is possible that a third (intervening) factor might account for the relationship.

The parenting experiences of individuals who have been maltreated are of interest for many reasons. The theory of intergenerational transmission of abuse asserts that parental abuse and/or neglect in childhood is the most powerful predictor of parents' abusive behaviours to their own children. Parents with a history of abuse in their childhood have nearly twice the risk of having a child on the child protection register, although the absolute risk is low, with only 1% of abused parents going on to maltreat their own children (Sidebotham and Heron, 2006). Most parents who have suffered abuse as children grow up to be loving, non-abusive parents (Herbert, 1998; Ferrari, 2002), although their experience of being a parent may be qualitatively different from that of individuals who have not been maltreated (Sneddon et al., 2010).

Prevention programmes

How can we prevent child maltreatment? Some prevention programmes aim to prevent the occurrence of abuse or further abuse by working with potential perpetra-

Research

tors. However, many of these have not been empirically evaluated in ways that allow for their effectiveness to be assessed. With respect to evaluating the effectiveness of programmes, there has been a shift towards randomized controlled trials (RCTs) and systematic reviews that summarize the results from these. Mikton and Butchart (2009) undertook a systematic review of programmes aiming to prevent child abuse and neglect, and identified seven different types of prevention programmes:

- early childhood home visitation
- parent education programmes
- child sexual abuse prevention programmes
- programmes to prevent abusive head trauma
- multicomponent interventions
- media-based interventions
- support and mutual aid groups.

The authors concluded that early childhood home visitation, parent education, abusive head trauma and multicomponent interventions were assessed as promising approaches for preventing child maltreatment. The evidence, in relation to actual child mistreatment, on the three remaining types was either insufficient or mixed. They also found that the RCTs reported significantly lower effect sizes than quasi-experimental or non-experimentally designed studies; this may be due to the artificial inflation of the effects of the latter research designs (Euser, 2009).

Another meta-analysis of prevention programmes on child abuse (MacLeod and Nelson, 2000) concluded that longer and more intense formats produced better results. The lowest effect sizes were found for programmes with a duration of less than six months and involving fewer than 12 home visits (Macleod and Nelson, 2000).

Evidence suggests that the effectiveness of programmes is increased when (Barlow et al., 2006):

- intervention is focused on the parent in their role as a person and concentrates on their personal attributes such as self-esteem
- programmes target a large number of the subsystems involved in abuse, such as the parent as an individual, the family, the school and the community. The large-scale RCT evaluation of Triple P in America provides evidence of its effectiveness in preventing maltreatment using a public health approach (Prinz et al., 2009)
- programmes include parallel cognitive behavioural interventions to help families to regulate their negative emotions and interaction patterns.

Less successful approaches to treatment have been identified as:

- inflexible therapeutic methods that make it difficult for the therapist to work with the different (often conflicting) elements within a family; examples would be found in approaches such as behavioural parent training or routine family therapy
- media-based interventions (such as leaflets), the organization of support groups and some forms of perinatal coaching, all of which have been found to be ineffective with high-risk families.

Some programmes aim to teach children how to escape from or avoid abusive situations, or encourage them to disclose abuse if it occurs; the aim is usually to teach children how to be more assertive. Such programmes are often delivered in schools and have been criticized for commonly assuming that the perpetrators of abuse tend to be strangers ('stranger danger'), whereas the weight of evidence suggests that the perpetrators of abuse are usually known to the victim (Barron and Topping, 2008). In spite of being adopted into the school curriculum by many counties, their effectiveness has not been proved. For example, Zwi et al. (2009) undertook a systematic meta-analysis of school-based education programmes for the prevention of child sexual abuse. They concluded that, while the programmes led to improvements in knowledge and protective behaviours, it is not known whether the benefits were sustained over time or whether the results would apply in respect of non-American populations. They noted that a worrying number of the studies reported potential harms such as increased levels of anxiety among the children, and they concluded that school-based programmes should preferably be used as a part of a community-based approach and that potential harms should be carefully monitored. There is some evidence that education programmes may be particularly effective in preschool children but that the learning may not be retained over time (Rispens et al., 1997).

Studies in which the perpetrators are interviewed about maltreatment can be useful in terms of offering insight into the strategies employed and how prevention programmes can help to prevent abuse. Elliott et al. (1995) interviewed 91 sex offenders about the methods they had used to target children, the age range of their victims, how they selected children and maintained them as victims, and what suggestions they had for preventing child sexual abuse. They found that the men:

- gained access to children through caring
- targeted children by using bribes, gifts and games
- used force, anger, threats and bribes to ensure their continuing compliance
- systematically desensitized children through touch, talk about sex and persuasion.

Elliott et al.'s research highlighted messages for prevention programmes aimed at children. For example, a clear consequence of what they were told by the offenders is that children should be wary of public toilets and never go into them alone. As one respondent said:

> A great place to hand out is in a toilet in a kiddies' hamburger-type restaurant. Little boys, especially, go into the toilets alone, and they aren't expecting someone to try to touch them. Most of the time they are too embarrassed even to shout. I would teach kids to run out of the toilets yelling the minute anyone tries to help them zip up or touch them. (Elliott et al., 1995, p. 591)

The research concluded that it is important for parents to realize that there are some people, even family members and friends, who could ask their children to do something sexual. As another respondent put it:

Research

Parents are so naive – they're worried about strangers and should be worried about their brother-in-law. They just don't realize how devious we can be. I used to abuse children in the same room with their parents and they couldn't see it or didn't seem to know it was happening. (Elliott et al., 1995, p. 590)

With respect to teachers and schools, the offenders' message was that schools should have prevention programmes for all children from a very young age: 'In the same way that we groom children from a young age to be victims, schools should groom them to tell automatically' (Elliott et al., 1995, p. 590).

Treatment programmes for the victims of maltreatment

Survivors of abuse may be offered therapeutic interventions soon after the maltreatment occurs during childhood, or they may not receive interventions for many years. Unfortunately, the effectiveness of treatment on maltreated children and their parents has rarely been studied by RCTs and Chaffin and Friedrich (2004, p. 1198) conclude that 'most services provided to abused children and their families are not based on any clear evidence that the services actually work'.

Effective treatment programmes for the victims of maltreatment have nevertheless been identified as:

- goal-directed programmes with a treatment plan addressing specific and measurable problems
- programmes that involve a structured approach, in the sense that specific techniques are used and therapeutic components follow sequential stages
- programmes that focus on building skills to enable victims to manage their emotional problems and behavioural disturbances. For children, additional areas for skill building may include emotional identification, processing and regulation, anxiety management, and the identification and alteration of maladaptive cognitions and problem-solving
- programmes that use techniques that repeatedly practise skills with ongoing feedback from the counsellor (Euser, 2009).

A meta-analysis by Saunders et al. (2004) identified trauma-related behavioural cognitive therapy as a proven treatment. Holding therapy, the common form of attachment therapy, was evaluated as a concerning treatment, with potentially harmful consequences.

Challenges for practitioners in using the evidence base

As in other areas of social work, it has been observed that within the field of child protection, practice wisdom has been the traditional basis of decision-making by practitioners. Research evidence most commonly influences policy and practice decisions when the research resonates with the *existing* tacit knowledge of decision-makers

(Lewig et al., 2010). Lewig et al. (2010, p. 470) noted a number of barriers to the use of research in child protection policy development: 'Time; the nature of the child protection evidence base; cultural constraints and political pressures'. Lewig et al. (2010, p. 470) comment:

> a lack of time to access and apply research is a commonly identified barrier to research use across a range of professionals, including health, education, social work and criminal justice (Hemsley-Brown and Sharp, 2003; Walter et al., 2003). In our survey of Australian child and family welfare policy-makers and practitioners it was noted that 79% of child protection practitioners and 62% of policy-makers had little time to read research reports or to apply research findings (Holzer et al., 2008).

In the context of their research in South Australia, Lewig et al. (2010) usefully summarize the professional barriers that seem to make it difficult for social workers to draw on research to enhance their practice. Discussing their research findings, they observe that:

> in general research was viewed as being peripheral to the child protection policy and practice environment. Child protection is applied in nature and the discipline of social work, more generally, places less reliance on research evidence than other professions. (p. 470)

Lewig et al. (2010, p. 470) list six points of interest emerging from their investigation:

- There was a perceived mismatch between research questions of interest to those working in the child protection field and those of interest to researchers.
- The qualified nature of child protection research (and research in general) and the sometimes contradictory findings in the evidence base were also a source of frustration for those participants who had attempted to find programmes and interventions that have been shown to work.
- The general inaccessibility of the child protection evidence base also presented a barrier to research use.
- The culture of the academic requires researchers to publish in academic journals that are often difficult to access and navigate.
- Unfortunately researchers often do not disseminate the results of their research through other means. This limits access to research findings to those with the skills and opportunity to search academic databases.
- Research dissemination bodies such as the 'Research in Practice' initiative in England and Wales (www.rip.org.uk/index.asp) and the EPPI-Centre (www.eppi.ioe.ac.uk/cms/) have attempted to address this issue by providing more accessible gateways to research evidence of interest to professionals working in child and family welfare fields, although providing easy access to research does not of itself ensure that research will be read or used.

Research

Conclusion

Maltreatment can take many forms – sexual, physical and emotional abuse and neglect. Children may be subjected to more than one type of maltreatment, and it can be argued that all maltreated children are the victims of some sort of emotional maltreatment (Lynch and Browne, 1997). All maltreatment can have serious detrimental consequences for the child, although not all types have received equal examination by researchers and not all individuals will show the same outcomes.

Different types of preventive programme and therapeutic intervention can be directed towards different forms of maltreatment: the focus may be on the child, the parent and/or the family unit. We need to better understand what sorts of intervention are best suited to which situations so that the right help can be targeted effectively and efficiently. By raising public and professional awareness of the factors that place children at risk of maltreatment and of who are most commonly the perpetrators, we may be better placed to protect children and stop maltreatment from occurring. This is an area where the research evidence is very much at odds with the generally held stereotypical assumption: we know from research that those most likely to perpetrate abuse are relatives, young people and those known to the child, whereas the common fear is much more focused on 'stranger danger'.

There is a need in research to highlight those factors that protect children from abuse and that make children more resilient, and we need to improve detection rates. By doing this, we will be able to offer early intervention programmes that build on the strengths of the child and reduce the long-term negative effects of maltreatment (Besharov et al., 1998).

Finally, there needs to be better engagement between practice and research. Research should focus on questions that are useful to practitioners; it needs to provide information in useable ways. Although much research has been done in the area of child

> **Making connexions**
>
> 'Research should focus on questions that are useful to practitioners.'
>
> Can you think of one example? What would be the practical and methodological problems of pursuing it?

maltreatment, investigations in this area are methodologically challenging. Child protection does not readily lend itself to the experimental methodology that evidence-based practice and programmes commonly require (Lewig et al., 2010). If we expect research to produce simple answers to such complex questions, it will be bound to fall short of our expectations because social research rarely provides such definitive answers (Nutley et al., 2007) and these are families with complicated lives and complex needs.

In summarizing the evidence base informing the provision of effective services in child protection cases, Thoburn (2010, p. 23) concludes that while there is a

> growing knowledge base about promising approaches to supporting families and changing harmful parenting practices, there is no clear message from research that any specific service approaches or method will be effective with abusing families. Each complex case has to be researched, both by the careful collection

and analysis of what is known, and also by matching that against the knowledge base of the approaches, methods and packages of services that may be effective in the particular child's and family's circumstances.

Practitioners need to be able to access such evidence, be skilled in how to assess its usefulness to their particular context, and empowered to be able to make judgements or instigate actions on the basis of their professional interpretation.

Further reading

■ Baker, A.J. and Charvat, B.J. (2008) *Research Methods in Child Welfare*. New York: Columbia University Press.

Looks at how best to tackle the complexities of research in the area of child protection in the light of methodological challenges and issues relevant to practice.

■ Newman, T., Moseley, A., Teirney, S. and Ellis, A. (2005) *Evidence-based Social Work: A Guide for the Perplexed*. Lyme Regis: Russell House.

Offers practical advice on how practitioners can access evidence that is useable and useful for their needs.

■ Robson, C. (2002) *Real World Research: A Resource for Social Scientists and Practitioner-researchers*. Oxford: Blackwell.

More methodologically focused but gives an accessible introductory overview of research methods for practitioners.

References

Akmatov, M.K. (2010) 'Child abuse in 28 developing and transitional countries: results from the Multiple Indicator Cluster Surveys', *International Journal of Epidemiology*, **40**(1): 219–27.

Barlow, J., Simkiss, D. and Stewart-Brown, S. (2006) 'Interventions to prevent or ameliorate child physical abuse and neglect: findings from a systematic review of reviews', *Journal of Children's Services*, **1**(3): 6–28.

Barron, I. and Topping, K. (2008) 'School based child sexual abuse prevention programmes: the evidence on effectiveness', *Journal of Children's Services*, **3**(3): 31–53.

Besharov, D.J., Robinson Lowry, M., Pelot, L.H. and Weber, M.W. (1998) 'How can we better protect children from abuse and neglect', *The Future of Children*, **8**(1): 120–32.

Budd, K.S. and Holdsworth, M.J. (1996) 'Issues in clinical assessment of minimal parenting competence', *Journal of Clinical Child Psychology*, **25**(1): 2–14.

Cawson, P., Wattam, C., Brooker, S. and Kelly, G. (2000) *Child Maltreatment in the United Kingdom: A Study of the Prevalence of Abuse and Neglect*. London: NSPCC

Chaffin, M. and Friedrich, B. (2004) 'Evidence based treatments in child abuse and neglect', *Children & Youth Services Review*, **26**(11): 1077–113.

Clark, A. and Clark, A. (2000) *Early Experiences and the Life Path*. London: Jessica Kingsley.

De Bellis, M.D. (2005) 'The psychobiology of neglect', *Child Maltreatment*, **10**(2): 150–72.

Dubowitz, H. (2007) 'Neglect of children's health care', in H. Dubowitz (ed.) *Neglected Children: Research, Practice and Policy.* Thousand Oaks, CA: Sage.

Elliott, M., Browne, K. and Kilcoyne, J. (1995) 'Child sexual abuse prevention: what offenders tell us', *Child Abuse & Neglect*, **19**(5): 579–94.

Euser, E.M. (2009) Child Maltreatment: Prevalence and Risk Factors, doctoral thesis, Leiden University.

Ferrari, A.M. (2002) 'The impact of culture upon child rearing practices and definitions of maltreatment', *Child Abuse & Neglect*, 26, 793–813.

Finkelhor, D. (1994) 'The international epidemiology of child sexual abuse', *Child Abuse & Neglect*, 18, 409–17.

Fonagy, P., Steele, M., Steele, H. et al. (1994) The Emmanuel Miller Memorial Lecture 1992: The theory and practice of resilience, *Journal of Child Psychology & Psychiatry*, 35, 231–57.

Heller, S.S., Larrieu, J.A., d'Imperio, R. and Boris, N.W. (1999) 'Research on resilience to child maltreatment: empirical considerations', *Child Abuse & Neglect*, **23**(4): 321–38.

Hemsley-Brown, J. and Sharp, C. (2003) 'The use of research to improve professional practice: a systematic review of the literature', *Oxford Review of Education*, **29**(40): 449–70.

Herbert, M. (1998) *Clinical Child Psychology: Social Learning, Development and Behaviour* (2nd edn). Chichester: John Wiley.

Higgins, D.J. and McCabe, M.P. (2000) 'Multi-type maltreatment and long-term adjustment of adults', *Child Abuse Review*, 9, 6–18.

Hobbs, C. (2005) 'The prevalence of child maltreatment in the United Kingdom', *Child Abuse & Neglect*, 29, 949–51.

Holzer, P., Lewig, K., Bromfield, L. and Arney, F. (2008) *Research Use in the Australian Child and Family Welfare Sector.* Melbourne: Australian Institute of Family Studies.

Jacelon, C.S. (1997) 'The trait and process of resilience', *Journal of Advanced Nursing*, 25, 123–9.

Jespersen, A.F., Lalumiere, M.L. and Seto, M.C. (2009) 'Sexual abuse history among adult sexual offenders and non-sex offenders: a meta-analysis', *Child Abuse & Neglect*, 33, 179–92.

Kelly, L., Regan, L. and Burton, S. (1991) *An Exploratory Study of the Prevalence of Sexual Abuse in a Sample of 16–21 Year Olds.* London: Child Abuse Studies Unit, Polytechnic of North London.

Kendall-Tackett, K.A. (1997) 'Timing of academic difficulties for neglected and nonmaltreated males and females', *Child Abuse & Neglect*, **21**(9): 885–7.

Kendall-Tackett, K.A. and Eckenrode, J. (1996) 'The effects of neglect on academic achievement and disciplinary problems: a developmental perspective', *Child Abuse & Neglect*, **20**(3): 161–9.

Kendall-Tackett, K.A., Williams, L. and Finkelhor, D. (1993) 'Impact of sexual abuse on children: a review and synthesis of recent empirical studies', *Psychological Bulletin*, 113, 164–80.

Lewig, K., Scott, D., Holzer, P. et al. (2010) 'The role of research in child protection policy reform: a case study of South Australia', *Evidence & Policy*, **6**(4): 461–82.

Lynch, M.A. and Browne, K. (1997) 'The growing awareness of emotional maltreatment', *Child Abuse Review*, 6, 313–14.

MacLeod, J. and Nelson, G. (2000) 'Programs for the promotion of family wellness and the prevention of child maltreatment: a meta-analytic review', *Child Abuse & Neglect*, **24**(9): 1127–49.

Maker, A.H., Shah, P.V. and Agha, Z. (2005) 'Child physical abuse: prevalence, characteristics, predictors and beliefs about parent child violence in South Asian, Middle Eastern, East Asian and Latina women in the United States', *Journal of Interpersonal Violence*, **20**(11): 1406–28.

Manly, J.T. (2005) 'Advances in research definitions of child maltreatment', *Child Abuse & Neglect*, 29, 425–39.

Manly, J.T., Kim, J.E., Rogosch, F.A. and Cicchetti, D. (2001) 'Dimensions of child maltreatment and children's adjustment: contributions of developmental timing and subtype', *Development & Psychopathology*, 6, 121–43.

Masten, A.S., Hubbard, J.J., Gest, S.D. et al. (1999) 'Competence in the context of adversity: pathways to resilience and maladaptation from childhood to late adolescence', *Development & Psychopathology*, 11, 143–69.

May-Chahal, C. and Cawson, P. (2005) 'Measuring child maltreatment in the United Kingdom: a study of the prevalence of child abuse and neglect', *Child Abuse & Neglect*, 29, 969–84.

Mikton, C. and Butchart, A. (2009) 'Child maltreatment prevention: a systematic review of reviews', *Bulletin of the World Health Organization*, **87**(5): 353–61.

NSPCC (National Society for the Prevention of Cruelty to Children) (2011) *Child Cruelty in the UK 2011: An NSPCC Study into Childhood Abuse and Neglect over the Past 30 Years.* London: NSPCC.

Nutley, S., Walter, I. and Davies, H.T. (2007) *Using Evidence: How Research can Inform Public Services.* Bristol: Policy Press.

Prino, C.T. and Peyrot, M. (1994) 'The effect of child physical abuse and neglect on aggressive, withdrawn and prosocial behaviour', *Child Abuse & Neglect*, **18**(10): 871–84.

Prinz, R.J., Sanders, M.R., Shapiro, C.J. et al. (2009) 'Population-based prevention of child maltreatment: the U.S. Triple P System Population Trial', *Prevention Science*, 10, 1–12.

Rind, B., Tromovitch, P. and Bauserman, R. (1998) 'A meta-analytic examination of assumed properties of child sexual abuse using college samples', *Psychological Bulletin*, **124**(1): 22–53.

Rispens, J., Alemon, A. and Goudena, P.P. (1997) 'Prevention of child sexual abuse victimization: a meta-analysis of school programs', *Child Abuse & Neglect*, **21**(10): 975–87.

Rutter, M. (1990) 'Psychosocial adversity: risk, resilience and recovery', *South African Journal of Child & Adolescent Psychiatry*, 7, 75–88.

Rutter, M. (1995) 'Clinical implications of attachment concepts: retrospect and prospect', *Journal of Child Psychology & Psychiatry*, **36**(4): 549–71.

Saunders, B.E., Berliner, L. and Hanson, R.F. (eds) (2004) *Child Physical and Sexual Abuse: Guidelines for Treatment.* Charleston, SC: National Crime Victims Research and Treatment Center.

Sidebotham, P. and Heron, J. (2006) 'Child maltreatment in the "children of the nineties": a cohort study of risk factors', *Child Abuse & Neglect*, 30, 497–522.

Sneddon, H. (2003) 'The effects of maltreatment on children's health and wellbeing', *Child Care in Practice*, **9**(3): 236–49.

Sneddon, H., Iwaniec, D. and Stewart, M. (2010) 'Prevalence of childhood abuse in mothers taking part in a study of parenting their own children', *Child Abuse Review*, 19, 39–55.

Thoburn, J. (2010) 'Towards knowledge-based practice in complex child protection cases: a research-based expert briefing', *Journal of Children's Services*, **5**(1): 9–24.

Research

Walter, I., Nutley, S. and Davies, S. (2003) *Research Impact: A Cross-sector Review*. St Andrews: Research Unit for Research Utilization, University of St Andrews.

Wilson, K.R., Hanse, D.J. and Li, M. (2011) 'The traumatic stress response in child maltreatment and resultant neuropsychological effects', *Aggression & Violent Behaviour*, **16**(2): 87–97.

Wyatt, G.E., Loeb, T.B., Solis, B. and Carmona, J.V. (1999) 'The prevalence and circumstances of child sexual abuse: changes across a decade', *Child Abuse & Neglect*, **23**(1): 45–60.

Zwi, K., Woolfenden, S., Wheeler, D.M. et al. (2009) 'School-based education programmes for the prevention of child sexual abuse (Review)', *Cochrane Database of Systematic Reviews*, 2007(3).

10

Child protection social work in practice

JOE SMEETON

This chapter raises issues about the nature of social work in child protection arenas through the description and discussion of four case scenarios. Each scenario deals with a different form of potential or actual harm to a child or children. I frame the scenarios in terms of harm rather than abuse because the idea of 'harm' relates to the experience of the child whereas 'abuse' focuses on the actions of the adult. This tension between *the needs and experiences of children* and *the risk posed by adults* forms the central debate in children and families social work practice today. They aren't mutually exclusive but ensuring a healthy balance between the two is the key to effective, safe and sensitive practice.

The discussion relies on a belief in what Wilson et al. (2008, pp. 463–9) describe as the principles of relationship-based practice in working with children and families:

- *Recognizing the 'child within'*: understanding that we all have an experience of being a child and being parented, whether positively or negatively, and that this experience informs our emotional and professional responses to the harm of children. Some of us go on to parent for ourselves and how we experience this can also massively affect our judgements and understandings of the families we work with, in positive and negative ways, which means it is not necessarily an advantage to be a parent, but it does introduce another slant to the values we bring to the relationship.
- *Listening to the voice of the child*: effective communication with children and the ability to understand what it is like to be *that child* within the context of *their family* is central to effective and ethical social work. If we don't recognize that children have voices and listen to those voices, we are adding to the construction of them as powerless victims.

Practice

155

■ *Working with children and families:* it is important to hold the child in mind and not be too distracted and enmeshed in dealing with the parents'/carers' issues and problems. But it is crucial to acknowledge that children are located in families and that recognizing strengths and tackling weaknesses in family systems is an important and effective way of promoting children's interests.

■ *Acknowledging power and purpose:* partnership working with families is extremely important, and when parents feel empowered and valued, they are more likely to engage positively with change processes. However, the social worker must be open and honest about their statutory role and the power the state is employing through them in all their dealings with families. Setting yourself up as a family friend and confidante is dishonest, as your ability to maintain that role is severely limited by your professional role; should you later need to shift the emphasis onto the statutory use of power, parents can feel betrayed and duped.

The other important preparation for approaching the scenarios is an understanding of what Reder and Duncan (1999, p. 101) describe as the 'dialectic mindset' necessary for child protection work; a way of interrogating the data and being open to a range of possibilities and explanations for the situation at hand. I think this idea is best developed by Taylor and White (2006) by asking the social worker to deal with the messy complexities and uncertainties of practice through maintaining a position of 'respectful uncertainty'. While it would feel safer to feel that we can uncover causal relationships through our assessment of families and therefore diagnose difficulties and prescribe cures, the realities of the complex dynamics of children nested within family systems with histories, impacted upon by external social, cultural and political forces, populated by individuals with psychological realities and the will to make unpredictable decisions and act in sometimes bizarre ways make this incredibly challenging.

I ask therefore that before approaching the discussion of interventions, you take a moment or two to consider your initial thoughts and assumptions, recognize where they come from and give yourself permission to challenge and question them for yourself ... before you hear me, challenging and questioning my own.

Practice example 1   Physical harm

Description

Margaret was a 45-year-old woman who lived alone with her children, Mark (aged 7) and Ellie (aged 4). Margaret and the children had no contact with the children's father who had left her four years before. She had a wide network of friends and family living locally who often helped out with the children, doing the majority of the school runs and having them around to play with their own children. Anne was one of these friends who, on one occasion, took the children swimming and noticed a number of bruises on Mark's back and bottom; this caused her to make a referral to social services asking for her identity to be kept confidential. Anne also alleged that she believes that Margaret drinks more than she should.

When the social workers visited, Margaret reacted angrily and initially refused permission for the social workers to see the children. However, after 10 minutes' discussion at the door, she reluctantly agreed to them coming in to the kitchen as she didn't want the neighbours to know what was happening. After the social workers were able to discuss their concerns openly and talk about the various options open to Margaret and themselves, Margaret agreed to both children having a medical examination that same day. The paediatrician found no marks on Ellie but felt that Mark's bruises were consistent with being repeatedly punched and slapped on the back and bottom by an adult. There were also bruises of different ages, which suggested that he had been assaulted on several occasions.

The police arrested and interviewed Margaret while the social workers acquired emergency protection orders, heard *ex parte*, and both children were placed in emergency foster care while the assessment was conducted. Margaret denied hurting Mark and said that he had been bullied by local boys on the estate and at school. When Mark was interviewed by the police, he couldn't say how the bruises had happened or when and didn't implicate his mother. The police didn't feel they had enough to charge Margaret and released her.

Mark remained very shy and withdrawn in the foster placement and found it difficult to relax. The foster carers described him as unable to maintain eye contact with them, and seemed unable to play or to have any enjoyment in anything at all. On the third night in care, he wet the bed and tried to hide it. When the foster carer was changing the sheets the next morning, Ellie said: 'He always does that and mummy gets cross and has to smack him for it.'

The police didn't feel that Ellie would be a credible witness and so charges weren't brought. Margaret, believing herself to be in the clear, asked for the return of her children, still denying any responsibility for Mark's injuries.

Intervention

While this seems to be a clear case of physical abuse towards Mark, the possible outcomes are still varied and the social worker's first task is to call a multi-agency child protection conference to consider whether Mark and/or Ellie can be returned to their mother's care with the support of a child protection plan. In preparation for this meeting, the core assessment required by the 'section 47 enquiry' (Children Act 1989) should endeavour to develop an honest and open working relationship with Margaret and her children so that as full an assessment as possible is available for the conference.

The social work decision may be that care proceedings need to be initiated immediately to secure the children's placement in foster care while the assessment and planning are carried out, but this shouldn't be undertaken in a way that necessarily assumes that permanent alternative care is the preferred plan. We are bound legisla-

Practice

tively, professionally and ethically to consider all options in a balanced and open way, which recognizes the strengths and weaknesses of all possible plans. While most looked after children receive a better standard of care than they would have had if they had remained with their birth parents, local authority care is not risk free and poor outcomes for looked after children are well documented. Advice on the likelihood of securing a permanent adoptive or foster placement would inform planning for that possible option. How likely is a sibling placement?

The assessment of Margaret needs to look at her entire history of parenting, as these children have only recently come to the attention of the local authority. We need to ask:

- Has there been a change or deterioration in their care and if so, what has triggered this?
- Can that be addressed or mitigated against by work with Margaret on her own mental health, her alcohol use, developing her support systems in the local area and within her extended family?
- What worked before and why?
- Are those factors retrievable?
- What is the nature of her relationship with both children?
- How is it different and why?
- What is Margaret's capacity to change and her understanding and motivation to make the necessary changes?
- Are these real and sustainable motivations or tokenistic moves to please the professionals but not rooted in realization of the harm caused?
- Does Margaret understand the needs of her children and have acceptable strategies for dealing with problems that arise, such as bedwetting? If not, does she have the capacity to learn and sustain new approaches to problems?

We must also establish the potential for the children's birth father to care for them. Although he doesn't have a current relationship, that does not mean that this isn't a real possibility. Men lose touch with their children for a range of emotional, cultural and structural reasons, yet we still have an ethical, legal and practical responsibility to ensure that children have opportunities to live within their birth family wherever possible. Establishing whether he has parental responsibility is important in establishing the legal basis for proceeding and can steer practice and process, but the emotional basis and possibilities of meeting the children's long-term needs should be the key drivers.

While the parenting assessment is crucial, the importance of hearing the children's voices in this scenario should not be sidelined and the social worker needs time to work individually and jointly with the children to reach as full an understanding as possible about their daily, lived experience of being parented by their mother. This is lengthy and skilled work that requires time and patience and a thorough understanding of child development and the creative application of a wide range of communication strategies. This work is often overlooked as the social worker focuses on the parent's capacity to parent, often without sufficient thought to the child's wishes and feelings. (For a more detailed description of assessing children's lived experience of being parented, see Horwath, 2007.)

What happened next?

Interim care orders were obtained for both children while the assessment proceeded; it concluded that neither parent was in a position to care for the children and they were successfully placed together in a long-term foster placement on full care orders with ongoing contact with both parents.

Practice example 2   Harm through neglect

Description

Hannah is 35 and has three children: Gemma aged 13, John aged 10 and Luke aged 12 months, and they each have different fathers. Hannah spent her adolescence in care after being sexually abused by her stepfather who still lives with her mother. Despite this, Hannah did fairly well at school and achieved five A*-C grade GCSEs; she has had a number of office jobs that she enjoys.

The two older children were made the subjects of care orders by another local authority. After five periods in care due to their mother's fluctuating mental health, they were permanently placed back with their mother two years previously but remained subject to care orders. Hannah then met her new partner Liam, and moved to Newtown to live with him. She quickly became pregnant and separated from Liam almost immediately. Hannah fled from domestic violence perpetrated by all three of the children's fathers and so she has had a number of changes of address.

When Luke was born, Hannah became severely depressed again and found it hard to care for him, often staying in bed all day. Gemma and John undertook most of the care and missed a lot of school, but Luke's health deteriorated quickly and the health visitor raised concerns over his failure to thrive as Luke's weight was falling. All three children were brought into foster care while Hannah accepted intensive outreach support from mental health services. The children and families social worker felt that a return home may not be in the children's best interests, and care proceedings were initiated for Luke. Gemma and John were found a permanent foster placement where they quickly settled and soon began performing well at school. Luke was placed in a separate short-term placement, where his weight recovered and he began to attach to his carer.

Six months later, Hannah began a part-time job in an office and felt well enough to ask for the children to be returned to her. By this time, Luke was subject to an interim care order while parenting assessments were concluded. Hannah felt that she had been severely postnatally depressed, but believed that her therapeutic support would sustain her in parenting all three children in the future. Her therapist was convinced she had the capacity to parent and that the loss of her role as mother was detrimental to her own mental health.

Luke had supervised contact with his mother at home three times a week. Hannah always welcomed Luke with a big hug and showed lots of affection. However, after 20 minutes or so, she would leave him to play on his own and enjoyed talking to the social worker about her office job. The home was usually cluttered and Hannah wouldn't accept advice about safety. The social worker had to step in on many occasions to stop Luke picking up sharp objects, standing on electrical extension sockets or putting unsuitable things into his mouth.

The social worker undertook some work with the older children who were loyal to their mother but also said they were happy in their placement, had lots of friends in their new school and didn't want to move again. They were also worried that they would end up having to care for Luke and still felt responsible for his poor health as they hadn't known how to look after him properly.

Intervention

At this point in the progress of the assessment, the social work decision is primarily around whether the children will return to Hannah or live in permanent alternative care, either through long-term foster care or adoption. These aren't easy questions, as the needs of four people in the immediate situation need to be fully assessed, understood and balanced in order for the best needs of all to be met as far as possible. We multiply this complexity when we extend the assessment to the fathers and extended birth families of each of the children. We could be dealing with four sets of potential birth family carers. While the allegations of domestic violence need to be taken seriously and are likely to reduce the chance of the birth fathers being successfully assessed as carers, these can't be dismissed out of hand and all should be offered full and honest assessments before permanent alternative care is considered.

The possibilities of supporting a return to Hannah's care also need to be fully considered. Are there professional and personal support systems available in the local community to enable this family to reach a level of stability that will enable the children to develop securely and safely? How viable are these in the long term, given the history of home and relationship changes? A key question for the social worker is not only 'What is Hannah's capacity to parent for the duration of the children's minority?' but also 'What is the likelihood of her sustaining the effort?' An assessment that a parent knows how to parent and understands the needs of their children does not necessarily translate into actual parenting. Some parents' own histories and complex needs mean that it can be difficult for them to consistently meet their children's needs. Understanding the ways this may manifest for particular families nested within particular social and cultural systems and recognizing the parents' strengths and the children's personalities and resilience factors are key to considering all the potential options.

The Children Act 1989 usefully focuses the social worker's mind on prioritizing the children's needs over those of the parents. Consideration of the fact that Hannah's role as a mother is extremely important to her own mental health is crucial but should not override the children's needs for a secure, stable and safe childhood. If we take the view that the best predictor of future behaviour is past behaviour (Munro, 2008), then we are likely to have severe doubts about Hannah's ability to provide this, despite assurances from her therapist, and it is likely that professional disagreement may arise. Both sides of this argument may not be resolvable and ought therefore to be put before the court. There is often a reluctance to have contested hearings through a desire to be seen to 'work in partnership' with families and between professionals, and also through a lack of confidence in decision-making. Provided that the children's needs are central to the case put before the court, a healthy contest that recognizes a parent's strengths may help the parent to feel that their voice has been heard.

The key voices in this decision-making progress need to be those of the children. We have clear indications from the older children that their needs are likely to be best met through continuation of their current placement where they can achieve stability in their relationships and education and be cared for rather than having the responsibility of caring. Their relationship with their mother is extremely important and serious consideration needs to be put into how this can be maintained through direct and indirect contact (MacAskill, 2002), which enables Hannah to maintain her identity as a mother but doesn't undermine the placement. Ensuring that foster carers receive good support is likely to be key in achieving these complex aims.

Luke's voice could easily be overlooked as he isn't, at this age, able to vocalize his thoughts and feelings. A social worker needs to employ all their skills of observation and interpretation of Luke's behaviour, emotional states and responses to the key people in his life. Judicious use of attachment theory (Howe, 1995) can inform this assessment through observation in the foster placement and in contact sessions with his mother and siblings, separately and together. The aim of the decision-making process is to form a plan for Luke's permanent care, where he can form secure and lasting relationships. It is likely that the preferred option for Luke, if this isn't achievable within his birth family, would be adoption. The viability of achieving an adoptive placement for Luke, given his particular history and circumstances, may be quite strong, but if we then consider the potential to maintain contact with his siblings and possibly with Hannah and maybe even with his birth father, we could be reducing the pool of potential placements. However, this should not be dismissed without due consideration, and careful thought needs to be put into how contact could be maintained safely within any potential placement. Drawing on the advice and skills of colleagues in adoption services would be crucial in forming this element of the plan.

What happened next?

Gemma and John remained in their long-term placement with ongoing contact with their mother. Luke was successfully adopted by his foster carer, with direct contact with his siblings and indirect contact with his mother.

Practice example 3 | Sexual harm

Description

Keith (35 years) and Eve (37 years) are both profoundly deaf parents of hearing children, Dan aged 10 and Poppy aged 5. Dan's friend Adam, who is also 10, has alleged that when he went into the toilet at their home, Keith followed him in and touched his penis. The police visited and have asked Keith to leave the family home while the joint section 47 investigation proceeds. They are aware of two previous similar allegations made against Keith 14 years ago.

The video interview that Adam gives is clear and compelling, and the police are able to quickly pass their evidence on to the Crown Prosecution Service (CPS) for a decision. While that decision is pending, the social work assessment continues with all the family members under section 47 of the Children Act 1989.

Early in the assessment, several sessions of direct work are conducted with Dan and Poppy separately. The social worker concludes that both children's knowledge of sexuality is age appropriate. They have the usual childhood names for their body parts and show due awareness of appropriate and inappropriate touching. No concerns are raised by this phase of the assessment and so after discussion with the police, it is agreed that the social worker will ask the children more direct questions as to whether they have been touched inappropriately. Both children say that they haven't. Both say how much they love and miss their father.

The assessment of Eve concludes that she is an organized, caring mother who has good emotional support from her own parents (who live 30 miles away) and from the deaf community, but has little practical support in the local area. Eve does say she struggles to maintain discipline with the children and usually leaves this to Keith, who she describes as a very good father who has a strong relationship with the children. Keith's continued absence from the home becomes increasingly problematic for Eve as the children become more and more challenging and naughty. She doesn't believe that her husband would commit this act as she feels they have an active and satisfying sex life. She explains the current and previous allegations as boys making fun of Keith and perhaps not understanding him because of his deafness.

The assessment of Keith is difficult. He completely denies the charges and is angry that he is being kept away from his children other than for supervised contact. He is currently in bed and breakfast accommodation, which doesn't have the environmental aids he relies on, he doesn't want the deaf community to know about the allegation as he feels he may be ostracized, and he is becoming increasingly isolated and depressed. Keith is extremely averse to discussing anything sexual with a woman and although the social worker is male, the only available, appropriately qualified interpreter is a 22-year-old woman. Part of the assessment therefore is conducted without an interpreter, with Keith's explicit agreement, and the discussions are held through a combination of lip-reading, rudimentary sign language, writing and drawing. Keith discloses having had some sexual contact with other adolescent boys when he was a boarder at a school for the deaf, but he says this was commonplace and part of growing up, insisting that he is heterosexual and no longer has sexual feelings for boys.

The social worker feels that Keith is unlikely to admit to being attracted by boys in the current situation and especially while still awaiting a decision from the CPS regarding prosecution. A child protection conference held after 15 days recommended that Dan and Poppy were made the subject of child protection plans due to concerns about a risk of sexual abuse while the core assessment continues.

Intervention

The social worker in this situation is dealing with complexity and uncertainty magnified by the pending decision about whether Keith will face criminal charges. In the meantime, the family as a unit and as individuals are finding it difficult to continue to function. If we think of the family as a system in which each family member has a role and each impacts on the others, then removing one key element (Keith) from that system can massively impact on how the whole system functions. However, the children's safety and right to live free from abuse are legitimate and real concerns.

How the social worker approaches this assessment can affect the information that is shared and subsequently the decisions made and the potential outcomes for all family members. To some extent, this is informed by the social worker's statutory role and available legislative powers and the social worker's theoretical stance, but mainly by the emphasis they and their organization place on balancing the assessment of *needs* and *risks*. In what is becoming an increasingly risk-averse profession, this seems to be a key scale on which we balance children's lives.

An emphasis on risk in this case would recognize that whether or not a criminal prosecution follows, the clear statement from Adam, combined with two previous similar allegations, would conclude that a safe working assumption was that Keith is sexually aroused by boys of a similar age to his son Dan and that he seems to have acted on those feelings on at least three occasions. Dan is clearly at risk, then, of being sexually abused by his father. This risk is compounded by Keith's denial, which reduces the capacity to engage with him in any meaningful work in recognizing and reducing the likelihood of his going on to abuse again. Keith is caught in a double bind – catch-22. If he admits to the abuse of Adam, he is certain to face criminal prosecution, and if he denies it, he is considered more of a risk to his own children. The risk is compounded by Eve's disbelief – if she can't consider that Keith is a risk to his own children, then can she be an effective safety element in this family? Eve's deafness may also mean that her awareness of activity within the house could be reduced. The simplest solution to reduce the risk of sexual abuse would be a requirement that Keith shouldn't live in the family home.

An emphasis on need in this case, however, would recognize that this family system is severely disrupted by Keith's absence. The children need stability and Keith seems to be the parent who maintained routines and discipline and is clearly loved

Practice

by both children who are suffering a significant loss. There is a possibility that Eve may not cope as a single parent and the outcomes for the children could be very poor as a result. The viability of the children remaining within their birth family has to be a key priority, and given the apparent lack of immediately available support in the local and deaf communities due to the nature of the allegations and the need for confidentiality, Keith's continued absence is likely to become increasingly problematic and restoring him to the family becomes an attractive option.

Balancing these two elements – risk and need – is difficult and requires a great deal of work with the entire family and the full multi-agency team including education, health and social service staff working directly with the children and the parents in the form of regular core groups. Again, the approach assumed by the social worker is likely to colour the possibility of work. If the social worker falls too readily into the role of 'investigator' – trying to uncover whether the abuse did or did not happen – this is likely to polarize the options and set up an adversarial stance against the parents. Conversely, if assuming the role of advocate for and champion of the parents, the social worker minimizes the significance of the risk and the children's right to a safe childhood. Working from the position of 'respectful uncertainty' – in which we keep alive the belief that the abuse could have happened and ask the family to cooperate on that basis, recognizing that we are never going to know with certainty whether it did or not – gives us the possibility of helping the family to set up routines that minimize the opportunities for abuse and also increases the possibility for any abuse that does occur to be disclosed or discovered through persistent involvement with the family. This would be predicated on the professionals feeling confident that the family are also able to cooperate on that basis and will fully engage in the plan, which may be difficult if Eve is unable to accept the possibility that this is a real concern and Keith has the potential to abuse.

What happened next?

The CPS eventually decided not to prosecute Keith. A comprehensive support package was put in place to enable Keith to remain at home with the children on a child protection plan, but the family had to move house as the allegations became public, resulting in a number of threats from neighbours.

Practice example 4	Emotional harm: domestic violence

Description

Westhaven School contacted social services with concerns about Eddie (aged 13) whose behaviour had changed dramatically over the previous six months. He had changed from being a confident, hard-working, successful and popular student to one who was withdrawn and anxious. His attendance had fallen dramatically and he had been caught sneaking out of school several times. His class teacher had tried to speak to him but he wouldn't discuss any worries and became agitated when the teacher suggested a home visit to meet his mother Jenny. Eddie became angry when the teacher referred to Eddie's stepfather Jack as his 'dad'. Jenny had missed several appointments with the education welfare officer and he had been unable to meet her at all.

A neighbour then made an anonymous call to the police describing shouting and screams coming from the family home. The police visited and found that Jenny had obviously been severely beaten. They asked Jack to leave the family home and took Jenny to hospital for treatment. Jenny refused to say who had caused her injuries and insisted that she had fallen down the stairs.

This prompted a referral to social services who visited two days later to find Jack back at home and Jenny saying all was now back to normal. The social worker, Clare, did some direct work with Eddie at school. He said that his mother had been beaten on a regular basis over the six months since Jack lost his job and that he was really scared that she would be killed. Eddie was clear that he had never been hit by Jack but said that Jack is always picking on him and calling him stupid. Eddie would like his mother to leave Jack but thinks she is too scared to do so. He asked that no one should tell Jack what he had said in case he took it out on his mother.

Clare asked to meet Jenny alone at the office to discuss their concerns about Eddie, but when Jenny arrived she had brought Jack with her, who refused to stay in the waiting room while the social worker spoke to Jenny. Jenny also said that she wanted Jack to come into the meeting as he was Eddie's new dad and had every right to be there. Clare found Jack to be intimidating and was anxious to avoid a confrontation that might put herself, Jenny or Eddie in danger; she chose to hold the meeting but kept away from the topic of domestic violence and discussed general concerns that the school had about Eddie. Jack dominated this discussion, saying that Eddie was lazy and not very bright. Jenny sat quietly agreeing. Clare strongly felt that Jenny was intimidated and scared.

Clare tried to meet Jenny alone on a number of occasions over the next week by calling in at odd times, but either there was no answer or Jack answered the door saying Jenny wasn't at home.

Intervention

The impact of witnessing domestic violence on children is now well documented (Kolbo et al., 1996) and the family court is predisposed to recognize it as meeting the threshold criteria for care proceedings. There are strong links with the physical abuse of children, yet often the most damaging element is the impact on children's emotional development. Children become preoccupied with worry and concern for the abused parent, mixed with fear for themselves. The longer term impacts, especially on boys, of regularly witnessing domestic violence are explained by social learning theory as often leading to them to go on to have difficulty forming and sustaining adult relationships or becoming abusive themselves (Sturge, 2003).

Practice

We are also aware of the devastating impact it has on the victims' – usually women's – mental and physical health, and that women often make many attempts to escape violence before they are successful. The nature and effect of domestic violence reduces their self-esteem, increases their reliance on the abusive partner, and reduces their ability to make effective decisions and take decisive actions. Why is it, then, that social work often puts the responsibility of keeping children safe onto the abused partner? Women are often faced with a choice of leaving the relationship or losing their children. We may think that this is a straightforward decision and that any reasonable parent would put their children's needs first, but that is to ignore the social, cultural, historical, financial and emotional ties that bind relationships (Featherstone et al., 2007).

What happens less often is that the responsibility is placed at the door of the abusive partner. Professionals often feel scared and intimidated by the risks posed to themselves by violent service users, which means that they are often not tackled about the effect their behaviour is having on all the members of the family and helped to make the necessary changes. The construction of men – usually – as dangerous therefore serves to marginalize them from child protection processes. I tend to agree with Munro's (1998, p. 93) comment that this scrutiny of women in child protection is 'surprising' since men are more likely to be violent and social workers should give them more rather than less attention than women.

This scenario is a difficult one to progress but avoiding tackling the issue is unlikely to lead to any resolution. The social worker needs to find a way to be open and honest about the concerns with Jack and Jenny. This needs to be done as safely as possible and will need careful consideration about the time and place where this difficult discussion is held. Planning how the issue is to be raised and anticipating potential responses will help to minimize risk, as will sensitivity. Again, adopting a stance as 'investigator' is not likely to be helpful as that is likely to produce a defensive response. Adopting the position of 'respectful uncertainty' helps us to recognize that we need to work on the real concerns about the emotional impact on Eddie; addressing these concerns is likely to involve individual and couple counselling with Jack and Jenny in order to resolve whatever conflicts there are in order to enable progress. There are many links to 'solution-focused' work here and although I am not advocating a straight solution-focused approach (Walsh, 2010), an emphasis on resolving the problems within the family is more likely to help them engage in a change process than one that seeks to attribute blame.

Of course, it is very likely that Jack will rebuff any attempts to engage with the family and that Jenny may feel so disempowered that she can't act independently of Jack, which is why it is important that the social worker works fully within the child protection system, conducting a thorough core assessment, with the expectation that the social worker is able to meet each parent and Eddie separately and conduct regular observations with a view to holding either a child protection conference or 'child in need' meeting to conclude and share the assessment.

The option of care proceedings is also alive throughout the assessment and at its conclusion. We need to consider the possible outcomes of a legal process and the possible care plans available and their potential impact on Eddie. His voice will be a major consideration in discussion of the

> **Making connexions**
>
> The children and families social worker requires 'a peculiar and highly developed skill set'. In respect of any one of the four case studies, can you identify which social work skills are employed?

plan as he may have strong feelings about where he wants to live and may especially have grave worries about leaving his mother in a dangerous situation. Serious consideration should be given as to whether his needs might best be met by remaining in the family home and working with the family through a supervision order. This level of intervention might help Jenny's resolution of issues. If we are unable to change the family situation satisfactorily, then a care order would still be available to protect Eddie, but again we need to balance the risks of him staying at home against the potential risks of local authority care, which wouldn't reduce his anxiety about his mother's safety and may make it more likely that he will find it difficult to settle in placement.

What happened next?

Unfortunately, Jenny was hospitalized again by Jack before she felt able to end the relationship, and she and Eddie moved to a refuge in a different local authority, where they relocated.

Conclusion

The reader will perhaps reflect that most of the discussion in this chapter relates to assessment and decision-making and there is little discussion about intervention strategies to effect change. This reflects the current emphasis in practice, but the profession recognizes the urgent need to free up social work time through systemic reform in order to allow social workers to intervene positively with families with a view to supporting them more effectively where possible, yet making timely decisions about alternative care when necessary (Munro, 2010).

Our exploration of these not untypical scenarios invites the reader to recognize the complexity of child protection practice and to give up any idea that there are simple, formulaic solutions to practice problems. Rather, what is required is an engaged, actively reflective and sensitive practitioner with access to supportive and challenging clinical supervision in which they can explore their values and assumptions and the needs and risks of individual children within particular family contexts. These activities require a peculiar and highly developed skill set in the children and families practitioner:

> let us educate for uncertainty, compassion, carefulness and wisdom ... I am convinced that only those with those qualities are able to work (relatively) safely and soundly with children and families placed in their charge. (White, 2009, p. 107)

Practice

Further reading

■ Broadhurst, K., Grover, C. and Jamieson, J. (eds) (2009) *Critical Perspectives on Safeguarding Children*. Chichester: Wiley-Blackwell.

Engages the reader in the wider debates about child protection and invites a reflexive approach to practice that will help social workers locate themselves in an ethical framework.

■ Ferguson, H. (2011) *Child Protection Practice*. Basingstoke: Palgrave Macmillan.

Probably the best book currently on the market about the everyday business of 'doing' child protection work. Helps practitioners to recognize the significance of the often overlooked smaller things they do that contribute to their overall practice confidence and competence.

■ Munro, E. (2008) *Effective Child Protection*. London: Sage.

Every social worker engaged in child protection work should have this on their bookshelf. Especially good at looking at the significant elements of decision-making and lays out a methodology for making recommendations relating to children's safety.

References

Featherstone, B., Rivett, M. and Scourfield, J. (2007) *Working with Men in Health and Social Care*. London: Sage.

Horwath, J. (2007) *Child Neglect*. Basingstoke: Palgrave Macmillan.

Howe, D. (1995) *Attachment Theory for Social Work Practice*. Basingstoke: Macmillan – now Palgrave Macmillan.

Kolbo, J.R., Blakely, E.H. and Engelman, D. (1996) 'Children who witness domestic violence: a review of empirical literature', *Journal of Interpersonal Violence*, 11, 281–93.

MacAskill, C. (2002) *Safe Contact?: Children in Permanent Placement and Contact with their Birth Relatives*. Lyme Regis: Russell House.

Munro, E. (1998) 'Improving social worker's knowledge base in child protection work', *British Journal of Social Work*, 28, 89–105.

Munro, E. (2008) *Effective Child Protection* (2nd edn). London: Sage.

Munro, E. (2010) *The Munro Review of Child Protection – Part One: A Systems Analysis*, http://www.education.gov.uk/munroreview/index.shtml.

Reder, P. and Duncan, S. (1999) *Lost Innocents: A Follow-up study of Fatal Child Abuse*. London: Routledge.

Sturge, C. (2003) 'Can violent parents be fit parents?', in P. Reder, S. Duncan and C. Lucey (eds) *Studies in the Assessment of Parenting*. London: Routledge.

Taylor, C. and White, S. (2006) 'Knowledge and reasoning in social work: educating for humane judgement', *British Journal of Social Work*, 36, 937–54.

Walsh, T. (2010) *The Solution-focused Helper: Ethics and Practice in Health and Social Care.* Maidenhead: OU Press.

White, S. (2009) 'Arguing the case for safeguarding', in K. Broadhurst, C. Grover and J. Jamieson (eds) *Critical Perspective on Safeguarding Children.* Chichester: Wiley-Blackwell.

Wilson, K., Ruch, G., Lymbery, M. and Cooper, A. (2008) *Social Work: An Introduction to Contemporary Practice.* Harlow: Pearson Education.

Practice

Part III

Social Work in the Field of Adoption and Fostering

Part III focuses on two important areas of policy and practice relating to child permanence. Any discussion of adoption and fostering inevitably requires us to engage with difficult questions regarding the role of the state in family life. This was illustrated in 2011 in the challenging and at times provocative paper prepared by Martin Neary for *The Times* (5 July 2011) newspaper on the need to increase numbers of adoptions in order to meet the best interests of vulnerable children. Whatever the benefits or risks associated with state interventions in family life, however, what cannot be denied is the profound and long-lasting impact of such interventions on the everyday lives of children, their immediate and extended birth relatives, and their adoptive and foster family members. The consequences of adoption and fostering can reach across families, across generations, across communities and across society. The direction set by the state also has an impact on those charged with implementing and interpreting government policy within legal and welfare systems. What begins to emerge, then, is a complex web of individuals and agencies involved in the difficult task of achieving successful outcomes for children in need of substitute families through adoption or fostering.

The five chapters in Part III carefully unpack some of this complexity. The authors do not aim to provide comprehensive analyses of adoption and fostering in all its forms. It would be almost impossible to deal adequately with all iterations of adoption – domestic or international, confidential or open, same-race or transracial – and all types of fostering – short term, emergency or long term – in a few thousand words. Instead, each chapter provides a window onto specific aspects of adoption and fostering, allowing the reader to reflect on this area of child and family social work from the different perspectives of policy, law, theory, research and practice.

In Chapter 11, John Simmonds provides a historical account of adoption in order to contextualize contemporary policies, practices and principles. He charts the trends in adoption policy and highlights the ongoing challenge of ensuring that adoption policies and legal and welfare systems operate in the best interests of the child. In Chapter 12, Caroline Ball provides a clear and helpful overview of the law as it relates to the placement of children in adoptive families or foster care. She, too, describes the historical context of current laws and suggests some policy and practice issues that will require urgent future attention. In Chapter

13, Christine Jones focuses on two theories with particular explanatory power within adoption and fostering: attachment theory and the social construction of family relationships. While these theories have developed within different disciplines and from very different research traditions, it is suggested that they can offer complementary ways of understanding family life following a child's placement for adoption or fostering.

Chapter 14 provides an overview of research milestones that have influenced thinking and practice in relation to adoption and fostering. Gary Clapton stresses the importance of hearing the voices of children and adults affected by adoption and fostering, and highlights the concepts, such as loss, resilience and difference, that have become influential within adoption and fostering as a result of empirical research. In Chapter 15, Sally Holland and Cecilia Love provide four insightful case studies that bring to life the day-to-day experiences of adopted and fostered individuals. Importantly, they are a reminder that an adoptive or foster placement does not simply mark a child's transition to a new family and new life. Instead, it sets children on a lifelong journey of making sense of relationships and exploring identity.

Taken together, the chapters in Part III weave an intricate story of individual experience and the wider cultural context within which adoption and fostering have developed in the UK. In true Millsian tradition, they bring together the personal, historical and social. They also remind us of the enduring ability of children and adults to create new and permanent family relationships in the face of adversity.

Christine Jones

11

Adoption: from the preservation of the moral order to the needs of the child

JOHN SIMMONDS

Adoption as a policy issue attracts the most intense public interest. There could not be a more emotive image than that of a child abandoned, abused or neglected by their parents and in need of a family who will love them and commit themselves for ever. There could not be a more powerful need than identifying the characteristics of parents who deserve or are able to 'properly' parent children in need of adoption. There could not be more ambivalence expressed about the circumstances and characteristics of, primarily, women who give up, or are forced to give up, their children for adoption. And lastly, there are the views and experiences of those affected by adoption, adults primarily but children certainly, often expressed through the experience of search and reunion. Adoption policy is not therefore some remote concern of central or local government bureaucrats but an issue that brings together the most basic of human concerns – children, parenting and the family and our attitudes towards these. It also raises a question about the role of the state in influencing and determining what should happen when a parent is unable to care for their child: To what extent is it a proper concern for the state when family life is usually recognized as something that is fundamentally a private matter?

The state recognizes that when a child is born, whatever the 'wisdom' or circumstances of the couple at the time of conception, childbirth is a fundamental right of the mother and father. The state will endeavour to support the parent/s through the provision of health, education and social care, including the provision of a range of practical resources such as housing and income. While the eligibility for and adequacy of these services are always subject to political and public scrutiny, the right to family life and the privacy of family life are well established as human rights. The exception to this will be the triggering of the threshold that invokes a child protection investigation but, even in such investigations, human rights issues continue to be important drivers. In making a decision and planning for a child to be adopted, however, every aspect of the process is subject to considerable legal, professional and bureaucratic scrutiny – certainly until the adoption order is made. The contrast between 'normal' conception and the birth of a child and adoption could not be starker. It is something that is in need of an explanation.

Since the *Prime Minister's Review of Adoption* (Performance and Innovation Unit, 2000), new primary legislation has been enacted in England and Wales – the Adoption and Children Act 2002 – and in Scotland – the Adoption and Children (Scotland) Act 2007. Northern Ireland still waits for new legislation as various contentious issues, such as the right of a gay or lesbian couple to jointly adopt, encounter public and political opposition. Significant secondary legislation, together with statutory and practice guidance, has accompanied the new Acts, plus financial incentives to local authorities by the former Labour administration to increase the numbers of children adopted by 38% or more (in England).[1] Other funding was ring-fenced to improve adoption support services, and a more rigorous inspection framework was and continues to be introduced, with the intention of driving up standards of practice. The first five years of reform in England and Wales – from 2000 to 2005 and up to the year when the English and Welsh legislation was enacted in 2005 – showed a significant increase in the number of children placed for adoption and children adopted. The planned increase was largely met. But from the point where the Act was implemented at the end of 2005, the figures in England show a decline in numbers over the following six years to 3,050. This is the opposite of what was intended and with a new coalition government in power, adoption has appeared high on the agenda, with a desire to reverse the trend by reinvigorating policy and practice, particularly around delay, the ethnic matching of children and adopters, and the use of the voluntary adoption sector.

Trends in adoption over a generation

Exploring the adoption figures over 25 years shows that the decline has been dramatic. From 1975 to the early 1980s, the number of adoption orders decreased from 22,502 to 10,240 in 1982; from the mid-1990s, numbers fell again to around 5,000; and since then, it has varied only slightly from year to year but remains at about 5,000. In itself, this overall trend is significant, but unpicking these figures reveals a major change in society and particularly in views about children, family life, and the role of the state in policy, law and practice. The figures in Figure 11.1 amalgamate four different kinds of adoptions – relinquished baby adoptions, children adopted from care, international adoptions and step-parent adoptions.

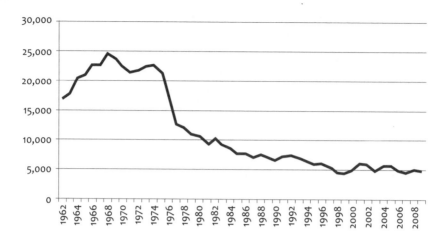

Figure 11.1 Number of adoptions, per annum, 1962–2008
Source: Office for National Statistics

The largest number of adoptions in the 10 years from 1974 are those children 'relinquished' by their mothers within the first few weeks or months of birth. These adoptions reflect a number of issues. The overarching, although not exclusive theme is the stigma of illegitimacy and the problem of children born outside wedlock. Society's attitudes prior to and during this period were harsh, reinforced by religious belief about the sanctity of marriage as core to family life. Single parenthood was a limited option, and, if chosen, was likely to result in social and personal stigma, which, when combined with the lack of availability of state housing or benefits, made it an option of considerable cost to the mother and baby. At the same time, the lack of reliable and effective contraception and the unlawfulness of abortion prior to 1967 made 'unwanted' pregnancies difficult to prevent, with the only option being to illegally terminate the pregnancy, often at considerable risk to the mother's health. If the pregnancy continued, it would often do so in secrecy, with the mother 'sent' to a religious or health-based 'mother and baby' home at some distance from her community to give birth. She would then have been under some, and maybe considerable, pressure to 'give up' her baby for adoption, with little support available for the painful and often long-lasting consequences of such decisions.

The introduction of effective and reliable forms of contraception in the early 1960s, the legal availability of abortion from 1968, and the gradual acceptance by society of a responsibility to support single parenthood if that is what the mother chose began to have an impact in the 1960s and 70s. Thus the period from the mid-1970s to the mid-1980s indicates much more than a significant drop in the number of adoptions; it shows a fundamental shift in society in personal and social attitudes towards women, pregnancy, children and the concept of the kinds of families needed to raise children. It also reflects developments in social welfare and in the state's relationship with and responsibilities towards its citizens. Policies were developed to support single parenthood as an acceptable choice, and laws and services were established that reflect these policies. Following on from the foundation of the welfare state in the 1940s and 50s, the development of adoption policy is therefore the coming together of a number of significant, interrelated strands that result in the fall in the number of adoptions, reflected in Figure 11.1. In order to understand this, we can focus our attention on the circumstances of individual women or children or on adopters – their personal stories; or we can focus our attention on society's attitudes and the way social control exerts itself to influence how people behave and what social mores they conform to; or we can focus our attention on understanding the nature of social problems and the way society at any one moment in time defines and tries to solve these problems.

What is central to any understanding of these issues is that children, parents and the family are fundamental to society. The meaning they have in any particular society is never static and we need to understand the way this changes over time. Meanings are socially constructed in relation to prevailing social norms, and the way society attributes meaning to the family at one point in time may radically change and seem less important or even meaningless at another point in time. When it comes to adoption, the solution it provides needs to be understood in relation to prevailing values and norms and this may well be very different to the solution it provides even a generation later.

Historical trends and influences: morality, inheritance and class

One of the strongest themes that can be identified in the history of adoption is the question of inheritance – title, family name and property; indeed, the first recorded adoption law from Greece in 594 BC focused on preserving family inheritance, including maintaining political alliances. Adoption was a means of ensuring that this happened. However, the issue of inheritance was seen quite differently in the UK in the early part of the twentieth century, with a fear that any child not 'naturally' born to the parents would risk bringing into the adoptive family inherited and unwelcome traits such as the 'immorality', fecklessness or lack of social grace of the child's birth parents. Social standing and class and the inheritance of property were values of such dominant importance that they had acted against any strong belief that adopting a child born to other parents was a morally or socially acceptable thing to do. So while many thousands of children were orphaned and/or illegitimate throughout Victorian and Edwardian times, where they survived, the solution was to care for them in poor-houses until such time they could be indentured to families for the work they could do in those families. It may be that, for some children, new relationships were established that enabled something close to creating a family life, but the barrier of social class would, for most, be impenetrable.

Following the end of the First World War (1914–18), with its decimation of all sections of society, the care of orphans and the problem of property inheritance rights led to a demand for a legal framework that could support a child becoming a full member of a new family. It was a social problem that demanded a formal and legal solution and resulted in the first adoption legislation in England and Wales, the Adoption Act 1926 (the Act did not apply in Scotland or Northern Ireland). Under the Act:

- an adopted child legally and irrevocably became a member of the new family
- their legal links with their birth family were extinguished, although they retained their inheritance rights in respect of their birth family
- they acquired the right of inheritance from the adoptive family.

The adoption decision was supervised by the court as a judicial process with the assistance of a guardian ad litem to safeguard the infant's interests. At the same time, a number of agencies were established to arrange adoptions.

Historical trends and influences: psychology

The acceptability of adoption slowly became established and, following the Second World War (1939–45), it came to be seen as a new solution to the problem of illegitimate children. At the same time, it became a socially acceptable solution to the problem of infertile couples, which, like contraception, lacked any reliable medical solution. However, while a change in society's views about the dangers of inherited traits and rights to inheritance were important, adoption practice was influenced by a dominant belief about the importance of adoption being a new start. The fear of contamination continued to be a significant influence over both policy and practice, with the idea that only 'perfectly healthy' babies could and would be adopted by 'perfectly respectable' couples. The assessment of the baby and the prospective adopters by medical staff and moral welfare workers (who were part of the emerging semi-profession of social work) was important in guaranteeing that the non-contamination principle drove practice. The matching of the physical appearance of the baby and the prospective adopters was also important along with the careful preservation of the child and the adopters' religious affiliation. The age of the child was the last important factor – the younger the better, in order to ensure that the process of integrating the child into the new family would run smoothly, which included the child having no memory of a relationship with or of being cared for by their birth mother. Adoption was about a new start unencumbered by any memory of the past and with a strong emphasis on secrecy. It was passed off as morally respectable and, but for the fact of infertility, the same as having a child of one's own. If infertility and illegitimacy were shameful and subject to social stigma, adoption practice ensured that all three parties were cleansed by the adoption process. The importance of voluntary adoption agencies affiliated to the Anglican, Catholic and nonconformist churches reinforced this.

At the time when adoption was becoming an acceptable and workable solution to the problem of infertility and illegitimacy, other developments started to become influential (Yelloly, 1980). Social work as a profession became established and was strongly influenced by psychological theories of human development, particularly those of Freud (Pearson et al., 1988). The child started to emerge as a subject in their own right, not a blank canvas. Freud had developed highly influential perspectives, which suggested that babies were born with an inner life made up of base instincts that needed to be tamed by the active influence of their psychologically mature parents. While morality was an important part of this framework, family life and adopted family life in the form of the nuclear family stressed the significance of close relationships in the development of the child; at the heart of these relationships were psychological explanations of what made this work. There was a fundamental change in the concept of what a child and a family was, and this had a profound impact on adoption. Morality was to give way to psychology, a profound change in the meaning that children, parenting and the family were to have for the rest of the century.

The current perspective on adoption

Adoption as a solution to society's problem with infertility and illegitimacy only had a relatively brief life. The 'sexual revolution' of the 1960s, the drive for the emancipation and equal rights of women, the legalization of abortion and the development of contraception, combined with the consolidation and strengthening of the postwar welfare state, rendered relinquished baby adoption almost irrelevant. Women had a 'right' to choose abortion and they had a right to keep their babies. Marriage started to become a choice rather than a baseline for family life and the Church was quickly losing its dominant hold on morality. The number of babies available for adoption started to decline dramatically, but other social problems started to emerge. Under the increasing influence of the psychological theories of Freud and Bowlby, and the decreasing influence of the 'moral contamination' framework, social workers had begun to see the potential of adoption for other groups of children – older children, children with disabilities, children from diverse ethnic backgrounds and sibling groups, children categorized as 'hard to place' or 'special needs' children.

These children were in need of a solution where their birth family could not care for them, and, for the most part, that solution had been in the form of long-term state care in children's homes or, for some, in foster care. But these were solutions that were being shown to lack the intimacy, consistency and commitment of family life that were at the core of a child's development. Films made by James and Joyce Robertson (Robertson and Robertson, n.d.), under the influence of Bowlby (1988), demonstrated the severe impact of separation and loss on children where they were placed in residential and foster care. Research by Rowe and Lambert (1973) demonstrated the unsatisfactory 'drift' of many children in state care. Adoption was identified as a solution with real hope for meeting the developmental needs of these children. Agencies began to believe that prospective adopters – suitably motivated, well prepared and supported – could be flexible and adaptable enough to provide the kinds of parenting and family environments that these children needed. A number of innovative and influential projects paved the way, supported by practice frameworks and practice material published by organizations like the British Association for Adoption and Fostering (Fahlberg, 1994). Other developments, such as the 'discovery' of the physical abuse of children in the 1970s, sexual abuse in the 1980s and then neglect through the 1990s, reinforced the need for adoption to be seen as a solution for a wide range of children in care. Adoption became identified as child centred, long-lasting and advantageous over other possible solutions and with significant cost advantages – certainly over the cost to the state of a child remaining in care. The beginnings of a framework for special needs adoption were identified in an influential text (Goldstein et al., 1980) and were enshrined in legislation – the Children Act 1975 and the Adoption Act 1976. Among other things, it became a requirement that every local authority should establish its own adoption agency, although the voluntary sector continued to be active and important. This new legislation marked a significant change in the interest the state was to have in the regulation and control of adoption activity. The voluntary sector, the Church and adoptive parents continued to have a role but, as with so many other societal issues, the state was to become increasingly influential in what and how things happened. The needs of the child became the dominant framework in adoption and this has remained the case in the first part of the twenty-first century.

The emergence of the birth family

While children, their development and the influence of psychological explanations had come to supersede a framework that was concerned with the management of social stigma and shame, other key issues were to have an important impact, in particular the position of the birth family in adoption. For the birth mother, adoption as a solution to the problem of illegitimacy was not without considerable personal cost. While the law required that the mother freely gave her consent to her child being adopted, the personal and social pressures to do so were immense. There are many individual testimonies of the personal and long-lasting pain involved and campaigns have been established to have the injustice of legal and societal processes recognized.

Other developments recognized that the 'new start' philosophy of adoption and the advocacy of secrecy were unhelpful, if not damaging. The experiences of many adopted children and their families demonstrated that the need to know why a child was placed for adoption was important (Simmonds, 2000, 2008). It was something that the adoptive family needed to be open to: in telling the child that they were adopted, having an explanation about why and what the circumstances were, and being able to address any feelings of loss that may be stirred up. Some children wanted to meet their birth parents and, after an exploration of the issues by the Houghton Committee, which began to sit in 1972, adoption records were opened for any adopted person when they reached 18, subject to prior counselling by an adoption practitioner. The adoption triangle of adopted person, adopters and birth parents became a 'to be lived' reality. Searching for birth parents by adopted adults and by birth parents for their now adopted children became a significant activity pursued by many. The resulting reunions were emotional and largely positive expe-

Policy

riences, although for most they did not replace the sense of belonging and commitment established in the adoptive family (Howe and Feast, 2003; Triseliotis et al., 2005).

Further exploration of these issues also established the significance of contact arrangements for children prior to their 18th birthday. Exchanges of information, photographs and birthday and Christmas cards became common, although usually mediated by the adoption agency to preserve confidentiality. Occasionally, direct contact arrangements were made with birth families. The drawing of the boundary around the 'nuclear family', a significant postwar phenomenon, became challenged by the experiences of adopted children with both a 'born to' family and a 'lived with' family. Concerns continued to be expressed by child development specialists about the risks posed by such arrangements: Could children, faced by all the challenges of adoption, develop 'normally' and do as well as children living with their birth parents in 'ordinary' circumstances? The answer to that question is largely 'yes, they do' – across a range of significant measures, including attachment, physical development, educational and cognitive development, self-esteem and wellbeing (van Ijzendoorn and Juffer, 2006). If one factor stands out from research about what contributes to this, it is that the younger the child is placed, the better the outcomes.

The one area where there has been significant controversy has been in respect of the adoption of black and minority ethnic children by white adopters – transracial adoption. A study by Gill and Jackson (1983) of children transracially adopted through the British Adoption Project (1965–69) caused a storm of protest when it established that, while the children had done well across a range of developmental measures, questions remained about the long-term impact on the child of being dislocated from their ethnic and cultural heritage. The study was published at a time when the UK was emerging from its colonial past and the reality of racism, oppression and discrimination was troubling society's conscience. The adoption of black children by white couples was seen as evidence of the colonization of the black community by removing its children and 'making them white'. Similar issues have arisen with intercountry adoption. In Europe and in many other countries in the world, this is the dominant form of adoption. In the UK, the numbers are relatively small. Again, the issue of transracial placements has significantly influenced the views about the acceptability of removing children from their family, country, culture, language and religion and placing them with adopters who are likely to be different in every respect. Arguments about the alternative of leaving these children in institutions, with all that that results in, have had some force but not sufficient to hold sway in the heated debates.

If there were earlier fears about the child's 'inheritance' contaminating the family through adoption, this then became a new fear about the adoptive family contaminating the child's ethnic and cultural inheritance. Social work quickly took up the racism at the centre of this argument and transracial adoption was vigorously and determinedly opposed. As a consequence, a commitment to same-race placements became a dominant and driving force in adoption policy and practice. It is only recently, as society has emerged into a more complex mix of established and newly arrived ethnic groups, that this policy has been challenged, especially in the light of the serious delays experienced by many minority ethnic children in care, which, in some cases, has meant that they are not placed for adoption at all.

The battleground is redrawn

Adoption has changed in other respects in its role of meeting the needs of 'hard to place' children. The Adoption Act 1976 (ss. 18(1)(b), 16(2)) reinforced the legal possibility of courts dispensing with the consent of the birth parents if specified conditions were met. These conditions focused on those parents who could not adequately care for their children where there was evidence that the children were being seriously abused and/or neglected. The earlier powerful motivational forces of social stigma and shame on the mother and the personal and societal belief that 'your child' could only have a happy and successful life if they were put up for adoption came to be replaced by the state taking a primary role in protecting children and, where necessary, legally separating them from their birth parents and placing them with state-approved adopters. An adoption system driven by social pressures became a state-driven system focused on the management of serious parenting deficits. Local authorities and the courts were charged with identifying qualities of parenting so detrimental to a child's safety and welfare that the child's future development could only be met if they were legally removed from their parents and placed for adoption.

While, in law, the parents' consent to adoption remained and remains legally possible and preferable, in the emerging context of abuse and neglect, this was less likely. Birth parents are likely to resist or oppose the local authority's case that they had abused or neglected their child and that there was little likelihood of them being able to change that. If adoption was the plan, then it was much more likely in these circumstances that consent would need to be dispensed with by the court, because the best interests of the child in the long term required it. The adoption process fundamentally changed into an active legal contest between the state and the birth parent/s, which centred around the culpability of the parent/s in respect of abuse and/or neglect and the likelihood that they will not or cannot change sufficiently to adequately care for their child. Given that the outcome of this legal contest is that the child is legally and irrevocably separated from their birth parents, it is one of the most severe sanctions the state can impose, albeit that it is justified for the greater good of the child whose interests are legally paramount. The emergence of the 'psychological' and the discovery of abuse have therefore combined with the legal to transform adoption primarily into a solution for child abuse and neglect. The contamination of the social classes through the adoption of 'lower class' children and the preservation of property, rights and title has been transformed into the restoration of abused and neglected children to a healthier developmental pathway available from psychologically mature adopters.

At the same time as adoption was changing its focus towards the restoration of family life for abused and neglected children, a more general development was taking place that created a framework of human rights designed to protect the individual

Policy

and the family from undue state interference. It was a framework that first became enshrined in the 1950 European Convention on Human Rights and subsequently in domestic legislation in the Human Rights Act 1998. In terms of children, the well-regarded Children Act 1989 in England and Wales reflected this in making the welfare of the child the paramount consideration in any decisions a court might make; it established a 'welfare checklist' that the court had to satisfy itself about in those decisions and a principle of 'no order' unless a resolution of the child's welfare interests could not be met in any other way.

A principle running through the Act was that of partnership between parents and local authorities. Local authorities were to provide a range of services for parents and their children, and parents were to avail themselves of those services. Social workers were key to ensuring that the links between services and families were made and had a key role in assessing needs and providing those services under the fundamental public service reforms of 'managerialism' and the 'purchaser/provider split'. The place of adoption in this emerging framework became less certain as the principle of partnership seemed fundamentally in opposition to the draconian steps of legal separation. Adoption figures were in decline over this period as a result. This was not helped by the absence of new adoption legislation that reflected the framework of the Children Act 1989. Indeed, despite a draft bill introduced in the mid-1990s, it was not until 2002 and the Adoption and Children Act that complementary legislation was enacted and that did not come fully into force until the end of 2005.

The modernization of the adoption agenda

The new Act resulted from the *Prime Minister's Review of Adoption* (Performance and Innovation Unit, 2000) and an adoption White Paper (DH, 2000). Before the Act was implemented, a considerable investment of money, targets and performance indicators was aimed at increasing the rate of adoption by 38%. The whole policy and legislative thrust was to increase the use of adoption, reduce delay in placing children for adoption, provide a modernized adoption support framework and generally tighten up on adoption processes – both domestically and internationally. While the welfare of the child was the dominant value of this reform programme, other changes reflected important social trends, particularly the idea of family life loosened from the model of a two-parent, heterosexual couple of middle-class values. Gay and lesbian couples were allowed to jointly adopt, and guidance stressed that agencies were to welcome applications from all sections of society, whether they were single or a couple, married, in civil partnerships or living together, young or old, well off or on benefits, able-bodied or disabled. The fundamental issue was parenting capacity not social status.

The long-term recovery of children from early adversity

The 2002 Adoption and Children Act further reinforced the dominance of the psychological in parenting and family life over social status. This was also reflected in another emerging issue – the recognition that adoption did not end at the making of the adoption order. While the order marked a significant transition for the child from state care to a private family life, the long-term consequences of abuse and neglect on the child's development and subsequently on the adoptive parent/s were identified as long-term issues. There was a real possibility that, for many adoptive families, access to specialist support services would be necessary to address emotional, behavioural and learning difficulties issues arising from contact arrangements with birth parents or other family members, or to receive financial and practical support. The Act acknowledged that these could be required at any point in the life of the child/adult or the other two parties in the adoption triangle. If earlier fears in the history of adoption had focused on the heritability of the values and standing of the lower classes and the spoiling of those issues for the adoptive family, this was now significantly reworked. There was an explicit recognition that, whether through inherited characteristics or the impact of early abusive experience, there was likely to be a long shadow cast over the child and the adoptive family that would need to be directly addressed through the psychological insights, strengths and flexibility of the adopters and their support systems. Contamination had become firmly built in to adoption policy and practice, although reformulated with a modern interpretation.

The impact of the adoption reform programme

The New Labour reforms were intended to provide an alternative route for children with the worst of possible starts in life. The first five years of that programme following the Prime Minister's Review in 2000 demonstrated a significant increase in the numbers of children placed and came close to the target set of increasing that number by 38%. However, the five years following implementation of the Act at the end of 2005 show a decrease (see Figure 11.2). A number of factors may account for this. Delays in the court system have become severe, caused by a number of factors:

- the level of demand
- the complexity of public law cases
- the severity of what is at stake when adoption is being considered
- the continual testing of parents' motivation and their capacity to change
- the exploration of alternative plans, particularly the placement of the child in their wider family or with friends – the availability of a new legal order, 'special guardianship', reinforced the potential for this type of alternative plan
- the lack of expertise and confidence among social workers in presenting a sound case in court.

Despite a continuing focus on reducing delay, the average age of children at the making of an adoption order has stubbornly remained around four years. The average length of time from the court agreeing that the child should be placed for adoption also stubbornly remained up to a year, with a significant number of cases averaging over a year. Most worrying of all, a significant number of children who had adoption as the plan were never placed for adoption. So, despite the clear lifelong advantages of adoption and the overriding principle of the welfare of the child, the law, the courts, local authorities and the professions had become so entangled in a system of endless complexity, with checks and balances impinging on every part of that process, that the primary objective had become too challenging in too many cases to deliver. The election of a new government in 2010 resulted in a new wave of adoption reform, albeit in the context of significant public spending cuts. The focus, as with the previous reform programme, was on reducing delay, the more explicit expectation that children from minority ethnic backgrounds would be placed with white adopters, and the greater use of the voluntary adoption sector. This was set within a major review of the family justice system and a review of child care social work.

> **Making connexions**
> 'The younger the child is placed, the better the outcomes.'
>
> Why, then, has the average age at adoption 'stubbornly remained around four years' and the 'average length of time from the court agreeing that the child should be placed for adoption stubbornly remained up to a year, with a significant number of cases averaging over a year'?

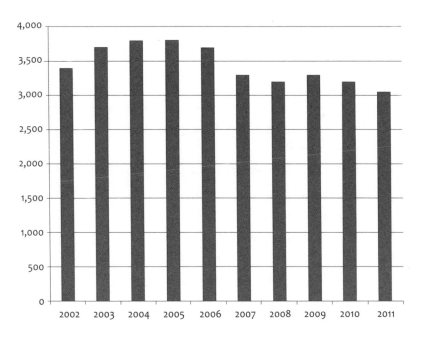

Figure 11.2 The number of children adopted from care in England, per annum, 2002–11
Source: Department of Education

Conclusion

As with every area of public policy, adoption reflects fundamental beliefs in the nature of society and, particularly, family life and the position of children. These beliefs change and adoption has changed as the definitions of childhood, the family and social order and social coherence have changed. Adoption practice also reflects wider policy shifts. In the past 20 years, the rise of a centralized state driven by a belief in managerial control, inspection, accountability and detailed guidance has had a significant impact on adoption and there is some evidence that this has not been to the advantage of children, especially when age at adoption is such an important evidence-based factor in establishing better outcomes.

It is important not to be drawn into simple technical debates about improving adoption policy and practice without setting them within the context of public policy and the drivers and context for that policy. Any debate at one moment in time will have strident advocates and detractors but maybe, even just a generation on, the arguments will have lost their meaning and sense. So much depends on one's perspective. The needs, rights and welfare of children and particularly those children who are most at risk have a powerful draw in policy. But theirs is not the only perspective. Perspectives change depending on the position one is viewing them from. Controversy and conflict have marked and will continue to mark the development of adoption policy and practice for years to come.

Note

1   At the time of writing and for the foreseeable future, no such incentives apply.

Further reading

■ Harris, P. (2008) *The Colours in Me: Writing and Poetry by Adopted Children and Young People*. London: BAAF.

Collection of writings and other material from young people who have been adopted.

■ Hindle, D. and Shulman, G. (eds) (2008) *The Emotional Experience of Adoption: A Psychoanalytic Perspective*. London: Routledge.

Collection of papers exploring the more recent psychological perspectives on adoption practice from a variety of personal and clinical perspectives.

■ Schofield, G. and Simmonds, J. (eds) (2009) *The Child Placement Handbook: Research, Policy and Practice*. London: BAAF.

Collection of chapters from leading researchers and practitioners on various aspects of child placement including comprehensive sections on adoption.

References

Bowlby, J. (1988) *A Secure Base: Parent-Child Attachment and Healthy Human Development*. New York: Basic Books.

DH (Department of Health) (2000) *Adoption: A New Approach*. London: DH

Fahlberg, V. (1994) *A Child's Journey Through Placement*. London: BAAF.

Gill, O. and Jackson, B. (1983) *Adoption and Race: Black, Asian and Mixed Race Children in White Families*. London: Batsford/BAFF.

Goldstein, J., Freud, A. and Solnit, A.J. (1980) *Before the Best Interests of the Child*. London: Burnett Books.

Howe, D. and Feast, J. (2003) *Adoption, Search and Reunion: The Long-term Experience of Adopted Adults*. London: BAFF.

Pearson, G., Treseder, J. and Yelloly, M. (eds) (1988) *Social Work and the Legacy of Freud: Psychoanalysis and its Uses*. Basingstoke: Macmillan Education.

Performance and Innovation Unit (2000) *Prime Minister's Review of Adoption*. London: Cabinet Office.

Robertson, J. and Robertson J. (n.d.) Robertson Films, http://www.robertsonfilms.info/useful_links.htm.

Rowe, J. and Lambert, L. (1973) *Children Who Wait: A Study of Children Needing Substitute Families*. London: BAFF.

Simmonds, J. (2000) 'The adoption narrative: stories that we tell and those that we can't', in A. Treacher and I. Katz (eds) *The Dynamics of Adoption*. London: Jessica Kingsley.

Simmonds, J. (2008) 'Developing a curosity about adoption: a psychoanalytic perspective', in D. Hindle and G. Shulman (eds) *The Emotional Experience of Adoption*. London: Routledge.

Triseliotis, J.P., Howe, D., Feast, J. and Kyle, F. (2005) *The Adoption Triangle Revisited: A Study of Adoption, Search and Reunion Experiences*. London: BAAF.

Van Ijzendoorn, M.H. and Juffer, F. (2006) 'The Emanuel Miller Memorial Lecture 2006: adoption as intervention. Meta-analytic evidence for massive catch-up and plasticity in physical, socio-emotional, and cognitive development', *Journal of Child Psychology and Psychiatry*, **47**(12): 1228–45.

Yelloly, M. (1980) *Social Work Theory and Psychoanalysis*. New York: Van Nostrand Reinhold.

Policy

12

Legal perspectives on social work in adoption and fostering

CAROLINE BALL

If, for whatever reason, a child cannot live with their own family, either temporarily or on a long-term basis, placement in another family rather than an institution has, since the seminal child care reforming statute, the Children Act 1948, been the preferred option. Fostering and adoption feature on a placement spectrum, ranging from the short-term provision of local authority accommodation in an emergency to securing an adoption order, which irrevocably and for life severs the legal link between the child and their birth family and vests all parental rights, duties and responsibilities in the adoptive family. Between the two extremes are other legally disparate arrangements that may better meet the individual needs of children and young people seeking the security of a permanent placement away from their birth family. The spectrum includes:

- foster care: accommodation for children 'in need'
- private fostering
- foster care under a care order
- residence orders
- special guardianship
- adoption.

This chapter explores the policy and legal development of the regulation of fostering and adoption in England and Wales. It goes on to consider the current legal framework within which social workers make decisions regarding the placement of children outside their birth families and concludes with a brief reflection on current concerns and possible developments.

Development of the regulation of fostering and adoption

Despite widespread recognition of the need for regulation, and several attempts with regard to fostering, there was little effective regulation of fostering and none of adoption in England and Wales until the second quarter of the twentieth century. The first law regulating the care of children, the Infant Life Protection Act 1872, was passed in response to the deaths of numerous children looked after for reward by so-called 'baby farmers'. Several statutory provisions followed, but none proved effective in terms of improving the lot of the children involved, least of all the transfer to the Poor Law guardians, under the Prevention of Cruelty to Children Act 1889, of parental responsibility for children removed from their parents on the grounds of mistreatment or neglect.

The regulation of foster care: 1900 to the present day

For most of the first half of the twentieth century, the majority of children 'deprived of a normal home life' (Curtis, 1946, p. 1) were maintained by local authorities under Poor Law provisions as persons in need of relief. The Poor Law Act 1930 consolidated earlier enactments for the relief of the poor, and was administered by local authorities generally acting through public assistance committees. The duty of the local authority in regard to children was expressed in bleak terms: 'To set to work or put out as apprentices all children whose parents are not, in the opinion of the Council, able to keep and maintain their children' (s. 15).

The 1930 Act also allowed local authorities to assume parental rights over orphans or abandoned children and those whose parents were deemed unfit to have care of a child.

Under all these provisions, children could be placed in a wide range of institutions, including many run by voluntary organizations. Certain children, initially orphans and deserted children and those over whom the local authority had assumed parental rights, could also be boarded out in foster homes. During and after the Second World War (1939–45), the rules regarding eligibility for boarding out were relaxed and finally abolished. The whole system for placing children away from their homes was one of infinite complexity, involving three government departments and a confusing web of local statutory and voluntary committees. In a letter to *The Times* (5 July 1944), Lady Allen of Hurtwood stated that within the institutions, many children suffered 'repressive conditions that are generations out of date', together with the 'chilly stigma of charity'. The campaigning of Lady Allen and others, and the public outcry that followed the death of Dennis O'Neill at the hands of his foster parents in January 1945, led to the setting up of the Care of Children Committee, chaired by Myra Curtis. Its terms of reference were (Curtis, 1946, p. 1):

> to inquire into existing methods of providing for children who from loss of parents or from any other cause whatever are deprived of a normal home life with their own parents or relatives; and to consider what further measures should be

taken to ensure that these children are brought up under conditions best calculated to compensate them for the lack of parental care.

The Curtis Committee made a large number of mostly unannounced visits to observe conditions in all types of institutions and foster homes across England and Wales, as well as minutely analysing the ways in which the system was administered. The committee's report describes, in measured but painfully graphic terms, 'a picture of administrative chaos and human suffering' (Griffith, 1966, p. 361). In particular, it identified:

■ the problems arising from the overlapping responsibilities of several government departments devolved to a confused network of local committees
■ the high numbers of children poorly cared for in low-quality, impersonal institutions
■ the lack of child care expertise among those working with children.

At a time when 86% of children maintained by public assistance authorities were placed in children's homes, voluntary homes and hospitals, the committee was in no doubt, as had been advocated by the Mundella Committee at the end of the nineteenth century (George, 1970), that the placement of choice should be foster care and, for those with no hope of returning to their families, adoption.

The committee's recommendations were robust and, it has been suggested, resulted in reforms considerably more radical than those appointing the committee intended (Cretney, 1997). As well as the shift away from the bleak duty in the Poor Law Act 1930, referred to above, there was to be a focus on the welfare of the individual child in decision-making. Other recommendations included:

■ a single department of state, the Home Office, to have overall responsibility for children cared for away from their homes
■ local authorities to appoint dedicated children's committees employing experienced and suitably qualified children's officers to exercise statutory powers and duties in regard to children in their area
■ a determined drive to recruit more foster parents, with the aim of ultimately phasing out institutional care.

The Children Act 1948 enacted most of the Curtis Committee's recommendations, and moving children from institutions into foster care, governed by Boarding Out Regulations made under the Act, resulted in a significant increase in the use of foster care (Packman, 1975).

Throughout the next 40 years, various statutory reforms impacted on foster care as on all other areas of child care practice.

Preventive powers

The provision of supportive services to prevent the need for children to be removed from their homes was identified by the Curtis Committee as an essential responsibility for local authorities. Unfortunately, its terms of reference precluded the committee making recommendations to that effect. Following a sustained campaign (Packman, 1975, Ch. 4), this deficit was remedied when the terms of reference for a Home Office committee under the chairmanship of Lord Ingleby, set up in 1956, included the direction to 'inquire into and make recommendations' on 'Whether local authorities should ... be given new powers and duties to prevent or forestall the suffering of children through neglect in their own homes' (Home Office, 1960, p. 1). In response to the Ingleby Committee's recommendations, provisions introducing the power to undertake preventive work with families were enacted in the Children and Young Persons Act 1963, section 1: 'It shall be the duty of every local authority to make available such advice, guidance and assistance as may promote the welfare of children by diminishing the need to receive children into or keep them in care.'

Local authorities' powers and responsibilities, 1969–89

The period 1969–89 saw the complete reorganization of local authority social services into generic social work departments (Local Authority Social Services Act 1970), with a consequent loss of social work child care expertise. This was followed by a raft of legislation (Children and Young Persons Act 1969, Children Act 1975, Adoption Act 1976 and Foster Children Act 1980), the effect of which was to considerably increase local authorities' responsibilities and discretion as to how their powers were exercised (Packman et al., 1986).

By the early 1980s, for a variety of well-explored reasons (see, for example, Ormrod, 1983; Ball, 1990), the state of public child law was seen to be frustrating rather than helping good child care practice. In the words of a group of lawyers and social workers giving evidence to the House of Commons Social Services Committee, which had chosen for its 1983/4 session the topic of 'children in care':

> The present state of children's legislation can only be described as complex, confusing and unsatisfactory ... The effect and implication of this on children is diverse with far-reaching consequences for their welfare. (House of Commons, 1984, para. 118)

The evidence for these assertions was well demonstrated by the findings of a substantial body of government-funded research into all aspects of social work decision-making within the existing statutory framework (DHSS, 1985). These studies identified a range of poor practice, including:

- defensive, ill-planned crisis interventions in families already well known to social services departments, with overuse of statutory provisions rather than voluntary care (Packman et al., 1986)
- the lack of active work to maintain links between children in care and their birth families, resulting in lengthy care episodes and many children losing all contact with their families (Millham et al., 1986).

Law

The need for root-and-branch reform of not only public child law, but all aspects of the private law relating to children, which had from the late 1970s been subject to scrutiny by the Law Commission, was accepted by government, and the reform process is well documented (see, for example, Ball, 1990; Masson, 2000; White et al., 2008, Ch. 1). The Children Act 1989 (CA 1989), described by the Lord Chancellor Lord MacKay as 'the most comprehensive and far-reaching reform of child law which has come before Parliament in living memory' (*Hansard*, 1988, HL Deb, 502, col. 488), came into force in 1991. It transformed public and private child law with shared concepts and a single set of principles, administered in a coherent court structure. The cornerstone of the CA 1989, Part III, which builds on and substantially expands previous preventive provisions, provides for services for children in need, including accommodation of the child, in partnership with families.

Developments relevant to foster care, 1991–2011

Many of the post-1991 amendments to Part III reflect a growing recognition of the extent to which the life chances of children growing up for most or part of their childhood as 'looked after' children in the public care, whether under care orders (Part IV) or on a voluntary basis under Part III, suffer grave social and educational disadvantage. The Children (Leaving Care) Act 2000 and the Children and Young Persons Act 2008 amended Part III of the CA 1989 to considerably extend the responsibilities of local authorities to previously looked after children. These responsibilities were further increased as a result of the House of Lords decision in the so-called 'Southwark judgment' that homeless 16- and 17-year-olds should be regarded as children in need under section 17 and accommodated by local authorities rather than being placed in bed and breakfast accommodation under homelessness legislation (*R (on the application of G)* v *London Borough of Southwark* [2009]).

The Children Act 2004 provides the statutory framework for implementation for the *Every Child Matters* agenda to improve outcomes with regard to health, staying safe, enjoying and achieving, making a positive contribution and achieving economic wellbeing for all children. However, when compared to all children, outcomes for looked after children were recognized to be very poor and in need of further statutory support (DfES, 2006). The Children and Young Persons Act 2008 enacted the proposals in the White Paper *Care Matters: Time for Change* requiring legislation (DfES, 2007).

The regulation of adoption: 1926 to the present day

The UK lagged well behind most of the rest of the world in recognizing legal adoption (Lowe, 2000). In practice, de facto adoption had always existed and was particularly well established in Scotland. Children were brought up outside their birth families by agreement and without any legal security for the 'adoptive' parents.

Without recourse to costly and risky litigation, the people who had raised the child were, unless extreme cruelty on the part of the birth parents could be proved, unable to resist demands for their return.

With the rise of concern about and professional interest in children's welfare in the 1920s came increased recognition of the unsatisfactory nature of unregulated adoption and a more vociferous demand for legal adoption that would spare children the stigma of illegitimacy and secure their place within adoptive families. Such demands met considerable opposition, and it was only after two departmental committee reports (Home Department, 1921, 1925) and six failed bills that the Adoption Act 1926 finally reached the statute book. Implemented in 1927, it introduced an order effecting the complete and irrevocable transfer of the child from the birth family to the adopters for all purposes apart from succession.

Reform of adoption law, after the introduction of legal adoption in 1926 and prior to 1975, was largely concerned with regulating the process of adoption to eliminate perceived abuses, and equating the adopted child's legal status within the adoptive family more closely with that of birth children for the purposes of inheritance. Lowe (2000) provides a detailed account of these developments and the increased professionalization of adoption practice.

The waxing and waning of adoption

Contrary to the expectations of the 1925 Tomlin Committee, which had anticipated that there would always be more people wishing 'to get rid of children by way of adoption' (Home Department, 1925, para. 19) than couples wanting children, adoption proved popular.

Adoption statistics, beyond the numbers of orders made annually (and even they are somewhat unreliable), are recognized to be woefully inadequate. Because of the failure to collect and record essential data, many of the vital questions properly asked by researchers and policy-makers remain unanswered and unanswerable (Dance, 1997; Triseliotis et al., 1997). Despite this, and some disparity between the numbers of adoption orders recorded according to the source of the statistics, there is no doubt about the overall trends over the last 75 years. The number of orders rose, with some fluctuations, from nearly 3,000 orders in 1927 to a high of almost 25,000 in 1968, before dropping to a little over 4,000 by the end of the twentieth century. The reasons for this remarkable shift are well understood – effective methods of contraception, the legalization of abortion, changing social mores, and the availability of social housing and benefits for unmarried mothers all contributed to a drastic reduction in the number of babies becoming available for adoption, and, over the same period, the age of children adopted rose (Lowe, 2000; Ball, 2002).

There were two quite separate but parallel responses to the rapid decline in the number of healthy white babies available for adoption in the 1970s. As in all other developed Western states, childless couples with means, and determined to adopt a baby, started to look to the developing world and Eastern Europe. Others were encouraged to accept older and 'hard to place' children with disabilities, or those children who were unable to return to their birth families from local authority care.

The Adoption Act 1958 was the last major reform of the law undertaken while the number of adoption orders made annually was still rising. The adoption reforms in the Children Act 1975, consolidated with the 1958 Act into the Adoption Act 1976, reflect some recognition of the changes in the adoptive population that were just starting and would accelerate throughout the rest of the century. However, by the time the 1976 Act was fully implemented in 1988, changes in adoption practice had overtaken not only the long-lasting provisions from earlier legislation but also many of the reforms in the 1975 Act. The need for a new legal framework for the adoption of children from care, often with continuing complex needs and a baggage of relationships with members of their birth family and others, was well supported by research (Lowe et al., 1999). It was also widely recognized and advocated by professional bodies and all the leading child care organizations, but still took nearly two decades to achieve (Ball, 2002).

Essentially what was demonstrated from 1992 onwards, with an increasing, research-informed understanding of the complexity of practice (Lowe et al., 1999), was the need for a regulatory framework, which:

- put children's welfare throughout their lives at the heart of agency and court decision-making
- aligned adoption law as far as possible with the principles and concepts in the CA 1989
- supported and encouraged adoption or other permanent and secure arrangements for children who could not return to their birth families
- required local authorities to support all those involved in adoption with a range of services available before and, for many, for long after the making of the adoption order
- encouraged the continuation of meaningful relationships from the past, while allowing for there to be no continuing contact where the child's welfare required there to be none
- respected the human rights of all parties, including relatives separated through adoption
- incorporated, very importantly, the regulation of intercountry adoption.

The Adoption and Children Act 2002 (ACA 2002) came fully into force on 30 December 2005. It substantially reformed adoption law in England and Wales and amended the CA 1989, most significantly in regard to this chapter, through the introduction of the new legal concept of special guardianship. Full details of the raft of regulations made under the ACA 2002 can be accessed on the website of the British Association for Adoption and Fostering (www.baaf.org.uk). Revised departmental guidance was published in February 2011 (DfE, 2011a).

It should be noted that, despite government targets to increase the numbers of children adopted from care prior to implementation of the ACA 2002 in 2005, the numbers have not increased and, by 2010, at 4,550, were at their lowest for a decade (ONS, 2010).

The spectrum of legal provision for the placement of children

Looked after children: Children Act 1989, Part III

Children are looked after by the local authority if they are provided with accommodation:

- on a voluntary basis as a child in need in the infinitely wide circumstances set out in section 20, which concludes with the catch-all: 'the person who has been caring for him being prevented (whether or not permanently and for whatever reason) from providing him with suitable accommodation or care'. Accommodation under section 20 is an arrangement about where a child will live made with the agreement of those with parental responsibility, who may remove a child at any time.
- under a care order made under section 31, which allows the local authority to exercise parental responsibility for the duration of the order (s. 33).
- in police protection, detention, or on remand.

The local authority, as a corporate parent, has a duty to safeguard and promote the welfare of looked after children, including a particular duty to promote educational achievement, and to make such use of services available for children cared for by their own parents as appear reasonable (ss. 22(3)(a), 22(3A)). As we have seen, the functions of local authorities in relation to children who are looked after by them, as set out in the CA 1989, have been significantly amended by subsequent legislation: Children (Leaving Care) Act 2000, Adoption and Children Act 2002, Children Act 2004, and the Children and Young Persons Act 2008.

Choice of placement

- The first choice is for placement with a parent or person with parental responsibility, unless it would not be consistent with the child's welfare or reasonably practicable (ss. 22C(3), 22C(4)).
- If placement under section 22C(3) is not possible, then the next choice is placement with relatives or friends who have been approved as local authority foster carers (ss. 22C(5), 22C(6)), or in an emergency situation and for a limited period have satisfied less stringent requirements, or
- placement with approved foster carers, or in a children's home or hostel.

The wishes and feelings of the child about the placement should be sought and given due consideration.

Law

Revised statutory guidance (DfE, 2011b, 2011c) and the consolidated Care Planning, Placement and Case Review (England) Regulations 2010, predicated on a set of 'good social care practice' principles that reflect the intentions in the CA 1989 (paras. 1.5, 1.6), came into force in 2011. The guidance and regulations provide a detailed framework regulating the planning, placement and regular review of all looked after children, as well as local authorities' duties to those who cease to be looked after (DfE, 2010).

Private fostering arrangements, Children Act 1989, section 66

A child is privately fostered if under 16 (18 if disabled) and cared for and accommodated by someone other than a parent, someone with parental responsibility, or close relative. The definition excludes children looked after in this way for less than 28 days when it is not intended that the arrangement should last for longer. These arrangements have been described as 'among the least controlled and most open to abuse of all the environments in which children live away from home' (Utting, 1997).

Enacting many of the recommendations of the inquiry into the death of Victoria Climbié, who was privately fostered, sections 44–47 of the Children Act 2004 amended the law on private fostering arrangements and the role of the local authority in respect of the Children (Private Arrangements for Fostering) Regulations 2005. The Act provides for a notification scheme, which has been in force since 2005 (Children (Private Arrangements for Fostering) Regulations 2005), and for a registration scheme, long called for by many commentators and all leading child care organizations (Philpot, 2001). There is a time-limited power to introduce a registration scheme, but it has not yet been implemented.

Many local authorities make considerable efforts to encourage the reporting of private fostering arrangements, but there is general recognition that the number of notifications is much lower than the actual incidence (www.privatefostering.org.uk).

Private law orders: Children Act 1989, Part II

Residence orders

Residence orders under section 8, settling the arrangements as to the person with whom a child under 16 (or, in exceptional circumstances, 18) is to live, are mostly, but not only, used in disputes between parents. They may also be applied for by relatives, foster parents or others, if they qualify under section 10 to make an application as of right, or with leave of the court. The residence order may be made in favour of one or more people and gives parental responsibility for the child for its duration. Parents who had parental responsibility prior to the making of the order do not lose it and may apply as of right to have the order discharged.

Law

Special guardianship

Special guardianship, enacted by the ACA 2002, amends the CA 1989 by the introduction of sections 14A–14F. A special guardianship order provides a more secure placement for a child than a residence order without the termination of the legal relationship with the birth family effected by adoption. The birth parents remain legally the child's parents but with minimal power to exercise parental responsibility. A special guardian may, in the same way as a parent with parental responsibility, appoint another person to be the child's guardian in the event of their death. Although, in contrast to an adoption order, special guardianship orders can be discharged or varied by a court, applications cannot be made within the first year of the making of the order, and after that only with leave 'if there has been a significant change of circumstances' since the order was made (s. 14D(5)). The process of approving and supporting special guardians is subject to the Special Guardianship Regulations 2005, which to a large extent mirror adoption regulations.

Adoption orders: Adoption and Children Act 2002, Part I

An adoption order effects the irrevocable legal transfer of a child from the birth family to the adoptive family. As we have seen, although originally a private law arrangement, it is now also the preferred outcome for many children in local authority care who are unable to return to their birth families. All local authorities are adoption agencies, and there are now very few approved independent adoption agencies. The whole adoption process is strictly regulated under the ACA 2002 and its accompanying regulations, guidance and the National Minimum Standards for Adoption. The first revision of the *Adoption Guidance: Adoption and Children Act 2002* (DfE, 2011a) provides detailed practice guidance relating to local authority adoption agency arrangements and all aspects of the adoption process before and after the making of an adoption order.

A detailed account of the legal requirements throughout the process is beyond the remit of this chapter (for more details, see Probert, 2009, Ch. 15; DfE, 2011a). What follows are the bare bones in regard to the adoption of looked after children.

Underlying principles

In provisions mirroring those in section 1 of the CA 1989, the ACA 2002 requires that every court and adoption agency, when coming to any decision relating to the adoption of a child, must:

- have the welfare of the child throughout his life as its paramount consideration
- 'bear in mind that, in general, any delay in coming to a decision is likely to prejudice the child's welfare' (s. 1(3))
- pay regard to the checklist of issues set out in section 1(4) regarding the child's

wishes and feelings, existing relationships, particular needs and so on, and the child's religious persuasion, ethnic origin and cultural and linguistic background

■ consider the whole range of powers available to it in the child's case, and not make any order unless it considers that 'making the order would be better for the child than not doing so' (s. 1(6)).

Eligibility to adopt and to be adopted

Under the ACA 2002, married or heterosexual or single-sex unmarried couples and single people are legally able to adopt a child. The suitability of prospective adoptive parents has to be decided by the local authority adoption panel or an approved adoption agency, and prospective adopters have a right of appeal against rejection of their application (DfE, 2011a, Ch. 2; Independent Review of Determinations (Adoption and Fostering) Regulations 2009).

Making connexions

The Adoption and Children Act 2002 requires any decision relating to the adoption of a child to 'have the welfare of the child throughout his life as its paramount consideration'.

In your opinion, is it likely that social workers will start from a presumption for or against adoption? What are the implications of this?

In a minority of cases, a birth parent will ask a local authority or voluntary adoption agency, possibly before the birth, to place a child for adoption. The majority of cases will involve children looked after by the local authority and not able to return to their birth family, for whom adoption is considered as part of the planning process (DfE, 2011a). The case should be referred to the adoption panel within six weeks of the decision regarding adoption as the preferred outcome being taken, and the panel should recommend whether the child should be placed for adoption within two months of a review where adoption has been identified as the permanence plan.

Placement for adoption by agencies

The ACA 2002 introduced new provisions for the placement of children for adoption, replacing the deeply unsatisfactory freeing for adoption provisions in the 1976 Act (see, for example, *Re C (Adoption: Freeing Order)* [1999]). Under the ACA 2002, an adoption agency may only place a child for adoption (except where the child is less than six weeks old, in which case the mother cannot give valid consent (s. 52(3)), or where it has placed a child, leave the child with the persons with whom they are placed as prospective adopters, with the consent of the parents or guardian, or under a placement order made by a court. Local authorities have the same responsibilities towards children placed for adoption as they do to other 'looked after' children (CA 1989, s. 23, see above).

Where parents are seeking their child's adoption, the child may be placed without a court order under section 19 and parents may give advanced consent to the making of an adoption order. Under section 19, they may subsequently withdraw agreement and require return of the child at any time before an application is made to court for an adoption order (ss. 36–40).

Where the child is an orphan, or parents with parental responsibility are not consenting, and the local authority is satisfied that the child ought to be placed for adoption, it must obtain a placement order. Even if consent to placement has been given, provided that the criteria for making a placement order are satisfied, the local authority may apply for a placement order in order to prevent parents withdrawing their consent and requiring return of the child, which they will only be able to do if the placement order is revoked.

Courts may only make a placement order if the child is an orphan, or the subject of a care order, or the court finds the 'significant harm' threshold conditions for making a care order under section 31(2) of the CA 1989 satisfied; and, except where the child has no parent or guardian, the parents consent or the court dispenses with their consent, and, in all cases, the section 1 welfare criteria are satisfied.

When a placement order is made, parents require leave to apply for revocation, and courts can only grant leave if satisfied that the circumstances have changed (ss. 24(2), 24(3)). Also, where there has been a placement order, parents cannot oppose the making of an adoption order without leave, with the same proviso (s. 47). For how the courts have interpreted this provision, see *M* v *Warwickshire County Council* [2007], and *Re P (Adoption: Leave Provisions)* [2007]).

Dispensing with parental consent to placement for, or adoption

Under section 52 of the ACA 2002, the list of grounds on which a court can dispense with parental consent under the 1976 Act – of which the most commonly relied on was 'unreasonably withholding' – was replaced by just two:

- that the parent or guardian cannot be found or is incapable of giving consent, or
- the welfare of the child requires the consent to be dispensed with.

Post-adoption contact

The value to the children concerned of some form of post-adoption contact with members of their birth family, or others of importance in their past, except those for whom such an arrangement would clearly not be in the interests of their welfare, is now generally recognized (Young and Neil, 2009). Before making an adoption order, the court has to consider any existing or proposed arrangements for contact and elicit the views of parties to the proceedings (s. 46(6)). The presumption is that such arrangements will be by agreement. In the exceptional cases in which an order for contact is made at the same time as the adoption order, or is needed if adopters have reneged on agreed contact, contact orders are made under section 8 of the CA 1989 – the section used for regulating disputed contact arrangements in all private law family proceedings. Post-adoption, applications by former parents and others for orders under section 8 can only be made with leave of the court (CA 1989, s. 10).

Step-parent adoptions

The adoption of a child by a parent and step-parent, which in the past accounted for a large number of adoption orders, was recognized by the Haughton Committee, as long ago as 1972, as being detrimental to children because it deprived the child of all legal connection with half of their birth family (Home Office/Scottish Education Department, 1972). Section 4A of the CA 1989, which allows a step-parent to acquire parental responsibility through a parental order either with the consent of all with parental responsibility, or a court order, without separating the child from the birth family, was a welcome development.

Access to information for birth relatives

Adopted adults have had the right since 1976 to access their original birth certificates, although actually tracing relatives has been fraught with difficulties (Triseliotis et al., 2005). For birth relatives searching for an adopted child or sibling, and with no corresponding right to information which might aid the search, the chances of success were remote in the extreme. The Adoption Contact Register, introduced under the CA 1989, took a tentative step in the direction of greater flexibility, but has achieved only modest success. Under sections 61 and 98 of the ACA 2002, adoption agencies, having consulted with the person about whom information is sought, are allowed to disclose otherwise protected information about an adopted adult to persons requesting such information. There is no duty on adoption agencies to respond, although many have made arrangements with adoption support agencies to undertake the work, which, given the number of birth relatives who are likely to search, may well be considerable. This is because the tens of thousands of babies adopted in the 1960s, when there was no post-adoption information, let alone contact, are now only in their forties or fifties (Howe et al., 1992).

Fostering and adoption: is the legal framework in need of reform?

This commentator would suggest that the answer to the question: 'Is the legal framework in need of reform?' is 'probably not'.

Legislation in regard to looked after children has recently, and significantly, been reformed. Following recognition of the extent to which outcomes for children and young people in care are demonstrably poorer than those of the general population, in terms of the whole range of life chances (DfES, 2006, 2007), the Children and Young Persons Act 2008 amends Part III of the CA 1989. Local authorities' responsibilities towards children who are looked after or cease to be looked after are considerably enhanced under the Act, the Care Planning, Placement and Case Review (England) Regulations 2010, and statutory guidance (DfE, 2011c). Additionally, performance in regard to looked after children forms a substantial element of Ofsted inspections of children's services. The extent to which foster care services and work with looked after children under the revised guidance, which accompanies the legislative developments (DfE, 2011b, 2011c), improves outcomes will be a matter for research in the future. Only if that research demonstrates further deficits in the legal framework will further reform of the law be required.

The ACA 2002 and its accompanying regulations, for the most part, provide a statutory framework within which the adoption of any child for whom adoption is the permanent placement of choice could be achieved, within a timescale appropriate to the child's needs. Seeking to address the lack of suitable and willing adopters, ensuring local authorities follow the recently revised Adoption Guidance (DfE, 2011a), and remedying the delays endemic in the adoption agency process and the family courts are all matters that urgently need to be addressed, but while they may need some amendment of regulations, they do not require primary legislation.

Appendix 12.1 Table of cases

M v Warwickshire County Council [2007] EWCA Civ 1084
R (on the application of G) v London Borough of Southwark [2009] UKHL 26
Re C (Adoption: Freeing Order) [1999] 2 FLR 202
Re P (Adoption: Leave Provisions) [2007] EWCA Civ 616

Further reading

■ Katz, S.N., Eekelaar, J. and McLean, M. (2000) *Cross Currents: Family Law and Policy in the US and England*. Oxford: Oxford University Press.

The chapters on adoption provide an exceptionally rich resource for readers interested in the development of adoption policy and law in England and the USA during the twentieth century.

■ Masson, J., Bailey-Harris, R. and Probert, R. (2008) *Principles of Family Law* (8th edn). London: Sweet & Maxwell.

The relevant chapters set the current law on fostering and adoption within the historical and policy context of its development.

■ Probert, R. (2009) *Cretney and Probert's Family Law*. London: Sweet & Maxwell.

The relevant chapters provide an informed and accessible analysis of current law on fostering and adoption.

References

Ball, C. (1990) 'The Children Act 1989: origins, aims and current concerns', in P. Carter, T. Jeffs and M. Smith (eds) *Social Work and Social Welfare Year Book 2*. Milton Keynes: Open University Press.

Ball, C. (2002) 'Regulating inclusivity: reforming adoption law for the 21st century', *Child and Family Social Work*, 7, 285–96.

Cretney, S. (1997) 'The Children Act 1948: lessons for today?', *Child and Family Law Quarterly*, **9**(4): 359–69.

Curtis, M. (1946) *Report of the Care of Children Committee*, Cmd 6922. London: HMSO.

Dance, C. (1997) *Focus on Adoption: A Snapshot of Adoption Patterns in England – 1995.* London: BAAF.

DfE (Department for Education) (2010) *The Children Act 1989 Guidance and Regulations*, vol. 3: *Planning Transition to Adulthood for Care Leavers*. London: DfE.

DfE (2011a) *Adoption Guidance: Adoption and Children Act 2002, First Revision*. London: DfE.

DfE (2011b) *The Children Act 1989 Guidance and Regulations*, vol. 2: *Care Planning, Placement and Case Review*. London: DfE.

DfE (2011c) *Family and Friends Care: Statutory Guidance for Local Authorities*. London: DfE.

DfES (Department for Education and Skills) (2006) *Care Matters: Transforming the Lives of Children and Young People in Care*, Cm 6932. London: DfES.

DfES (2007) *Care Matters: Time for Change*, Cm 7137. London: DfES.

DHSS (Department of Health and Social Security) (1985) *Social Work Decisions in Child Care: Recent Research Findings and their Implications*. London: HMSO.

George, V. (1970) *Foster Care*. London: Routledge & Keegan Paul.

Griffith, J.A. (1966) *Central Departments and Local Authorities*. London: Allen and Unwin.

Home Department (1921) *Report of the Committee on Child Adoption*, Cmd 125. London: HMSO.

Home Department (1925) *Report of the Child Adoption Committee*, Cmd 2401. London: HMSO.

Home Office (1960) *Report of the Committee on Children and Young Persons*, Cmnd 1191. London: HMSO.

Home Office/Scottish Education Department (1972) *Report of the Departmental Committee on the Adoption of Children*, Cmnd 5107. London: HMSO.

House of Commons (1984) *Children in Care: Second Report from the Social Services Committee, 1983/84*, 360-1. London: HMSO.

Howe, D., Sawbridge, P. and Hinings, D. (1992) *Half a Million Women: Mothers who Lose their Children by Adoption*. London: Penguin.

Lowe, N. (1997) 'The changing face of adoption: the gift/donation model versus the contract/services model', *Child and Family Law Quarterly*, **9**(4): 371–86.

Lowe, N. (2000) 'English adoption law: past, present and future', in N. Sandford, J. Katz, J. Eekelaar and M. Maclean (eds) *Cross Currents: Family Law and Policy in the US and England*. Oxford: Oxford University Press.

Lowe, N., Murch, M., Borkowski, M. et al. (1999) *Supporting Adoption: Reframing the Approach*. London: BAAF.

Masson, J. (2000) 'From Curtis to Waterhouse: state care and child protection in the UK 1945–2000', in N. Sandford, J. Katz, J. Eekelaar and M. Maclean (eds) *Cross Currents: Family Law and Policy in the US and England*. Oxford: Oxford University Press.

Millham, S., Bullock, R., Hosie, K. and Little, M. (1986) *Lost in Care: The Problems of Maintaining Links between Children in Care and their Families*. Aldershot: Gower.

ONS (Office of National Statistics) (2010) *Historic Adoption Tables*. London: ONS.

Ormrod, R. (1983) 'Child care law: a personal perspective', *Adoption and Fostering*, 7(4): 10.

Packman, J. (1975) *The Child's Generation*. Oxford: Blackwell and Robertson.

Packman, J., Randall, J. and Jacques, N. (1986) *Who Needs Care?* Oxford: Blackwell.

Philpot, T. (2001) *A Very Private Practice: An Investigation into Private Fostering.* London: BAAF.

Probert, R. (2009) *Cretney and Probert's Family Law*. London: Sweet & Maxwell.

Triseliotis, J., Feast, J. and Kyle, F. (2005) *The Adoption Triangle Revisited: A Study of Adoption, Search and Reunion Experiences*. London: BAAF.

Triseliotis, J., Shireman, J. and Hundleby, M. (1997) *Adoption: Theory, Policy and Practice*. London: Cassell.

Utting, W. (1997) *People Like Us: The Report of the Review of Safeguards for Children Living Away from Home*. London: TSO.

White, R., Carr, P. and Lowe, N. (2008) *The Children Act in Practice* (4th edn). London: Butterworths.

Young, J. and Neil, E. (2009) 'Contact after adoption', in G. Schofield and J. Simmonds (eds) *The Child Placement Handbook: Research, Policy and Practice*. London: BAAF.

Law

13

Two theoretical fields relevant to social work practice in adoption and fostering

CHRISTINE JONES

Adoption and fostering is an area of social work that is fraught with ethical dilemmas and has seen great changes over the past three decades. It is crucial, therefore, that the knowledge base (both the theory and empirical evidence) guiding legal decisions, social policy and professional practices relating to adoption and fostering is explicit, open to debate and keeps pace with people's experiences. In this chapter, I outline two key theories of importance to adoption and fostering law, policy and practice: attachment theory; and the social construction of family relationships.

It is not my expectation that these will provide a comprehensive account of the concepts drawn on by social work in the area of adoption and fostering. Instead, I have focused on these domains of theoretical endeavour for two reasons. First, they offer different yet potentially complementary ways of understanding the complex, multilayered nature of adoption and fostering; and second, they both deal with what is at the heart of social work with children and families, that is, the importance of personal relationships.

I begin by outlining attachment theory, its origins and some of the theoretical developments that have taken place over the past 50 years. I discuss the emerging critique of attachment theory, particularly the concerns relating to the empirical basis for the diagnosis of attachment disorders and therapeutic interventions. I then provide an overview of sociological approaches to the study of the family before describing in more detail the social constructivist approach to family relationships and its relevance to adoption and fostering.

Attachment theory

Attachment theory has come to have an important place within adoption and fostering. The theory has its roots in the work of John Bowlby (1953, p. 13), who highlighted the importance of 'a warm, intimate and continuous relationship' with a primary carer for healthy child development and the long-term consequences of poor early experiences. Bowlby's theory developed from his observations of troubled and delinquent children and his studies of children's experiences of maternal deprivation, that is, extended or permanent separation of the child from the mother. From these observations, he described the grieving process experienced by separated children (Bowlby, 1976).

When developing attachment theory, Bowlby drew on ethology, the scientific study of animal behaviour and evolutionary biology to explain the innate need of infants to seek proximity to a primary carer or 'attachment figure' in order to receive protection and care. The attachment figure is said to provide a 'secure base' (Ainsworth et al., 1978; Bowlby, 1988) from which the child can safely move out to explore the world and in so doing develop a sense of competence and self-esteem. Much of the early work on attachment focused on the process of attachment in the period when an infant is between 6 and 30 months old. Bowlby, however, stressed the importance of attachment as a lifelong process affecting intimate relationships in adulthood and old age.

Ainsworth et al. (1978) developed the strange situation test in order to study attachment behaviours in child/mother dyads. From this work, new categories of attachment behaviour were developed, namely, secure, insecure ambivalent and insecure avoidant (Ainsworth et al., 1978). The secure child's experience of responsive and sensitive parenting provides them with confidence in the carer's ability to meet their need for comfort when distressed. The insecure ambivalent pattern of attachment is characterized by the child being anxious, clingy and rejecting of the carer's attention. In the insecure avoidant pattern of attachment, the child lacks curiosity to explore and is undemanding and disengaged. Later, the concepts of disorganized and organized attachment (Main and Solomon, 1986) were developed to distinguish patterns of attachment behaviour that were chaotic or unpredictable from those that appeared to be more coherent strategies used by children to cope with day-to-day stresses such as strange environments and illness. Both secure and insecure attachment behaviours were considered to be examples of coherent strategies adopted by children and were therefore categorized as organized attachment behaviours. The category 'disorganized attachment' captured the incoherent and unpredictable nature of behaviours demonstrated by some children who had experienced inadequate care. The children were said to face an 'irresolvable dilemma' – experiencing fear in a strange situation yet being unable to seek comfort from a carer who is also a source of fear.

The early work of Ainsworth and colleagues also focused on the identification of antecedents to the development of a secure attachment. Four dimensions of caring were identified as important in this process: sensitivity, availability, cooperation and

Theory

acceptance (Ainsworth et al., 1971, 1978). More recently, a re-examination of the dimensions of caring that contribute to the development of secure attachments has been undertaken. Fonagy et al. (1991) and Meins (2001) have suggested that maternal behaviours that demonstrate attunement to an infant's mental states are more reliable predictors of secure attachment than a mother's responsivity to emotional and physical needs. Meins (1997) has introduced the concept of 'mind-mindedness', that is, the ability to see things from the child's point of view. She suggests that mind-mindedness differs from the concept of maternal sensitivity in that it requires caring to be not only prompt or contingent but also appropriate, that is, to match the need of the child (an aspect emphasized by Bowlby in his early work but later given less emphasis when operationalized in empirical studies). This requires the carer not only to respond to a child's behaviour but also to accurately infer intention. Attempts have also been made to develop the theory so that it better fits the experience of adopted and fostered children. For example, Schofield and Beek (2006) have suggested a fifth dimension of caring in addition to those described by Ainsworth and colleagues: 'promoting belonging', which, they suggest, is particularly important for children joining new families. Mary Dozier (2005) has also revisited the concept of carer 'commitment' in Bowlby's early work in her studies of foster care. She suggests that a child's confidence in a carer's long-term and deeply held commitment to the child is at least as important to the attachment relationship as is a carer's ability to comfort the child when distressed (Dozier and Lindheim, 2006).

One source of controversy within attachment theory relates to the presumed association between insecure or disorganized attachment and psychopathology. In a review of Bowlby's work and the empirical evidence, Sroufe et al. (1999) assert that Bowlby did not suggest such a simplistic causal relationship between attachment and child outcomes but instead emphasized the complex interplay and cumulative effect of past experiences, current experiences and broader social factors such as socioeconomic status. Sroufe et al. (1999) borrow Bowlby's concept of developmental pathways and the metaphor of the tree to explain the various directions that a child's development can take as they are exposed to various environmental factors and experiences. They suggest that associations between anxious or disorganized attachment and psychopathology must therefore be considered probabilistic rather than predictive and understood as playing a role in a dynamic system of child development (Sroufe et al., 1999). In the specific case of adopted children, insecure or disorganized attachment relationships in infancy cannot be said to predict psychological or relationship problems later in childhood but are instead just one source of vulnerability and must be considered alongside other risk factors, such as previous emotional or physical deprivation and current experiences (Barth et al., 2005).

A key question surrounds the ability to influence attachment style and therefore to avoid 'intergenerational transmission' of insecure attachment styles and to reduce vulnerability to risk. Evidence suggests that attachment styles are not inflexible and can be reshaped by new experiences. This is possible even in adolescence and adulthood, although early change is more easily accomplished (Sroufe et al.,

1999). Two key tools have been developed to explore the current attachment representations of children and adults, namely, the story stem technique (Bretherton et al., 1990; Green et al., 2000) and the adult attachment interview (Main and Goldwyn, 1985–95; Hesse, 1999). These tools uncover the 'internal working models' or mental representations of attachment relationships used by individuals having been developed through repeated interactions with carers. The adult attachment interview acknowledges the ability for internal working models to change over time, focusing on individuals' current attachment relationships rather than past experiences of attachment. This approach accommodates the experiences of adults who have had difficult life experiences and yet have worked through these to achieve autonomous states of mind.

The application of attachment theory to the experiences of children who are adopted and fostered has received special attention. Dozier et al.'s work (2001) has shown that previously abused and neglected infants were able to adapt quickly when placed with foster mothers with secure autonomous 'states of mind'. Steele et al. (2009) show the same rapid adaptation for late placed adopted children. However, this change is not straightforward. The work of Hodges and Steele and colleagues (Hodges et al., 2003; Steele et al., 2009) has also demonstrated that while positive parent characteristics represented in adopted children's story stem completion increased over time, negative parent characteristics did not decrease. Their work suggests that children find it easier to take on new positive internal working models than to extinguish negative representations.

A further criticism levelled at Bowlby's work was his primary focus on the mother figure. While Bowlby (1976) did acknowledge the importance of fathers and other key individuals as attachment figures, historically, a greater focus was placed on maternal caring, particularly in empirical research, and the assumption persisted of the importance of the mother as the 'primary' figure. Rutter (1972, 1979) instead suggested that it is the norm for children to develop multiple attachments. Recent research has focused on the father's role in encouraging exploration through play and giving praise and encouragement (Grossman et al., 1999, 2005).

Clinical work, real-world observation and hypothesis testing have all contributed to the continuing development of attachment theory, and there are a number of ways in which the theoretical field is of value to the field of adoption and fostering today (see Box 13.1).

Theory

Box 13.1

The contribution of attachment theory to social work practice in the field of adoption and fostering

- It provides an explanation of the importance of a 'secure base' in promoting healthy child development.
- It raises awareness of the deep significance of attachments for children and

the sense of loss felt by children when these attachments are severed, even in cases where relationships between the child and carer are problematic and stressful.

■ It provides an explanation of the processes through which maltreated children can develop adaptive attachment styles in order to cope with danger, fear or inadequate care.

■ It identifies caring characteristics that can contribute to the promotion of healthy attachments such as sensitivity, mind-mindedness and commitment to the child.

■ It highlights a degree of risk associated with children's experiences of inadequate care, separation from attachment figures and multiple transient carers.

■ It provides an optimistic account of the ability of children to overcome adversity, shift internal working models and develop healthy attachment relationships in new and positive caring environments.

While attachment theory's contribution to the field of adoption and fostering is significant, much still remains uncertain. Concern has been expressed regarding an apparent overreliance on attachment theory to explain the difficulties experienced by children requiring substitute care and a tendency to pathologize children's attachment experiences (Barth et al., 2005). Given the evidence that attachment relationships are just one source of vulnerability for children requiring adoption and fostering, an emphasis on attachment issues to the exclusion of others seems to be a rather narrow approach to take. Within adoption and fostering, there has been much emphasis on identifying children with disorganized attachment patterns in order to intervene. However, deep concern has been expressed about the use of 'attachment therapy', also known as holding therapy, to 'treat' attachment disorders despite these lacking scientific testing and being highly intrusive (Dozier, 2003). In response to such concerns, a call has been made for greater acknowledgement of the lack of a current evidence base relating to the assessment, diagnosis and treatment of attachment disorders (Steele, 2003) and the need to ensure that interventions are sensitively delivered (Dozier, 2003). A distinction is necessary between 'attachment therapy' and 'attachment-based therapies'. While 'attachment-based therapies' have been slow to develop, there is now emerging evidence of the effectiveness of some of these programmes. For example, the attachment and biobehavioural catch-up intervention, an attachment-based training programme for foster carers, has been demonstrated to be effective in helping foster children to develop trusting relationships with foster carers (Dozier et al., 2009).

While attention to attachment issues remains a core element of adoption and fostering practice, there is still much empirical work needed to guide professional interventions in this area.

The social construction of family relationships

The first part of this chapter focused on attachment theory, a key theory relating to the development of close personal relationships or, as Bowlby describes them, 'affectional bonds'. In the second part, the focus shifts to sociological understandings of intimate relationships, more specifically, family relationships. While adoption and fostering are clearly concerned with the welfare and development of the child, they are also unavoidably concerned with families. So it is important that 'family' as a concept is critically examined. Sociological theories of family have much to offer in terms of advancing understandings of the family relationships that result from adoption and fostering arrangements. Much of this section will focus on a strand of the sociology of the family that can broadly be called 'the social construction of family relationships'. I begin with a brief outline of the sociological theories of family that preceded the social constructivist approach before going on to describe the approach in more detail and to look at its relevance to adoption and fostering.

Shifts in the sociology of families have broadly followed more general shifts in sociological theorizing. Structural functionalism took an interest in the family as a social institution and charted the rise, out of industrialization, of the nuclear family (Parsons and Bales, 1956). Marxist analyses of the family have also been prevalent, characterizing the nuclear family as the servant of capitalism (Engels, [1884]2010). Feminist theories began to dominate the field from the 1970s onwards, building on the earlier work of writers such as Hannah Gavron (1966). Their analysis exposed the operation of patriarchy within families and the pervasive nature of family ideology (Oakley, 1974).

More recently, theories of risk and individualization became prominent. Individualization theory emphasized the role of agency in the creation of relationships and characterized contemporary society as one in which people are able to follow their own individual life projects (Beck and Beck-Gernstein, 1995, 2002; Bauman, 2003). The theory distinguished family relationships that were 'given' or fixed and those that were 'made' or elective. From this starting point, however, two distinct schools of thought emerged. One strand of individualization theory associated the freedom to act with conflict, selfish self-determinism, instability within relationships and the decline and fragmentation of the family (Beck and Beck-Gernstein, 1995). The second strand of individualization theory associated choice with the potential for greater equality in relationships (Giddens, 1992). Both schools of thought have faced criticism regarding the lack of empirical evidence for the assumptions on which they are built (Jamieson, 1998; Silva and Smart, 1999; Lewis, 2001; Williams, 2004).

This section focuses on current sociological thinking in relation to families and relationships in Britain, particularly the work of sociologists such as Smart, Morgan, Finch, Mason and others who have been at the forefront of developments in the sociology of families and personal life. Their work follows on from, but also challenges, individualization theory, particularly the more pessimistic aspects of the theory. Much of this analysis has developed from empirical studies of reconstituted families

Theory

following divorce (Smart and Neale, 1999) and gay and lesbian families or 'families of choice' (Weston, 1991; Weeks et al., 2001), two family forms that have challenged conventional ideas about what counts as family. The studies of 'friends as family' by Pahl and colleagues (Pahl, 2000; Pahl and Spencer, 2003) have also been influential.

The role of human agency, that is, the ability of individuals to make choices and act upon these, albeit within the context of cultural expectations and social structures, continues as a central theme in contemporary sociological theorizing in relation to families. An emphasis is placed on the meanings individuals attach to relationships and the creative abilities of both adults and children to craft family relationships (Edwards et al., 2005; Mason and Tipper, 2008). This contemporary work challenges the assumed inevitable connection between family and biological relatedness or co-residence. Families are no longer solely defined in terms of blood-lines, the marriage contract and shared households. Instead, an emphasis has been placed on the ability of individuals to define relationships as 'family' relationships regardless of biological relatedness or legal status. There is also a recognition of the fluidity and mobility of family relationships (Smart, 2007) and the role of negotiation in the process of family construction (Finch and Mason, 1993). This work also emphasizes the continuing importance of 'connectedness' (Smart, 2007) and an ethic of care and commitment (Williams, 2004) within increasingly diverse family forms. This contrasts with the more pessimistic forecasts of writers such as Bauman and Beck and Beck-Gernstein of increased atomization within society and the disintegration of the family.

The theoretical work of David Morgan (1996) has been highly influential in relation to this shift towards viewing families as socially constituted, particularly his development of the concept 'family practices'. Drawing on the work of Bourdieu (1990), Morgan conceptualized family as a set of practices, that is, regular and repeated day-to-day actions and interactions that have a 'family' quality. These may be familiar family practices such as the conventions around mealtimes or more subtle family practices such as a family mobilizing support when a loved one faces a crisis. This conceptualization represents a fundamental move away from viewing the family as a fixed institution, a predefined and clearly demarcated structure, to viewing family as a fluid set of relationships that are created and re-created over time through our active participation in day-to-day family life.

Put simply, 'families "are" what families "do"' (Silva and Smart, 1999, p. 11). Morgan (1996) emphasizes the importance in the construction of family relationships of both the meaning attached to practices by individuals and the social and historical significance of practices. He uses the example of feeding children to indicate the range of possible biographical, social and historical influences on practice such as previous feeding experiences, gendered expectations or commercial and advertising pressures. Following on from Morgan's work, Finch (2007) has emphasized the importance of the visibility of family practices and has advocated the use of the concept of 'displaying family' to capture the elements of 'doing and being seen to do' family in order to convey meaning.

There has been relatively little attention to the application of sociological theories of family relationships within adoption and fostering research, yet the concepts and ideas developed within the field appear to have much to offer (see Box 13.2).

Box 13.2

The contribution of a social constructionist approach to family relationships in the field of adoption and fostering

- It addresses both micro- and macro-aspects of family relationships, focusing on agency and daily practices at the same time as historical, structural and cultural influences on family life.
- It creates the possibility for new definitions of family relationships to exist alongside more traditional biological or legal relationships.
- It directs attention to the resourcefulness and active engagement of those involved in adoption rather than focusing on risk or pathology.

The breaking of the link between family and biology that is central to the constructivist thesis of family life also leaves room for diverse forms of relatedness to exist. This should not imply a devaluing of biological relatedness but instead an equal valuing of 'given' and 'made' family relationships. It creates space for children to hold 'multiple families in mind' (Rustin, 1999) rather than having to choose this family over that. Jones and Hackett (2011a, 2011b) have described the careful and lifelong process through which family relationships are crafted between adopters and their adopted children following domestic stranger adoption and the parallel process of retaining a sense of connectedness to the child's birth family.

The emphasis on agency does not, however, imply unfettered choice. For example, Carsten (2004), a social anthropologist, has written about the assumed inferiority of 'made' family relationships or 'fictive' kinship following adoption within Western culture in contrast to 'real' biological relatedness. Her study of adopted adults' experiences of search and reunion with birth relatives has highlighted the contradictions faced by such adults when confronted with an enduring Western cultural belief in the primacy of biological connectedness and yet a feeling of irreparable distance from birth relatives from whom they've been estranged for many years. Jones and Hackett's (2011a, 2011b) empirical work has also highlighted the challenges to legitimacy faced by both adoptive families and birth families. The legitimacy of adoptive families is challenged by the Western cultural assumption that adoptive families are second best, while the legitimacy of birth families is challenged by their lack of legal recognition as a family.

The emphasis on agency within a historical and cultural context directs policy-makers and providers of adoption and fostering services to consider the creative power of adopters and foster carers, adoptees, foster children and birth relatives to resist cultural norms and expectations and to make adoption and fostering work. This

Theory

Making connexions

This chapter suggests that 'the possibilities offered by the new sociological approaches to the study of adoption and fostering are just beginning to be recognized'. What are they, and how might they influence practice?

contrasts with the usual emphasis on risk and vulnerability within placements. While outcome research has helpfully identified important risk and protective factors in terms of children, adopters and placement characteristics, it has done little to explain the placements that survive despite pessimistic expectations and those that disrupt despite indications being positive. A focus on agency, practices and the negotiation of relationships offers an alternative approach within the field of adoption and fostering research, creating the potential to provide new insights.

Contemporary sociological theories of family relationships offer exciting possibilities for understanding the process through which families and family-like relationships are created following adoption or fostering. While there has been some interest in the application of anthropological theories of kinship to adoption over a number of years (Modell, 1994; Carsten, 2000; Howell, 2006), the possibilities offered by the new sociological approaches to the study of adoption and fostering are just beginning to be recognized.

Conclusions

Theories provide an essential framework for social work law, policy and practice. I suggest that there is much value in drawing widely from biological, psychological and social sciences in order to understand an area as complex as substitute family care and family relationships. Together, attachment theory and a social constructivist approach to family relationships provide a helpful framework for such an endeavour. They provide a window onto the personal and political dimensions of people's experiences of relationships when involved in adoption and fostering.

Good theories also move with the times, are constantly revised and updated and, if necessary, are replaced with better theories as evidence develops and the needs of society change. Both attachment theory and sociological theories of the family have continued to capture the imagination and to accommodate new evidence as it emerges. The challenge for legal and welfare professionals and adoptive families is to apply such theories thoughtfully, drawing on current evidence but acknowledging gaps, engaging with theories critically and always working with a degree of uncertainty.

Further reading

■ Jones, C. and Hackett, S. (2011) 'The role of "family practices" and "displays of family" in the creation of adoptive kinship', *British Journal of Social Work*, **41**(1): 40–56.

Introduces the reader to sociological concepts relating to family relationships and explores their relevance to adoptive family life.

■ Schofield, G. and Beek, M. (2006) *Attachment Handbook for Foster Care and Adoption.* London: BAAF.

Highly accessible and comprehensive overview of attachment theory and its application to adoption and fostering practice.

■ Smart, C. (2007) *Personal Life: New Directions in Sociological Thinking.* Cambridge: Polity Press.

Provides interesting sociological insights into various dimensions of family and personal relationships including emotions, family secrets and personal possessions.

References

Ainsworth, M., Bell, S. and Stayton, D. (1971) 'Individual differences in strange-situation behavior of one year olds', in H. Schaffer (ed.) *The Origins of Human Social Relations.* New York: Academic Press.

Ainsworth, M., Blehar, M., Waters, E. and Wall, S. (1978) *Patterns of Attachment: A Psychological Study of the Strange Situation.* Hillsdale, NJ: Erlbaum.

Barth, R., Crea, T.M., John, K. et al. (2005) 'Beyond attachment theory and therapy: towards sensitive and evidence-based interventions with foster and adoptive families in distress', *Child and Family Social Work,* **10**(4): 257–68.

Bauman, Z. (2003) *Liquid Love.* Cambridge: Polity Press.

Beck, U. and Beck-Gernstein, E. (1995) *The Normal Chaos of Love.* Cambridge: Polity Press.

Beck, U. and Beck-Gernstein, E. (2002) *Individualization.* London: Sage.

Bourdieu, P. (1990) *The Logic of Practice.* Cambridge: Polity Press.

Bowlby, J. (1953) *Child Care and the Growth of Love.* London: Pelican Books.

Bowlby, J. (1976) *The Making and Breaking of Affectional Bonds.* London: Routledge.

Bowlby, J. (1988) *A Secure Base: Clinical Applications of Attachment Theory.* London: Routledge.

Bretherton, I., Ridgeway, D. and Cassidy, J. (1990) 'Assessing internal working models of the attachment relationship: an attachment story completion task for 3-year-olds', in M.T. Greenberg, D. Cicchetti and E.M. Cummings (eds) *Attachment in the Preschool Years.* London: University of Chicago Press.

Carsten, J. (2000) "Knowing where you've come from": ruptures and continuities of time and kinship in narratives of adoption reunions', *Journal of the Royal Anthropological Institute,* **6**(4): 687–703.

Carsten, J. (2004) *After Kinship.* Cambridge: Cambridge University Press.

Dozier, M. (2003) 'Attachment-based treatment for vulnerable children', *Attachment & Human Development,* **5**(3): 253–7.

Dozier, M. (2005) 'Challenges of foster care', *Attachment & Human Development,* 7(1): 27–30.

Dozier, M. and Lindheim, O. (2006) 'This is my child: differences among foster parents in commitment to their young children', *Child Maltreatment,* **11**(4): 338–45.

Dozier, M., Chase-Stovall, K.K. and Bates, B. (2001) 'Attachment for infants in foster care: the role of caregiver state of mind', *Child Development,* 72, 1467–77.

Theory

Dozier, M., Lindhiem, O., Lewis, E. et al. (2009) 'Effects of a foster parent training program on young children's attachment behaviors: preliminary evidence from a randomized clinical trial', *Child and Adolescent Social Work Journal*, 26, 321–32.

Edwards, R., Hadfield, L. and Mauthner, M. (2005) *Children's Understanding of their Sibling Relationships*. London: National Children's Bureau.

Engels, F. ([1884]2010) *The Origin of the Family, Private Property, and the State*. London: Penguin Classics.

Finch, J. (2007) 'Displaying families', *Sociology*, **41**(2): 65–81.

Finch, J. and Mason, J. (1993) *Negotiating Family Responsibilities*. London: Routledge.

Fonagy, P., Steele, M., Steele, H. et al. (1991) 'The capacity for understanding mental states: the reflective self in parent and child and its significance for security of attachment', *Infant Mental Health Journal*, 12, 201–18.

Gavron, H. (1966) *The Captive Wife*. London: Routledge & Kegan Paul.

Giddens, A. (1992) *The Transformation of Intimacy. Love, Sexuality and Eroticism in Modern Societies*. Cambridge: Polity Press.

Green, J.M., Stanley, C., Smith, V. and Goldwyn, R. (2000) 'A new method of evaluating attachment representations on young school age children: the Manchester Child Attachment Story Task', *Attachment & Human Development*, **2**(1): 42–64.

Grossman, K.E., Grossman, K. and Kindler, H. (2005) 'Early care and the roots of attachment and partnership representation in the Bielefeld and Regensburg longitudinal studies', in K.E. Grossman, K. Grossman and H. Kindler (eds) *Attachment from Infancy to Adulthood: The Major Longitudinal Studies*. New York: Guilford Press.

Grossman, K.E., Grossman, K. and Zimmerman, P. (1999) 'A wider view of attachment and exploration: stability and change during the years of immaturity', in J. Cassidy and P.R. Shaver (eds) *Handbook of Attachment: Theory, Research and Clinical Applications*. London: Guilford Press.

Hesse, E. (1999) 'The adult attachment interview', in J. Cassidy and P.R. Shaver (eds) *Handbook of Attachment: Theory, Research and Clinical Applications*. London: Guilford Press.

Hodges, J., Steele, M., Hillman, S. et al. (2003) 'Changes in attachment representations over the first year of adoptive placement: narratives of maltreated children', *Clinical Child Psychology and Psychiatry*, **8**(3): 351–67.

Howell, S. (2006) *The Kinning of Foreigners: Transnational Adoption in a Global Perspective*. New York: Berghahn Books.

Jamieson, L. (1998) *Intimacy: Personal Relationships in Modern Societies*. Cambridge: Polity Press.

Jones, C. and Hackett, S. (2011a) 'Redefining family relationships following adoption: adoptive parents' perspectives on the changing nature of kinship between adoptees and birth relatives', *British Journal of Social Work*, doi:10.1093/bjsw/bcr060.

Jones, C. and Hackett, S. (2011b) 'The role of "family practices" and "displays of family" in the creation of adoptive kinship', *British Journal of Social Work*, **41**(1): 40–56.

Lewis, J. (2001) *The End of Marriage?: Individualism and Intimate Relations*. Cheltenham: Edward Elgar.

Main, M. and Goldwyn, R. (1985–95) The Adult Attachment Interview Classification and Scoring System, unpublished manuscript. University of California, Berkeley.

Main, M. and Solomon, J. (1986) 'Discovery of an insecure-disorganised/disoriented attachment pattern', in T.B. Brazelton and M.W. Yogman (eds) *Affective Development in Infancy*. Norwood, NJ: Ablex.

Mason, J. and Tipper, B. (2008) 'Being related: how children define and create kinship', *Childhood: A Global Journal of Child Research*, **15**(4): 441–60.

Meins, E. (1997) *Security of Attachment and the Social Development of Cognition*. Hove: Psychology Press.

Meins, E., Fernyhough, C., Fradley, E. and Tuckey, M. (2001) 'Rethinking maternal sensitivity: mothers' comments on infants' mental processes predict security of attachment at 12 months', *Journal of Child Psychology and Psychiatry*, **42**(5): 637–48.

Modell, J. (1994) *Kinship with Strangers: Adoption and Interpretations of Kinship in American Culture*. Berkeley: University of California Press.

Morgan, D. (1996) *Family Connections: An Introduction to Family Studies*. Cambridge: Polity Press.

Oakley, A. (1974) *The Sociology of Housework*. Oxford: Martin Robertson.

Pahl, R. (2000) *On Friendship*. Cambridge: Polity Press.

Pahl, R. and Spencer, L. (2003) *Personal Communities: Not Simply Families of 'Fate' or 'Choice'*. Colchester: Institute for Social and Economic Research.

Parsons, T. and Bales, R.F. (1956) *Family: Socialization and Interaction Process*. London: Routledge & Kegan Paul.

Rustin, M. (1999) 'Multiple families in mind', *Clinical Child Psychology and Psychiatry*, 4, 51–62.

Rutter, M. (1972) *Maternal Deprivation Reassessed*. Harmondsworth: Penguin.

Rutter, M. (1979) 'Maternal deprivation, 1972–1978: new findings, new concepts, new approaches', *Child Development*, **50**(2): 283–305.

Schofield, G. and Beek, M. (2006) *Attachment Handbook for Foster Care and Adoption*. London: BAAF.

Silva, E.B. and Smart, C. (1999) 'The "new" practices and politics of family life', in E.B. Silva and C. Smart (eds) *The New Family?* London: Sage.

Smart, C. (2007) *Personal Life: New Directions in Sociological Thinking*. Cambridge: Polity Press.

Smart, C. and Neale, B. (1999) *Family Fragments?* Cambridge: Polity Press.

Sroufe, L.A., Carlson, E.A., Levy, A.K. and Egeland, B. (1999) 'Implications of attachment theory for developmental psychopathology', *Development and Psychopathology*, **11**(1): 1–13.

Steele, H. (2003) 'Holding therapy is not attachment therapy: editor's introduction to this invited Special Issue', *Attachment & Human Development*, **5**(3): 219.

Steele, M., Hodges, J., Kaniuk, J. et al. (2009) 'Attachment representations and adoption outcome: on the use of narrative assessments to track the adaptation of previously maltreated children in their new families', in G.M. Wrobel and E. Neil (eds) *International Advances in Adoption Research for Practice*. Chichester: Wiley-Blackwell.

Weeks, J., Heaphy, B. and Donovan, C. (2001) *Same Sex Intimacies*. London: Routledge.

Weston, K. (1991) *Families We Choose: Lesbians, Gays, Kinship*. New York: Columbia University Press.

Williams, F. (2004) *Rethinking Families*. London: Calouste Gulbenkian Foundation.

Theory

14
Milestones in adoption and fostering research

GARY CLAPTON

Many of the developmental milestones that have shaped social work thinking and practice in adoption and fostering have been derived from small-scale qualitative studies, tentative explorations or have been 'magpied' from disciplines such as psychology. As will be seen, in true social work eclectic manner, autobiography and fiction have been gathered in for inclusion in this chapter. 'Research' has thus been defined broadly in order to capture all the creativities that have gone into works that constitute significant contributions to the development of good practice in adoption and fostering.

The main messages that emerge from the choices presented fall broadly into five areas:

1 There are writings that talk directly to us of the experiences of the people who receive or have received an adoption and fostering service. These include two reports from the Office of the Children's Rights Director, *Being Fostered* and *About Adoption* (Morgan, 2005, 2006), Graham Gaskin's (2005) story of his life in care and Jacqueline Wilson's (1991) expertly written account of the world of a girl living in a residential home.

2 There are works that give us an understanding of experiences and provide us with new knowledge. These are the studies of Jenkins and Norman (1972) and Howe et al. (1992). They can be read for a grasp of the pain of loss communicated by those interviewed, but they also offer theorization, contextualization and suggest implications for practice for those working with loss, grief and feelings of disenfranchisement.

3 There is work that has taken our grasp of the dynamics of adoption to a new theoretical level. Kirk (1964) and Triseliotis (1973) have changed thinking, policy and practice, and law in the case of Triseliotis's work on adopted adults' access to original birth information. Kirk's pinpointing of 'differentness' of the adoptive

216

family and Triseliotis's discussion of curiosity about origins tell us something about human nature that perhaps we may have intuitively grasped but didn't know and couldn't verbalize or put into practice.

4   There are three studies that draw on research and provide clear practice guidelines: Rowe and Lambert (1973) on the misery of children who couldn't be cared for by their families and had been 'waiting in care'; the attachment research-based work of Gilligan's (1997) promotion of resilience; and Fahlberg's (1991) meticulous guide for professionals. All three give us delight when we see a perfect connection between theory and practice.

5   I have included one study that speaks to us directly of the wider social and economic context – Bebbington and Miles's (1989) uncontestable fact that care entry is linked inextricably to poverty and deprivation.

Research milestones in the development of fostering

Filial Deprivation and Foster Care (Jenkins and Norman, 1972)

In 1972, Jenkins and Norman produced a rare and seminal work (*Filial Deprivation and Foster Care*) on the grief experienced by parents who lose their children into care. They coined the term 'filial deprivation' to describe parents' feelings and reactions to the loss of a child into care. Most parents were sad, about half were angry and a third felt guilty and ashamed. The removal of their children and the associated stigma was often only one episode in a lifetime of difficulties. While the experiences and feelings of birth parents whose children are adopted have been studied since 1972, little further work has been done on the sense of loss felt by parents whose children are deemed to be in need of public care.

A Child's Journey through Placement (Fahlberg, 1991)

In 1991, our knowledge and practice in fostering made a great leap forward with a book that provided practitioners with research-informed tools for a holistic approach to working with children in care. Now reprinted many times over, *A Child's Journey through Placement* (Fahlberg, 1991) starts by describing the bonding and attachment process and then gives a thorough description of the developmental tasks of childhood and how those tasks can be disrupted by separation and loss. Ways to mitigate the harmful effects of multiple moves on children in the foster care system are offered, one of which was 'life story book' work. Life story work with a child in care had an outcome – the compilation of a chronology of memories and important artefacts, for example photographs, that would contextualize events, provide solace and offer some kind of comprehension for a hurt child. It was also a rehabilitative process because it was done together with a carer and this allowed for the therapeutic expression of emotions and pain evoked by recollections.

Life story work, however, was just one of the attractions of *A Child's Journey through Placement*. During the 1980s, there was a change in the demography of children coming into UK public care. The proportions of children entering the system for reasons that had purely to do with delinquency and poor school attendance reduced and the care system began increasingly to concentrate on children who had experienced abuse and neglect. These children were older and some would experience a range of interventions, including temporary foster care, spells of return to care within their families, readmission to public care and possible long-term fostering or adoption. Some children experienced all these, including multiple moves within foster care (Fisher et al., 1986). The phrase 'care careers' emerged to describe mounting concern about children's experiences in the system (Thorpe, 1988) and evidence emerged of the depth of disturbance of children in foster care (Rowe et al., 1984).

So when *A Child's Journey through Placement* appeared, UK fostering and adoption practice was receptive to a step-by-step handbook for children, with case scenarios, that artfully combined the theory of attachment and loss with real practice that was trying to engage with a new raft of problems facing children in care. Fahlberg delivered Bowlby's work on attachment and loss in bite-sized, practice-shaped chunks in a book that could be taken down from the shelf above the desk of a busy social worker or the pages photocopied and passed on to foster parents. Because of its structure and frequent posing of questions and use of practice scenarios, *A Child's Journey through Placement*, with its section-by-section progress through all ages and developmental stages of children, was perfect for in-service training days; sections from the book are regularly included in guides to contemporary social work practice (for example Wilson et al., 2008).

The Story of Tracy Beaker (Wilson, 1991)

In 1991, the child's perspective was beautifully captured in fiction. The fictional story of a child Tracy Beaker, who lives in residential and foster care, came out in the same year as Fahlberg's work. *The Story of Tracy Beaker* (Wilson, 1991) provides an account of a child's journey through placement – told by an expert storyteller. The book has been passed around among children in foster care and read and used by foster carers and social workers around the world. According to Random House, it has sold over 750,000 copies, and Public Lending Right says it is the most borrowed book of the 2000s. It has been translated into over 30 languages, turned into a BBC drama, a game, a song and a website that gives agency to children in care.

'Beyond permanence? The importance of resilience in child placement practice and planning' (Gilligan, 1997)

In 1997, Gilligan wrote about the practical application of the concept of resilience to social work with children in care. Resilience as a concept emerged, like much of social work thinking does, from the disciplines of psychology and psychiatry (Rutter,

1985), but Gilligan (1997) was one of the first to write about the practical application of the concept to social work with children and young people and thus to precipitate a major practice innovation. His work was developed into a guide, *Promoting Resilience: A Resource Guide on Working with Children in the Care System* (Gilligan, 2001, updated 2009).

The idea of promoting resilience may seem like common sense – 'accentuate the positive' – yet the idea arrived as a fresh way of thinking about work with children:

> Ideas about attachment and trauma enabled us to make sense of the problems we encountered, but did not account adequately for the determination and grace with which the children applied themselves to the work of their lives. The concept of resilience delighted us. Here was a way of thinking about the process of living a life that embraced the many strands of vulnerability and resources that interact to produce the individuality of each person's response to adversity. (Cairns, 2002, p. 12)

Resilience in a child is their capacity and ability to adapt constructively to life after stress, adversity or harm, and, crucially, it can be enhanced. The concept emerged at a point when social work had been refocused from work with families towards a greater emphasis on individuals, especially children (Cabinet Office, 2008). If social workers were to engage meaningfully with children who had suffered great pain and were estranged from their families, and had neither the skills of child psychiatry nor wide access to the service, then an intervention that could be understood and simply practised rapidly became a valued component of the social worker's 'toolkit'.

Cairns (2002, p. 12) puts the value of resilience well:

> Helping a child do well with a piece of schoolwork, for example, could have benefits at all these levels. It might enable the child to reflect on and change their internal self-concept, create some change in the cultural setting of school friends and peers through being perceived by others as more able to achieve success, and the combination of the achievement and the change in self-presentation might also enhance the interaction between the child and the formal structures of the school. Such small steps and incremental changes do seem to have the potential to create much larger changes in the personal and social resources available to the child. The positive chain reaction that interrupts the downward spiral in the life of a child can grow from very small beginnings.

More than comprehension and simplicity, resilience offered hope, especially to social workers:

> However, as our study also suggests, some specific changes or single events in a child's life, such as a new attachment relationship, a change of school, a change of contact arrangements or the discovery of a child's particular talent, do have the potential to alter the direction significantly for better or for worse … This notion of significant turning points can raise anxiety about the long-term impact of, say,

Research

a placement move, but it can also leave room for hope, as social workers and foster-carers work patiently to achieve small but influential and catalytic changes. (Schofield and Beek, 2005, p. 1298)

As befits such a dynamic concept, the theory and practice of resilience has continued to develop. Gilligan (2004) has provided refinements and Ungar (2008, p. 225) has suggested that resilience ought to be seen as an interactive and holistic process that includes the capacity of the child's environment (family, community, culture) to respond positively to the child as they 'navigate and negotiate' their resilience-promoting behaviour.

Today, resilience promotion is a widespread feature of social work training and a central feature of fostering and adoption practice. Social workers can and do help a child build 'islands of competence' in an ocean of confusion (Brooks, 1994).

Fostering Now (Sinclair, 2005), *Being Fostered* (Morgan, 2005)

In the twenty-first century, the voices of fostered children have begun to be heard: the first step in crafting a service that properly places the child's views at the centre.

In a summary of *Fostering Now* (Sinclair, 2005), Berridge (2005, p. 6) notes that

the studies reveal that children want their views to be taken seriously; they want a normal family life without conflict between their birth and foster families; they want the same opportunities that other children have; and they do not want to be made to feel uncomfortable by being singled out, such as at school.

Being Fostered (Morgan, 2005) is the result of a national survey that included an exploration of the views of 410 children and young people in foster care. Over a thousand were sent the questionnaire and the response rate was 37%. The youngest was 4 years old and the oldest was 18 years. The average age was 13, so children under 10, as the report acknowledges, are less well represented. However, the number of replies makes this one of the largest polls of what fostered children think and so the findings are of great interest. They provide an authentic child's voice that remarkably echoes messages that are emerging from contemporary fostering research. The report's 'top findings' are:

1 A third of foster children said they were not told enough about their current foster family before they went to live there. Children said they wanted much more information about their future carers (including, for some, information about their race and religion). They also wanted information about other children who would be living in the foster home.

2 Two-thirds of foster children had had no choice in the decision of which foster home they were placed in.

3 Over a quarter of the foster children said they weren't asked about what their care plan should say. Over a quarter didn't know what their care plan said.

4 The 'best things about being fostered' were 'the care and support you received,

the opportunities it gave you, liking your foster family, and living in a family rather than another sort of placement' (p. 8).

5   The 'worst things about being fostered' were 'missing your birth family and past friends, the rules and punishments in your foster home, and feeling you are the odd one out because you are in care' (p. 8). A third of children said 'nothing' is the worst thing about being fostered.

The report notes that 'the most usual worry for foster children about the future was about what sort of support they would be getting when they left care' (p. 9). It is a telling remark that reminds us that young people continue to grow up in foster care and that sorting out what happens to them when they are 'discharged' – with all its connotations of the state being relieved of an obligation – remains a huge priority.

In his summary of *Fostering Now*, Berridge (2005, p. 7) suggests that the following are the key messages for practitioners:

■   *normality:* fostering should be as 'normal' as possible. For example, arriving at school in a taxi could be a source of embarrassment

■   *family care:* to feel that they belonged in the foster home and that they were treated the same as other children: 'They valued treats, opportunities for their hobbies and, in most cases, a room of their own' (Sinclair, 2005, p. 50)

■   *respect for their origins:* children had different opinions about the relationships they wanted with their birth families and with whom they wanted to be in touch. These views should be respected

■   *influence:* children wanted greater attention paid to their views and to have some influence over future plans

■   *future opportunity:* foster children mainly had the same aspirations for their future as other children: to do well at school, get a good job, have a happy family and children. Foster care should provide a springboard to get their lives back on track and provide an opportunity for these achievements, which most take for granted.

A Boy Called Graham (Gaskin, 2005)

In 2005, Graham Gaskin wrote about his successful battle to secure access to his records in *A Boy Called Graham*.

From the time he came into local authority care in 1959, Graham Gaskin experienced many moves within foster care; he had 14 different foster homes before the age of eight. During his 18 years in care, he was sent to over 20 institutions – borstals, remand homes and prisons (*Hansard*, 1981, HC Deb, vol. 12, 282–8). Gaskin repeatedly but unsuccessfully sought access to his records and eventually appealed to the European Court of Human Rights in Strasbourg. In 1989, the court decided that Gaskin's Article 8 right to have his private and family life respected by the state had been breached and that people in Gaskin's position, who had been in public care as children, should not be obstructed from accessing their care records.

Graham Gaskin's case was a milestone victory and led directly to the provisions in the Data Protection Act 1998 enabling access to social services records by people who had been in public care (*Hansard*, 2000, HL Deb, 99W). The story of Graham Gaskin's life (2005) is salutary reading for us all.

Research milestones in the development of adoption

Shared Fate (Kirk, 1964)

In 1964, by questioning some of the central assumptions of adoption, Kirk's *Shared Fate* made adoption a significant issue in the sociological literatures on family and mental health.

The 'shared fate' of adoptive parents and children was the acceptance of difference. Kirk's argument was that simulating a biological relationship was detrimental to adoptive parents and adoptive children. For adoptive parents, difference meant that they were not and could not be biological parents. For the adopted child, difference was that they were not the biological offspring of their parents. Kirk argued that the struggle with difference (whether to ignore it, deny it, or accommodate it) was the single most defining feature of the adoption experience.

Prior to the emergence of Kirk's radical rethink of adoption relations, the denial of difference was dominant (even in the face of physical difference). This was justified on three main grounds:

1   Adoptive parents would be protected from any distress associated with notions of raising an illegitimate child and would avoid awkward discussion about infertility. Agencies went to great lengths to achieve a match of physical characteristics and presumed intellectual ability in order to make the notion of 'as if born to' the adoptive parents as tenable as possible (Kellmer-Pringle, 1972).

2   An adoption that was 'closed', that is, made confidential and records permanently sealed, would help adopted children be raised with the stigma of 'bad blood' put behind them (Samuels, 2001, p. 385).

3   If it were arranged so that the infant's transfer from birth parent to adoptive parent was as early and concealed as possible, unmarried mothers would be shielded from societal opprobrium (van Bueren, 1995). As much help as possible was given to ensure that the birth could take place away from the mother's home surroundings (Petrie, 1998).

Despite all this – some would say – subterfuge, the 'shared fate' of adoptive parents and children was difference – not worse, not better, just different. Acknowledging this was less comfortable but far better for everyone involved.

Ten years after Kirk's case for the recognition of the obvious – difference – in adoption, the notion that the adoptive family cancelled out the birth family remained predominant. In a discussion of the Irish Adoption Bill in 1974, the then Irish Minister for Justice Mr Cooney, arguing against access to birth records, declared that:

It is basic to our adoption code that the adopted child becomes the child of the adoptive parents in everything except the natural blood. It would be contrary to that principle if we allowed to be introduced into that relationship curiosity or questions concerning the natural ancestry of the child. We want to ensure that the family together with the adopted child becomes as far as possible a natural family, bonded in terms of natural love as the Minister for Posts and Telegraphs said. We want to achieve that aim and it would be going against that if we were to facilitate information regarding the ancestry of the adopted child to be given to him. So far as possible we want to make him the child of the adoptive parents and this is the reason for having our code of adoption as is, preserving the secrecy of his origin from the child. (quoted in Clapton, 2008, pp. 132–3)

This thinking resulted in attitudes expressed by an adoption lawyer in the early 1970s when he told an adopted person: 'You have no right to any information whatsoever. You were adopted legally … You had no other parents' (quoted in Fisher, 1973, p. 84).

So, while Kirk's work is included as a milestone, it is fair to say that, as a US publication, the implications of it took time to transfer to UK practice. Today, the notion of practising 'as if born to' and the denial of difference are outmoded because of a general erosion of a belief in adoption secrecy, the reality of older children being adopted from care with memories and perhaps continuing contact with birth family members, and intercountry adoption.

Children Who Wait (Rowe and Lambert, 1973)

In 1973, Rowe and Lambert revealed how many children in care were left 'waiting for something to happen'. Their study *Children Who Wait* found evidence of children who lacked any legal or emotional security and were left 'waiting' for something to happen. It rarely did.

There was widespread drift and delay when it came to securing the future permanent care of these children. The views of social workers were researched and it was found that social workers frequently failed to make timely care plans, and were slow to implement those they did put in place. Rowe and Lambert provided the first comprehensive picture of what was happening in child care services since the establishment of the welfare state. The key conclusion of *Children Who Wait*, that those children who remained in care for any length of time were likely to remain in care even longer, unfortunately still holds true.

In Search of Origins (Triseliotis, 1973)

In 1973, Triseliotis's research demonstrated that adopted children would one day grow up to be adults with a wish to know more about their origins.

Should a youngster ever raise the question [Who are my birth parents?], it is important, of course, to make it very clear that a search is unrealistic and can lead to unhappiness and disillusionment. (*You and Your Adopted Child*, Public Affairs Pamphlet, New York, 1958, quoted in Clapton, 2008, p. 133)

This view was the prevalent attitude throughout the 1950s, 60s and 70s. *In Search of Origins*, Triseliotis's (1973) study of the experiences of adopted adults who had accessed their birth records, refuted the notion that adopted people who expressed more curiosity about their natal backgrounds were more highly clustered in the 'high-problem' group (Jaffee and Fanshel, 1970). Triseliotis's findings were that a wish to know more about one's origins was legitimate, understandable and not an expression of a pathology arising from the adopted person's upbringing. This countered a view that was widespread at the time – that an adopted person's indifference to genealogy was a sign of success. Adoption agencies encouraged adoptive parents in the maintenance of 'a blank and impenetrable wall between the identities of natural and adopting parents' (quoted in Samuels, 2001, p. 399). Drawing on research into adoption agency practices, Samuels goes on to quote from one agency's manual that characterized a searching adopted adult as:

a person who has had many unhappy past experiences and … is so intent upon finding the natural parent that he is not able to consider his request in a realistic or rational way. (p. 410)

The manual advised caseworkers to discourage the search and then, if necessary, to refer the person for psychological treatment (p. 410). Betty Lifton, a prominent campaigning adopted person, recounts being told by a psychiatrist when she was in the early stages of seeking information about her origins that 'your need to look for your mother is neurotic' (quoted in Samuels, 2001, p. 403).

The consequences of this standpoint could be dismaying and debilitating for those involved: dismay for the adoptive parents when it seemed as though their parenting had not been sufficient to 'quell' their child's curiosity about their origins – especially since they had been assured that 'instances of extreme curiosity and concern almost never happen' (*You and Your Adopted Child*); debilitating for the adopted person because of their sense of betraying their parents by wishing to know of their birth family origins. The result was often the maintenance of everyone's (unhealthy) silence on the matter. This meant that the adopted person either suspended their wish to access their birth records until the death of their adoptive parents or was required to conceal their quest for information.

The key implication of Triseliotis's findings was that knowledge of background information was a deeply felt psychological need, and that the absence of such information can lead to consequences ranging from negative feelings of incompleteness, loss and anger through to severe difficulties in establishing a sense of personal identity.

In Search of Origins (the work for which was conducted in Scotland where adopted people were allowed access to their birth record) pioneered widespread openness regarding adoption records and led directly to the provision to do so contained in the Children Act 1975 and the Adoption Act 1976.

Half a Million Women (Howe et al., 1992)

In 1992, research by Howe et al. highlighted the importance of birth mothers' experiences and needs. *Half a Million Women* (Howe et al., 1992) was concerned with the experience of birth mothers in 'stranger' adoptions, that is, those in which an infant was relinquished to non-relatives. It contextualized these (generally secret) adoptions, detailing the stigma and societal and familial attitudes facing unmarried, pregnant women and the lack of choice that gave them no option but adoption of their child.

A review at the time noted that:

> Previously it was assumed to be in the interest of all concerned for an adopted person's two families by birth and by adoption to have no contact during the transfer of the child from one to the other and thereafter to lead entirely separate lives. For social workers there was no role after the adoption order since the newly created family merged with the general population, hopefully to live happily ever after. (Hill, 1992, p. 597)

Howe et al.'s book is skilfully structured with one foot in practice (that of the Post Adoption Centre in London) and another in theory in a highly readable combination of interviews, case histories and analysis. Prior to the 1990s, the post-adoption services that existed were generally concentrated on the adoptive family except for a handful of voluntary agencies. *Half a Million Women*, with its message that birth mothers experienced enduring loss and pain, was instrumental in ensuring that birth mothers took their place at the table; the term 'the adoption triangle' (adopted people, adoptive parents and birth mothers) came into popular usage. Most importantly, local authority after-adoption services have now expanded to include birth parents support. *Half a Million Women* was not solely responsible for this. Practice responses to birth parent demands for help, birth mother organizations such as the Natural Parents Network and other research findings all contributed to a process that began in the early 1980s in the UK. But *Half a Million Women* accelerated the process.

Later, birth fathers' experiences were to come to the fore, with Witney (2005) making explicit reference to *Half a Million Women* when she titled her paper 'Over half a million fathers'.

About Adoption (Morgan, 2006)

In 2006, research by Morgan gave us access to the views of over 200 adopted children. Morgan's report, *About Adoption* (Morgan, 2006), discloses what adopted children themselves think about adoption – about the way they were adopted, about being an adopted person and whether that makes a difference at home or at school, and about what might be special about being adopted.

Similar in tone and structure to *Being Fostered* (Morgan, 2005) and from the same team, *About Adoption* stands out for the number who responded to the questionnaire – 208 children and young people aged between 6 and 22; the average age was 11.

Sections include 'The best things about getting adopted' (42% answered 'joining a new or real family' and 46% said 'being part of a family') and 'The worst things about getting adopted' (20% answered leaving your old family; another 8% spoke of being sepa-

> **Making connexions**
>
> 'The key conclusion of *Children Who Wait*, that those children who remained in care for any length of time were likely to remain in care even longer, unfortunately still holds true.'
>
> Why do you think that is? What can the practising social worker do to improve matters?

rated from their brothers and sisters and 'missing your own family').

The report does all it can to bring out the views of the children and young people and makes fascinating reading that sums up in a paragraph what academics often take pages to say. The children's top ten ideas for improving adoption were:

1 make it quicker
2 involve and support the child more
3 keep the child in touch with what is happening – in their birth family as well as in the adoption itself
4 give more information about adoption
5 don't change social workers in the middle of being adopted
6 don't separate brothers and sisters
7 go to only one foster home before being adopted
8 make the process more enjoyable and fun
9 have more trial days with the new family
10 let children themselves make the final decision on their new parents.

In addition, the report offers guidance on how social workers should check whether children are happy in new families:

- ask the child, but listen to the answers
- make visits to see the child
- speak to the parents and the child, both alone and together
- spend time talking to the child away from the family home
- check how the child is fitting in at home and at school.

And finally ...

'The background of children who enter local authority care'
(Bebbington and Miles, 1989)

In 1989, Bebbington and Miles described the background of children who enter local authority care. Their paper was about the influence of socioeconomic factors on the risk of children coming into care. They compared the backgrounds of children who had entered out-of-home care with children who had not entered care and found that having a single parent was the greatest risk factor for care placement. They concluded that if a child came from a white, two-parent family, with three or fewer children, who owned a home with more rooms than family members and who did not receive welfare benefits, the odds of entering local authority care were 1 in 7,000. However, if a child had a mixed ethnic background, lived in a single-parent family that received welfare benefits and rented a home with less rooms than there were family members, the odds of entering care were 1 in 10.

Having agreed that poverty is a major determinant, 16 years later, Little (2005, p. 11) notes the gulf between the poor whose children come into care and those who work in care or write about it: 'What cannot be said, because the research is not set up to show it, is that most people working in or commentating on the care system would not let their own children anywhere near it.'

Bebbington and Miles's work still serves as a reminder that if child and family poverty were abolished, the numbers of children in the care system would be far fewer than at present.

Further reading

■ Fahlberg, V. (2008) *A Child's Journey through Placement*. London: BAAF.

Beautifully accessible handbook that guides workers, step by step, through the caring process.

■ Howe, D., Sawbridge, P. and Hinings, D. (1992) *Half a Million Women: Mothers who Lose their Children by Adoption*. London: Penguin.

Played a major part in the emergence of birth mothers as key players in the sequence of events before, during and after adoption.

■ Kirk, D. (1964) *Shared Fate: A Theory of Adoption and Mental Health*. New York: Free Press.

Because of its emphasis on 'differentness', one of the most influential books in the history of adoption.

References

Bebbington, A. and Miles, J. (1989) 'The background of children who enter local authority care', *British Journal of Social Work*, **19**(5): 349–68.

Berridge, D. (2005) '*Fostering Now: Messages from Research*: a summary', *Adoption & Fostering*, **29**(4): 6–8.

Brooks, R. (1994) 'Children at risk: fostering resilience and hope', *American Journal of Orthopsychiatry*, **64**(4): 545–53.

Research

Cabinet Office (2008) *Think Family: A Literature Review of Whole Family Approaches.* London: Cabinet Office.

Cairns, K. (2002) 'Making sense: the use of theory and research to support foster care', *Adoption & Fostering*, **26**(2): 6–13.

Clapton, G. (2008) 'The right to information in practice: adoption records, confidentiality and secrecy', in J. McGhee and C. Clark (eds) *Private and Confidential? Handling Personal Information in the Social and Health Services.* Bristol: Policy Press.

Fahlberg, V. (1991) *A Child's Journey through Placement.* Indianapolis: Perspectives Press.

Fisher, A. (1973) *The Search for Anna Fisher.* New York: Fawcett Crest Books.

Fisher, M., Marsh, P., Phillips, D. and Sainsbury, E. (1986) *In and Out of Care: The Experience of Children, Parents and Social Workers.* London: B.T. Batsford.

Gaskin, G. (2005) *A Boy Called Graham.* London: Blake Publishing.

Gilligan, R. (1997) 'Beyond permanence? The importance of resilience in child placement practice and planning', *Adoption & Fostering*, **21**(1): 12–20.

Gilligan, R. (2001) *Promoting Resilience: Supporting Children and Young People Who are in Care, Adopted or in Need.* London: BAFF.

Gilligan, R. (2004) 'Promoting resilience in child and family social work: issues for social work practice', *Journal of Social Work Education*, **23**(1): 93–104.

Gilligan, R. (2009) *Promoting Resilience: Supporting Children and Young People Who are in Care, Adopted or in Need* (2nd edn). London: BAFF.

Hill, M. (1992) 'Book review', *British Journal of Social Work*, **22**(5): 597–8.

Howe, D., Sawbridge, P. and Hinings, D. (1992) *Half a Million Women: Mothers who Lose their Children by Adoption.* London: Penguin.

Jaffee, B. and Fanshel, D. (1970) *How They Fared in Adoption.* New York: Columbia University Press.

Jenkins, S. and Norman, E. (1972) *Filial Deprivation and Foster Care.* New York: Columbia University Press.

Kellmer-Pringle, M. (1972) 'A place of one's own', in J. Seglow, M. Kellmer-Pringle and P. Wedge (eds) *Growing Up Adopted.* London: National Foundation for Education Research.

Kirk, D. (1964) *Shared Fate: A Theory of Adoption and Mental Health.* New York: Free Press.

Little, M. (2005) 'Time for a change: a review of *Fostering Now* and other programmes of research on children in need', *Adoption & Fostering*, **29**(4): 9–22.

Morgan, R. (2005) *Being Fostered: A National Survey of the Views of Foster Children, Foster Carers, and Birth Parents about Foster Care.* Newcastle: Office of the Children's Rights Director.

Morgan, R. (2006) *About Adoption: A Children's Views Report.* Newcastle: Office of the Children's Rights Director.

Petrie, A. (1998) *Gone to Aunts.* Toronto: McClelland & Stewart.

Rowe, J. and Lambert, L. (1973) *Children Who Wait: A Study of Children Needing Substitute Families.* London: Association of British Adoption Agencies.

Rowe, J., Cain, H., Hundleby, M. and Keane, A. (1984) *Long-term Foster Care.* London: Batsford.

Rutter, M. (1985) 'Family and school influences on cognitive development', *Journal of Child Psychology and Psychiatry*, 26, 683–704.

Samuels, E. (2001) 'The idea of adoption: an inquiry into the history of adult adoptee access to birth records', *Rutgers Law Review*, 53, pp. 367–437.

Schofield, G. and Beek, M. (2005) 'Risk and resilience in long-term foster care', *British Journal of Social* Work, **35**(8): 1283–301.

Sinclair, I. (2005) *Fostering Now: Messages from Research*. London: Jessica Kingsley.

Thorpe, D. (1988) 'Career patterns in child care: implications for service, *British Journal of Social* Work, **18**(2): 137–53.

Triseliotis, J. (1973) *In Search of Origins*. London: Routledge & Kegan Paul.

Ungar, M. (2008) 'Resilience across cultures', *British Journal of Social Work*, **38**(2): 218–35.

Van Bueren, G. (1995) 'Children's access to adoption records: state discretion or an enforceable international right?', *The Modern Law Review*, **58**(1): 37–53.

Wilson, J. (1991) *The Story of Tracy Beaker*. London: Doubleday.

Wilson, K., Ruch, G., Lymbery, M. and Cooper, A. (2008) *Social Work: An Introduction to Contemporary Practice*. Harlow: Pearson.

Witney, C. (2005) 'Over half a million fathers: an exploration into the experiences of fathers involved in adoption in the mid-20th century in England and Wales', *Journal of Social Work*, **5**(1): 83–99.

Research

15
Adoption and fostering in practice

SALLY HOLLAND AND CECILIA LOVE

This chapter introduces and discusses four practice examples that represent real-life episodes and reflections from the life stories of young adults who were adopted or lived in foster care. These accounts were generously shared with us in two recent life history research projects. These real-life (anonymized) examples give a vivid sense of the challenges, achievements and complexities of working constructively with children and young people who are adopted or looked after in foster care. Because they are real, they are not simple stories with neat endings, but they do raise important issues regarding family and professional relationships, culture, 'race', and responding in a critical and reflective manner.

The first research project aimed to gain an in-depth understanding of how transracial adoptive family life had been experienced for both the child and the adoptive mother. The study deployed psychosocial interview methods (Stopford, 2004) in order to gain an in-depth understanding of how transracially adopted adults remember their childhood experiences and how these family experiences have affected them as young adults. There was a diverse range of ethnicities involved in the study, but all the adoptive mothers were of white ethnicity. Although adoptees involved in the study were placed for adoption up to 30 years ago, and contemporary transracial adoption policy and practice has changed and evolved, many of the issues raised by the participants in the study remain timeless and relevant to consider when working with transracial placements. This includes the complexity involved in understanding and managing feelings around acceptance, negotiating the difference of the adoptive family status in a context of the 'naturalness' of the biological family, and managing two sets of racially different parents (Tessler et al., 1999). While these themes of differentiation and acceptance may be relevant to consider when working with transracial adoptive contexts, they can also be understood in an increasingly interconnected globalized world where questions around 'roots', national and racial identities are being asked by many parts of contemporary society (Feigelman, 2000; Yngvesson, 2003).

The second research project involved life history interviews with 16 care leavers. All eight young men and eight young women had left care since the implementation of the Children (Leaving Care) Act 2000 and at the time of interview in 2009 were aged 17–24. They had experienced a wide range of experiences and settings while looked after and subsequent experiences included parenthood, university, employment, unemployment, prison and acting as advocates and educators. Most took part in two lengthy semi-structured interviews about their lives and experiences and early findings were developed in consultation with a wider group of care leavers.

Contemporary families in the UK are increasingly characterized by the diverse ways in which they are formed and practised. Alongside same-sex, single carer, mixed 'race' or heritage and step-parent families, looked after and transracial adoptive families are other examples of family forms that contribute to this increasingly diverse family landscape.

All looked after and adopted children and young people have experienced separation from a birth parent and some have experienced multiple losses. The majority will have experienced some form of abuse or neglect in early childhood. Many will have experienced stigma and a sense of being an 'outsider' at home, at school or in their local community. Many will feel that they have not had aspects of their experiences properly explained to them. Such emotional and material experiences will often have some impact on behaviour and physical and emotional health. Practitioners and carers need to be tuned into such needs and respond as needed. However, we also wish to emphasize the diversity of experience and responses by young people who are looked after or adopted. Many young people who have been looked after or adopted go on to lead conventionally successful lives (Chase et al., 2006). Above all, we need to recognize those who are looked after or adopted as children and young people first, with the needs, joys, sadnesses and potential of all other children and young people. Practitioners can play a pivotal role in advocating, and indeed demanding, excellent care and education, in the way we would for our own children.

Transracial adoptive families

Since its conception, the practice of joining 'racially' different and nonbiological children and parents has remained an ideological battlefield. Located in what Galvin (2003) describes as the vortex of race, culture, class and gender, the contentious debates that surround transracial adoption not only touch on established norms of individual identity, but, as Rushton and Minnis (1997) articulate, also encroach on political identities of communities as a whole. It is inescapable that we as practitioners are also influenced by these often contentious broader social and political debates that surround the practice of transracial adoption. The first two case studies aim to encourage critical reflection on how our own racial, national and class identities as practitioners may impact on the way in which we assess and provide interventions for transracial adoptive families.

Practice

Practice example 1 Rebecca

Culture and 'race'

Rebecca is a young woman who was adopted as a baby from the UK public care system in the 1980s into a transracial adoptive context. At the time of interview, Rebecca has just gained a first class honours degree and is preparing to complete a vocational masters in London. She describes herself as having many friends, and a very close relationship with her adoptive parents.

Rebecca is of East Asian ethnicity and has grown up in an adoptive family where her adoptive father is also of Asian ethnicity and her adoptive mother and adoptive sister are white. Rebecca grew up in a rural and predominantly white part of the UK where she describes herself as having often been the only non-white person among her friendship group and wider community. By discussing aspects of how Rebecca experienced her racial identity in a transracial adoptive context, the case study aims to increase understanding of some of the potential difficulties involved in having a racially different body, but inside feeling culturally the same as her peers and family. Rebecca describes this 'mismatch' as resulting in her having to manage difficult feelings around not being able to fully take ownership of the cultural practices of the people she is close to – such as her parents and friends – largely because of what she describes as responses from other people. Indeed, a prominent theme in Rebecca's life story has involved her managing some of the complex feelings that arise from the way in which she feels the visible difference between herself and her family is often responded to in subtle and nonverbal ways.

In Rebecca's description of her going to support her national team at a sporting event with her friends, it becomes possible to gain an insight into the potential emotional complexities involved in terms of the relationship between how someone may feel about their race and how the race of their body may prevent them from fully gaining access to the national identity of their adoptive parents. Rebecca describes how her friends wear the national shirt 'without even thinking about it', but, for Rebecca, being able to wear the rugby shirt is described as being a much more complex act. Her adoptive family nationality and geographical place of her childhood means she has a legitimate right to wear the shirt of the team she is supporting. But when she has worn it in the past, she has felt a sense of embarrassment – 'of being always conscious of it', of feeling 'awkward', and feeling as though something is not quite right. Instead, she chooses to 'wear a little bit of red, but won't go all the way and wear the official shirt', because for her she describes it as always being aware of the national shirt on her 'non-white body'.

For practitioners, this short and simple description of Rebecca's everyday experience can make us think about how crucial the appearance of the body is to feeling accepted and having ownership of a national identity. It is important for practitioners, when working with people of non-white ethnicity, to consider how cultural practices, including our own, may unintentionally create a sense of exclusion for people of ethnicity, which can be experienced as being differentiated. As practition-ers, it may be helpful to advocate for interventions that take into account transracial adoption and fostering not simply as an issue involving one-on-one parent–child relationships across racial lines, but to consider the significance of the way in which race may be experienced in the broader context of society and specific geographical places (Perry, 2006). Perhaps an important point for practitioners to note is to try to avoid imposing a national, racial or cultural identity on the transracial adoptee/looked after child or their adoptive or foster parents, and to facilitate an assessment or intervention that enables members of the transracial adoptive family to articulate how race and ethnicity come to have personal meaning for members of the transra-cial family. The crucial social work skill needed to facilitate this articulation is the ability to listen and demonstrate empathy towards an individual articulating an account of what their racial identity means to them. To demonstrate this ability to empathize potentially requires critical reflection on how the transracial adoptive or foster family identity may implicitly impact on our own sense of national, racial and cultural identity.

Contact with birth families

We know that children and young people will have individual needs and preferences around contact with birth family members (see SCIE, 2004; Morgan, 2009). These will include extended family members such as grandparents, aunts and uncles. Needs and preferences will change over time and may be ambivalent. In other words, chil-dren and young people may desire contact but also find it upsetting. Contact is also rapidly changing with the use of social networking sites such as Facebook. Siblings are as important as parents to many children, and some feel particularly sad that they have lost touch when siblings have been adopted. Children and young people wish to be consulted about contact, but most understand that sometimes decisions against their preferences will need to be made to keep them safe. Children and young people often want to maintain contact, or at least hear news about, former foster carers and other non-related young people they have lived with in the past.

Research findings do not point to improved outcomes for looked after young people related to contact, but there is a legal presumption that contact will be promoted if safe and beneficial (Children Act 1989).

Practice example 2   Catherine

Birth family experiences

Central to all adoptive contexts is that the child is born to one family, but grows up in a different family setting and therefore becomes part of a family involving two sets of parents, birth parents and adoptive parents. In same-'race' placement adoptive settings, the adoptive status is much less visible to the outside world, which provides

Practice

a higher level of autonomy around when and to whom the adoptive or looked after status is disclosed. For the transracial parenting relationship, the racial difference potentially places an additional dimension of complexity in terms of how the adoptive status is negotiated and managed. Nearly all the participants involved in the transracial adoption study describe experiences involving this central theme of having to manage outside responses to the racial difference between their adoptive parents. Participants described experiencing a sense of being looked at twice when participants referred to their adoptive parents as 'mum' or 'dad' in public settings, or being mistaken for girlfriends or boyfriends of their adoptive parents. These experiences were described as heightening a sense of ongoing connection with birth parents because of outside responses to the visual difference of the transracial parenting relation, even where participants had not physically met their birth parents. They provide just some examples that illustrate the potential complexity involved in negotiating the powerful racial norms of families.

In Catherine's descriptions of her experience of returning to birth family contexts, she provides an insight into the complexity of feelings involved around how that original disconnection from birth parents is experienced when there is a reconnection through having contact with birth family members; it highlights some of the difficulty in being between two different parental and racial worlds.

Catherine is of Jamaican ethnicity and was the only child adopted out of a birth family where she has two other birth siblings who stayed in the birth family. She attends the wedding of her birth brother where members of his wider birth family are present. What is prominent in her description of this experience is how a sense of her disconnection from her birth family is communicated in subtle and invisible ways. She describes feeling that just her presence in groups at the wedding changes the dynamics. For example, she describes approaching a group of her birth cousins where

> everyone was laughing and joking and the conversation was quite bubbly, but as I approached, everyone kind of, not in a bad way, but changed, you can see it in their faces when I'm there, you can see the way they look, you feel like you're objectified in a sense.

She describes feeling a heightened sense of uneasiness with her 'blackness', and becomes aware of the social position she has gained through her adoption in terms of her education, her profession and cultural capital, which, in relation to her birth family, is now quite different. A more obvious differentiating experience at this wedding is when she is mistaken for one of the waitresses by a member of her birth family. To assume someone wearing a white shirt and black trousers is one of the waiting staff is potentially an easy mistake to make for anyone, and perhaps for some people it is an incident that could be laughed or brushed off. However, for Catherine being misrecognized as a waitress in this birth family context is painful and further consolidates her sense of disconnection from a sense of belonging to this group. Being misrecognized is already familiar to her from her transracial adoptive context where the blackness of her body and the whiteness of her adoptive parents has meant that her family status has been questioned many times before. At this wedding, Catherine also describes how frustrated she feels when her birth mother presents her to other members of the family by her Jamaican birth name rather than her adopted name of Catherine. Some of the women in her birth family at the wedding make comments on the way she dresses, refer to her Afro hair as being styled in a 'white way' and say that 'she's lost our black ways'. The way Catherine describes herself dealing with these comments at the time is to 'laugh them off, and say nothing, just smile'. However, the way she actually feels is angry and hurt and these comments confirm to her that members of her birth family do not accept her for who she now is, so that she feels part of herself is denied by them.

These are just some examples of the potential complexity involved in forming relationships with birth families for practitioners to be aware. What is important to consider as practitioners working with children or young adults returning to birth family contexts is some of the complex and potentially painful feelings involved. We recommend creating reflective spaces in which young people going through these kinds of experiences can talk to practitioners about some of the feelings these encounters may bring up.

Making connexions

Having read about Rebecca and Catherine's experiences, consider how these visibly different child and parent relationships make you feel. How does your own experience of or encounters with people of a different ethnicity from yours influence the way you think about transracial adoption or fostering? Where do you sit in the ideological debates that surround transracial adoption, and why have you taken this position?

Relationship-based social work with looked after young people

A key issue for many looked after young people is the lack of stable relationships in their lives. In our care leavers' life history study, many of the young people had not had a positive, sustained relationship with an adult carer or professional adult throughout their childhoods. Social workers, in particular, were often seen as distant and ever changing. Many studies of young people's experiences have found that young people value reliability, honesty, humour and empathy. Most young people (at least in retrospect) valued having clear boundaries laid down, as long as they already had a trusting relationship with the social worker or carer. Relationship-based social work places emphasis on the quality of the relationship between social worker and service user. This can be marginalized in practice that is overfocused on completing paperwork for assessments and reviews. Practitioners need to search for, highlight and bolster strengths as well as tackling difficulties, and also recognize that many looked after young people provide care, love and assistance to birth family members and foster carers as well as being recipients of care. Foster carers need support and guidance on how to keep in touch with young people after they leave their care and it should be recognized that many young people want to have some contact with

Practice

former social workers, who may remember them when they were younger and have important connections with their past (see Holland, 2010).

Practice example 3 Rhian

Behaviour and emotions in foster care

Rhian is a young woman of 22. She works in social care, is married and has a young child. She describes her current life as happy and settled, but her entire childhood and youth were marked by a series of difficult experiences. She experienced serious abuse and neglect at the hands of her birth parents and extended family members. Social workers were involved intermittently throughout her early childhood and she had a brief period in foster care at a young age and a few further periods of respite care. She was permanently removed into care in her early teens. By this time Rhian was acting as a primary carer for her younger siblings. She was separated from all her large sibling group and found separation from the younger siblings, who called her 'mum', traumatic. Rhian lived in a series of foster homes and later spent time in residential care and hostels. Rhian gave a detailed and reflective account of her life experiences. There are many practice points that could be explored through her experiences, but here we have chosen to focus on Rhian's account of her behavioural and emotional responses to her experiences and how she feels that the responses of those around her helped or hindered.

Rhian's initial period in foster care was experienced by her as caring and warm. Her emotional and practical need to be cared for was met by her first two carers. The first temporary carer 'was really like soft and calming and she was really like happy and bubbly and stuff as well'. This helped Rhian who says she had no idea what family life should feel like, and who was desperately missing her siblings. The second, longer term carer looked after Rhian for 18 months. Rhian feels that she taught her how to 'feel and look normal', buying her new clothes, showing her how to style her hair and about personal hygiene. Nonetheless, Rhian's behaviour began to deteriorate; she recalls that she began to be violent and to run away. Her experienced foster carer was apparently calm and forgiving, but Rhian eventually asked to be moved after a violent fight with another child in the foster home.

In her next period in a residential home, Rhian began to self-harm and get involved in substance misuse. Another stable period in a foster home followed, with the carer encouraging Rhian's creative writing skills, but Rhian began drinking heavily and the placement ended. Rhian then moved between a series of children's homes, where she appears to have led a chaotic life of partying and heavy drinking, which culminated in a two-week 'bender' when she was 16. She was moved to a care leavers' hostel and lived in hostels for three years (interspersed with a three-month period of street homelessness). Against the odds, Rhian has found stability and some degree of success in early adulthood, demonstrating the resilience that many individuals are able to muster despite difficult experiences (Chase et al., 2006). Rhian sums up her deteriorating behaviour and feelings while looked after: 'It was just sort of like a flower that just sort of come out and the petals just fell off everywhere and just went off in every direction.'

In Rhian's account of her life she gives us insights into what she feels caused her behaviour problems. Rhian suggests that some of her challenging behaviour was related to the kinds of feelings experienced by many teenagers, that is, they were normal responses to her life stage: 'I was still a quiet sort of teenager that didn't really know what was going on around her kind of thing.' On the other hand, her teenage feelings were amplified by a number of factors. Primarily, she felt intensely conflicting feelings towards her mother, who was waging a court battle to regain the care of her children. She is able, in retrospect, to chart her changing feelings towards her mother, from profound longing to anger and then disappointment. Second, she rebelled against the intense involvement of social services in her life. She says that she was influenced by the negative portrayal of social services that she had been brought up with and grew irritated that she had no control over the timings and contents of meetings about her. Third, she was also strongly influenced by her peer group:

> In the end I just thought 'stuff it', I'd seen other foster children violent, I'd seen them throwing chairs, I'd seen them going out and smoking pot, and I'd seen them running away and not coming back – so it was like I sort of went down that road then, for like, about a year or two, that was when we had them 15/16 placements afterwards.

There are no easy answers to helping an angry and upset young person lead a stable and less destructive life. By the time she was about 15, Rhian must have felt she had nothing to gain from conforming or living a more stable life. However, she also analyses, in retrospect, the care that she received.

Helpful aspects of Rhian's care were attention to her physical needs and comfort. This felt nurturing and warm (Rees and Pithouse, 2008) and helped her to feel 'normal'. She had strong memories of these early experiences in foster care that appear to have sustained her through later chaotic periods. Second, at least one teacher and one foster carer recognized that she had a talent for writing and encouraged her to write down her thoughts and feelings. A teacher allowed her to sit in her room and write when she needed to. Recognition by others that she had worth and abilities appears to have helped her maintain and develop her self-esteem and confidence. Rhian identifies a turning point of her life when she became involved in leaving care services. A training programme kept her occupied and gave her positive experiences. The leaving care team manager wrote to her personally and humorously in response to a tongue-in-cheek complaint she had sent about her social worker's car. Her leaving care worker was firm in supporting her when she was doing well and showing open disapproval when she 'went off the rails'. Both responses showed a human face and point of connection to social services. Finally, Rhian was helped by volunteering as an adult with a user-led advocacy group for looked after children.

Practice

Hindrances to Rhian's progress were, in her view, the poor peer relationships she developed in foster and residential settings. She portrays a pretty chaotic environment in the latter with few effective boundaries. Second, she was confused and upset over her experiences and relations with her birth family. She does not report any therapeutic intervention that helped, nor life story work, although she received mental health interventions on at least two occasions.

Rhian's main messages for practitioners are that young people need to be helped to understand their situation, to be shown genuine care and love, to have special talents or interests encouraged, to have effective boundaries and to have carers who can stick with young people through 'thick and thin'.

Life story work and understanding the past

Life story work has been used with looked after and adopted children since the 1960s (see Ryan and Walker, 2007; Baynes, 2008). It is used to help children and young people understand their past and present living circumstances and to provide a record that they can add to and look back on in the future. It might take the form of a book, a box of mementos and/or a digital record. There is little research on the effectiveness of life story work, but a small-scale study found that the process was valuable to young people for both factual information and emotional support (Willis and Holland, 2010). Many looked after young people lack access to the anecdotes and photographs about their early lives that most of us take for granted. Many care leavers in our life history study were unclear about their early histories and several felt that barriers were put in the way of them accessing their case files as young adults.

Photographs and items of emotional value may be lost when young people make multiple moves. Practitioners and carers should consider how to support young people in making sense of their past and keeping material items safe.

Practice example 4   Calvin

Multiple losses and the search for explanation

Calvin is in his early twenties. He currently attends a further education college and lives alone in a flat. He spent nearly all his childhood in foster care, having been accommodated as a baby. His parents misused drugs and his father died when Calvin was a young child. Calvin was in a stable foster home until he was seven. At that point the local authority decided that he deserved a chance to be adopted and his foster family were not in a position to adopt him. Unfortunately, none of the prospective adoptive homes worked out for Calvin. Calvin feels that this was because he had been so attached to his first foster carers and could not allow himself to become so attached again. He had stopped having contact with his mother, with whom he had had intermittent contact until he was four. Calvin explains how he felt during this period and the implications he felt it had for his relationships and self-confidence in the longer term:

And so, I went, and then I started doing this whole going into different families but because I was so settled, there was no way of me being settled in the other homes … It was quite distressing and a lot of the rejection I went through, through meeting people, I met people and they would … I would stay with them one weekend and they would say things and that, and I'd never see them again. I never had a reason why … I've never been able to understand why I wasn't liked and why I was rejected. But now growing up I sort of understand a little bit, because I was so settled, it was hard for them to move me. But I didn't know growing up that it was that.

Calvin experienced a strong sense of rejection and being disliked as a young child. He had several meetings at the age of 10 with potential long-term foster carers, but the meetings stopped without warning or explanation, and Calvin thought

there was something wrong with me for that, sometimes I used to think it was because maybe they found out more about my mum and dad, that they were drug addicts and they thought that I'd grow up to be this crazy drug addict. I don't know, I became very self-conscious.

As a teenager, Calvin experienced a period of stability with an experienced carer, but had secretly started making contact with his mother whom he had contacted through an older sibling. This contact became negative and anxiety-provoking for Calvin and led to the breakdown of yet another foster home. Later, after a further series of foster placements and hostel places, Calvin gained and maintained his own flat and gradually carved out a stable life for himself. Like Rhian above, he demonstrates extraordinary resilience. His reflective account allows us to draw lessons for practice and here we concentrate on issues of caring relationships and the need for an adequate understanding of one's situation.

Calvin appears to have had some experiences of positive caring relationships in his childhood and youth, and he was able to describe in his life history interview how good it felt to be cared for by his first long-term carers, his last foster carer and by one social worker who worked with him for 10 years – an unusual length of time in contemporary children's services. These relationships may have helped sustain him through the series of losses – from his birth parents, his foster carers and that long-term social worker who left suddenly and without any explanation. In common with many of the young people in our research study, Calvin did not have a sustained relationship with any single adult throughout his childhood. Birth family members came and went over the years and there was a series of different foster carers. This meant that he did not have anyone with whom he could reminisce or even ask for basic information. He was left with a sense of inadequacy and being unloved. In the course of our interviews, we were able to witness the difference that information and connections with one's early history can make. In Calvin's first interview, he explained that he had not understood why his first, and primary, foster carers had stopped caring for him. A few weeks later, in his second interview for the research project, he reported that he had made contact with these carers through a social networking site. He now understood why he had had to leave them and had been told how upset they had been to lose him. Knowing that they had cared for him deeply and had not intentionally rejected him, but allowed him to be moved on in his 'best interest', led Calvin to report that he felt this was a 'turning point' and that he felt more at peace with his early life history.

Calvin's account powerfully brings home the significance of multiple moves on a young child's life and the need for adequate explanations. It is possible that he did receive more explanation and support than he recalls, but his lack of memory of any form of help to make sense of his experiences suggests the need for repeated explanation over the years, and perhaps a written account, such as a life story book or memory box, that a young person can return to in their own time. Calvin was unusual in having one social worker for a long period of time, but when that social worker left without any explanation that Calvin can recall, Calvin had no helping professional who remembered him as a young boy. Subsequent social workers may have assumed that Calvin had been given sufficient explanations of his situation. Children and young people need to be enabled to ask questions throughout childhood, when and if they are ready to, rather it becoming some big 'revelation' when they turn 18.

Conclusion

There is an ongoing debate as to whether substitute care is an adequate response by contemporary society to families facing extreme difficulties (Forrester et al., 2009; Little, 2010; Sinclair, 2010). Nonetheless, removing a child from their birth family is sometimes the only, and indeed best, option when that family is unable to provide the care that a child needs. Only one of the 16 young people in the care leavers' life histories study expressed the view that it had been wrong to remove them from home. However, accommodating a child or young person does not, of course, end their relationship with their birth family. For many young people, the changing relationship with their birth family and the often confusing emotions associated with attempting to maintain interpersonal relationships across several households and with those about whom they may feel ambivalent can have an enormous impact on behaviour and general wellbeing. We have seen in these case examples that young people need to be given an opportunity to understand their background, make sense of their current situation and have hope about the future. They may need to be given repeated opportunities to discuss their living situation and the reason for them being in care, and this includes adequate access to their records when they are adults. We believe that enormous efforts should be made to help young people maintain positive relationships with adults, whether relatives, carers or formal or informal helpers, over sustained periods of time. Many will have complex and dynamic relationships with birth family members and they may well need help in navigating their practical and emotional responses.

Practitioners' response to these issues will be enhanced if attention is paid to class, 'race' and other issues of cultural difference. How these affect individuals will vary greatly, but acknowledging that these may be an issue may help carers and young people reflect on and share their experiences. As practitioners, we need to reflect on our own social identities and family experiences in order to understand and work constructively with others.

Acknowledgements

With thanks to Voices from Care Cymru, to Anne Crowley, Emma Renold and Valerie Walkerdine for their contributions to the research studies reported in this chapter, and to the anonymous research participants.

Further reading

■ Chase, E., Simon, A. and Jackson, S. (2006) *In Care and After: A Positive Perspective.* Abingdon: Routledge.

Reports results from a number of important research studies and avoids a deficit approach to understanding looked after children's experiences.

■ Forrester, D., Goodman, K., Cocker, C. et al. (2009) 'What is the impact of public care on children's welfare? A review of research findings from England and Wales and their policy implications', *Journal of Social Policy*, **38**(3): 439–56.

Important article that prompts us to re-examine the case for public care.

■ Treacher, A. and Katz, I. (2000) *The Dynamics of Adoption, Social and Personal Perspectives.* London: Jessica Kingsley.

Useful generic book on adoption that also contains a chapter on transracial adoption

References

Baynes, P. (2008) 'Untold stories: a discussion of life story work', *Adoption & Fostering*, **32**(2): 43–9.

Chase, E., Simon, A. and Jackson, S. (2006) *In Care and After: A Positive Perspective*. Abingdon: Routledge.

Feigelman, W. (2000) 'Adjustments of transracially and inracially adopted young adults', *Child and Adolescent Social Work Journal*, **17**(3): 165–84.

Forrester, D., Goodman, K., Cocker, C. et al. (2009) 'What is the impact of public care on children's welfare? A review of research findings from England and Wales and their policy implications', *Journal of Social Policy*, **38**(3): 439–56.

Galvin, K.M. (2003) 'International and transracial adoption: a communication research agenda', *Journal of Family Communication*, 3, 237–53.

Practice

Holland, S. (2010) 'Looked after children and the ethic of care', *British Journal of Social Work*, **40**(6): 1664–80.

Little, M. (2010) 'Looked after children: can existing services ever succeed?', *Adoption and Fostering*, **34**(2): 3–7.

Morgan, R. (2009) *Keeping In Touch*. London: Ofsted.

Perry, T.L. (2006) 'Transracial adoption and gentrification: an essay on race, power, family and community', *Boston College Third World Law Journal*, **26**(25): 25–60.

Rees, A. and Pithouse, A. (2008) 'The intimate world of strangers: embodying the child in foster care', *Child and Family Social Work*, **13**(3): 338–47.

Rushton, A. and Minnis, H. (1997) 'Annotation: transracial family placements', *Journal of Child Psychology & Psychiatry*, **38**(2): 157–9.

Ryan, T. and Walker, R. (2007) *Life Story Work* (2nd edn). London: BAAF.

SCIE (Social Care Institute for Excellence) (2004) *SCIE Guide 7: Fostering*, http://www.scie.org.uk/publications/guides/guide07.pdf.

Sinclair, I. (2010) 'Looked after children: can existing services ever succeed? A different view', *Adoption and Fostering*, **34**(2): 8–13.

Stopford, A. (2004) 'Researching postcolonial subjectivities: the application of relational (postclassical) psychoanalysis to research methodology', *International Journal of Critical Psychology*, 10, 13–35.

Tessler, R. Gamache, G. and Liu, L. (1999) *West Meets East: Americans Adopt Chinese Children*. Westport, CT: Greenwood.

Willis, R. and Holland, S. (2009) 'Life story work: reflections on the experience by looked after young people', *Adoption and Fostering*, **33**(4): 44–52.

Yngvesson, B. (2003) 'Going "home": adoption, loss of bearings, and the mythology of roots', *Social Text*, **21**(1): 7–27.

Part IV
Residential Child Care

243

The chapters in Part IV all highlight the continuing tensions and ambivalence in the development of residential child care. Throughout its history, from the days of the Poor Law, there has been a contrast between the 'institutional' setting of residential care and the primacy of the family setting. This contrast in the nature of the different forms of care, the scandals of abuse in residential care and questions about the effectiveness of residential care have all led to the development of policy and legislative frameworks, which have highlighted procedures, standards and regulation. This is exemplified in Chapter 16 by Jonathan Stanley's discussion of the diversification of ownership and specialization in the residential child care sector, and the reaction to this in the form of commissioning, procurement and finance. Residential child care is part of a complex, hierarchical structure of organizations. It is important to recognize the tensions in dealing with organizational issues and how they affect the way in which we address the needs of individual children and young people.

The variation in residential child care across the UK is highlighted in Robin Sen's Chapter 17 on differing legislative contexts in England and Wales, Northern Ireland, and Scotland. The legislative frameworks, however, are based on the overarching principles of the United Nations Convention on the Rights of the Child, and define the duties of carers and the rights of children and young people. The focus on regulation has affected all care settings, not just residential child care, and there is no question that the highlighting of historical abuse in residential care from the 1980s onwards was a major driver in wider developments in social work and social care.

Robin Sen also identifies the varying groups of children and young people in residential child care, and this is picked up in Andrew Kendrick's overview of research in Chapter 19. Residential child care is a complex sector and a diverse range of residential establishments address the needs of a heterogeneous group of children and young people. This means that care needs to be taken about making sweeping generalizations about the effectiveness of residential care, and there needs to be a more subtle approach, acknowledging that some forms of residential care have been underresearched and there is a need to develop a more rigorous evidence base.

That said, one of the clear messages running through this part is the increasing recognition of the importance of the relationship in the group setting. This is highlighted in the research evidence that has focused on the critical influence of relationships on the outcomes for children and young people. In Chapter 18, Mark Smith shows how relationships have been central to the development of theory in residential child care, and outlines this in relation to the psychodynamic approach, work in the life space, care ethics, and social pedagogy.

Everything is brought together in Janine Bolger and Jeremy Miller's account of Jennifer's time in residential child care in Chapter 20. Drawing on extracts from Jennifer's diary, they succeed in placing the young person at the centre of their discussion of residential child care practice. They show how successful and effective residential child care work needs to understand the young person's life experiences, traumas, strengths and resilience. They highlight how residential practice draws on theory and research evidence, and uses day-to-day activities and routines to address Jennifer's varied and varying emotions, experiences and behaviours. Policy and legislation is used as a framework to promote Jennifer's best interests.

Residential child care has a continuing and important role in the provision of services for vulnerable children and young people. It is essential that there is clear and explicit support for this work to ensure that Jennifer's story can be replicated across the sector.

Andrew Kendrick

16
Residential child care policy

JONATHAN STANLEY

This chapter begins by reviewing the history of residential child care in England and Wales and seeks to explain how social concepts have shaped our thinking and become enshrined in legislation. We move from the Poor Law, through Victorian refinements, to consider a range of policy influences in the twentieth century.

The Poor Law

Many Victorian buildings reflected the reality of industrial wealth and served as manifestations of civic pride – museums, baths, railway stations. The same stability and prosperity also led to the building of workhouses, prisons, hospitals, asylums, barracks, boarding schools, industrial schools, refuges and homes for the poor. Such social institutions, in size frequently almost social factories, reflected the movement of people into the towns and were felt to be a demonstration of the ethic of the industrial age (Parker, 1989).

Even today, residential child care is frequently seen as 'institutional', although with the majority of registered children's homes in England now being for five young people or fewer, this is no longer the case in terms of numbers. Any child care can be institutional if it does not start from a commitment to meeting the needs of the young people living there.

In the Victorian era, people feared having to be admitted to one of the institutions. They were perceived as deterrents, with the workhouse offering the poor only a discouraging level of meagre provision and 'relief'. In time, local 'boards of guardians' began to remove children from the workhouse to 'workhouse schools', where education and training were provided in order to break the cycle of pauperism through the development of skilled labour. In fact, education was compulsory for paupers before it was for other children. In Scotland, the system was notably different, with children being 'boarded out' by the board of guardians – often with poor farming families who were thankful for the allowance they received and the additional pair of hands.

Policy

By the 1850s, courts were able to commit offending children to reformatory or industrial schools set up by philanthropic bodies, on the grounds of sensibilities, moralities and law, being parentless, begging or gang membership. When schooling became compulsory, the industrial school was used as a punishment for truancy.

Industrialization diminished the need for child labour. Hours were long for the parents, and with families no longer working and living together, children were often unsupervised, compulsory education only coming with the 1870 Education Act. Social disorder was always seen as a potential risk, and voluntary societies were empowered by legislation and government grants to remove young people from debilitating family and social circumstances and offer the prospect of rehabilitation – an ethic frequently founded on religious beliefs. As far as institutional care was concerned, these factors led to a long-stay mentality, very different from today where young people tend to stay in residential settings for two to three years. It would be the introduction of probation in 1907 that would signal the decline in importance and numbers of these schools.

The 1860s and 70s saw a number of voluntary children's organizations emerge and, with them, the residential home. With boarding out now commonly used for younger children, the homes took on the business of training, along with the provision of religious instruction. The voluntary societies had no shortage of referrals made to them, suggesting that this was a 'vocational' paradigm shared by the public imagination – a light compared with the shadow of the workhouse or the industrial schools. Desperation brought about by poverty was behind many admissions, but in 1889, legislation allowed courts to place children whose parents were found to be abusive with voluntary societies. These factors, along with the religious roots that ensured financial and political support, strengthened the public view that only with more residential places available could children be 'rescued'. Attracting funds required what would now be called marketing; 'saving' children needed the buildings to be a symbol of sustained success; greater numbers and more homes led to further funds coming in. Children did not return home. Numbers had to be finite, but turning children away could affect how the success of the home was evaluated by benefactors. Preventive work and fostering had no such attraction in this age.

The 'vocational' view of child care lingers long in the public memory. Child care is still struggling towards professionalism and maybe the roots of this can be seen in these times. Many women acquired accommodation through working in a child care setting; it was one of the few accommodation options open to unmarried women. This was also a 'win' for the voluntary societies as it led to low staffing costs and in-built loyalty. Later, when religious commitment declined, and with other employment opportunities available, the provision of residential child care would increase in cost and the reduction in provision begin.

It needs to be emphasized that these were *voluntary* societies. The Poor Law 'deterrence' ethic was based on the idea that support was not assumed to be a municipal responsibility. Local authorities did not provide homes in the way that was done by the voluntary societies; 'boarding out' was a preferred option. Eventually, fostering would be developed in response to the criticism that 'institutional' residential life resulted in poor outcomes – a notion that lingers today, despite the data of children's homes in England compliance with national minimum standards being 95% satisfactory or better (Ofsted, 2009). There were concerns over the educational outcomes in the schools too, another theme that persists.

By the 1890s, the boards of guardians had changed their composition, with the appointment of more women along with representatives of self-made men and the guilds of the labouring classes. Compulsory schooling had entered the lives of all children. Voluntary societies were increasingly attracted to fostering, and gradually, from being a provision for the overspill, it was seen as more efficacious than a residential resource in providing 'love' – in addition to it being a more economic use of funds.

The twentieth century – to 1948

Numbers in public care fell during the 1920s, the result of a falling birth rate and mass unemployment, obliging the government to assume more responsibility for the workless; as a consequence, fewer families met Poor Law terms. This should have led to the closure of children's homes, and although many did close, others took their place. Small boards of guardians were abolished and their work was taken on by local authorities; homes could then be used effectively for other purposes. Infant mortality fell; neglect and abuse were more visible; expectations of child care rose in what we might now view, through Maslow's (1943) hierarchy of needs, as being beyond shelter, food, bed and training. There was a new zest for quality, usually achieved by investment in smaller homes as a response to the criticisms of 'institutional' life.

The period 1918–45 saw the rise of administration rather than evangelism in the provision of residential options for children. Central government began to inspect and register, and to lay regulations that would be built on in later decades. Post-1945, the responsibility for providing care for children was uncoupled from the relief of the destitute, which depended on national social insurance and, eventually, the benefit system.

The year 1948 saw new children's departments being established in local authorities, care separated from cash, and an increased focus on 'boarding out'; the first national training programme for 'child care officers' was established, although there was no equivalent programme for residential care staff.

The mid-twentieth century was a seminal time in residential child care development, and it is worth pausing to consider the debate that took place between John Bowlby and Donald Winnicott in the context of the Curtis Committee and its report. Here we can see what was to determine the 'social' in social policy relating to the placement of children in care, and its relationship to the psychosocial. Bowlby and Winnicott are often thought of as thinking along the same lines; but, as Table 16.1 shows, they may be singing the same tune but not in unison, not in harmony; there was even a degree of disharmony between them. Maybe counterpoint is a good way to describe it. Reeves (2005) refers to them as ploughing the same furrow from different ends. Their public discussion concerned the nature of relationship and upbringing. The root cause of need was differently situated. Winnicott had been alerted to the importance of environmental influences by Bowlby, but thought that he had 'an impoverished concept of unconscious mental life'.

Table 16.1 Comparison between Bowlby and Winnicott

Bowlby	Winnicott
Circumstance, character, disposition of parents	Internal disposition of infant
Quality of care central to infant experience of self and world is objective – immediate cause and explanation of later character, disposition and behaviour of child	Infant experience is objective and subjective – environment is proximate
Emphasis on extrapsychic as formative of internal	Emphasis on intrapsychic
Effects of absence and loss	Affects – the *experience* of loss
Emphasize preventive over remedial – concentrate on home life	Imaginative recreation was possible
'Better a bad home than a substitute home'	Non-family settings (hostels) – residential care as therapy
Delinquency as pathology to be removed	Delinquency as sign of hope to be understood
Child to demonstrate concern	Society to demonstrate concern

Source: Drawn from Reeves, 2005

Bowlby favoured family-based care even extending to 'cottage homes', but, Reeves (2005, p. 194) observes, was 'reluctant to fully endorse the sort of therapeutic benefits to be derived from systematic, specialized hostel-type provision'. Bowlby had the aim of reducing, if not totally removing, the potential for young people to be 'taken into care' by removing the causes and thus the need for cure of deprivation.

Winnicott's experience in paediatrics and psychoanalysis led him to the view that deprivation was never going to go away completely. He was not confident of the resilience of the ordinary family in all circumstances to provide the required structures for deprived children or young people. Winnicott thought that a small well-supported residential home – 'primary home provision' – could provide a suitable 'facilitating environment' for young people.

The Curtis Report (1946, p. 5), prompted by concern for 'boarded out children', concluded that 'measures should be taken to ensure that these children are brought up under conditions best calculated to compensate them for the lack of parental care'. It proposed family-based 'homely' care, and saw the need for residential child care rather than therapeutic child care. It was optimistic that most children would respond.

Nonetheless, fostering did not develop quickly. In this respect, we can see the pragmatic limits to evidence-based policy and practice. More women were in employment, housing was scarce, and the separation and loss experienced by wartime evacuees was perceived as a national phenomenon, not an individual misfortune. So the continuing use of residential child care was inevitable, however much there was a policy wish for the increased use of foster care.

This was the thinking that lay behind the Children Act 1948 and that underpinned many of the developments over the next 50 years. Residential child care came to be seen not as a place simply for the upbringing of young people, but as an intervention, to be used only when personal or social circumstances made it essential.

The twentieth century – post-1948

While residential child care remained a place where some children would spend their childhood, it would need to be increasingly innovative, employing specialist skills to meet what were seen not as elemental needs of human society, but as exceptional need. According to the National Centre for Excellence in Residential Child Care (NCERCC, 2006), it was given the task of caring for two groups of children:

- children or families with deep-rooted, complex or chronic needs with a long history of difficulty or disruption, including abuse or neglect – children requiring more than simply substitute family care
- children with extensive, complex and enduring needs compounded by difficult behaviour requiring more specialized and intensive resources – children requiring particular care and specialist settings for their serious psychological needs and behavioural problems.

The title of a government document, *Care and Treatment in a Planned Environment* (Advisory Council in Child Care, 1970), shows that the focus was on meeting need in a planned way. As such, the cost of the residential care setting was not uppermost in the thinking of policy-makers. Budgets were set and costs largely determined by what had happened in the previous years and by emerging need. Local authorities accepted that needs had to be met: they provided for them or collaborated with others to support regional planning to ensure a wide range of provision.

Changes in the age and range of children in care could be seen in a residential sector that now encompassed therapeutic communities, observation and assessment centres, adolescent psychiatric units, and secure children's homes. The intent and degree of the development can be seen in the changes of terminology used in the descriptors employed in the allied sector of 'special educational needs' between the 1960s and 1980s. For example, what had been 'maladjusted' in the 1981 Education Act became 'emotional and behavioural difficulties' or 'behavioural, educational and social difficulties'. These were still wide categories, and it is only relatively recently that we have had knowledge of more specific conditions, such as 'autistic spectrum' needs or 'attention deficit hyperactivity disorder'; or take the importance of 'attachment' into account both socially and educationally.

Young people followed a care, education or health route, depending on where their needs were first identified; often the disposing factor would dominate all others.

Planning was by people who had been in residential work for a long time and inspections were carried out by a similar group of people: experienced managers became inspectors. Local authorities had the responsibility of providing, advising and inspecting. Sometimes, because of longstanding relationships and/or common understanding, this had good results, but sometimes it did not: there were several inquiries into abuse in residential care that called the close managerial/inspectoral relationship into question.

At this time, older children were less readily placed in foster care. Family restoration was both a principle and a practice that was growing, but foster care would need reshaping before being able to supplant residential care. Eventually, changes would affect the work of the voluntary agencies and see them develop in different directions, for example by making specialist provision for what are now called 'high cost/low incidence' needs or by engaging in community-based working, as in Sure Start.

The continuing expansion of community-based sentencing for offenders also had an impact on residential care. Approved schools that had become 'children's homes with education' closed. From the 1980s onwards, there was a confluence of community-based policy and pressure on local authorities to manage all cost centres efficiently. Unit costs relating to direct care, staffing and training, heating and lighting were all rising year by year, and this meant that financial comparisons between fostering and residential care began to take precedence over the identification of differing needs of young people placed in the comparative sectors of care.

The turn of the century

Around the late 1980s, there emerged a small residential private sector that provided an alternative to local authority or voluntary society provision. It was used initially for emergency or 'bridging' placements but also for very specific needs, such as the victims of sexual or physical abuse, or for autistic spectrum disorder. The small numbers and high levels of care needed made such homes a viable business proposition.

Gradually in the 1980s and 90s, the involvement of business backers or entrepreneurs gained ground, and they were able to employ experienced care and education professionals. Local authorities began to appreciate that private providers could offer what they needed either at better quality as a result of gathering together the best staff, or at the same quality but at lower cost. Many local authority residential schools and children's homes closed, and sometimes the private sector would replace them in the same buildings.

It had become clear that it was possible to provide a private sector for care and education in large numbers, but because they were not part of the local authority, one consequence was that they were under no obligation to accept all referrals and they could refuse admission to identified children. This led to the growth of yet another part of the private sector – the opening of small homes for a very high level of need, requiring intensive staff–resident ratios. These were often set up by experienced professionals who believed they could provide a better quality than 'in-house' provision and who could offer their skills without experiencing the sense of compromise they had felt as part of the local authority. Often, the manager and the owner were the same person, and they now became an employer. Part of the funding stream changed, now coming from banks.

In the local authorities, new posts were established in order to respond to the demands posed by the phenomenon of diverse ownership: 'placement officers' and 'access to resources teams', people whose task it was to find places to match need. National minimum standards were introduced as a part of the Care Standards Act 2000. Compliance was to be achieved by means of inspection by an independent regulator, an adjunct to but separate from government. A basic child care ethic of creativity, while not replaced fully by compliance, was at least was being balanced or challenged.

On the back of this profit opportunity came new entrants into the field. Although small and solo providers continued to make up most of the residential care provision, there began to emerge larger corporate concerns, sometimes backed by insurance companies or other similar financial concerns such as pension funds, who were able to market their service, subsidize their homes and buy up smaller homes that were becoming unviable. The larger operators could benefit from economies of scale and advertising; they could offer hundreds of beds within the framework of a national service; and they could give discounts for block bookings. Sovereign trusts entered the market, buying quality provision partly as an investment and partly to enable them to relocate knowledge and practice through using experienced staff in other countries. A market had been formed where price, quality and need were active. Now, of nearly 2,000 settings, 70% are privately owned and the number is increasing; 25% remain in the hands of local authorities but their number is falling; and 5% are run by the voluntary sector, and that number is also decreasing (Ofsted, 2009).

To help to organize this market, a national contract was developed in order to provide a single efficient format. As a 'framework contract', it incorporated research findings that indicated what makes for good residential child care. However, although it was developed by local authorities and providers together, it never gained the universal approval of the local authorities themselves. There were two clauses that provoked their opposition:

- one that would provide for an identified leaving phase including local authority funding beyond the end of the residential phase – an idea that was based on good child care principles allowing relationships to be supported
- another that sought the possibility of increased fees year on year in order to meet additional expenditure arising out of the rising cost of living.

Placement officers and access to resources teams now became 'commissioning teams' supported by a new quasi-government organization, the Commissioning Support Programme (CSP). The role of the CSP was to support and shape the market, and it has drawn heavily on personnel and ideas from the financial sector. An imported health economics perspective is apparent. While this has brought clarity of thinking to the situation, it has little connection to the reality of providing care for children. It may have helped the development of administrative and financial systems, but it has been at the cost of the central task of residential child care as an expression of corporate parenting.

In the 1980s, compulsory competitive tendering in local government had introduced us to the 3Es – economy, efficiency and effectiveness. But by the beginning of the twenty-first century, in the wake of the Gershon Report (2004), these might have been replaced by the 4Cs – challenge, comparison, consultation and competition.

Finance and performance indicators came to dominate activity in the management and inspection of homes. As defined in Gershon terms, commissioners are successfully meeting their primary task; statements from commissioners report the effectiveness of the approach in terms of savings. These parameters led us to procurement, purchasing and contracting, which can easily become an end in themselves and do not necessarily lead on to the more sophisticated developmental stage of commissioning.

Through an emphasis on procurement, administration and financial demands have come to be major factors in the shaping of placement provision. We have been able to do the relatively easy task of making the system maintain its focus on cost, but we have struggled with establishing true measures of cost-effectiveness; types of placement in different settings are represented as alternatives or competitors, whereas evidence tells us that each type will be better used by matching it to the assessed needs of individual young people.

Commissioning, seen as a separate part of 'corporate parenting', has the potential to become an activity in isolation from good child care practice. In attempting to follow a purely objective line, quality assurance can become an 'end in itself' rather than a 'means to an end'. This is explored more fully in *Commissioning is a Parenting and Child Care Activity* (NCERCC, 2009). In planning placements for children, quality assurance appears to be rational. But it does not appear to function well when we look at what we do currently. Commissioning needs to be able to take the strengths of finance and administration and combine them with care values and practice. A strategy for the achievement of this may hinge around the development of relational commissioning and require the current style of commissioning to be transformed:

- shifting from product to learning
- developing explicit skills, attitudes and abilities as well as knowledge
- developing appropriate assessment procedures
- rewarding transformative practice
- encouraging the discussion of practice of both commissioner and provider
- providing transformative learning for all commissioners and providers
- fostering new collegiality
- linking quality improvement to learning
- auditing improvement.

The Labour government of 1997–2010 led a major turnaround in thinking about the provision of all services for children. A universalist view of 'children's services' required people from different disciplines to work together. In local government, separate education and children's departments came to an end, and each local authority created a multidisciplinary children's service, later developing the idea for looked after children of a 'team around the child.' In central government, the relevant department became the Department for Children, Schools and Families (DCSF). Schools were seen as the vehicle for promoting the development of children and there was renewed impetus given to improving the quality of learning for all children. On the one hand, this meant funding new schemes to promote literacy and, on the other, an enhanced inspection and rating system for schools, with all the results being published. An early intervention approach was taken for all children aged 0–5 years, with money put into nursery school places for all and, for families in assessed need, support to parents and day provision through a system called Sure Start.

A policy document *Every Child Matters* (DfES, 2003) outlined universal ambitions for every child and young person whatever their background or circumstances. The aim of improving outcomes and narrowing the gap between disadvantaged children and their more privileged peers was reflected in the identification of five goals for all young people – be healthy, stay safe, enjoy and achieve, make a positive contribution, and achieve economic wellbeing.

There emerged a set of national minimum standards for fostering and residential settings. In England and Wales, these were largely created by bringing together previous regulations rather than looking at research and starting from the life of a child – resulting in very different results to those developed in Scotland or Norway.

One consequence of taking the universalist approach and combining education and the children's service in a single department is that it increases the risk that specialist or exceptional need services will be overshadowed or marginalized. *Every Child Matters* is based on the idea that child development and chronological expectations run smoothly together. Sadly, this is not always so with respect to the young people the residential sector is concerned with: their emotional stage of development does not always correspond to normal chronological development and, as a result, the usual social, emotional and academic expectations are not always achievable.

The perspective of the coalition government, elected to office in 2010, clearly places overwhelming emphasis on the role of the family and on the need for specialist resources in the community. In the coalition's national prospectus on the subject, *Improving Outcomes for Children and Young People and Families* (DfE, 2010), there was no mention of residential child care.

Group care and individual care, however, need not be distinct. What is needed is to match the care setting to the needs of the young person, whether that be through foster care or group care. The starting point in any setting, whether in a children's home or the community, lies with the close relationship between child and carer. In residential child care, this is provided by the key worker. The key worker may have a co-worker, and certainly will have more than one young person for whom they are 'key'. So there begins the formation of a sibling group. This group in itself is part of a larger group – often no bigger than a large family.

With this understanding of young people and their needs, we can see how residential child care can structure their development, moving from a close circle to another bigger circle and then into wider social living. Residential child care provides a successful space for young people to explore successfully these different spaces, each with different expectations. This success can be transferred to other arenas.

There are young people for whom a family setting is not right at a particular time. Group care can allow a young person to be supported to see behind and beyond the dynamics of their own family; it can help them explore and understand their own earlier experiences that may be driving them to repeat traumatic situations and events. To do this requires a setting that can withstand – through understanding – the actions of a young person, even where those actions would be deemed unacceptable in other settings. Good leadership, well-motivated and trained staff who are well supported and supervised, and a clear vision, ethos and philosophy of care all add up to good outputs from residential child care, irrespective of the setting or size.

The residential care task

What, then, is the task for residential child care? Is it caring or parenting? Winnicott (1966) observed: 'There is no such thing as a baby, only a baby and someone.' But what sort of someone? The 'eight pillars of parenting' listed by Cameron and Maginn (2009) explore this territory, and it would be impossible not to argue that all eight can be represented as legitimate aspirations for young people in residential care:

1 primary care and protection
2 secure attachments, making close relationships
3 positive self-perception
4 emotional compliance
5 self-management skills
6 resilience
7 a sense of belonging
8 personal and social responsibilities.

In *The Residential Solution*, Ann Davis (1981) categorized residential units on the basis of their attitude to family life. She distinguished between three models of residential care.

1 *substitute family care:* in which staff try to create a family-like atmosphere
2 *family alternative care:* here, positive aspects of communal life, rather than those of the family, are used as an appropriate model for residential care. For example, many boarding schools see themselves as residential communities, quite separate from the children's family life
3 *family supplement care:* this model contains three main concepts: the need to rehabilitate families; the need to rehabilitate individuals to family life; and the need to share care with families.

This last model may be of most congruence with the government view of family support. Such community-based, short-term residential care allows for care to be shared rather than substituted entirely. One child may spend all week at a children's home, while another is admitted to care at weekends: the arrangement made is dependent on the family situation. Instead of being seen as isolated from communities, residential establishments would be seen as part of the neighbourhood in which they are located, as focal points of community-oriented social work. The emphasis is on flexibility. For example, there may be a range of accommodation and support services: day attendance, part-time residence; full-time care; open visiting hours; flexible staff roles; and a willingness to respond appropriately to the specific needs of each individual family. There is also an emphasis on purposeful intervention with the family. For example, there may be clear plans for time-limited family work, for rehabilitation, or for the maintenance of family responsibility and close links between the family and the child. It may provide help with factors such as income, housing or employment, which affect the family's capacity to care for the child.

Those commissioning the future shape of residential child care will need to take into account how organizational attitudes influence children's service systems. One study with a focus on predicting children's service performance found a significant link between the organizational climate and outcomes, with respect to both process and results, at the individual and organizational levels (Glisson and Hemmelgarn, 1998). Young people's psychosocial functioning was significantly better if the system was served by offices with a more positive climate; appropriate services did not by themselves lead to better outcomes.

Positive climates were associated with fairness, role clarity, cooperation, job satisfaction and personal accomplishment; and they were less likely to be linked with role conflict, emotional exhaustion or depersonalization.

Organizations displaying a positive climate were better able to focus on uniqueness and needs, to be flexible and to make individualized responses rather than programmed responses; they were able to step outside protocol in order to meet needs, perhaps by going to a particular provider to suit the interests of a particular child.

Further reading

■ Clough, R., Bullock, R. and Ward, A. (2006) *What Works in Residential Child Care*. London: NCB Books.

Includes a literature review that draws on research in the UK and the USA and reviews the state of residential child care for children and young people, highlighting what is known and the limits of knowledge, with a view to developing effective policy and practice.

■ Shaw, R. (n.d.) *The Key Texts: An Overview*, http://www.childrenwebmag.com/c/articles/key-child-care-texts.

A series of key texts from the past offering a 'digested read' of selected texts, books, research reports, papers, chapters and government policy documents. The digests cover a standard pattern, setting the context of the text, describing its contents, analysing its impact then and its relevance now, and suggesting further reading.

■ Smith, M. (2009) *Rethinking Residential Child Care: Positive Perspectives*. Bristol: Policy Press.

Sets present-day residential child care policy and practice within a historical, political and organizational context. Highlights the importance of personal relationship in helping children to grow and develop. Other areas discussed include the impact of inquiries, assessment, care planning and programming; and traditions of practice such as social pedagogy and North American models of child and youth care.

References

Advisory Council in Child Care (1970) *Care and Treatment in a Planned Environment: A Report of the Community Home Project*. London: HMSO.

Cameron, R.J. and Maginn, C. (2009) *Achieving Positive Outcomes for Children in Care*. London: Sage.

Curtis Report (1946) *Report of the Care of Children Committee,* Cmd 6922. London: HMSO.

Davis, A. (1981) *The Residential Solution*. London: Routledge & Kegan Paul.

DfE (Department for Education) (2010) *Improving Outcomes for Children and Young People and Families: A National Prospectus*. London: TSO.

DfES (Department for Education and Skills) (2003) *Every Child Matters*. London: TSO.

Gershon, Sir Peter (2004) *Independent Review of Public Sector Efficiency*. London: HM Treasury.

Glisson, C. and Hemmelgarn, A. (1998) 'The effects of organisational climate and interorganisational coordination on the quality and outcomes of children's service systems', *Child Abuse and Neglect*, **22**(5): 401–21.

Maslow, A. (1943) 'A theory of human motivation', *Psychological Review*, **50**(4): 370–96.

NCERCC (National Centre for Excellence in Residential Child Care) (2006) *What Works in Residential Child Care:* A Review of the Research and Implications for Practice. London: NCB.

NCERCC (2009) *Desire, The Link Between Intention and Achievement: Commissioning is a Parenting and Child Care Activity*. London: NCB.

Ofsted (2009) *The Annual Report of Her Majesty's Chief Inspector of Education, Children's Services and Skills 2008/09*. London: TSO.

Parker, R.A. (1989) 'Aspects of the history of residential child care in Britain', Address to Residential Child Care in England and the Carolinas: History, Choices and Alternatives.

Reeves, C. (2005) 'Singing the same tune? Bowlby and Winnicott on deprivation and delinquency', in J. Isroff, C. Reeves and B. Hauptmann (eds) *Donald Winnicott and John Bowlby: Personal and Professional Perspectives*. London: Karnac.

Winnicott, D.W. (1966) *The Family and Individual Development*. New York: Basic Books.

17
Residential child care: the legal foundations and requirements

Robin Sen

This chapter examines the legal duties and powers that residential workers, social workers and local authorities have in respect of children placed in residential child care. It also considers the legal rights that children and young people in residential child care have.[1]

'Residential child care' covers a relatively broad range of child care provision connected by the fact that it provides 'group care' to children in establishments that are staffed by employees, rather than care in a family-based setting. Traditionally, residential child care facilities were run by charities or local authorities, although an increasing number of facilities are now run by private sector companies. Where a local authority uses residential child care facilities for a child in an establishment that it does not itself run, it fulfils its legal duties to provide care to children outside parental care by purchasing the placement from the establishment in question.

The most common type of residential child care establishments are community children homes. Typically, education is not provided 'on site', so children attend school outside the children's home. Additionally, there are a number of residential boarding schools that do provide both care and education 'on site', and there are 'special' residential boarding schools for children with disabilities who have enhanced care and educational needs. Where young people have committed serious criminal offences or pose a significant risk to themselves or others, residential provision can be provided through young offender institutions, secure training centres or secure children's homes. Finally, residential child care also includes the use of residential beds for children in hospital and psychiatric settings.

The Children Act 1989, the 1995 Children Order (NI) and the Children (Scotland) Act 1995 all suggest that children should normally be cared for within their

258

families, unless it is clearly the case that removing them will be in their best interest. The factors to be considered in such a decision are:

- whether a child has experienced, or is likely to experience, significant harm, and that this harm will arise from the care provided to them by their parent(s) or carer(s)
- or that a child is beyond the control of their parent(s) or carer(s) and may cause significant harm to themselves or others.

The process by which children enter the care system will vary according to the country in which children are resident, but in all four parts of the UK there are two main routes: via a 'voluntary' admission with parental consent and via a more formalized judicial process involving a court ruling. In Scotland, children may also enter the care system via the children's hearing system. The hearing system considers cases both where children have committed offences and where they are in need of care and protection; children's hearing panels comprise three trained members of the public who volunteer to undertake that role, rather than a paid judicial official (Lockyer and Stone, 1998).

Law

Box 17.1

The different legal systems in the UK

There are three different legal systems in the UK:

1. 'English law' operating in England and Wales
2. Northern Ireland law operating in Northern Ireland since partition in 1921
3. Scottish law operating in Scotland, which has developed distinctly over several centuries.

While some areas of law, for example those concerning national welfare benefit payments and immigration, apply across all the four constituent countries, in other areas, such as around child and family law, there are differences. The most important statutes in all four home countries regarding child law – the Children Act 1989 in England and Wales, the 1995 Children Order (NI) and the Children (Scotland) Act 1995 – are broadly similar in tone and import, although the wording of the Scottish legislation is substantially different. Additionally, since the establishment of the Scottish Parliament, the Welsh Assembly and the re-establishment of the Northern Ireland Assembly in 1998, there have been increasing divergences in legislation and policy between the four home countries and this has led to greater complexity when discussing the law relating to social work in the UK. This chapter is primarily based around English law, given that this applies to the largest number of people in the UK, but some significant national variations are noted.

On coming into the care system, there is no definitive legal guidance as to when a child should be placed in residential child care, as opposed to foster care or kinship care. However, in considering where a child should reside, courts should take due account of a child's own wishes as appropriate to their age and stage of development, their needs, gender and any other relevant background and characteristics. Wherever possible, a local authority should seek to place children within, or close to, their own communities and with their siblings. Statutory guidance also suggests that when considering admitting a child to residential child care, due consideration should be given to the needs of the child in question, the needs of other children in the residential unit, and the capacity of the staff team to meet those needs.

In practice, residential child care is principally used for young people aged 12 and over, and, typically, only when foster or kinship care is not considered suitable due to a young person's high level of needs, their behaviour, their preference against foster care, or because they have already had a number of foster placement breakdowns (Sinclair, 2006). Since 1945, there has been an increasing preference for using foster care rather than residential care for children under 12. There has also been a general move away from the use of residential child care provision in the UK: in the mid-1970s, there were more children in residential care than in foster care (Skinner, 1992), whereas in the last decade only 10–15% of 'looked after' children have been placed in residential child care, with approximately two-thirds in foster care (Clough et al., 2006; Scottish Government, 2010). The move away from the use of residential child care has been based on policy and practice decisions but is not enshrined within law. The emergence of this clear trend highlights the fact that, despite the importance of legal requirements in social work, policy and practice decisions can also shape the character of social work within its given legal context.

From the mid-1980s, there were a significant number of high-profile inquiries into allegations of abuse perpetrated by staff in residential child care establishments. There are ongoing debates about the true scale of the abuse, the methods used to investigate it, and the extent to which there has been a tendency to focus a disproportionate amount of attention on abuse in residential child care establishments as opposed to other child care settings. Nonetheless, it is the case that various inquiries documented a range of physical, emotional and sexual abuse that occurred within residential child care establishments in the UK (Sen et al., 2008).

Part of the response to these findings has been the enhancement of the system of regulatory and inspection regimes and the introduction of minimum standards for residential child care establishments. These developments were intended to try and ensure that standards of care are maintained, that children's rights are safeguarded and that they are protected from negligent care and abuse. Each unit providing residential child care services is subject to inspection by an inspection body, the name and exact functions of which differ in the constituent countries. In each case, they inspect residential units against explicit standards, and, where standards are not being met, have the power to issue correction notices for relevant changes to be made. In the final analysis, they can close units down if they fail to address identified concerns.

Law

Legal duties, powers and children's rights

The UN Convention on the Rights of the Child (UNCRC) sets out broad fundamental rights which all children in the world should have. It was ratified by the UK in 1991. Articles within the UNCRC that are of particular relevance to those in residential child care include:

- children's rights to express their views in matters relating to them so far as they are capable – Article 12
- children's rights to periodic review of their treatment – Article 25
- state duties to protect children from 'physical or mental violence, injury or abuse, neglect or negligent treatment, maltreatment or exploitation, including sexual abuse' – Article 19
- state duties to provide 'special protection' to children who are outside the care of their family – Article 20
- state duties to promote the 'physical and psychological recovery and social integration' of any child who has experienced abuse, degrading treatment or armed conflict – Article 39.

In looking after children, a local authority must have regard for their religious views, their ethnicity and their cultural and linguistic background. Social workers should consult children about decisions affecting them wherever this is possible, and their care should be formally reviewed by the relevant local authority within four weeks of them becoming looked after,[2] then in a further three months, and thereafter at least every six months. Article 37 of the UNCRC states that children have the right to maintain contact with family members except in exceptional circumstances, and the relevant child care legislation in the UK supplements this by giving local authorities a duty to actively facilitate contact between children, their families and significant people in their lives so far as it is consistent with their welfare.

Where children in residential care are unhappy with the services they are receiving, they have the right to complain about those services, and the local authority must provide a response to those complaints within 28 days. They are entitled to have an independent person involved in the investigation of the complaint should they wish this (Willow, 1996).

In terms of the care provided, *National Minimum Standards – Children's Homes Regulations* (DH, 2002)[3] set out that children should be given targeted support and guidance to meet their needs, including medical care and education, and that they should be protected from abuse. Residential workers should be appropriately qualified, skilled and supported to be able to meet children's needs in the unit. Support should also include the opportunities to participate in a range of leisure activities; and the residential establishment itself must be maintained to a good physical standard.

Residential workers should respect the privacy and confidentiality of children in the residential establishment as far as is consistent with good and appropriate caring.

This includes respecting children's space in the way in which their rooms are entered and providing scope for children to make telephone calls privately.

Residential workers may restrain a child but only to prevent an injury to that child or to others or to prevent serious damage to property. The residential establishment is required to keep a record of each restraint, which includes:

> the name of the child, the date, time and location, details of the behaviour requiring use of restraint, the nature of the restraint used, the duration of the restraint, the name of the staff member(s) using restraint, the name(s) of any other staff, children or other people present, the effectiveness and any consequences of the restraint, any injuries caused to or reported by the child or any other person. (DH, 2002, p. 33)

Increasing attention has been given to the support of young people in residential care in preparation for when they leave care. This focus has arisen out of recognition that, in the past, the levels of support provided were inconsistent and inadequate (Dixon and Stein, 2002) and that there is a correlation between the provision of such support and the achievement of better outcomes by young people once they have left care. New legislation gives social workers and residential workers enhanced duties to provide support, guidance and assistance to young people leaving residential child care at least until the age of 21, including the duty to assess the needs of a young person preparing to leave care and to implement a plan to meet those needs. Where a young person is in full-time education, the local authority's duty to provide support continues until they are 24.

Secure establishments

There are different types of secure residential accommodation where children have committed serious offences:

- Young offender institutions are penal establishments, run by the prison service, for those aged 15 to 21.
- Secure training centres, run by private sector organizations, provide more structured education and care programmes where young people can be placed until the age of 17.
- Secure residential accommodation, usually directly provided by local authorities, provides more individually tailored support for young people until the age of 16; it is normally used for younger teenagers, teenagers who are particularly vulnerable, and girls under the age of 16 (Clough et al., 2006).

The Utting review of residential child care in England and Wales (1997) reported evidence that secure care provided substantially better standards of care than penal institutions and provided a clear message: 'Prison is not a safe environment' (Utting, 1997, p. 3). Despite this, from the mid-1990s to the early 2000s, there was a substantial increase in the number of young people in England and Wales in penal institutions.

While this has been followed by a reduction in more recent years, England and Wales still have one of the largest proportions of young people in penal institutions in Western Europe, with three-quarters of young people reoffending on their release (Howard League for Penal Reform, 2010).

According to section 25 of the Children Act 1989, there are two situations in which young people can be placed in secure children's homes even where they have not committed offences:

1   where there are well-founded concerns that they will abscond, and they are likely to experience significant harm after doing so
2   when, if placed elsewhere, they would be likely to injure themselves or others.

In such situations, the Children (Secure Accommodation) Regulations 1991 state that a child can only be kept in secure accommodation for a maximum of 72 hours in a 28-day period without the agreement of a court. It is rare for younger children to be placed in secure care, and children under 13 can only be placed in secure care with the agreement of the relevant secretary of state. A court ruling to place a child in secure care must be reviewed by the court after three months, and thereafter no later than six monthly.

Practice example 1   Michael's story

Michael is from the north of England. He was originally placed in foster care on a care order at the age of 10 along with his older sister, Becky. His mum was a single carer with severe mental health difficulties, and there had been long-standing concerns about the neglect of both Michael and his sister. The initial plan was for both Michael and Becky to return to their mum's care, but her mental health deteriorated further, making this impossible. Michael failed to settle in his foster placement and went through three foster placement break-downs before being placed in a residential home run by his local authority just before his twelfth birthday. During this time, he continued to attend main-stream school, with additional support provided to him by a classroom assistant as he had fallen behind his peers academically.

After initially settling into the children's home, Michael started to abscond, running away from the home on more than 15 occasions in eighteen months. When he did so, he usually returned to the home intoxicated with either drugs and/or alcohol, refusing to state where he had been. However, on one occasion, staff were contacted by the police after Michael had been arrested and charged with criminal damage, assault and theft; he was subsequently sentenced by the local youth court to a six-month referral order. The local authority supported Michael's continued placement at the children's home, but he absconded again and on this occasion, having taken ecstasy, cannabis and alcohol, he needed hospital treatment after he had been found uncon-

Law

scious in a bus shelter by a member of the public. Following the last incident, the local authority applied to the court for Michael to be placed in secure care, supported by Michael's social worker's assessment that he would be likely to abscond from any community home and, if he did so, would be likely to cause harm to himself or others.

Michael instructed a solicitor to oppose this application. His solicitor argued that Michael's placement in secure care was not consistent with the Children Act 1989 'welfare principle', and that a move to secure care was disproportionate, as no other community residential resource had been tried. The judge, however, accepted the social worker's assessment and Michael was placed in secure care for an initial three-month period.

Michael was placed in a specialized, secure unit with a ratio of 1:2 staff to young person at all times. Educational facilities were provided within the secure unit, and Michael continued to study for his GCSEs, although he had fallen further behind in his studies during the time he was in the previous children's home; in the secure unit, he followed the curriculum for a smaller range of subjects. The unit provided the same care facilities as a children's home, but there were locked doors within the unit which prevented the young people moving around freely; at night the door to Michael's room was locked with night staff on duty. Some leisure facilities (sports, computer games) were provided within the unit, although the young people were not allowed out of the premises. Other than the restriction to his liberty, Michael retained the same rights to care and protection as any other child. Michael was allocated a key worker within the secure unit to undertake targeted work with him on substance misuse, anger management and his offending behaviour. Michael established a close relationship with his key worker and made some progress in the work they did together; but there remained concerns about Michael's aggression and his willingness to address his offending behaviour. Michael's social worker visited him at the unit every three to four weeks and was in phone contact with residential staff and Michael in between this. Michael continued to have contact with his mum on a monthly basis at his request, although both Michael and his mum found these meetings difficult. Michael did not have any contact with Becky, who remained in foster care.

At the time of writing, Michael's placement in secure care will shortly need to be reviewed in court as he is approaching the end of his first three months there. If the court approves his placement on this occasion, it will be a further six months before it is reviewed in court again. A recent 'looked after review' meeting considered Michael's care plan and decided that the local authority should recommend to court that Michael continue to be placed in the secure unit because of the need for him to undertake further work regarding his aggression, his offending behaviour and his understanding of his alcohol and drug use. However, it was agreed that, if the court approves Michael's continued placement in the secure unit, a further review would be held earlier than usual – in three months – to see if there has been clear progress in the areas where Michael's behaviour is currently giving rise to concern. If there is, the local authority will seek to move Michael from secure care to a non-secure community residential unit. At his 'looked after review', Michael requested that his sister visit him at the secure unit. It is unclear why Becky has not visited Michael. The meeting decided that Michael's social worker should speak to Becky and her carers about the possibility of her visiting Michael as soon as possible and then give feedback to Michael about whether this will happen.

Key legal dimensions behind the case of Michael

1 Young people can be placed in secure care where they have committed serious criminal offences. However, they can also be placed in secure care on 'welfare grounds' in very specific circumstances. Where this is for more than a three-day period, a court must sanction the young person's move to secure care and periodically review the decision.
2 Other than the restriction to their liberty, young people in secure care retain all the same rights in respect of the care they receive as any other young person.

Children with disabilities

Under child care legislation (the Children Act 1989), a child with a disability is automatically defined as a 'child in need' with particular entitlements to support and services from the local authority. Children with disabilities may be placed in residential respite care for short periods in order to give some support to their parents. However, the most common reason for children with disabilities to be living away from home on a long-term basis is attendance at a residential boarding school, often some distance from their home area, despite the policy emphasis on developing local services that can meet the needs of children within their home environment. Children with a disability in residential care tend to be 14 and over and have multiple and/or profound disabilities. The majority of families from which they come will, like the families of other looked after children, be more likely to be experiencing a range of difficulties, including suspected child neglect and abuse, parental substance misuse and mental health issues (McConkey et al., 2004).

Under section 23 of the Children Act 1989, the local authority must make sure that the accommodation provided to children with a disability is suitable to their needs, but this is within the bounds of what is 'reasonably practicable' and consequently provides relatively minimal specific legal duties as to what adjustments must be made. There have been questions about the lack of data, policy and research focus on disabled children in residential care, and there is some evidence that not all the legal requirements in respect of their care, for example the need to periodically review their care or for social workers to regularly visit them as children living away from home, are met (McConkey et al., 2004). This is of particular concern, given that disabled children are especially vulnerable, and more likely than other children to experience all forms of abuse (Stalker and McArthur, 2010).

Practice example 2 | Nila's story

Nila is 18 and from Belfast. She has a severe learning disability and communication difficulties: she has spoken language with limited vocabulary, but can clearly express preferences and understand and give instructions. Nila also exhibits some behavioural difficulties, which have in the past included striking out at others, self-harming through scratching herself and biting her tongue.

Until she was 14, Nila's parents cared for her at home. She attended schools for children with learning disabilities in her local area. To support the family's care of Nila, respite care was also provided where Nila would go to a residential respite unit for a one- or two-night stay every fortnight. Nila's school found her level of needs increasingly hard to manage and requested that her placement be reviewed. An educational psychologist's assessment suggested that a more specialized educational placement be found with a highly structured and supervised environment. In order to meet this need, a specialist residential school providing round-the-clock care, 365 days a year, was recommended by a joint education and child care services panel.

Nila's parents were extremely unhappy with this recommendation as the school is in Derry/Londonderry, a four-hour, 150-mile round trip from their home. They argued that the failure to provide appropriate educational provision to Nila within her own locality was in contravention of Article 9 of the UNCRC, which states that a child has a right to live with their family, and in contravention of the authority's duties to Nila as a 'child in need' under the 1995 Children Order (NI). However, they reluctantly consented when Nila's then school refused to continue her placement after she struck out at a classroom assistant.

The residential school to which Nila was sent has 24-hour care and on-site educational provision, catering for a range of children with profound and multiple disabilities. Nila followed an adapted curriculum for pupils with learning disabilities, which included academic learning and life skills, such as self-care, cooking and basic budgeting. Nila's key worker in the school, who was responsible for implementing Nila's overall care plan, undertook work with her on her behaviour and social skills. There are on-site sports facilities, a TV room and a library and the residents go on outings outside the school a couple of times a month. Nila settled very well at the school. Staff described her as a lively, energetic and thoughtful person who gets on well with staff and other young people. While Nila continued to scratch herself, there were increasingly fewer aggressive outbursts to others.

At the time of writing, Nila's parents are generally happy with the placement, but they are distressed that they find it hard to visit every week due to other family commitments and the cost of the travel. They are frustrated that it is nearly a year since Nila's last 'looked after review', knowing that these reviews should occur at least every six months. However, Nila's social worker has periodically visited her and has been in contact with her parents. Under education law, Nila is entitled to stay at the residential school until she is 19. Nila's social worker, aware that the local authority has a legal responsibility to support Nila's transition from school, has suggested that she could move to a supported independent living unit for adults with learning disabilities in her local area. Nila is excited about this idea and her parents want her to move closer to them, but feel she will need greater support than this; they do not, however, think that her returning to the family home is a realistic option.

Key legal dimensions behind the case of Nila

1   Every child looked after in a residential unit should have their situation periodically reviewed by the responsible local authority in order to consider their care and whether their needs are being met. Their social worker should keep regular contact with the child and the residential unit.

2   Local authorities have responsibilities to support the care of any young person who is looked after by them at the age of 16. Such support must last until the young person is at least 21.

Unaccompanied asylum-seeking children

Children who arrive in the UK after becoming separated from those with caring responsibilities for them have the right, like adults, to claim asylum in the UK due to a 'well-founded fear' of persecution in their home state under the 1951 UN Convention Relating to the Status of Refugees. While their claim is being adjudicated, they are classed as 'asylum seekers'; if their claim to stay in the country is granted, they become 'refugees'. Where separated children claim asylum in the UK, the relevant local authority has responsibilities to provide them with services, advice and guidance as a 'child in need', but also, where appropriate, to provide them with accommodation as a 'looked after child', according to the Children Act 1989. In 2003, there were 2,400 unaccompanied children in the UK, of whom just over three-quarters were boys and just under a quarter girls – 70% were placed in foster care, 20% in children's homes or hostels, and 10% were living independently (Kohli, 2007).

There have been serious questions about whether the treatment of unaccompanied children is consistent with the principle in British child care legislation that the welfare of the child should be the paramount consideration in any decisions about their care. It is notable that when the UK signed the UNCRC in 1991, it reserved the right not to apply the convention to asylum-seeking children. This position was only reversed in 2008 when the then government agreed to sign the UNCRC in full, meaning that, for the first time, an asylum-seeking child's welfare must be the primary consideration in decisions about their detention and deportation.

Although it is difficult to generalize about a group of children whose experiences and needs are so diverse, it is recognized that unaccompanied children are especially vulnerable. They are, by definition, separated from their carers; they may have experienced or witnessed violence, war or torture in their home country; and they may have experienced deprivation in their journey to the UK. They are likely to be unfamiliar with the indigenous culture, systems within the UK, and possibly also the English language. They may be subject to discrimination based on their ethnicity and their status as asylum seekers or refugees (Kohli, 2007). Finally, their stay in the UK, beyond the age at which they become adults, is not assured: unaccompanied children are often given 'discretionary leave' to remain until they are 18, with the possibility that they may be deported to their country of origin on becoming an adult (Dennis, 2007).

Part of the challenge for local authorities in responding to unaccompanied children is accurately estimating their age. On the one hand, it would be inappropriate for asylum seekers who are actually adults to be placed in care facilities alongside other looked after children. Recent case law suggests the factors that can be considered in age determination include physical appearance and behaviour, medical evidence, personal history and documentary evidence (Brammer, 2010). On the other hand, it is difficult for asylum-seeking children to 'prove' their age, because in some cases they have had to travel on documents stating that they are several years older than they claim, and in others because getting hold of any documents proving age can be hard if not impossible (Dennis, 2002).

Practice example 3 | Ariana's story

Ariana is 17 and originally from Helmand Province, Afghanistan. She arrived in the UK two years ago in the company of an agent who had been paid by her family to smuggle her out of Afghanistan. This followed the abduction and murder of her father by a local militia in Helmand because her father had worked as an interpreter for the British Army. The agent had been paid to take Ariana to London where her family had a contact, but, in fact, he left her in Glasgow where, via the police, she was taken to the local social work department children and families team and then placed in a children's home. Initially, the UK Border Agency raised questions about whether Ariana was 'unaccompanied', alleging that the agent who had accompanied Ariana was, in fact, a member of her extended family who had caring responsibilities for her. They did, however, go on to accept her status as an unaccompanied young person, supporting Ariana's right to receive the same care and treatment as any other looked after young person.

Ariana struggled to settle in the unit, finding it hard to adjust to the different care arrangements, unable to find food that she liked and having difficulty communicating. Ariana speaks Pashto (her mother tongue), Persian and English fluently, but for the first months she was in Glasgow, she had great difficulty with the regional accent. Her key worker reported her to be withdrawn and isolated in the children's home. Her social worker, concerned that she was exhibiting signs of post-traumatic stress disorder and that she was struggling with issues of trauma and loss, referred her to the child and adolescent mental health service. In this, she was recognizing the local authority's duties to provide appropriate services to her as a looked after child. Early on, Ariana asked her social worker to transfer her to a children's home in London, so she could try and find her family's contact. Her social worker explained that this would not be possible as Glasgow was legally responsible for her care as she had first presented there.

> **Making connexions**
>
> With regard to unaccompanied asylum-seeking children like Ariana, what are the challenges for the practitioners who work with them?

After a number of months, Ariana was awarded discretionary leave to remain until she is 18 and she started to adapt to her new situation better. She attended a local secondary school that has a strong tradition of supporting asylum-seeking children because of the significant proportion of asylum-seeking members within the local community. She made good progress in school, following an adapted curriculum.

At the time of writing, Ariana has a good relationship with her social worker and her key worker in the children's home, both of whom she trusts; but she knows that neither of them has the power to influence the decision of the UK Border Agency, which still has to make a decision on whether she will be allowed to stay in the UK when she reaches 18. If she is given leave to remain after 18, Ariana will be entitled to the same leaving care support as any other 'looked after' young person leaving care, and her social worker and key worker have put in place a plan to support Ariana once she leaves the children's home, in the event of her being given leave to remain.

Ariana's solicitor is hopeful of a positive decision, although the wait for the decision has caused Ariana some distress, including flashbacks of her father's abduction and her transit to the UK.

Key legal dimensions behind the case of Ariana

1   Local authorities have duties to meet the needs of unaccompanied asylum-seeking children who arrive in the UK. Their welfare should be the principle consideration in any decision taken in respect of their care.
2   On reaching 18, asylum-seeking young people have the same rights to post-care support as any other young person. However, they do not have an automatic legal entitlement to stay in the UK on becoming an adult and as a result may face removal to their home country at this point.

Law

In conclusion

In the second decade of the twenty-first century, the residential child care sector occupies an ambiguous space within UK child and family social work. Despite efforts to promote residential child care as a positive placement choice, it tends to be used for children who are unable or unwilling to be cared for in a family setting. This gives rise to a conundrum that the least favoured sector cares for the most vulnerable and marginalized children, with the highest level of need. While policy and practice, rather than legal requirements, have created this conundrum, legal requirements are there to help ensure that these children's needs are met and their welfare is safeguarded during their time in residential child care. These requirements provide a framework in which local authorities, social workers and residential workers have explicit duties in respect of the care they provide, and children in residential child care have explicit rights in respect of the care they receive. However, such a framework does not guarantee that children's needs will actually be met or that their welfare will be safeguarded, nor could it. The only guarantor of these things is informed, ethically sound and reflective practice.

Acknowledgement

Thanks to Andy Thompson, specialist practice teacher, youth justice, Sheffield, for helpful feedback on Practice example 1.

Notes

1 This chapter will use the terminology 'child' when referring to those under 12 and when referring to both those under 12 and over 12. 'Young person' will be used when referring only to those aged 12 and over.
2 Six weeks in Scotland.
3 These only apply in England and Wales, but similar requirements apply in Northern Ireland through the Children's Homes Regulations (NI) 2005 and, in Scotland, via National Care Standards for care homes for children and young people.

Further reading

■ Sinclair, I. (2006) 'Residential care in the UK', in C. McAuley, P.J. Pecora and W. Rose (eds) *Enhancing the Well-Being of Children and Families through Effective Interventions: International Evidence for Practice*. London: Jessica Kingsley.

Succinct and useful chapter that sets out the historical context and outlines contemporary research and policy in respect of the residential child care sector in the UK.

■ Utting, W. (1997) *People Like Us: The Report of the Review of the Safeguards for Children Living Away from Home*. London: TSO.

Seminal report commissioned by the government to look at the care of and legal safeguards for children living away from home in England and Wales.

■ Willow, C. (1996) *Children's Rights and Participation in Residential Care*. London: National Children's Bureau.

Slightly dated, but readable and detailed book focusing on the particular rights of children in residential child care.

References

Brammer, A. (2010) *Social Work Law* (3rd edn). Harlow: Pearson.

Clough, R., Bullock, R. and Ward, A. (2006) *What Works in Residential Child Care: A Review of Research Evidence and the Practical Considerations*. London: National Children's Bureau.

Dennis, J. (2002) *A Case for Change: How Refugee Children in England are Missing Out*. London: The Children's Society/Save the Children/Refugee Council.

Dennis, J. (2007) 'The legal and policy frameworks that govern social work with unaccompanied asylum seeking and refugee children in England', in R. Kohli and F. Mitchell (eds) *Working with Unaccompanied Asylum Seeking Children*. Basingstoke: Palgrave Macmillan.

DH (Department of Health) (2002) *Children's Homes: National Minimum Standards – Children's Homes Regulations*. London: TSO.

Dixon, J. and Stein, M. (2002) *Still a Bairn: Throughcare and Aftercare Services in Scotland*. Edinburgh: Scottish Executive.

Howard League for Penal Reform (2010) *Life Inside 2010: A Unique Insight into the Day to Day Experiences of 15–17 Year Old Males in Prison*. London: Howard League.

Kohli, R. (2007) *Social Work with Unaccompanied Asylum Seeking Children*. Basingstoke: Palgrave Macmillan.

Lockyer, A. and Stone, F. (1998) *Juvenile Justice in Scotland: Twenty-five Years of the Welfare Approach*. Edinburgh: T & T Clark.

McConkey, R., Nixon, T., Donaghy, E. and Mulhern, D. (2004) 'The characteristics of children with a disability looked after away from home and their future service needs', *British Journal of Social Work*, **34**(4): 561–76.

Sinclair, I. (2006) 'Residential care in the UK', in C. McAuley, P.J. Pecora and W. Rose (eds) *Enhancing the Well-Being of Children and Families through Effective Interventions: International Evidence for Practice*. London: Jessica Kingsley.

Scottish Government (2010) *Children Looked After Statistics 2008–09*, http://www.scotland.gov.uk/Publications/2010/02/22133946/9.

Sen, R., Kendrick, A., Milligan, I. and Hawthorn, M. (2008) 'Lessons learnt? Abuse in residential child care in Scotland', *Child & Family Social Work*, **13**(4): 411–22.

Skinner, A. (1992) *Another Kind of Home: A Review of Residential Child Care*. Edinburgh: Scottish Office.

Stalker, K. and McArthur, K. (2010) 'Child abuse, child protection and disabled children: a review of recent research', *Child Abuse Review*, doi: 10.1002/car.1154.

Utting, W. (1997) *People Like Us: The Report of the Review of the Safeguards for Children Living Away from Home*. London: TSO.

Willow, C. (1996) *Children's Rights and Participation in Residential Care*. London: National Children's Bureau.

Law

18
Theory in residential child care

MARK SMITH

Residential child care is described as 'a physical setting in which children and young people are offered care – physical nurturing, social learning opportunities, the promotion of health and wellbeing and specialized behaviour training' (Fulcher, 2001, p. 418). Steckley and Smith (2011) argue that moral and relational considerations are also central to any notion of care. Theoretical frameworks that might cast some light on the nature and aims of residential child care need to reflect all these dimensions.

Theoretical influences on residential child care were traditionally informed by psychology and principally reflected strands of psychodynamic and behaviourist thinking. Following the professionalization of UK social work in the early 1970s, residential child care was claimed to be part of social work. But it has struggled to find a home within what might be considered to be social work theory, mirroring perhaps a wider ambivalence in the relationship between residential child care and social work more broadly defined. Later in the chapter, I identify theoretical perspectives that I think do 'fit' with residential child care, specifically the idea of life space and the emerging interest in care ethics, before concluding that European models of social pedagogy may provide an appropriate theoretical and practice paradigm within which to locate residential child care.

Theory and residential child care

Clough et al. (2006) argue that residential child care has been adequately researched but inadequately theorized. Indeed, theory and residential child care can be uneasy bedfellows. There are several reasons for this. First, the experience of care is universal; we all, irrespective of the quality of that experience, have been cared for and most of us have had some responsibility for caring for others. The everydayness of such practices can render the giving and receiving of care seemingly atheoretical and thus not requiring conceptual analysis. Another reason is that residential workers are regularly presented with theories, often transposed from disciplines such as psychology and social work, that don't 'fit' with their understanding of the task and that can be experienced as overly abstract and impractical (Phelan, 2001a).

Despite this, residential child care cannot escape theory. Theories, according to Moss and Petrie (2002, p. 17), whether in the form of academic, political or professional ideas, or offered in the guise of 'common sense', shape our understandings and govern our actions, whether we recognize this or not . They underpin the daily practices of residential child care, even if just in the oft-repeated assertion from workers that there needs to be some consequence to an action, a crude form of behaviourism, which, although widely adhered to, isn't particularly helpful or theoretically robust. In more extreme cases, theory can be misunderstood and misapplied with serious consequences. Frank Beck, subsequently convicted of numerous counts of physical and sexual abuse committed when officer in charge of children's homes in Leicestershire during the 1980s, was able to dress up his actions as psychoanalysis and regression therapy. The practice of pindown in Staffordshire during the early 1990s, which was essentially an unreflective behavioural regime, degenerated into an oppressive one.

Theory over time

In the nineteenth and early twentieth century, views of care were consistent with a commonsense assumption that it could be provided by anyone of good standing and moral character. The emphasis was on building similar character in those children placed in care, to be achieved through austerity, hard work and religious instruction – a training of the soul if you like. Children's emotional life was rarely understood or even acknowledged and to pander to it would have been considered detrimental to their moral upbringing.

Psychodynamic theories

Following the work of Freud in the early twentieth century, the focus of intervention with children shifted, gradually, from their souls to their psyches. Psychoanalytic approaches identify the centrality of a child's emotional life, rooted in their early relationships, particularly those with their mothers, in shaping current behaviour. While gaining a foothold at an academic level, the influence of psychoanalytic thinking on practice, notwithstanding some experiments in free schooling such as A.S. Neill's Summerhill and early therapeutic communities, was for a long time marginal. It did, however, begin to shape the discourse on residential care, primarily through the influence of the child guidance movement, which was instrumental in informing the Curtis and Clyde Reports (1946) into children in state care following the Second World War (1939–45). These reports expressed a preference for smaller homes based around a 'family' model that might respond to children's emotional needs.

The family as the template for residential child care was given a shot in the arm by Bowlby's (1951) work on attachment. This had an influence on reports such as *Children Who Wait* (Rowe and Lambert, 1973), which identified the family as the option of choice for all children. In that respect, it was used to make a case that residential child care could not provide sufficiently strong attachment opportunities for children (Milligan, 1998), contributing substantially to the decline in its use.

Over time, psychoanalytic thinking moved away from its early biological language of 'drives' and 'instincts' towards a greater social focus on how a sense of self evolves and is maintained in relationship with others. In that respect, the term 'psychodynamic' rather than psychoanalytic is perhaps more appropriate as it embraces ideas that go beyond the clinical to incorporate relational aspects of human development.

A central idea in psychodynamic thinking is of the need for adults to be able to manage a child's anxiety. In babies, this happens when carers respond to an infant's distress by providing physical and emotional comfort. If this occurs sensitively and consistently, then children form an attachment bond with their carers. If this bond is what Donald Winnicott (1965) terms 'good enough', it allows infants to form what attachment theorists call an 'internal working model' of the world as benign and trustworthy. They learn to regulate their emotions and to explore their worlds, confident of the existence of a secure base to which they can return. 'Good enough' parenting figures provide what Winnicott (1965) called 'the facilitating environment' – a stable physical and emotional environment where a child is safe yet allowed sufficient space to grow and to build healthy trusting relationships that will provide the template for subsequent relationships.

The failure to provide such an environment in early childhood gives rise to anxieties and fears, some of which may be unconscious (Sharpe, 2006). Anglin (2002) identifies much of the behaviour of children in residential child care as being pain based. Children seek to defend themselves against anxiety and emotional pain by employing a range of psychological defence mechanisms. They may 'project' onto others what is too difficult for them to hold inside. Unhappy children often express the fears and frustrations of their past by acting out or 'transferring' their emotional distress onto residential workers. The experience of being confronted by expressions of a child's anxiety and anger can, in turn, arouse primitive anxieties in the worker, a dynamic known as 'countertransference'. Responses to children based on countertransference reactions can lead workers to react to aggression with aggression and to meet anxiety with further anxiety. The task for workers in such situations is, like good parents, to try and understand why a child might be behaving in a particular way, to process their feelings and give them back to the child in a way that will reassure them (Sharpe, 2006).

Wilfred Bion (1970) offers another helpful psychodynamic concept – that of 'containment', which is similar to Winnicott's facilitating environment. The concept provides a way of understanding the process by which the primary carer receives the projected, intolerable feelings of an infant, but modifies and returns them in such a way that they become tolerable; thus the carer is termed the 'container' and the infant is 'contained'. Early, ongoing experiences of containment enable a child to manage emotions. By contrast, when experiences of containment are inadequate or significantly interrupted, children's cognitive and emotional development and their capacities to manage emotions are adversely affected (Steckley, 2010). The implications of this for practice are that workers need to assume the role of the 'good enough' parent and to seek to create a 'facilitating' or 'containing' environment.

Ward (1995) identifies the need children have for both literal containment, in terms of basic care and the setting of boundaries, and metaphoric containment, which involves the worker holding a child's uncontainable feelings. Staff teams need to create and maintain cultures that are strong enough to withstand and contain the projections of uncontained children and to give them tools to establish healthy and intimate relationships in their adult lives. Interventions should thus seek to focus on the development and maintenance of containing relationships rather than directly on control.

Within a psychodynamic model, workers cannot retreat into some ostensibly 'therapeutic' counselling-type role. Therapeutic relationships depend on the promotion and modelling of responsive, authoritative and supportive relationships that may at times involve conflict between adults and children. In this regard, Winnicott's notion of 'good enough' rather than perfect parenting is an important one, especially in political and professional cultures that demand some technical/rational notion of 'best practice'.

Such a state of 'best practice' is probably neither possible nor desirable in working with children, where questions of contingent understandings and human fallibility are central to practice. Internal and external organizational cultures that recognize the need to contain staff anxieties in order that they might do likewise with children are essential.

Behaviourist theories

Psychodynamic approaches are currently enjoying a resurgence in social work (Ruch et al., 2010), although for a long while they had fallen out of favour. They were deemed too complex for many staff to understand, a problem that became more pronounced with the lowering of aspirations for a professionally qualified workforce and an increasing reliance on vocational qualifications. Psychodynamic approaches were also considered too tenuous in their conclusions and thus dissonant with the emerging political drive to measure the outcomes of interventions. In those respects, behaviourist ideas offered something a bit more concrete. Where the aim of psychodynamic approaches is to try and understand an individual's intrapsychic processes, the focus of behaviourism shifts to the external environment and the outward expression of behaviours.

Behavioural theories are associated, historically, with the work of B.F. Skinner (1953). The basic premise of behavioural theories is that behaviours are learned and therefore can be unlearned. In addition, it is believed that new and more adaptive behaviours can be substituted for maladaptive behaviours. The notion of 'operant conditioning' posits that behaviour can be controlled by its consequences: acceptable behaviours are rewarded and thereby reinforced; unacceptable behaviours can be eliminated if they result in punishment. Many residential establishments in the 1970s adopted behaviourist approaches based around operant conditioning principles. A number, perhaps best known of which was Aycliffe School in County Durham (Hoghughi, 1979), operated token economy systems, whereby young people had to earn points to gain access to particular areas of a unit's programme, such as activities or home leave.

There is a commonsense logic to behaviourism. It can be intellectually and emotionally easier to seek to address a child's outward behaviour rather than trying to work out what is going on below the surface, with the inevitable uncertainty and possible distress to the worker this might entail. It may also fit with a primitive impulse to punish and a modernist desire for certainty and rationality. In both senses, it may be consonant not only with the inherited worldviews and social mores of many residential care staff but also with a political culture that seeks technical/ rational solutions to complex social problems. Punishment and reward alone, however, have not been found to be particularly effective in changing behaviour. Behaviourism in its crudest form has been largely discredited for this reason and because it fails to acknowledge the complexity of human behaviour. Even when behaviourist approaches might be seen to have positive effects in the residential environment, they face the problem of 'wash-out', whereby behaviours learned in residential care are not maintained when children move out of that environment.

Criticisms of some of the cruder applications of behaviourist theory led to the adoption of other psychological theories. One of these was social learning theory, most often associated with the work of Albert Bandura (1973), who argued that behaviour can be learned by observing and imitating other people. Suitable adults (and peers) were required to model prosocial behaviour in the belief that it would be replicated. Given the nature of residential child care and the opportunities for role modelling, it is easy to see the attraction of social learning theory in informing practice in this field and such approaches became popular during the 1980s.

Cognitive behavioural approaches represent another development from classic behavioural theory. They focus on the links between thoughts, feelings and actions, positing that a change in one area can lead to changes in the other two. They are based on a cognitive model of emotion, which dictates that it is not simply what happens to a person that causes particular reactions. Rather, it is the meaning they attach to an experience that leads them to feel and behave in certain ways. The focus of intervention is to tackle what are identified as cognitive distortions that lead people to behave in maladaptive ways. Cognitive behavioural ideas emerged primarily from the criminal and youth justice fields, where they became manifest in a range of programmed interventions and techniques around areas such as social skills training, anger management and addressing offending behaviour, often undertaken on a structured groupwork basis.

While they were initially thought to promise much in changing behaviours, claims made for programmed interventions are now far more modest; criminal and youth justice work in particular has witnessed a shift from the 'what works' focus of programmes back to a greater awareness of the importance of relationships in any change process. Stevens (2004) suggests that cognitive behavioural approaches are open to the same sort of questions regarding the longevity and generalizability of any behavioural changes once children have left care that can be asked of more classical behaviourist regimes.

Theory within social work

Following the professionalization of social work in the late 1960s, the Central Council for Education and Training in Social Work declared that residential child care was social work. This view prompted some discontent, perhaps with good reason. Social work drew on two dominant strands of thinking: the first a clinical orientation deriving from the profession's medical roots and, second, an emerging structural perspective drawing on a literature, of which Goffman's *Asylums* (1968) was perhaps the foremost example, that was hostile to institutional care. Wolfensberger's (1972) theory of normalization became influential in this regard.

A consequence of this was that, in pursuit of the 'normal', residential child care became stripped of any meaningful theory, its usage identified as increasingly short term and instrumental, undertaken in smaller community-based homes (or 'units' as they became known). In place of theory, social work placed its faith either in abstract notions such as rights, protection and the promotion of independence (Smith, 2009), or the various technologies of care represented by increasingly formulaic assessment frameworks. In fact, the very notion of care was identified as suspect: discourses of independence, empowerment and anti-institutionalization became totems of a profession that could consider itself 'so tainted by its associations with care that the word should be expunged from its lexicon and its rationale' (Meagher and Parton, 2004, p. 4).

Group care

In an attempt to stake a claim for residential child care within social work, Ainsworth and Fulcher (1981) and Fulcher and Ainsworth (1985) developed the concept of group care. The basic features of group care involve a group of children being cared for by a group of staff within a defined physical space with all the possibilities and complex dynamics that such environments give rise to. These two books contain contributions that are classics in the field: for example, chapters such as Henry Maier's 'Essential components in care and treatment environments for children' and Jim Whittaker's 'Major approaches to residential treatment'. Drawing on a North American as well as a UK literature, they bring to our attention a number of crucial themes:

- the concept of life space
- the importance of rhythm, ritual and routine
- the importance of the purposeful use of time, space and activity.

These are ways of thinking about residential child care that remain relevant and fresh today.

Ainsworth and Fulcher also introduced Uri Bronfenbrenner's (1979) theory of the ecology of human development, long before ecological models of assessment became standard fare in social work. For a while, group care became accepted as an area of social work practice and was given something of a boost by the publication of Adrian Ward's book *Working in Group Care* (1993). Ward's idea of opportunity work in some respects rebranded the idea of the life space intervention. This, again, enjoyed a brief flurry of respectability within the canon of social work thinking.

For the most part, though, there has been a paucity of useful theorizing of residential child care within social work. If anything, theoretical expositions of care became subsumed beneath an increasingly descriptive and policy-based literature during the 1990s. In that respect, the Ainsworth and Fulcher volumes remain foundational in grounding residential child care within a body of relevant theory. One legacy of them that is finding its way now into the everyday language of residential child care is the concept of life space.

Life space approaches

With the rise of child psychology and psychiatry from around the 1930s, treatment came to be thought of as being distinct from care. Children encountering emotional or behavioural difficulties would receive counselling from outside experts such as psychologists, psychiatrists or social workers. The job of residential workers was one of providing everyday care, a task that was not professionally valued.

A number of developments challenged this separation of care from treatment. In the mental health field, Maxwell Jones established therapeutic communities that identified the importance of group living in addressing psychiatric disorder; in child care, Barbara Dockar-Drysdale established the Mulberry Bush School as a therapeutic community; and in America, Bruno Bettleheim (1950) believed that the difficulties experienced by the children in his Orthogenic School in Chicago were so extreme that they required a round-the-clock psychotherapeutic environment or 'milieu' which brought together treatment and care. The idea of treatment happening alongside care was further developed by Redl and Wineman (1951, 1957).

The classic text setting out a life space approach is *The Other 23 Hours* (Trieschman et al., 1969). The title of the book conveys the relative importance of what happens in the hours of the day when children are not involved in formal treatment. While planned interventions may have their place, they are only one aspect of work with children. Life space theory suggests that everyday life events or experiences, from getting children up in the morning to putting them to bed at night, offer opportunities to enhance their growth and learning that are at least as powerful as more formal interventions.

Life space is the total physical and emotional arena in which workers and young people interact. The main factor distinguishing residential child care from any other kind of work with children is that 'practitioners take as the theatre for their work the actual living situations as shared with and experienced by the child' (Ainsworth, 1981, p. 234). Working in the life space requires the conscious use of everyday life events as they occur for therapeutic purposes: 'therapy on the hoof', as Redl (1966) described it.

Henry Maier's paper 'The core of care' (1979) stands as a seminal contribution to life space approaches. It offers a framework within which to conceptualize the relational basis of care, introducing seven components essential to the provision of developmental care:

1 Maier's starting point is to ensure children's *bodily comfort*, the provision of good basic care.
2 This needs to take into account the differences or *differentiations* between children. Maier describes some children as 'human radars', others as 'go-go kids': the first are the active scanners; the second are those children who only make sense of their world by bumping into it. Interventions that might suit one are unlikely to suit the other, thus requiring individualized responses.
3 Responses or interventions that 'fit' allow worker and child to enter into a unique *rhythmic interaction*, to get onto a similar wavelength. This process might be helped through involvement in some common interest or activity.
4 Out of the experience of rhythmicity comes a level of *predictability*, where children become able to anticipate how a worker might respond in any given situation.
5 Once they have reached this stage they can begin to experience *dependency*. Notions of dependency can be frowned on in social work, where the emphasis, too often, is on promoting independence. Maier argues, however, that it is only through the experience of a healthy dependency that children can achieve meaningful independence or interdependence.
6 Moreover, he claims that it is only with the development of appropriately dependent and reciprocal relationships that workers can usefully address questions of *personalized behaviour training*. In such a model, acceptable behaviour does not come from sets of house rules or contracts, but through developing personal relationships.
7 The final element is *care for the carer*. Just as parents need support in bringing up children, so too do care workers need to feel safe and supported in the task if they are to provide an appropriate quality of care for young people. At one level, this can be provided by organizational supports such as supervision, but more importantly it requires organizational cultures in which they feel safe and valued and able to make mistakes.

Life space approaches form the basis of the child and youth care profession in North America and in other countries including South Africa. There is a growing body of literature developing features of a child and youth care approach. Fulcher and Garfat (2008), for example, identify a long list of characteristics and principles of such an approach, all of which centre around the development of relationships in

Making connexions

This chapter argues that the idea of 'treatment' is generally inappropriate in a group care setting. Do you agree? Do you think that the life space approach offers a better framework?

a life space context. Garfat (2003) extends the scope of these features of child and youth care to working with families. In many respects, life space approaches constitute an orientation to practice rather than a particular theoretical approach. Different homes might be informed by psychodynamic, behavioural or any other theoretical model. What they have in common is that the very nature of the work demands that they operate within a life space context and it is the ideas that flow from this that can help workers name what it is they do beyond the merely tending.

Reclaiming a moral dimension to care

The emergence of psychodynamic thinking shifted the focus of care from children's souls to their psyches. A psychological paradigm has been dominant ever since and has encouraged a quest for scientifically based ways through which to understand care. Scientific reductionism intensified from the 1970s onwards, with political pressure to demonstrate measurable outcomes from care and to identify interventions that might be claimed to 'work'. Increasingly legalistic and instrumental approaches became reified in legislation to regulate care across the different countries of the UK in 2001. While this legislation specifies who is to provide care, where, and the penalties for failing to do so, it neglects to say what care might be. Nor does it give any attention to why we might care.

Approaches to care based on psychological or managerial reductionism fail to ascribe any ethical dimension to it. Yet it is just such a dimension that Webb (2006) argues ought to characterize social work in this late modern period. There has, in fact, been a discernible ethical turn in the social work literature in recent years (see Gray and Webb, 2010). In the particular context of how we care for children, Moss and Petrie (2002) pose several ethical questions:

■ What do we want for our children?
■ What is a good childhood?
■ What kind of relationships do we want for children, with other children, with adults and within society?

Such questions perhaps set the direction for the future theorizing of residential child care. The nature of caring relationships becomes a central concern. According to Brannan and Moss (2003, p. 202), caring relationships

> are predicated upon an expressive rather than instrumental relationship to others. They are based upon trust, commitment over time and a degree of predictability.

One set of ethical ideas that might provide some insight into care and caring relationships is provided in the growing interest in care ethics (Steckley and Smith,

2011). Care ethics seek to make 'relational realities explicit – how to live in relationship with others' (Gilligan, 1982, p. xiv). They are associated with Carol Gilligan, a research student of Lawrence Kohlberg, the psychologist associated with the development of what has become the dominant theory of human moral development. Gilligan (1982) claimed that Kohlberg's thesis reflected a particularly male way of thinking about morality. She reinterpreted his data to argue that, rather than being less moral than men, women applied different ways of thinking to moral decision-making; they spoke in a different moral voice, one that emphasized qualities of care, compassion, context and intuition. Men, by contrast, inclined towards decision-making based around qualities of justice, objectivity and reason. From Gilligan's initial work, a whole literature has built up around what has become known as care (or feminist) ethics.

Joan Tronto (1994, p. 126) identifies care as

a practice, rather than a set of rules or principles … It involves both particular acts of caring and a 'general habit of mind' to care that should inform all aspects of a practitioner's moral life.

Sevenhuijsen (1998) suggests that an ethic of care is concerned with responsibilities and relationships rather than rules and rights; bound to concrete situations, rather than being formal and abstract, it is a moral activity rather than a set of principles to be followed.

According to Ricks (1992, p. 54), care ethics take

professional caring into the personal realm and requires that both parties show up, be present, be engaged at a feeling level for each other. The presence of feeling(s) provides the link which connects the worker and client. Very simply put, without this connection, without the feeling(s) in the relationship, the people do not matter to each other.

Maier (1979) makes a similar point, arguing that physical care needs to be transformed to caring care. In this context, Noddings draws on Bronfenbrenner's oft-quoted assertion that a child needs 'the enduring, irrational involvement of one or more adults in care and joint activity … Somebody has to be crazy about that kid' (cited in Noddings, 2002, p. 25). When an adult is crazy about a kid and that kid knows it, children can, in Noddings' terms, 'glow and grow'.

According to Held (2006, p. 4), 'a caring person not only has the appropriate motivations in responding to others or in providing care but also participates adeptly in effective practices of care'. The need to participate in effective practices of care may go some way towards distinguishing between the respective roles of direct care workers and social workers. Noddings (1984, 2002) differentiates between 'caring about' and 'caring for'. 'Caring about' involves taking a stance on an issue; it does not require the provision of direct care but reflects a general predisposition to see that children are well treated. However, 'caring about' isn't enough on its own. One can profess to be a caring person without getting one's hands dirty in the messy business

Theory

of 'caring for'. As Noddings (1984) says in her earlier work, 'caring about' can involve a certain benign neglect; it is empty if it does not result in caring relations.

Residential child care, by contrast, requires that workers are primarily called to 'care for' children. They work at the level of the face-to-face encounter, engaging in tangible practices of care such as getting children up in the mornings, encouraging their personal hygiene, engaging in a range of social and recreational activities with them and ensuring appropriate behaviours and relationships within the group. They are also confronted with the intensity of children's emotions and are involved in the messy and ambiguous spaces around intimacy and boundaries. An inevitable messiness and ambiguity enters the fray when workers become involved in 'caring for' (Steckley and Smith, 2011). As such, care ethics begin to reframe relationships away from the clinical and instrumental focus of a psychological discourse, and instead emphasize their practical and moral nature.

Social pedagogy

In recent years, and in many respects acknowledging the poor state of residential child care in the UK, there has been growing interest in European models of social pedagogy. These may offer a more promising paradigm for theorizing residential child care than social work. Social pedagogy is concerned with bringing up children through broadly socioeducational approaches, education being considered in its widest sense. This notion of education in its widest sense is perhaps encapsulated in the German concept of *bildung*, which incorporates but transcends formal teaching and learning to include a sense of character formation and preparation for citizenship. For residential child care, the adoption of a broadly educational, or pedagogic, way of thinking has the attraction of shifting the focus away from the child's psychological deficits; in its place, the emphasis is on the child's growth and development or, more generally, on what is needed to promote the child's upbringing.

The principles of social pedagogy would seem to offer a framework within which to locate essential features of residential child care (see Petrie et al., 2006). Social pedagogic practice happens in the life space. It involves elements of head, hands and heart – intellectual, practical and emotional activity on the part of the worker. The relational aspects of care are illuminated in the social pedagogic idea of 'the 3Ps', representing professional relationships, personal relationships and private relationships. In social pedagogy, it is only private aspects of the self that are kept from children; an inevitable and healthy crossover of the professional and the personal is acknowledged to be central to effective caring.

Another feature of social pedagogy is that it stresses the purposeful use of activities (the hands part of the 3Ps), which is a central feature of residential child care practice. The importance of activities might be illuminated by the concept of 'the common third', whereby worker and child come together in planning for and joint participation in activities, whether sporting, creative or recreational. Activities provide what Phelan (2001b) calls 'free spaces' where normal boundaries and hierarchies are dissipated, allowing for more equal relationships to form. These relationships then become the medium for children's growth and development.

Social pedagogic work is a self-in-action task; it requires that workers continually reflect on what they are doing and why, taking differing contexts into account. In that and indeed in many other respects, such as its stress on the importance of close personal relationships between workers and children, it is dissonant with the instrumental, procedure-bound and risk-averse cultures of residential child care in the UK.

Conclusion

What might be distilled from this brief overview of theory in residential child care? First, that the field, perhaps in pursuit of professional status, has for too long laboured after the psychological silver bullet that might lead it to some behavioural or therapeutic promised land. This hasn't happened, nor is it going to. Therapy may have a place in residential child care but too often the term is ill-defined and promises more than it can deliver. Fritz Redl had the right idea when he defined therapy as not putting poison in (children's) soup. It is about providing children with living experiences that nurture and sustain them without doing them further harm. This points towards theories of the everyday, and, in this respect, life space approaches are at the heart of practice and provide practitioners with a set of ideas that resonate with what they do.

It is, however, not just what the workers do but why they do it that needs to be addressed in theorizing residential child care; this has rarely been achieved or perhaps even attempted. To do so requires that ethical and relational ideas be brought into the frame. The soul or at least those bits of the human spirit that are not amenable to psychological or material reductionism need to be brought back to centre stage. In this respect, emerging moral theories that move beyond abstract rules and principles and programmed interventions to encompass ideas grounded in everyday caring relationships come into play.

Abstraction has not served residential child care well. The field needs to build a body of ideas that reflect the everyday realities of caring for children. This has not happened within a social work paradigm. Indeed, many of the theories applied to residential child care from social work have been singularly unhelpful. In this respect, social pedagogy may provide a more fertile paradigm for useful theory-building in residential child care.

Further reading

■ Cameron, C. and Moss, P. (eds) (2011) *Social Pedagogy and Working with Children and Young People: Where Care and Education Meet*. London: Jessica Kingsley.

Reflecting the growing interest in ideas of social pedagogy, offers a comprehensive introduction to its background, theory and practice.

■ Noddings, N. (2002) *Starting at Home: Caring and Social Policy*. Berkeley, CA: University of California Press.

Although not specifically focused on residential child care, this book by a philosopher of education provides a stimulating and well-grounded account of how to bring children up, rooted in the everyday experiences of care.

■ Smith, M. (2009) *Rethinking Residential Child Care*. Bristol: Policy Press.

Explores how residential child care has got to where it is, and considers how it might now develop – based around broad ideas of care and upbringing.

References

Ainsworth, F. (1981) 'The training of personnel for group care with children', in F. Ainsworth and L.C. Fulcher (eds) *Group Care for Children: Concept and Issues*. London: Tavistock.

Ainsworth, F. and Fulcher, L.C. (eds) (1981) *Group Care for Children: Concept and Issues*. London: Tavistock.

Anglin, J. (2002) *Pain, Normality, and the Struggle for Congruence: Reinterpreting Residential Care for Children and Youth*. New York: Haworth Press.

Bandura, A. (1973) *Social Learning Theory*. London: Prentice Hall.

Bettelheim, B. (1950) *Love is Not Enough: The Treatment of Emotionally Disturbed Children*. Glencoe, IL: Free Press.

Bion, W.R. (1970) *Attention and Interpretation*. London: Tavistock.

Bowlby, J. (1951) *Child Care and the Growth of Love*. Harmondsworth: Penguin.

Brannan, J. and Moss, P. (2003) *Rethinking Children's Care*. Buckingham: Open University Press.

Bronfenbrenner, U. (1979) *The Ecology of Human Development*. Cambridge, MA: Harvard University Press.

Clough, R., Bullock, R. and Ward, A. (2006) *What Works in Residential Child Care? A Review of Research Evidence and the Practical Considerations*. London: National Children's Bureau.

Clyde, Lord (1946) *Report of the Committee on Homeless Children*. Edinburgh: HMSO.

Curtis, M. (1946) *Report of the Care of Children Committee*. London: HMSO.

Fulcher, L.C. (2001) 'Differential assessment of residential group care for children and young people', *British Journal of Social Work*, 31, 417–35.

Fulcher, L.C. and Ainsworth, F. (eds) (1985) *Group Care Practice with Children*. London: Tavistock.

Fulcher, L.C. and Garfat, T. (2008) *Quality Care in a Family Setting: A Practical Guide for Foster Carers*. Capetown: Pretext.

Garfat, T. (ed.) (2003) *A Child and Youth Care Approach to Working with Families*. New York: Haworth.

Gilligan, C. (1982) *In a Different Voice: Psychological Theory and Women's Development*. Cambridge, MA: Harvard University Press.

Goffman, E. (1968) *Asylums*. Harmondsworth: Penguin.

Gray, M. and Webb, S. (2010) *Ethics and Value Perspectives in Social Work*. Basingstoke: Palgrave Macmillan.

Held, V. (2006) *The Ethics of Care: Personal, Political, Global*. Oxford: University Press.

Hoghughi, M. (1979) 'The Aycliffe token economy', *British Journal of Criminology*, **19**(4): 384–99.

Maier, H. (1979) 'The core of care: essential ingredients for the development of children at home and away from home', *Child Care Quarterly*, **8**(4): 161–73.

Meagher, G. and Parton, N. (2004) 'Modernising social work and the ethics of care', *Social Work and Society*, **2**(1): 10–27.

Milligan, I. (1998) 'Residential care is not social work', *Social Work Education*, **17**(3): 275–86.

Moss, P. and Petrie, P. (2002) *From Children's Services to Children's Spaces*. London: Routledge/Falmer.

Noddings, N. (1984) *Caring: A Feminist Approach to Ethics and Moral Education*. Berkeley, CA: University of California Press.

Noddings, N. (2002) *Starting at Home: Caring and Social Policy*. Berkeley, CA: University of California Press.

Petrie, P., Boddy, J., Cameron, C. et al. (2006) *Working with Children in Care: European Perspectives*. Maidenhead: Open University Press.

Phelan, J. (2001a) 'Notes on using plain language in child and youth care work', www.cyc-net.org/cyc-online/cycol-1101-phelan.html.

Phelan, J. (2001b) 'Experiential counselling and the CYC practitioner', *Journal of Child and Youth Care Work*, 16, 256–63.

Redl, F. (1966) *When we Deal with Children*. New York: Free Press.

Redl, F. and Wineman, D. (1951) *Children who Hate*. Glencoe, IL: Free Press.

Redl, F. and Wineman, D. (1957) *Controls from Within: Techniques for Treatment of the Aggressive Child*. New York: Free Press.

Ricks, F. (1992) 'A feminist's view of caring', *Journal of Child and Youth Care*, **7**(2): 49–57.

Rowe, J. and Lambert, L. (1973) *Children Who Wait: A Study of Children Needing Substitute Families*. London: BAAF.

Ruch, G., Turney, D. and Ward, A. (eds) (2010) *Relationship-based Social Work: Getting to the Heart of Practice*. London: Jessica Kingsley.

Sevenhuijsen, S. (1998) *Citizenship and the Ethics of Care: Feminist Considerations on Justice, Morality and Politics*. Abingdon: Routledge.

Sharpe, C. (2006) 'Residential child care and the psychodynamic approach; is it time to try again?', *Scottish Journal of Residential Child Care*, **5**(1): 46–56.

Skinner, B.F. (1953) *Science and Human Behaviour*. London: Collier Macmillan.

Smith, M. (2009) *Rethinking Residential Child Care: Positive Perspectives*. Bristol: Policy Press.

Steckley, L. (2010) 'Containment and holding environments: understanding and reducing physical restraint', *Children and Youth Services Review*, **32**(1): 120–8.

Steckley, L. and Smith, M. (2011) 'Care ethics in residential child care: a different voice', *Ethics and Social Welfare*, **5**(2): 181–95.

Theory

Stevens, I. (2004) 'Cognitive-behavioural interventions for adolescents in residential child care in Scotland: an examination of practice and lessons from research', *Child and Family Social Work,* **9**(3): 237–46.

Trieschman, A., Whittaker, J.K. and Brendtro, L.K. (1969) *The Other 23 Hours: Child-care Work with Emotionally Disturbed Children in a Therapeutic Milieu.* New York: Aldine de Gruyter.

Tronto, J. (1994) *Moral Boundaries: A Political Argument for an Ethic of Care.* New York: Routledge, Chapman and Hall.

Ward, A. (1993) *Working in Group Care: Social Work in Residential and Day Care Settings.* Birmingham: Venture Press.

Ward, A. (1995) 'The impact of parental suicide on children and staff in residential care: a case study in the function of containment', *Journal of Social Work Practice,* **9**(1): 23–32.

Webb, S. (2006) *Social Work in a Risk Society: Social and Political Perspectives.* Basingstoke: Palgrave Macmillan.

Winnicott, D.W. (1965) *Maturational Processes and the Facilitating Environment Studies in Theories of Emotional Development.* London: Tavistock.

Wolfensberger, W. (1972) *The Principle of Normalization in Human Services.* Toronto: National Institute on Mental Retardation.

19
What research tells us about residential child care

ANDREW KENDRICK

The role of residential child care in the UK and around the world is much contested. Over many years, there has been a continuing ambiguity about its place in the continuum of child care services, and this manifests itself in social work policy and practice. This has been driven by evidence of abuse and neglect of children and young people in residential care, the issue of the poor outcomes of children and young people who leave the care system, questions about the effectiveness of residential child care, and the focus on the family as the placement of choice.

It is important, however, to acknowledge the diverse nature of residential care for children and young people. Even within the four countries of the UK, there are distinct differences in the scale of the residential sector, the range of providers, and the characteristics of the children and young people who use residential child care. Residential child care for children and young people cuts across professional and agency boundaries, and health, education and justice are also involved in the provision of residential child care. Official designations for residential establishments vary not only across the countries of the UK but even across different agencies within countries. The main types of residential care include:

- children's homes and residential homes without education
- children's homes with education, residential schools and therapeutic communities
- residential establishments for disabled children including respite and shared care services
- secure accommodation services.

According to Forrester et al. (2009, p. 449):

> 'Residential care' is a complex sector of care for children. It includes local authority and private homes, secure accommodation and specialist boarding schools,

small institutions with a handful of children and large residential units; residential care can also range from a short-term emergency placement through to permanent placement in a therapeutic community.

Trends in the use of residential child care

The policy and practice debates of the 1970s and 80s led to significant reductions in the number of children in residential care (Kendrick, 2008a; Bullock and McSherry, 2009). Mainey et al. (2006) highlight how the residential sector has declined across the UK over the past 30 years. In England, for example, placements in community homes fell from over 25,000 to less than 2,000 between 1981 and 2000, and in Wales the fall was from 1,445 to 211 between 1980 and 2001. The numbers in residential care in Scotland also fell but to a lesser extent, from over 6,300 to less than a third of this number from the mid-1970s to the end of the 1980s. There has been a marked shift in the balance between the use of residential and foster care, and a major change in the age of children in residential care as now it tends to be used predominantly for older children, although there is recent evidence that it is being used increasingly for younger children.

If we look at the current figures, we find differences in the proportions of children and young people in residential care across the UK:

- At 31 March 2010, there were 64,400 children looked after in England and 8,170 (13%) were in residential care (DfE, 2010).
- At 31 July 2010, there were 15,892 looked after children in Scotland and 1,480 (9%) were in residential care (Scottish Government, 2011).
- At 31 March 2010, there were 5,162 looked after children in Wales and 351 (7%) were in residential care (Welsh Assembly Government, 2010).
- In 2009, there were 2,463 children looked after in Northern Ireland, and 308 (13%) were in residential care (DHSSPS, 2010).

In addition, there are a significant number of children who are looked after in at least one planned series of short-term placements. In England, for example, 10,000 children were looked after during the year to March 2010 on this basis; the vast majority (8,300) were disabled children (DfE, 2010).

There are, however, a significant proportion of children who remain in residential care long term. Generally, there has been a reduction in the length of time that children and young people spend in residential placements (Bullock and McSherry, 2009). In a study of local authority children's homes in Scotland, Milligan et al. (2006) found that nearly half of the residential placements lasted for less than three months, and one-third lasted less than one week. Reflecting the purpose of short-term care pending rehabilitation with the family, almost half of the children and young people (47%) returned to their family.

Making connexions

Why do you think the numbers of children in residential care have fallen so dramatically?

Within each country, there is also a great deal of variability in the use of residential child care across different local authorities (Sinclair et al., 2007; Hill, 2009). Sinclair et al. (2007, p. 148) stated that:

> one particular council said that it was proudly investing in its own residential care. Almost all the others appeared to be trying to keep children out of such provision if possible. Despite this view there was a grudging acceptance that some children need residential care either because of their impairment(s) or because this was seen as the only way to manage their behaviour.

The reasons for children being placed in residential care

The reduction in the use of residential care means that it deals with some of the most troubled and troublesome children and young people. Berridge and Brodie (1998, p. 83) found that most young people had experienced severe difficulties in several aspects of their lives and it 'therefore appears that the current children's home population is much more complex and problematic than in 1985'. There has been a long recognized link between poverty and entry into local authority care (Bebbington and Miles, 1989; Kendrick, 2005). Research has also highlighted the high incidence of mental health difficulties of children and young people in residential care (Meltzer et al., 2003; Kendrick et al., 2004; van Beinum, 2008).

Three main issues have been identified for placement in residential care: school-based difficulties; offending or behavioural issues; and family problems and child protection (Kendrick, 1995; Triseliotis et al., 1995). Sinclair and Gibbs (1998, p. 19) found that the main reason for most children and young people being placed in children's homes was 'breakdown of relationship between young person and family' (53%). One in five (21%) were admitted because of the young person's behaviour', and other reasons were 'potential/actual abuse of young person' (10%), 'neglect of young person' (4%) and 'family illness/housing problem' (2%).

Sinclair et al. (2007) found that children in residential care were more likely to be aged 11 or over, and also to have entered care for the first time when they were aged 11 or over. They were also more likely to be disabled, have acute family stress, or difficult behaviour, but less likely to have been abused. Children and young people in residential care had worse school performance and higher challenging behaviour scores.

Sinclair et al. (2007) also found that those seeking asylum are more likely to be in residential care, and Thoburn et al. (2005) highlighted that a significant proportion of unaccompanied asylum-seeking children spend much of their adolescence in residential care and hostels. Some local authorities have developed specialist children's homes for this group, although there are conflicting views about whether this is an appropriate model (Wade et al., 2005).

More generally, in relation to black and ethnic minority children, early research identified disproportionate placement in residential care. Later studies, however, identified different patterns, with equal proportions of, or more, white children being placed in residential care (Kendrick, 2008b). Sinclair and Gibbs (1998) found wide variation in the proportion of black and minority ethnic children across local authorities.

We saw above that Sinclair et al. (2007) found that disabled children are more likely to be in residential care. Stalker (2008) highlights that disabled children in residential care are a largely hidden group and that basic information is lacking. One issue concerns some of the complexities related to legal status, as not all disabled children in residential care will be looked after, and placements funded by education authorities may attract little or no attention from social services. The most detailed figures that Stalker could identify were from a report by the then Department for Education and Skills (DfES, 2003). In 2002, there were 1,320 disabled children with 'looked after' status in residential settings in England and Wales, just under half were in residential schools and a similar number were in children's homes. A far larger number of disabled children – 10,500 – attended residential special schools:

> The largest group in all types of school were children with EBD [emotional and behavioural difficulties], followed by those with learning disabilities. Children with physical and/or sensory impairments were a relatively small proportion. (Stalker, 2008, p. 109)

Research suggests that there are two main factors in the admission of disabled children to residential schools: an inability to meet a child's educational needs locally, and the impact of the child's impairment on the family.

Another significant sector in residential care consists of secure accommodation services. Locking up children is contentious and the role of secure care is riddled with ambiguity and contradictions. Secure accommodation primarily caters for two populations: those who present a risk to others, and those who present a risk to themselves. The first group is seen as requiring control or punishment, while the second requires care or treatment (Barclay and Hunter, 2008). Such distinctions, however, can become confused by the role of parenting and socialization in offending, and the similar characteristics and needs of the two groups (Goldson, 2000). O'Neill (2001) also reports the particularly poor experiences and short-term outcomes for girls placed on welfare grounds, given the different needs of boys and girls.

Research has also highlighted that despite the rhetoric of secure accommodation addressing the problems and issues of young people, its primary and predominant function is to contain (Kelly, 1992; Goldson, 2002). The routes by which children and young people enter secure care are a product of child-related factors and decisions and actions taken by professionals (Bullock et al., 1998; Walker et al., 2006). Bullock et al. (1998) differentiate between the life *route*, which refers to children and their families' actions, and *process*, which encompasses actions taken throughout the child's life by professionals in health, social work and education or by courts and children's panels.

Relationships in residential child care

If relationships are at the core of residential child care work, they also evidence the extremes of behaviours; relationships highlight both the best and worst aspects of residential child care. The abuse of trusted relationships is at the core of the scandals in residential care, while positive relationships are central to effective work with children and young people.

Relationships between staff members and young people

This contrasting nature of relationships can clearly be seen in the relationships between staff members and children and young people. At one end of the spectrum is the damaging impact of abuse and neglect in residential care; the misuse of power by members of staff who are in a position of trust. It is difficult to know the full extent of this abuse and there continue to be heated debates from different perspectives (Kendrick, 1998; Stein, 2006a; Sen et al., 2008; Smith, 2009). What cannot be contested is that over the years children and young people have suffered direct physical, sexual and emotional abuse, systematic organized abuse, and programme abuse. The issue of acknowledgement and accountability for historical abuse has been worked through in different ways across the UK. In Scotland, for example, the Time to Be Heard pilot forum gave former residents of Quarriers the opportunity to recount their experiences – and some are talking about this for the very first time (Hawthorn and Kendrick, 2011). An interdepartmental task force has been established in Northern Ireland to consider the nature of an inquiry into historical institutional abuse, and to review the immediate needs of survivors and provide a clear means of resolution and provision of services.

There continue to be concerns about poor relationships between staff members and young people, and about the physical and sexual abuse of children and young people in residential care – as there are concerns across a range of settings (Gallagher, 2000). One context in which this manifests itself is in respect of the physical restraint of children and young people. There have been child deaths due to improper physical restraint in secure settings in England (Smallridge and Williamson, 2008). Steckley and Kendrick (2008) also identify physical abuse of children and young people in the process of physical restraint. This same research has, however, also identified the importance of positive relationships between staff members and young people. More generally, children and young people often identify positive relationships with staff members as central to their experiences of care (Sinclair and Gibbs, 1998; Hill, 1999). Across a range of social work settings, there has been a 'rediscovery' of the importance of the therapeutic relationship (Burnett and McNeill, 2005; Ruch, 2005). The network of relationships has been identified as one of the distinctive features of group care (Ward, 2003).

Whitaker et al. (1998, p. 170) identify a number of features of good practice in working directly with individual young people:

- being ready to listen, both to the evidently momentous and to the apparently mundane
- being sensitive to a young person's readiness, or not, to talk and to share feelings and experiences
- combining nonverbal or symbolic forms of caring with verbal, explicit ones
- noticing good or admirable behaviour and crediting a young person for it
- marking special occasions in a young person's life with a celebration.

Berridge (2002) concluded that several studies have 'explained successful residential care according to the quality of the interaction between young people and adults. Terms used include: empathy; approachability; persistence; willingness to listen; reliability.' Houston's action research study (2011) highlighted the importance of relationship-based social work as a response to the psychosocial and practical needs of children and young people in residential care. The study explored residential social workers' experience of enhancing resilience in young people living in a children's home, and identified the development of a range of innovatory practices that addressed both the needs of children and young people and 'the agency's administrative imperatives for accountable and safe practice (for example the attention to recording and planning)' (Houston, 2011, p. 127). Daniel (2008) and Gilligan (2005) have identified the importance of resilience as a conceptual framework for residential child care practice.

Relationships between staff members and young people, then, are central to defining the residential experience as a negative or positive one:

> The caring individuals who frequently make enormous sacrifices for the children in their care are in large part responsible for the broadly positive pattern of welfare outcomes identified in the research. (Forrester et al., 2009, p. 451)

Peer relationships

The relationships between children and young people in residential child care also highlight the extremes of positive and negative behaviour.

Bullying and peer violence have long been identified as a major issue by children and young people in residential child care, but have tended to have less focus than abuse by staff members (Kendrick, 2011). Sinclair and Gibbs (1998) found that almost half of the 223 young people interviewed had been bullied during their residential placement, although many had also been bullied prior to their entry into residential care. Similarly, 23% of residents were taken sexual advantage of before they moved into the children's home compared to 13% after; the young people may generally live in a context of violence.

Barter et al. (2004, see also Barter, 2008) identify a spectrum of behaviours of peer violence. Four different forms of peer violence were derived from the young people's accounts: direct physical assault; physical 'non-contact'; verbal abuse; and unwelcome sexual behaviour. These could be *low-level* attacks, which were infrequent, did not involve severe use of force and were seen as having little impact; or *high-level* attacks, which were frequent, used severe force and had significant impact. Peer group hierarchies or 'pecking orders' within residential homes were linked to this abuse of power – and young people saw this as an inevitable aspect of residential life.

Another aspect of peer influence that has been raised is the criminogenic effect of residential care – the notion of 'schools of crime'. Although the issues around residential care being a criminalizing experience are broader than peer relationships, there is concern that delinquent subcultures in residential care can in some cases propel young people into crime (Taylor, 2006). We have seen, however, that offending and behavioural problems are a major factor for placement in residential care. Sinclair and Gibbs (2008) report that the pressures to take drugs, drink alcohol and steal were actually less in residential care than before young people had been placed there. Darker et al. (2008) studied the association between local authority care and offending behaviour for 250 looked after young people aged 10 and over. They concluded that 'this study shows no evidence that care itself promotes offending behaviour' (Darker et al., 2008, p. 146). While the study found that there was little difference in offending outcomes and types of placement overall, there was some evidence that offending behaviour was more common in certain residential homes than in other placements, partly because offenders were more likely to be placed in residential care but also because a criminalizing culture had developed in some residential homes.

Emond's ethnographic study of life in a residential establishment in Scotland (2002, 2003, 2005) contrasts markedly with what has gone before and highlights the ways in which children and young people in residential care form a support system for other members of the group. Young people 'regarded the resident group as an important force in their day-to-day lives, their view of themselves and of their social world' (Emond, 2003, p. 326). There was no fixed group structure; status was granted as a result of subtle negotiation between young people and their social context. This involved young people offering a range of support and advice through knowledge of the system, insider knowledge, humour and external networks (Emond, 2002). While Emond did identify negative features of the peer group such as verbal and physical aggression, these were used much less than the positive social currencies. Emond concludes that young people, as a group, are an untapped resource in residential care for positive influence on individual children and young people (see also Carter, 2011).

Working with parents and families

Over many years, there have been issues with regard to collaborative working relationships with parents and the families of children in residential care. We saw above that entry into residential child care often takes place because of a breakdown in family relationships, or, in the case of disabled children, because of pressure on the family. The move into residential care might mean that connections with the family may weaken even further. One-fifth of children and young people in Sinclair and Gibbs's study (1998) had no contact with their family or had 'no family', while a further fifth

Research

had contact on a two-weekly to monthly basis. While the remainder had more frequent contact with family members, just over a third of children said that they did not see their families enough. The study found that contact was not related to length of time in care or long-term placement. An earlier study of parental contact found that the proportion of children in residential care having regular contact with their parents was higher than for those in foster care (Bilson and Barker, 1995).

They also found that for children aged 10 and over, the longer children were in residential care, the more likely there was to be contact with parents, while the opposite was the case in foster care. That said, it can be difficult for parents to maintain regular contact with children in residential care, particularly if children are placed far from home, and parents lack or cannot afford transport. Communication may be more difficult for disabled children (Stalker, 2008).

Morgan's (2008) report on the views of the parents of looked after children does not focus on residential care but identifies a number of relevant issues. While almost three-quarters of the parents thought that their children were being well looked after, parents wished to have more of a say in their child's care plan and about placement, education and family contact. Bullock and McSherry (2009) see this lack of involvement of parents and families as a weakness in many interventions.

The residential environment

Good design in health, education and work settings has been shown to have a range of positive effects. The design of residential care facilities has traditionally been driven by statutory and health and safety considerations, usually resulting in an 'institutional' look and feel. Children and young people have spoken tellingly about the impact of their environment on their experience of care. Sinclair (2006) notes, however, that little research has looked at the effects of buildings on outcomes.

Docherty et al. (2006) identified three key themes in their study of design in children's homes: personalizing space, aesthetics and functionality. Personalizing space is important in terms of children taking ownership and thus respecting the environment; it is therefore an important determinant in the success of the design. Young people and staff differed in their response to design issues. In particular, young people were more descriptive, commenting on aesthetics (colour schemes, accessories), while staff opinions tended to focus on functionality (durability). What staff considered appropriate for a residential care home and what young people liked or chose to comment upon often differed. Consultation is a useful way of engaging young people and staff, and ensuring that their needs are recognized and involving them in the process.

Morgan (2009) found that children and young people thought that buildings that are big and spacious, in a good state of repair, which feel homely and where children have plenty to do are seen as good buildings to live in as children's homes:

> In general, the excellent accommodation and physical resources in these [outstanding] homes created a homely and welcoming environment for young

people. By having good and well-maintained surroundings, the young people felt they were treated with respect and wanted to treat their environment with respect in turn. (Ofsted, 2011, p. 11)

Research in Scotland has highlighted how food can play an important role in how residential workers aim 'to create an environment which closely replicated what was often referred to as "ordinary" family life' (Dorrer et al., 2010, p. 250). Food provided a safe medium for communicating emotional care and as a feature of the social relationships and culture of the residential home. The food preferences of young people are identified on entry to care, mealtimes build relationships between staff and young people, and food practices can reflect the routines of family life. Notwithstanding the ambiguities and tensions that could surround food practices in residential care, this research concluded that:

> food is central to the caring environment within each of the residential homes we studied and to the form and development of a range of relationships. (Punch et al., 2009, p. 169)

There has been some research on the impact of the size of residential homes, although we have seen that there has been a trend for residential homes to get smaller and now it is not unusual to provide residential services for single young people. Sinclair and Gibbs (1998, p. 207) found that:

- 19 homes had six places or less and their 'good home' score averaged 2.7
- 13 had seven to nine places and the average score was −0.5
- 7 homes had ten plus places and their average score was −6.4.

They conclude that these results 'provide strong support for the policy of reducing the size of homes'.

Berridge and Brodie (1998) studied 12 children's homes. The number of residents ranged between 4 and 11, with the average being 6.2. Berridge and Brodie (1998, p. 156) found that size was not a key factor: 'In fact our largest home ... was also the most impressive, while the three smallest ... came seventh, eighth and fourth.' They suggest that an important point is that all the homes in the study tended to be relatively small. Sinclair and Gibbs suggest that the range of services provided by homes in the Berridge and Brodie study is important. The large home mentioned above was a local authority home offering short-term breaks for young people with severe learning disabilities and additional health needs: 'The association between size and outcome may be easier to detect in homes that are serving similar populations' (Sinclair and Gibbs, 1998, p. 217). Carter (2011), in discussing therapeutic communities, suggests the need for size to support the group element of the work.

Effectiveness and quality in residential child care

As with many areas of social work practice, there have been major debates about the effectiveness of residential child care and 'what works' in residential care interventions (Clough et al., 2006). It is in relation to these debates that we need to be most careful in relation to the complexity and diversity of residential care, and to avoid broad generalizations in favour of a more nuanced approach about what works for whom in what circumstances. As Forrester et al. (2009, p. 449) highlight, residential care is a complex sector and 'it is therefore not possible to make generalized statements about the effectiveness of "residential care"'. That said, Forrester (2008) concluded that generally children did better following time in residential care than they were doing beforehand.

Knorth et al. (2008) carried out a review and selective meta-analysis on the outcomes of residential child and youth care. The main conclusion they made was that children and youth, after a period of residential care, on average, improve in their psychosocial functioning – the 'effect sizes that we found are in most cases positive and can often be characterized as "medium", sometimes as "large"' (Knorth et al., 2008, p. 135). They identified behaviour modification components and family-focused components in the residential interventions as achieving positive results (see also Curry, 1991; Whittaker, 2004). Knorth et al. also identified that specific training aimed at social cognitive and socioemotional skills of young people can generate a significant strengthening of a treatment effect.

A major concern has been the variation in the quality of residential child care establishments and the impact on outcomes (Berridge and Brodie, 1998; Sinclair and Gibbs, 1998; Sinclair et al., 2007). Research (Brown et al., 1998; Sinclair and Gibbs, 1998; Whitaker et al., 1998; Anglin, 2002) has stressed the importance of leadership in developing positive cultures in residential care, with clarity of roles and congruence in aims and objectives: 'homes are effective when they develop clear methods of work, provide continuity and nurture members of staff and staff teams' (Berridge and Brodie, 1998, p. 95).

Ofsted's (2011) report on 'outstanding' children's homes identified a number of key characteristics. In brief, these were:

- leaders who are hands-on and unite their staff behind a shared purpose
- clarity of vision focused on the experience of children and young people
- a commitment to continual improvement
- the passion and energy of staff who are deeply committed to their work, and the systems to identify these staff and support them
- understanding which young people will benefit from living in the home and creating the conditions most likely to make the placement a success
- meticulous planning that engages young people, combined with a commitment to never 'give up'
- time spent with children and young people individually and in groups
- absolute consistency in the management of behaviour
- an unwavering commitment to support children and young people to succeed
- working with each child or young person to build their emotional resilience and self-confidence.

Sinclair et al. (2007) found that children who had been placed in residential care did 'worse' than expected on their 'doing well' measure but comment that these poor 'doing well' scores are not surprising given that these young people had to be very troubled to get there. They found that if 'one takes account of behaviour, age and age at entry, children's homes are not significantly less "successful" than other placements' (Sinclair et al., 2007, p. 208).

Other forms of residential care have been underresearched and there is an important need to develop the evidence base across the range of provision. Research on therapeutic communities, for example, indicates promising outcomes for some young people (Little and Kelly, 1995; Carter, 2011). Stalker (2008) also highlights the lack of research on disabled children in residential settings, although Berridge and Brodie (1998) highlight positive practice in short-break homes for disabled children.

Transitions and leaving care

When we look at the outcomes for children and young people in residential child care, it is important to be clear about the point (or points) at which children leave residential care, and where they go. The transition of young people back into the community is absolutely crucial in our consideration of the role of residential care, both in terms of moving on to independent living and in returning home at a younger age.

Knorth et al. (2008) acknowledge that outcomes for young people were mainly examined over the short term. It has long been a concern that residential interventions may not have long-term benefits once young people leave the residential setting (Cornish and Clarke, 1975; Little et al., 2004). Walker et al. (2006), for example, tracked young people from admission to secure accommodation over a 24-month period. Social workers generally attributed a good outcome more to an appropriate placement and education being offered when the young person left secure accommodation rather than simply the placement itself. The term 'step-down approach' was used to refer to the practice of gradually returning young people to a more open and less supportive setting (see also Whittaker, 2004). Research has also identified stability as an important factor in positive outcomes (Biehal et al., 1995; DH, 1998; Jackson and Martin, 1998).

A main focus of the research on the outcomes of residential child care has been the outcomes of young people who move out of residential care to independence (Stein and Munro, 2008), and research 'has demonstrated the high risk of social exclusion faced by young people leaving care' (Wade and Munro, 2008, p. 215). A first concern about this has been the age at which this happens, with most young people leaving care to independent living at 16–18 years compared to most young people leaving home in their mid-twenties (Stein, 2006b). This has also raised major concerns about the maturity and preparation of young people leaving care:

> Of equal importance to age, therefore, is that young people are well prepared, are able to leave care in a planned and supported manner, and, given that a third of the residential group said they had no choice when they left care, that they are able to have a say in when they leave. (Dixon, 2008, p. 80)

Research

The most recent research on the outcomes for care leavers from residential child care reflects the findings of earlier studies. Relatively few care leavers gain educational qualifications, and those who do have fewer than the national average. Educational disadvantage further impacts young people's progress after they leave care. Studies have shown that a significant proportion of care leavers are unemployed, with about a quarter in further education and training and between 10 and 13% in casual or permanent work (Wade and Dixon, 2006; Dixon, 2008). Accommodation was another aspect of life where care leavers fared relatively poorly, although young people's experiences are varied, some maintaining their own tenancies, living with family, or in some form of supported accommodation. However, instability in housing and accommodation was also evident (Wade and Dixon, 2006). Dixon (2008) found that those leaving residential care had particular difficulties in settling after care, over a third had experienced homelessness, and they also tended to fare worse in relation to employment. Another particularly vulnerable group of care leavers was those with mental health, emotional or behavioural difficulties (Wade and Dixon, 2006).

Leaving care legislation enacted across the UK to tighten the duties of local authorities has led to a further expansion of leaving care services and improvements in pathway planning and support for young people (Wade and Munro, 2008). Specialist leaving care services have been shown to improve outcomes for care leavers (Stein, 2006b; Wade and Dixon, 2006). According to Stein (2006b, p. 276; see also Stein, 2008):

> Leaving care services can also help young people to some extent in furthering social networks, developing relationships and building self-esteem, although these dimensions are also closely connected with young people having positive, supportive, informal relationships with family members or friends.

Conclusion

This chapter has attempted a broad overview of the research on residential child care. In doing so, it hopes to have identified the complex issues in providing group care for an increasingly vulnerable group of children and young people. There have been many calls for a reduction in the use of residential child care and, in some cases, calls for its abolition. The tension between residential care as a positive choice and as a last resort is apparent in policy and practice. It seems that with each inquiry that argues for the development of residential child care as one element of a continuum of child care provision, there is another headline about poor practice or scandal. The research evidence would suggest that there is a place for residential child care and that it performs an important function for a number of children and young people. There is evidence that residential care can be effective in addressing the needs of this population of children and young people. However, there are also clear indications that there needs to be more focus on the transitions of children and young people to ensure that the benefits of good quality residential care can be supported when they move on – to home, to other placements or to independence. There need to be elements of stability in these transitions and it is clear that social workers must take a primary role in this.

Further reading

■ Anglin, J.P. (2002) *Pain, Normality, and the Struggle for Congruence: Reinterpreting Residential Care for Children and Youth.* Binghamton, NY: Haworth Press.

This classic research study of residential care in Canada develops a sophisticated conceptual framework for residential care, and highlights the voices of residential staff and children and young people.

■ Courtney, M.E. and Iwaniec, D. (eds) (2009) *Residential Care of Children: Comparative Perspectives.* Oxford: Oxford University Press.

Provides an excellent comparison of residential child care around the world, highlighting its different roles, functions and development.

■ Kendrick, A. (ed.) (2008) *Residential Child Care: Prospects and Challenges.* London: Jessica Kingsley .

Addresses the range of complex issues facing residential child care across the UK, and the priorities for developing best practice, policy and improved outcomes for children and young people.

References

Anglin, J.P. (2002) *Pain, Normality and the Struggle for Congruence: Reinterpreting Residential Care for Children and Youth.* Binghamton, NY: Haworth Press.

Barclay, A. and Hunter, L. (2008) 'Blurring the boundaries: the relationship between secure accommodation and "alternatives" in Scotland', in A. Kendrick (ed.) *Residential Child Care: Prospects and Challenges.* London: Jessica Kingsley.

Barter, C. (2008) 'Prioritising young people's concerns in residential care: responding to peer violence', in A. Kendrick (ed.) *Residential Child Care: Prospects and Challenges.* London: Jessica Kingsley.

Barter, C., Renold, E., Berridge, D. and Cawson, P. (2004) *Peer Violence in Children's Residential Care.* Basingstoke: Palgrave Macmillan.

Bebbington, A. and Miles, J. (1989) 'The background of children who enter local authority care', *British Journal of Social Work,* 19, 349–68.

Berridge, D. (2002) 'Residential care', in D. McNeish, T. Newman and H. Roberts (eds) *What Works for Children. Effective Services for Children and Families.* Buckingham: Open University Press.

Berridge, D. and Brodie, I. (1998) *Children's Homes Revisited.* London: Jessica Kingsley.

Biehal, N., Clayden, J., Stein and Wade, J. (1995) *Moving On: Young People and Leaving Care Schemes.* London: HMSO.

Research

Bilson, A. and Barker, R. (1995) 'Parental contact with children fostered and in residential care after the Children Act 1989', *British Journal of Social Work,* **25**(3): 367–81.

Brown, E., Bullock, R., Hobson, C. and Little, M. (1998) *Making Residential Care Work: Structure and Culture in Children's Homes.* Aldershot: Ashgate.

Bullock, R. and McSherry, D. (2009) 'Residential care in Great Britain and Northern Ireland: perspectives from the United Kingdom', in M.E. Courtney and D. Iwaniec (eds) *Residential Care of Children: Comparative Perspectives.* Oxford: Oxford University Press.

Bullock, R., Little, M. and Millham, S. (1998) *Secure Care Outcomes: The Care Careers of Very Difficult Adolescents.* Aldershot: Ashgate.

Burnett, R. and McNeill, F. (2005) 'The place of the officer-offender relationship in assisting offenders to desist from crime', *Probation Journal,* **52**(3): 221–42.

Carter, J. (2011) 'Analysing the impact of living in a large-group therapeutic community as a young person – views of current and ex-residents: a pilot study', *Journal of Social Work Practice,* **25**(2): 140–63.

Clough, R., Bullock, R. and Ward, A. (2006) *What Works in Residential Child Care: A Review of Research Evidence and the Practical Considerations.* London: National Children's Bureau.

Cornish, D.B. and Clarke, R.V. (1975) *Residential Treatment and its Effects upon Delinquency.* London: HMSO.

Curry, J.F. (1991) 'Outcome research on residential treatment: implications and suggested directions', *American Journal of Orthopsychiatry,* 61, 348–57.

Daniel, B. (2008) 'The concept of resilience: messages for residential child care', in A. Kendrick (ed.) *Residential Child Care: Prospects and Challenges.* London: Jessica Kingsley.

Darker, I., Ward, H. and Caulfield, L. (2008) 'An analysis of offending by young people looked after by local authorities', *Youth Justice,* **8**(2): 134–48.

DfE (Department for Education) (2010) *Children Looked After in England (Including Adoption and Care Leavers) Year Ending 31 March 2010.* London: DfE.

DfES (Department for Education and Skills) (2003) *Disabled Children in Residential Placements.* London: DfES.

DH (Department of Health) (1998) *Caring for Children Away from Home: Messages from Research.* Chichester: Wiley & Sons.

DHSSPS (Department of Health, Social Services and Public Safety) (2010) *Children Order Statistical Tables for Northern Ireland.* Belfast: DHSSPS.

Dixon, J. (2008) 'Young people leaving residential care: experiences and outcomes', in A. Kendrick (ed.) *Residential Child Care: Prospects and Challenges.* London: Jessica Kingsley.

Docherty, C., Kendrick, A., Lerpiniere, J. and Sloan, P. (2006) *Designing with Care: Interior Design and Residential Child Care, Full Report,* Glasgow: Farm7/Scottish Institute for Residential Child Care.

Dorrer, N., McIntosh, I., Punch, S. and Emond, R. (2010) 'Children and food practices in residential care: ambivalence in the "institutional" home', *Children's Geographies,* **8**(3): 247–59.

Emond, R. (2002) 'Understanding the resident group', *Scottish Journal of Residential Child Care,* **1**(1): 30–40.

Emond, R. (2003) 'Putting the care into residential care: the role of young people', *Journal of Social Work,* **3**(3): 321–37.

Emond, R. (2005) 'An outsider's view of the inside', in D. Crimmens and I. Milligan (eds) *Facing Forward: Residential Child Care in the 21st Century.* Lyme Regis: Russell House.

Forrester, D. (2008) 'Is the care system failing children?', *The Political Quarterly,* **79**(2): 206–11.

Forrester, D., Goodman, K., Cocker, C. et al. (2009) 'What is the impact of public care on children's welfare? A review of research findings from England and Wales and their policy implications', *Journal of Social Policy,* **38**(3): 439–56.

Gallagher, B. (2000) 'The extent and nature of known cases of institutional child sexual abuse', *British Journal of Social Work,* 30(6): 795–817.

Gilligan, R. (2005) 'Resilience and residential care for children and young people', in D. Crimmens and I. Milligan (eds) *Facing Forward: Residential Child Care in the 21st Century.* Lyme Regis: Russell House.

Goldson, B. (2000) '"Children in need" or "young offenders"? Hardening ideology, organizational change and new challenges for social work with children in trouble', *Child and Family Social Work,* **5**(3): 255–65.

Goldson, B. (2002) *Vulnerable Inside: Children in Secure and Penal Settings.* London: The Children's Society.

Hawthorn, M. and Kendrick, A. (2011) *Time to Be Heard Pilot Forum Evaluation: A Chance to Say More,* www.survivorscotland.org.uk/downloads/ 1298549265-Pilot-Process-Review-SIRCC_Time_to_be_Heard_Evaluation_Final.pdf.

Hill, M. (1999) '"What's the problem? Who can help?": The perspective of children and young people on their wellbeing and on helping professionals', *Journal of Social Work Practice,* **13**(2): 135–45.

Hill, M. (2009) *Higher Aspirations, Brighter Futures: NRCCI Matching Resources to Needs Report.* Glasgow: Scottish Institute for Residential Child Care.

Houston, S. (2011) 'Using action research to enhance resilience in a children's home: an exploration of need, experience and role', *Child Care in Practice,* **17**(2): 115–29.

Jackson, S. and Martin, P.Y. (1998) 'Surviving the care system: education and resilience', *Journal of Adolescence,* 21, 569–83.

Kelly, B. (1992) *Children Inside: A Study of Secure Provision.* London: Routledge.

Kendrick, A. (1995) *Residential Care in the Integration of Child Care Services.* Edinburgh: Scottish Office.

Kendrick, A. (1998) 'In their best interest? Protecting children from abuse in residential and foster care', *International Journal of Child & Family Welfare,* 3(2): 169–85.

Kendrick, A. (2005) 'Social exclusion and social inclusion: themes and issues in residential child care', in D. Crimmens and I. Milligan (eds) *Facing Forward: Residential Child Care in the 21st Century.* Lyme Regis: Russell House.

Kendrick, A. (ed.) (2008a) *Residential Child Care: Prospects and Challenges.* London: Jessica Kingsley.

Kendrick, A. (2008b) 'Black and minority ethnic children and young people in residential care', in A. Kendrick (ed.) *Residential Child Care: Prospects and Challenges.* London: Jessica Kingsley.

Kendrick, A. (2011) 'Peer violence for provision for children in care', in C. Barter and D. Berridge (eds) *Children Behaving Badly: Peer Violence Between Children and Young People.* Chichester: Wiley-Blackwell.

Kendrick, A., Milligan, I. and Furnivall, J. (2004) 'Care in mind: improving the mental health of children and young people in state care in Scotland', *International Journal of Child & Family Welfare*, 7(4): 184–96.

Knorth, E.J., Harder, A.T., Zandberg, T. and Kendrick, A. (2008) 'Under one roof: a review and selective meta-analysis on the outcomes of residential child and youth care', *Children and Youth Services Review*, 30, 123–40.

Little, M. and Kelly, S. (1995) *A Life without Problems? The Achievements of a Therapeutic Community.* Aldershot: Arena.

Little, M., Kohm, A. and Thompson, R. (2005) 'The impact of residential placement on child development: research and policy implications', *International Journal of Social Welfare*, **14**(3): 200–9.

Mainey, A. Milligan, I., Campbell, A. et al. (2006) 'Context of residential child care in the United Kingdom', in A. Mainey and D. Crimmens (eds) *Fit for the Future: Residential Child Care in the United Kingdom.* London: National Children's Bureau.

Meltzer, H., Corbin, T., Gatward, R. et al. (2003) *The Mental Health of Young People Looked After by Local Authorities in England.* London: TSO.

Milligan, A., Hunter, L. and Kendrick, A. (2006) *Current Trends in the Use of Residential Child Care in Scotland.* Glasgow: Scottish Institute for Residential Child Care.

Morgan, R. (2008) *Parents on Council Care: A Report on Parents' Views by the Children's Rights Director for England.* London: Ofsted.

Morgan, R. (2009) *Life in Children's Homes: A Report of Children's Experience by the Children's Rights Director for England.* London: Ofsted.

Ofsted (2011) *Outstanding Children's Homes.* Manchester: Ofsted.

O'Neill, T. (2001) *Children in Secure Accommodation: A Gendered Exploration of Locked Institutional Care for Children in Trouble.* London: Jessica Kingsley.

Punch, S., McIntosh, I., Emond, R. and Dorrer, N. (2009) 'Food and relationships: children's experiences in residential care', in A. James, A.T. Kjørholt and V. Tingstad (eds) *Children, Food and Identity in Everyday Life.* Basingstoke: Palgrave Macmillan.

Ruch, G. (2005) 'Relationhip-based and reflective practice: holistic approaches to contemporary child care social work', *Child & Family Social Work,* **10**(2): 111–23.

Scottish Government (2011) *Children Looked After Statistics 2009–10.* Edinburgh: Scottish Government.

Sen, R., Kendrick, A., Milligan, I. and Hawthorn, M. (2008) 'Lessons learnt? Abuse in residential child care in Scotland', *Child & Family Social Work*, **13**(4): 441–22.

Sinclair, I. (2006) 'Residential care in the UK', in C. McAuley, P. Pecora and W. Rose (eds) *Enhancing the Well Being of Children and Families through Effective Interventions.* London: Jessica Kingsley.

Sinclair, I. and Gibbs, I. (1998) *Children's Homes: A Study in Diversity.* Chichester: Wiley.

Sinclair, I., Baker, C., Lee, J. and Gibbs, I. (2007) *The Pursuit of Permanence: A Study of the English Care System.* London: Jessica Kingsley.

Smallridge, P. and Williamson, A. (2008) *Independent Review of Restraint in Juvenile Secure Settings.* London: Ministry of Justice/DCSF.

Smith, M. (2009) *Rethinking Residential Child Care: Positive Perspectives.* Bristol: Policy Press.

Stalker, K. (2008) 'Disabled children in residential settings', in A. Kendrick (ed.) *Residential Child Care: Prospects and Challenges*. London: Jessica Kingsley.

Steckley, L. and Kendrick, A. (2008) 'Physical restraint in residential child care: the experiences of young people and residential workers', *Childhood*, **15**(4): 552–69.

Stein, M. (2006a) 'Missing years of abuse in children's homes', *Child and Family Social Work*, **11**(1): 11–21.

Stein, M. (2006b) 'Research review: young people leaving care', *Child and Family Social Work*, **11**(3): 273–9.

Stein, M. (2008) 'Resilience and young people leaving care', *Child Care in Practice*, **14**(1): 35–44.

Stein, M. and Munro, E.R. (eds) (2008) *Young People's Transitions from Care to Adulthood: International Research and Practice*. London: Jessica Kingsley.

Taylor, C. (2006) *Young People in Care and Criminal Behaviour*. London: Jessica Kingsley.

Thoburn, J., Chand, A. and Proctor, J. (2005) *Child Welfare Services for Minority Ethnic Families*. London: Jessica Kingsley.

Triseliotis, J., Borland, M., Hill, M. and Lambert, L. (1995) *Teenagers and the Social Work Services*. London: HMSO.

Van Beinum, M. (2008) 'Mental health and children and young people in residential care', in A. Kendrick (ed.) *Residential Child Care: Prospects and Challenges*. London: Jessica Kingsley.

Wade, J. and Dixon, J. (2006) 'Making a home, finding a job: investigation early housing and employment outcomes for young people leaving care', *Child and Family Social Work,* **11**(3): 199–208.

Wade, J. and Munro, E.R. (2008) 'United Kingdom', in M. Stein and E.R. Munro (eds) *Young People's Transitions from Care to Adulthood: International Research and Practice*. London: Jessica Kingsley.

Wade, J., Mitchell, F. and Baylis, G. (2005) *Unaccompanied Asylum Seeking Children: The Response of Social Work Services*. London: BAAF.

Walker, M., Barclay, A., Hunter, L. et al. (2006) *Secure Accommodation in Scotland: Its Role and Relationship with 'Alternative' Services*. Edinburgh: Scottish Executive.

Ward, A. (2003) 'The core framework', in A. Ward, K. Kasinski, J. Pooley and A. Worthington (eds) *Therapeutic Communities for Children and Young People*. London: Jessica Kingsley.

Welsh Assembly Government (2010) *Adoptions, Outcomes and Placements for Children Looked After by Local Authorities: Year Ending 31 March 2010*. Cardiff: Welsh Assembly Government.

Whitaker, D., Archer, L. and Hicks, L. (1998) *Working in Children's Homes: Challenges and Complexities*. Chichester: John Wiley & Sons.

Whittaker, J.K. (2004) 'The re-invention of residential treatment: an agenda for research and practice', *Child and Adolescent Psychiatric Clinics of North America*, **13**(2): 267–79.

Research

20
Residential child care in practice

JANINE BOLGER AND JEREMY MILLAR

Residential child care shares some characteristics with other types of social work but is also unique in that 'staff witness and at times are part of other people's lives. They will see residents as they live their lives: getting up, bathing and eating; relaxing and busy; happy and sad; angry, confused or excited' (Whitaker et al., 1998, p. 25). The nature of the task itself is complex as the worker fulfils a range of roles within the group care setting.

Several functions have been attributed to those who work in group care around the tasks of caring, boundary and limit setting (Hyatt-Williams, 1971). The first task of providing the care, affection and nurturing necessary for the emotional, physical and psychological development of the child is not only complex in its own right but will not always be well received. The young person is often experiencing the loss of family, routines and familiar places, while confronting life as an adolescent and attempting to establish an identity of their own. Boundary and limit setting, a normal aspect of parenting, assists the child in understanding and anticipating the dangers that they might face and guides them towards more socially acceptable behaviours. It is the worker's task to help the young person navigate through their defences in order to face their emotional pain so that they might make sense of their past and inform their future (Collins and Bruce, 1984).

The residential child care task

Menzies-Lyth (1988) has written extensively with regard to the task, its organization and the responsibility and subsequent authority awarded to workers. The primary task, according to Menzies-Lyth, is simply defined as that which the agency or service must provide to guarantee survival. However, it must be defined in practice if the institution is to perform its task effectively. Personal uncertainty and group conflict can arise from a lack of clarity. Due to the complex nature of residential provision, no one task will be awarded primacy, although any number of tasks might be given priority at different times. Responsibility for task definition should not, however, be avoided because of a lack of resources or because the task is thought to be too difficult to achieve.

The knowledge required by residential child care workers, in order to ensure that they are able to undertake the tasks required of them, could be divided into that of 'head' knowledge and working knowledge. The first can be gained without the latter but the latter relies upon an element of the first. It is important that workers have a sound knowledge of the developmental stages of children and young people, as well as knowledge about how groups function and group dynamics – from large organizations such as social services to smaller family groups. Finally, the worker will need to know about residential systems, the legislative and social policy context, and the maintenance and administration of the unit.

Much of the good work carried out within group care settings is based on sound theoretical principles that the worker may or may not be knowledgeable about. There is a big difference between 'knowing that' and 'knowing how'. Training courses often focus on the delivery of conceptual rather than practice-based knowledge, but to maximize the benefit to the participants, the training should assist the worker in translating that information into working knowledge (Beedell, 1976).

In order to achieve a positive culture in residential child care settings, the creation of a unified organization where all members are supported and accept responsibility for the safety and wellbeing of others' needs is desirable (Maier, 1987, cited in Fulcher and Ainsworth, 2006). Flexibility and creativity of programme design should be encouraged, while rigidity and reactivity should be discouraged. Creativity is further encouraged through the fostering of a democratic environment where staff are encouraged to try new things, offer suggestions and participate in decision-making within the context of the shared values of their organization.

Supporting the task

A good environment will support the task. By providing a suitable environment for a child, it is hoped that recovery can be part of that reality (Tomlinson, 2004). The young person's experience of the residential environment will depend on the milieu, a term used to denote 'surroundings, location or setting'. We are usually concerned with the impact of the environment on the emotional rehabilitation of both the individual and the group. In addition to the concept of the milieu there exists a school of thought that there is 'something more than the sum of the parts that is important in determining what happens in a home' (Brown et al., 1998, p. 6). Such features might be associated with the 'culture' of group care, while aspects that include buildings, roles, policies and so on would be thought of as the 'structure' – mechanisms by which goals are achieved (Brown et al., 1998). The term 'institution' can be used to describe the building used by an organization or a society but it is clear that such a concept can refer to the processes taking place within the physical setting, including organizational structure, function and ethos (Jack, 1998).

It is not difficult to understand how the physical environment might impact upon the life space. Keenan (1991, cited in Lishman, 1991, p. 220) defines the life space as

> a therapeutic and institutional environment wherein residents or attenders enact both existential and historical aspects of their lives in the context of relations with each other, professional and other staff, their systems and sub-systems.

In other words, the residential context or 'the life space' includes external factors, for example atmosphere or location, and internal factors, for example experiences or perceptions, and the interplay between the two.

The organization, physical environment, structure and regime of a unit will, therefore, have an impact on the behaviour of residents and staff alike. These cultures and subcultures of the group will influence therapeutic outcomes significantly. The environment should promote the opportunity for growth while allowing for the possibility of failure underpinned by the presence of caring adults able to provide protection and support.

Having introduced the context of residential child care, we now turn to Jennifer, a young person about to begin her journey through the care system. She has shared some of her diary entries to illustrate how the experience of care impacted on her life.

Jennifer's diary

The social worker came to visit today. I heard her tell mum that I haven't been to school for three months. The social worker thinks I'm working as a prostitute! I told her I would have slept with that guy for nothing but he insisted on giving me money. Mum laughed at that. She's back on the smack again! I spent it on **********, just to take the edge off. Mum doesn't love me – I heard her say she can't look after me. She admitted that I'd been away for three days even though she knew I was at my boyfriend's. I was hiding out cos I'd beaten up a girl from down the road. Her gang's after me now. The social worker said I will end up in care. I told them I don't care but I'm scared. Mum's all I've got.

The social worker took me to a hearing today. Mum had forgotten about it cos she's obsessed with her new boyfriend so I had to go on my own. They said that I should come into care until mum can sort herself out. I am now on a supervision order. This means I have to go to the kid's home to live for a while. I don't want to go. I want to stay with mum. I know she's useless but she's all I've got.

Jennifer would be provided with accommodation under section 25(1)(c) of the Children (Scotland) Act 1995 through the children's hearing system, which is the care and justice system for Scotland's children and young people. In England and Wales, accommodation would be provided under section 20(1)(c) of the Children Act 1989.

The life experiences that we offer Jennifer should be as close to that of any of her contemporaries even though the method of delivery may need to be more flexible. The aim for residential child care workers is to help Jennifer connect with who she is and what is happening to her and to assist her in repairing and reconstructing her inner world (Trieschman et al., 1969). We would do this primarily through the provision of a secure base at the children's unit. Such a level of security offers both containment (Bion, 1961) and holding (Winnicott, 1964) and can be established within a relationship built up through attachment. As workers encourage Jennifer to form secure attachments from the time she moves in, they can consider ways of helping her promote her resilience through developing an understanding of her life experience and inherent strengths. Workers must help her understand that losses occur naturally and that she must try to learn to accept, understand, overcome and seek to replace those she loses.

Jennifer's diary

The social worker took me to the kid's home. I had to put my clothes in a bin bag – mum was wasted so she couldn't come with me. All the kids were showing off, losers! The staff smiled a lot and told me that I would have to go to school and be in by 10.30 at night. I told them where to go.

I tried to leave but they stopped me. I don't know anyone here. It's so noisy and everyone disses the staff. Help me!

The worker needs to remember that the experience of moving into care can reinforce and repeat the losses that Jennifer has already experienced. She will feel dispossessed of familiar roles, smells, people and so on. All changes might feel like a frightening separation. New routines might provoke anxiety but can be used to offer predictability and security. Special rituals to help Jennifer settle and feel understood need to be discussed, agreed and employed (Maier, 1991), for example playing a CD that has meaning for Jennifer at bedtime. The reliability and continuity brought by such rituals are crucial.

Life in residential care

Jennifer is encountering the behaviours of other troubled children who have incomplete and interrupted emotional experiences. This is as a result of the people who have come and gone from their lives, often with little awareness of the impact and the awfulness of the changes and the losses they have imposed on the child. Unintegrated children can demonstrate apparently irrational behaviour often characterized by violence and destructiveness (Dockar-Drysdale, 1968). They have no concept of boundaries and will attack organizational systems. They often display a wide range of behaviours and symptoms depending on and triggered by present or past circum-

Practice

stances (Kelly, 2003). The causes of not achieving emotional integration can be attributed to not good enough parenting in the first year of life resulting in a lack of attachment to a primary carer.

The worker can provide Jennifer with emotional experiences through day-to-day living and activity to help her become more complete. Small residential units with a stable staff group and firm boundaries can begin to offer experiences akin to a family model. Special attention and care can be offered through a key worker system. However, Jennifer's growth will depend, in part, on the ability of the staff team to understand the nature of and work with the distress and demanding behaviour of both the individual and the group.

The rhythms of our everyday life can provide Jennifer with opportunities for friendship and intimacy even when the day-to-day life of the unit appears chaotic. The repetition of these rhythms suggests predictability and even permanence (Maier, 1991). Opportunities for the creation and the discovery of rhythm need to be provided. Routines, such as morning rise and bedtimes or clearing up after meals, should be put in place to accomplish specified tasks in the most time-limited and effortless manner in order to achieve temporary order and security. Rituals can be created to prolong the process but personalize the activity, making it meaningful for the individual. As a child care worker, it is important to consider what meaning Jennifer might attach to a particular routine such as how she is woken each morning, for example waking her quietly and leaving her with a cup of tea and her music playing quietly rather than pulling back her curtains and loudly calling for her to get up. Routines from Jennifer's past that might resurrect feelings of being cared for, neglected or abused should be discussed and new routines put in place so that she can feel safe and secure.

Jennifer's diary

I've been here six months now. I've hardly seen mum. Her new bloke keeps beating her up just like I said he would. I've run away a couple of times to try and find her but the staff just call the police and I get grounded when I come back. School is good though. Miss Sood is cool and I can always talk to her. Staff at the kid's home help me with homework. I get to use the quiet room. It's still a wind-up with the other kids in my face and sometimes I still lose it. I hit out at my key worker last night. That didn't go down too well. Respect is a big word here and I'm going to respect me. I'm not a slag!

Responding to the child

Whatever the assessment of Jennifer might be and however skilled workers have proved themselves in intervening, it should be remembered that she is using her behaviour to ensure her survival. Survival can be strongly linked with fear as a mode of protecting the individual. Responses will usually involve withdrawing from the feared or unknown and moving towards the familiar or where there is a trusting relationship. The desire to survive can overflow into violence. The communication of violence is a symbolic way of finding someone willing to contain such feelings for you. Violence can therefore be viewed as a breakdown in communication. The causation of behaviour in one child will not necessarily be the same as in another child. In order to ensure that all children leave care with a broader repertoire of behaviours appropriate to the challenges they will face in life, they must be allowed frequent opportunities to practise new, more desirable behaviours across a range of settings, which will also sustain them in other environments (Fulcher and Ainsworth, 2006). So Jennifer might be helped to develop the skill of talking about her frustration rather than acting it out through aggressive behaviour.

Jennifer's behaviour should be viewed in relation to any developmental patterns from her past, the current manifestations of any such patterns and their future ramifications. Her view of past, present and future experiences is crucial. Such a view is inextricably linked with her sense of self, family and peers. The key relationships between past and present, particularly around attachment, detachment and death, are crucial in helping us understand Jennifer's present pattern of relationship formation. Links between past and present will also help us in our search for the meaning of the behaviour we experience each day. Through our understanding of these concepts, we can attempt to identify Jennifer's unresolved conflicts and adapt our intervention accordingly.

Workers are required to become attuned to the trauma history of the child. When the child or young person resists our intervention, they are likely to end up in conflict with staff members. In our attempts to deal with the conflict, workers may find themselves unwittingly involved in the re-enactment of the trauma. As the child replays their past struggles, staff need to understand the dynamic so that they might respond appropriately, while being aware of any past trauma they themselves may have experienced (Farragher and Yanosy, 2005). Shared decision-making between staff and young people results in shared power and in the resolution of feelings of anger and discontent. As workers, we cannot help people to change their behaviour unless their perceptions, feelings and expectations of self, family and peers have been explored and altered (Maier, 1991).

It is necessary to draw on concepts such as the influence of the past on the present, defence mechanisms and the way in which the unconscious influences our responses. Psychodynamic theorists believe that behaviour is only a

> surface characteristic and that true understanding of development requires analysing the symbolic meanings of behaviour and the deep inner workings of the mind. (Santrock, 2004, p. 39)

Jennifer has created defence mechanisms – such as hitting out, saying she doesn't care or running away – to protect her from the things that make her anxious, and, as such, they need to be understood as vital aspects of her coping mechanisms. It is the worker's challenge to support the young person in developing new, more appropriate coping strategies.

Practice

The workers response may evoke within them a range of feelings – unexplained anger, mistrust, disgust – which in turn may leave them critical of themselves for responding or thinking unprofessionally. In order to understand their own responses, workers needs to face up to the basic, internalized assumptions of their own upbringing and life experiences, which inevitably surface as a result of the work they are engaged in. Workers must also reflect continuously on their own responses to ensure that they are not employing defence mechanisms in order to avoid difficult situations. Workers must be aware of their own capacity to react angrily or by switching off, and their use of punishment, which is often only a rationalization of violence. Workers should be aware of what they are responding to and why, that is, 'transference' – the term used to explain the symbolic way in which the service user responds to the worker. How we respond to those we work with is also important, that is, 'countertransference' – the symbolic manner in which the worker perceives or responds to the service user. Transference helps us to identify distorted perceptions, while countertransference provides us with clues to what is being evoked by ourselves.

Working with the group

We should be mindful that Jennifer's anxieties can be lessened by dependable care for her daily needs through feeding, clothing, washing and so on. Physical care must be seen as a contributing factor in meeting Jennifer's psychological and emotional needs, while value is attributed to good standards of personal care through the building of relationships.

For many working in residential care, the prospect of a quiet shift is a good one, but this might mean that issues experienced by the residents have merely gone undetected or unresolved. Chaotic shifts where young people feel unsafe and act out their disturbance are also undesirable. A day that is neither too quiet nor boiling over but gently simmering is most likely to mean that the needs of the young people are being met (Whitwell, 2002).

When working with Jennifer in a group care setting, it is helpful to consider the psychology of the group and the task of individual integration within the group. Jennifer's experience of managing groups can be related to her level of emotional integration, which occurs as a direct result of the nature of her relationship with the primary carer. Children who have developed a basic level of trust and have moved on from a state of dependency to become a separate person, with a sense of self, self-control and internal boundaries, will find it easier to function in groups (Winnicott, 1960). However, this is not to suggest that the experience of groups cannot be helpful for less integrated children. In fact, the group can provide a level of emotional holding for such individuals. If this is the case, then it is likely that the value of the work carried out comes from the holding situation rather than from the input of individuals. A group can also offer a climate of hope for change, which can allow people the possibility of altering feelings and behaviour. For instance, alternatives to usual behaviour management strategies might be considered in a less threatening way within the group setting (Anglin, 2002).

Jennifer's diary

I've been here a year now, so much for the promises. A lot of kids have moved on and that's hard. I hate my mum, I hate her and all her empty ******** promises. All the staff do here is nag me when I get things wrong. I'm on a behaviour chart where I earn treats when I don't swear, break things or hit out at people. Big deal!

I'm doing better at school. I'm still a bit behind but the teachers say I might be able to take some exams next year and go to college. Apparently I've got 'potential'!

Young people within residential care are experienced in failing, so it is important that Jennifer is not led to believe that she can avoid facing up to difficult issues or relationships through destructive, dangerous or damaging actions. Inappropriate behaviour should be followed by clear consequences and the opportunity for reparation must be built in. The programme offered should incorporate the modelling of desirable behaviour from staff within a context that reflects the changing needs of the individual child and the group (Whittaker, 1979).

Provision must reflect the age, stage, culture and ability of each child. The level of structure required, the amount of responsibility, the expectations placed upon children and young people at different points in their development should be built into the 24-hour programme (Whittaker, 1979). A proactive, responsive (using well-considered judgement) stance from adults is more helpful in dealing with young people than a reactive (hasty and unconsidered) posture might be (Ward, 2002). Crisis and conflict should not be avoided altogether. As previously stated, Jennifer will need to be supported to acquire the skills for managing difficult situations in her life:

> Rehearsal of new and different ways of managing specific events can be addressed at moments of little stress, in a context of fun and interest-awakening procedures, and, above all, in a situation where residents and staff can become fully engaged with each other. (Maier, 1991, p. 23)

Moving on

The challenges facing Jennifer in the next stage of her journey through care cannot be underestimated. Research (Dixon and Stein, 2002, 2005; Jackson et al., 2003; Broad, 2005; Jackson, 2006) tells us that the outcomes for young people with experience of care tend to be poorer on any dimension that you care to measure. In Jennifer's case, we are alerted to risk-taking behaviours such as substance and alcohol misuse and staying out late at a young age. There are also indications of emotional

Practice

pain and grief (Marris, 1974; Murray-Parkes, 1996) expressed through aggressive acts towards others. It could be inferred that Jennifer has mental health difficulties that looked after young people experience to a disproportionate level (Meltzer et al., 2003, 2004). There exists the potential for Jennifer's future to encompass other negative outcomes often associated with young people exiting the care system, such as the increased likelihood of self-harm, substance misuse leading to dependency, early pregnancy and sexual health concerns. Other areas to be considered when working with young people moving on from care are the suitability of accommodation, access to further education, training and employment, promoting health and wellbeing, poverty and social exclusion, and reconciling the emotional and psychological damage from early life experiences that have led to their entering public care.

That outline may be bleak but if we ignore the body of evidence regarding outcomes for care leavers, we run the risk of condemning them to a life of poverty, distress and unrealized potential.

The starting point is understanding the duties and powers contained in the Children (Scotland) Act 1995, the *Regulations and Guidance on Services for Young People Ceasing to be Looked After by Local Authorities* (Scottish Executive, 2004) in Scotland

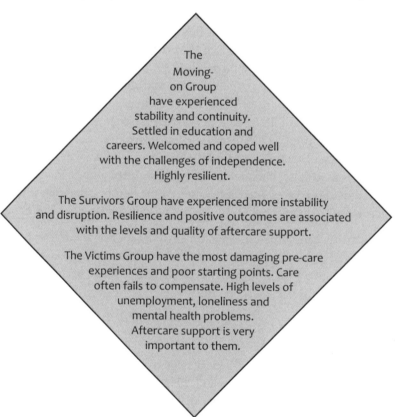

Figure 20.1 The resilience diamond
Source: Stein, 2005, p. 20

and the Children Act 1989 and Leaving Care Act 2000 in England and Wales. The legislation clearly states that local authorities are responsible for all looked after children and should discharge their duties of care in the manner of a good enough parent. This is often referred to as the role of the 'corporate parent':

> Local authorities have a role as corporate parents to these young people, particularly those who cannot return to their families. This means that the local authority should look after these children as any other parents would look after their own children. The provision of care and support for young people by their parents does not generally cease at a particular age and may continue long after a young person has reached adulthood. It adapts to meet the changing needs of the young person as they grow up, and will, at different times, include accommodation and financial support as well as advice and assistance. (Scottish Executive, 2004, p. 1)

A good question for workers to ask themselves and those charged with delivering services is 'Would this be good enough for my own child?' Should the answer be short of 'yes', further questions should be asked.

Stein (2005) utilizes the resilience diamond as a tool for assessing the young person and anticipating areas of their life that will require more focused resources and longer term therapeutic support (Figure 20.1).

Attention to resilience factors builds on our understanding of the impact, on later development, of early attachment experience (Rutter, 1999; Daniel et al., 1999; Gilligan, 2001). In respect of Jennifer's life, we are aware of significant loss and disruption to her assumptive world (Marris, 1974), evidenced by the loss of her birth father, the introduction of her mother's boyfriend and the addition to the household of a stepbrother, all compounded by the negotiation of early adolescence (Erikson, 1950).

Jennifer's diary

Typing this on my ace new laptop. I got the grades, bring on year 5. Dina and the staff have been sooo supportive. Curfew lifted and I got to stay over at Jackie's.

Mum has a new b*****d baby, totally blanking me. The waster hasn't changed a bit. Where is the social? She isn't fit to be a mother!

The focus of Jennifer's care plan shifts to look at throughcare and preparation for aftercare. These terms feature in the *Regulations and Guidance on Services for Young People Ceasing to be Looked After by Local Authorities* (Scottish Executive, 2004). 'Throughcare' refers to the period during which the young person remains looked after and accommodated, while 'aftercare' commences when the young person is no longer subject to supervision. The policy and procedures for care leavers in Great Britain are underpinned by the 'Pathways model' of service delivery. This approach provides for assessment, planning and progress review from a person-centred perspective.

Practice

Jennifer has hopes and dreams and benefits from a supportive relationship with her key worker. These are key elements in starting a Pathways assessment but, first, there should be a discussion regarding Jennifer's views on when and how she would like to move on from the children's home. The changes to the legislation contained in the Leaving Care Act 2000 and the *Regulations and Guidance on Services for Young People Ceasing to be Looked After by Local Authorities* (Scottish Executive, 2004) assume that the young person would remain in the residential unit until reaching at least the age of 18 unless their best interests would be served by moving on sooner. Jennifer's desire to stay on at school and study for the entrance qualifications required for nursing is a powerful argument for her to continue in the placement. The educational outcomes for children in care are extremely poor and the best indicators of future success in life are linked to good educational outcomes (Jackson, 2006). The fact that Jennifer has only had one placement adds to her potential for a smoother transition into living more independently in the community. Repeated placement moves negatively impact on outcomes for young people due to the impact on their ability to develop and sustain nurturing attachment experiences (Broad, 2005; Dixon and Stein, 2005).

The Pathways process

The Pathways materials will address the following areas of Jennifer's life:

- lifestyle
- family and friends
- health and wellbeing
- learning and work
- where I live
- money
- rights and legal issues.

These headings were drawn up in consultation with young people with experience of living in care and are specifically focused around the young person's own perspective and goals in life. A plan can be drawn up that clearly identifies who is responsible for doing what within set timescales. The Pathways process is dynamic, flexible and responsive to unexpected changes. The nature of adolescence is one of experimenting with new experiences, often holding unrealistic expectations and generally struggling with relationships, especially those with adult carers. For workers seeking clear care plans that are followed without dispute or deviation, the Pathways approach will be challenging. This is where the worker's awareness of and practical application of their understanding of attachment, loss and trauma and adolescent development is a critical skill (Stein, 2005).

The use of the Pathways material is inconsistent across local authorities despite training for staff being provided and its integration with holistic approaches to child care. The staff team supporting Jennifer understand that it is a statutory duty to undertake a Pathways assessment and subsequently put in place a Pathways plan. They recognize that the duties of the corporate parent commence when a child or young person enters care and that they have a duty to plan for when they are no longer looked after (Children Act 1989; Children (Scotland) Act 1995). Once Jennifer attained the statutory school leaving age, she came off supervision as her legal right to full advice, guidance and assistance as a care leaver would be protected under the relevant sections of the Children Act 1989, the Leaving Care Act 2000, the Children (Scotland) Act 1995 and the *Regulations and Guidance on Services for Young People Ceasing to be Looked After by Local Authorities* (Scottish Executive, 2004). Seldom would the best interests of the young person be served by coming off supervision prior to attaining the statutory school leaving age and workers should be vigilant regarding this crucial transition age.

Jennifer and her key worker share an interest in cooking and their time together often involves trying out new recipes. This way of utilizing their time demonstrates imaginative and productive residential care practice. For example, a typical session will include:

■ looking up the recipe and making a shopping list – discussion of ingredients, where they come from, which shops might have the items, doing rough budgeting sums
■ walking to the local shops – relaxed conversation, exploring the neighbourhood, physical exercise
■ purchasing the items – arithmetic, handling money, finding bargains, social interaction
■ return to the home to cook the meal – more discussion, often relating to memories that food holds for people, Jennifer has happy memories of cooking with her granny
■ and finally, serving the food to others – enjoyment of the meal, caring for others, a strong resilience protective factor, enhancing self-esteem and status in the group.

This practice illustrates the structured use of everyday life events (Ward and McMahon, 1998; Garfat, 2003) to support a range of developmental opportunities. It incorporates ongoing assessment and has clear links to the Pathways materials, making what could be an onerous procedural task (Pathways assessment) an empowering, fun and relationship-building daily event.

Jennifer's diary

Job going well down the caf and I'm minted for the first time. Dina's well impressed. Got my eye on a smart phone.

Visited the uni, shown round by cool guy, been in care himself. Jackie looking at courses too. We could share a flat, stop dreaming Jenn!

Spoke with Dina about finding my dad. Mum went in a bigtime sulk when I asked her about dad. No change there then!

Practice

The Pathways assessment and review

Prior to Jennifer's penultimate statutory review, the Pathways assessment was embarked upon and her key worker was identified as the Pathways coordinator. This assessment was informed by Jennifer's goals and aspirations. The careers service was involved to offer support and guidance with making an application for university. The school provided a staff member whose role was to support Jennifer in continuing her studies at school and achieve the necessary entrance qualifications. Both these professionals liaised with the university to ensure that Jennifer, as a formerly looked after young person, was supported by the Frank Buttle Trust (see www.buttletrust.org) to settle into university life. Prior to this review, Jennifer was informed of her right to have a person to support her at the regular reviews of her progress and she chose an older cousin who had kept in contact with her over the years.

From the age of 16, the Pathways reviews for Jennifer took place every six months. Her life was running smoothly according to her goals and aspirations, until at Christmas, Jennifer experienced further rejection from her mother, resulting in her taking an overdose in the children's home. A Pathways review was convened at the earliest opportunity in the new year and Jennifer was supported to talk about the pain she felt as a result of the rejection and the anger arising from the situation with her mother. The staff team and her key worker supported this process. From these discussions, it was established that Jennifer felt ongoing confusion over her mixed race identity. Her mother had consistently refused to discuss her father and within the wider family it was a taboo topic. This latest setback led to her resolve to find her birth father. The review updated the Pathways plan to support this important new focus and Jennifer asked that her key worker assist her in this piece of work. The children's home manager agreed to find additional staff cover to free the worker up to undertake this task. This is an excellent example of the dynamic and person-centred principles behind the Pathways planning process. Furthermore, we gain a sense of the corporate parent recognizing their ongoing responsibilities to Jennifer.

The period following Jennifer's overdose was extremely fraught, with Jennifer struggling to study in the run-up to her exams. The unstructured study time was particularly difficult as the home contained a number of younger residents who constantly disrupted Jennifer's attempts to settle into a routine. An additional setback was that Jennifer's journey to find her father faltered. It was discovered that he was an African Caribbean sailor who had never settled in the UK.

The team supporting Jennifer continued to offer practical and emotional support. Along with her key worker, Jennifer visited the university, looked at the student accommodation and spoke to student mentors provided for new students. Jennifer's journey to explore her family and her identity in the absence of her father involved visits to childhood places and conversations with family members. Jennifer took photos and kept a diary. Through this emotional journey, it became clear that the death of her much loved granny at the age of 12 was pivotal in informing her anger, coupled with her mum's new relationship and the addition of half-siblings, resulting in Jennifer feeling pushed out and struggling to make sense of her life. Undertaking life story work of this nature is complex and the structure of the ongoing supports inherent in the Pathways planning can be extremely useful in coordinating and providing resources to accomplish the work (Fahlberg, 2008).

It is through this therapeutic work and the power of a strong relationship that Jennifer started to reconcile these past losses and could begin to understand the complex emotions involved in the grieving process. Her key worker's ability to contain Jennifer's pain and provide an interpretative role on their shared journey highlights the necessity of working with an understanding of psychodynamic principles (Dockar-Drysdale, 1968; Maier, 1991). Young people, when they discuss the experience of leaving care, often offer feedback that reveals that staff have been supportive in practical matters but have struggled with the ongoing emotional impact of the transition (Dixon and Stein, 2005; Office of the Children's Rights Director, 2006).

Educational aspirations

Jennifer's aspirations to study for a degree place her in a relatively unique position among the population of looked after and accommodated young people. According to research, barely 2% of them go on to university compared with 40% of the general population of young people (Jackson et al., 2003; Stein, 2004; Francis, 2004). This disappointingly low proportion reflects a number of factors related to growing up in areas of poverty and deprivation, poor school experiences compounded by an absence of family role models who have had positive educational experiences and gone on to university. Jennifer was fortunate in her care experience as the home she was accommodated in had a learning culture. (For a description of an environment supportive of a child's learning, see Gallagher et al. 2004.) The staff team were motivated to obtain the relevant qualifications to enhance their roles. In addition, Jennifer's key worker was studying for a degree in social work through a distance learning course. Jennifer witnessed staff with academic books and they also consistently spent time with her and the other young people assisting with homework and helping with project work. The value of this social learning cannot be overstated (Jackson, 2006; Smith, 2009) because it offers insight into a world that looked after and accommodated children might otherwise have dismissed as not being for them.

The respective leaving care sections of the English and Welsh and Scottish child care legislation make provision for the support of young people going on into further/ higher education and training. This can be utilized to fund items required for studying such as laptops and essential tools of the trade like a set of knives for someone entering the catering trade. The funds can also be spent on providing travel expenses

Practice

or paying for accommodation if the student is studying away from home. Sonia Jackson (2006) has written extensively on the challenges facing care leavers continuing with their studies and her research clearly states that a learning environment coupled with positive role models and a local authority willing to invest in the young person produces the best outcomes.

In their research for the report *Still a Bairn*, Jo Dixon and Mike Stein (2002, p. 159) gathered these comments from the young people in relation to education:

> Lyn observed: 'I would say education is the big thing now. It's very important and it will always be something you've achieved in your life.'
>
> …
>
> Heather told others: 'If you're advised to go to college, force yourself to follow even if you don't like it because it will pay off in the end.'

Jennifer's diary

Coffee with Dina, she came round to the flat. The group photo picture she brought is ace. It's going up in my room.

Mark's been staying but he ain't moving in! Not yet anyways. Night out with the girls, Jackie is getting engaged. Should be a good one. Thankfully no classes on Friday!

Saw mum in Lidl, she asked for a sub till Friday. What am I, a charity?

One of the greatest challenges faced by care leavers is loneliness and isolation as they move into their own accommodation at an early age relative to the majority of the population (Dixon and Stein, 2005; Office of the Children's Rights Director, 2006). This often leads to the breakdown of the tenancy. Innovative practice can reduce the impact of this transition and in Jennifer's case the Pathways planning process discussed a range of options, including a supported lodgings scheme, Foyer-type bedsit or own tenancy, before opting for the student halls. This decision was informed by Jennifer's desire to mix with other new students and hopefully form friendships away from the care setting, which would offer her the chance to feel included in university life.

Now living in a shared flat with a social life distanced from the care system, Jennifer keeps in touch with her key worker and other supportive staff through social media and going for coffee. Jennifer is a welcome visitor to the children's home, one who can model and stand testimony to positive outcomes that can be achieved from being accommodated in residential child care.

Making connexions

Jennifer's story, although having many highs and lows, has a positive ending. What qualities in Jennifer herself and in the care experience do you think contributed to this?

Conclusion

Residential child care practice has a rich history of innovative and transformative impacts on the lives of children and young people. In this sphere of residential care, we can look to the therapeutic communities movement (Kahan and Banner, 1969; Fulcher and Ainsworth, 2006) and the influence of relational approaches (Maier, 1979; Ward and McMahon, 1998; Smith, 2009). Sadly, for formerly looked after children and young people, there is also a history tainted by institutionalized practices, emotional neglect and horrific abuse. We all know which history makes the headlines and as a result of the negative media portrayal of the experience of kids in care, the positive outcomes struggles to gain a hearing.

This chapter presents Jennifer's journey through care as one in which great personal challenges around loss and abandonment were addressed and overcome by staff and other professionals. They nurtured, cared for and supported Jennifer by utilizing their knowledge of child development theory and the profound importance of understanding the impact on later life of early attachment issues, and the impact of loss and trauma on a child's sense of self and identity. They consistently listened to Jennifer and placed her goals and aspirations to the forefront. The role of the legislation and policy was utilized to promote the core principles of working in Jennifer's best interests. The staff did not allow the procedural aspects to divert their attention and they fulfilled as best they could the corporate parenting role, insofar as they provided the resources for Jennifer to grow and flourish, particularly in respect of her educational achievements. It can be asserted that, in Jennifer's case, the state provided the level of care that could be expected from a 'good enough' parent.

Further reading

■ Smith, M. (2009) *Rethinking Residential Child Care: Positive Perspectives*. Bristol: Policy Press.

A classic in the making and offers a comprehensive, thought-provoking insight into the application of an ethical and radical approach to residential childcare.

■ Trieschman, A., Whittaker, J.K. and Brendtro, L.K. (1969) *The Other 23 Hours: Childcare Work with Emotionally Disturbed Children in a Therapeutic Milieu*. New York: Aldine de Gruyter.

Classic text that details the complexities of working the life space with troubled and troublesome children.

■ Ward, A. and McMahon, L. (ed.) (1998) *Intuition is not Enough: Matching Learning with Practice in Therapeutic Child Care*. London: Routledge.

Offers excellent guidance on how to practise in a therapeutic community milieu with an introduction to opportunity-led practice.

Practice

References

Anglin, J.P. (2002) *Pain, Normality and the Struggle for Congruence*. Binghamton, NY: Haworth Press.

Beedell, C. (1976) *Residential Life with Children*. Woking: The Gresham Press.

Bion, W.R. (1961) *Experience in Groups and Other Papers*. London: Tavistock/Routledge.

Broad, B. (2005) *Improving the Health and Well Being of Young People Leaving Care*. Lyme Regis: RHP.

Brown, E., Bullock, R., Hobson, C. and Little, M. (1998) *Making Residential Care Work: Structure & Culture in Children's Homes*. Aldershot: Aldgate.

Collins, T. and Bruce, T. (1984) *Staff Support and Staff Training*. London: Tavistock.

Daniel, B., Wassell, S. and Gilligan, R. (1999) *Child Development for Child Care and Protection Workers*. London: Jessica Kingsley.

Dixon, J. and Stein, M. (2002) *Still a Bairn: Throughcare and Aftercare Services in Scotland*. Edinburgh: Scottish Executive.

Dixon, J. and Stein, M. (2005) *Leaving Care: Throughcare and Aftercare in Scotland*. London: Jessica Kingsley.

Dockar-Drysdale, B. (1968) *Therapy and Child Care*. London: Longmans, Green.

Erikson, E.H. (1950) *Childhood and Society*. New York: Norton.

Fahlberg, V. (2008) *A Child's Journey Through Placement*. London: BAAF.

Farragher, B. and Yanosy, S. (2005) 'Creating a trauma-sensitive culture in residential treatment', *Therapeutic Community: The International Journal for Therapeutic and Supportive Organizations*, **26**(1): 97–113.

Francis, J. (2004) 'Failing Children? A Study of the Educational Experiences of Young People in Residential Care', PhD thesis, University of Edinburgh.

Fulcher, L.C. and Ainsworth, F. (2006) *Group Care Practice with Children and Young People Revisited*. Binghamton, NY: Haworth Press.

Gallagher, B., Brannan, C., Jones, R. and Westwood, S. (2004) 'Good practice in the education of children in residential care', *British Journal of Social Work*, **34**(8): 1133–60.

Garfat, T. (2003) *Four Parts Magic: The Anatomy of a Child and Youth Care Intervention*, http://www.cyc-net.org/cyc-online/cycol-0303-thom.html.

Gilligan, R. (2001) *Promoting Resilience: A Resource Guide on Working with Children in the Care System*. London: BAAF.

Hyatt-Williams, A. (1971) *The Occupational Risk for the Workers in the Field of Adolescent Psychiatry*. Guildford: Association for the Psychiatric Study of Adolescents.

Jack, R. (ed.) (1998) *Residential versus Community Care*. Basingstoke: Macmillan – now Palgrave Macmillan.

Jackson, S., Ajayi, S. and Quigley, M. (2003) *By Degrees: The First Year, from Care to University*. London: Frank Buttle Trust.

Jackson, S. (2006) 'Looking after children away from home: past and present', in E. Chase, A. Simon and S. Jackson (eds) *In Care and After: A Positive Perspective*. London: Routledge.

Kahan, B. and Banner, G. (eds) (1969) *Residential Task in Child Care: The Castle Priory Report.* Banstead: Residential Care Association.

Keenan, C. (1991) 'Working within the life space', in J. Lishman (ed.) *Handbook of Theory for Practice Teachers.* London: Jessica Kingsley.

Kelly, P. (2003) 'Growing up as risky business? Risks, surveillance and the institutionalised mistrust of youth', *Journal of Youth Studies*, **6**(2): 165–80.

Lishman, J. (ed.) (1991) *Handbook of Theory for Practice Teachers in Social Work.* London: Jessica Kingsley.

Maier, H.W. (1979) 'The core of care', *Child Care Quarterly,* **8**(3): 161–73.

Maier, H.W. (1987) *Developmental Group Care of Children and Youth: Concepts and Practice.* Binghamton, NY: Haworth Press.

Maier, H. (1991) 'Essential components in care and treatment environments for children', in F. Ainsworth and L. Fulcher (eds) *Group Care for Children: Concepts and Issues.* London: Tavistock.

Marris, P. (1974) *Loss and Change.* London: Routledge & Kegan Paul.

Meltzer, H., Gatward, R., Corbin, T. et al. (2003) *The Mental Health of Young People Looked After by Local Authorities in England.* London: TSO.

Meltzer, H., Lader, D., Corbin, T. et al. (2004) *The Mental Health of Young People Looked After by Local Authorities in Scotland.* London: TSO.

Menzies-Lyth, I. (1988) *Containing Anxiety in Institutions: Selected Essays*, vol. 1. London: Free Association Books.

Murray-Parkes, C. (1996) *Bereavement: Studies of Grief in Adult Life* (3rd edn). London: Routledge & Kegan Paul.

Office of the Children's Rights Director (2006) *Young People's Views on Leaving Care: What Young People in, and Formerly in, Residential and Foster Care Think About Leaving Care*, http://www.rip.org.uk/files/prompts/p5/yps%20views%20on%20leaving%20care%202006.pdf.

Rutter, M. (1999) 'Resilience concepts and findings: implications for family therapy', *Journal of Family Therapy*, 21, 119–44.

Santrock, J.W. (2004) *Child Development.* New York: McGraw-Hill.

Scottish Executive (2004) *Supporting Young People Leaving Care in Scotland: Regulations and Guidance on Services for Young People Ceasing to be Looked After by Local Authorities.* Edinburgh: Scottish Executive.

Smith, M. (2009) *Rethinking Residential Child Care: Positive Perspectives.* Bristol: Policy Press.

Stein, M. (2004) *What Works for Young People Leaving Care?* Barkingside: Barnardo's.

Stein, M. (2005) *Resilience and Young People Leaving Care: Overcoming the Odds.* York: Joseph Rowntree Foundation.

Tomlinson, P. (2004) *Therapeutic Approaches in Work with Traumatised Children and Young People.* London: Jessica Kingsley.

Trieschman, A.E., Whittaker, J.K. and Brendtro, L.K. (1969) *The Other 23 Hours: Child Care Work in a Therapeutic Milieu.* Chicago: Aldine de Gruyter.

Ward, A. (2002) 'Opportunity led work: maximising the possibilities for therapeutic communication in everyday interactions', *Therapeutic Communities*, **23**(2): 111–24.

Practice

Ward, A. and McMahon, L. (eds) (1998) *Intuition is Not Enough: Matching Learning with Practice in Therapeutic Child Care*. London: Routledge.

Whitaker, D., Archer, L. and Hicks, L. (1998) *Working in Children's Homes*. Chichester: John Wiley & Sons.

Whittaker, J. (1979) *Caring for Troubled Children*. London: Jossey-Bass.

Whitwell, J. (2002) 'Therapeutic child care', in K. White (ed.) *Re-Framing Children's Services*. London: NCVCCO.

Winnicott, D. (1960) 'The theory of the parent-child relationship', *International Journal of Psychoanalysis*, 41, 585–95.

Winnicott, D. (1964) *The Child, the Family and the Outside World*. Harmondsworth: Penguin.

Name index

Subject index